D0802248

Remaking Muslim Politics

PRINCETON STUDIES IN MUSLIM POLITICS

DALE F. EICKELMAN AND JAMES PISCATORI, EDITORS

Remaking Muslim Politics

PLURALISM, CONTESTATION, DEMOCRATIZATION

Robert W. Hefner, Editor

PRINCETON UNIVERSTY PRESS

PRINCETON AND OXFORD

Copyright © 2005 by Princeton University Press
Published by Princeton University Press, 41 William Street, Princeton,
New Jersey 08540
In the United Kingdom: Princeton University Press, 3 Market Place,
Woodstock, Oxfordshire OX20 1SY
All Rights Reserved

Library of Congress Cataloging-in-Publication Data

Remaking Muslim politics : pluralism, contestation, democratization /
Robert W. Hefner, editor.
p. cm.—(Princeton studies in Muslim politics)
Includes bibliographical references and index.
ISBN 0-691-12092-7 (cl : alk. paper) — ISBN 0-691-12093-5 (pbk. : alk. paper)
1. Islamic countries—Politics and government—20th century. 2. Islam and politics—
Islamic countries. 3. Religion and politics—Islamic countries. 4. Islamic renewal—Islamic
countries. I. Hefner, Robert W., 1952– II. Series.
DS35.69.R46 2005
320.917'67'09045—dc22   2004050522

British Library Cataloging-in-Publication Data is available
This book was printed in part through the generosity of the Pew Charitable Trusts

This book has been composed in Sabon

Printed on acid-free paper. ∞

www.pupress.princeton.edu

Printed in the United States of America

1 3 5 7 9 10 8 6 4 2

CONTENTS

ACKNOWLEDGMENTS

THIS VOLUME IS THE PRODUCT of a collaborative project entitled "Civic Pluralist Islam: Policies and Prospects for a Changing Muslim World." The project was funded by a grant from the Pew Charitable Trusts to the Institute on Culture, Religion, and World Affairs (CURA) at Boston University, and carried out from January 2002 to September 2003. I wish to thank Luis Lugo at the Pew Charitable Trusts for his generous support of this project, in which he had expressed a strong interest well before the world-changing events of September 2001. I also want to thank Peter L. Berger, the Institute director, for his unfailing support of this and other Institute projects on Islam, as well as for the intellectual inspiration he has provided on so many of my own reflections on religion and modernity.

As is always the case in a collaborative project of this sort, none of the effort would have been possible without the support, insights, and criticism of colleagues and friends. James Piscatori of Oxford University and Ali Banuazizi of Boston College participated in the first of our Working Group meetings, and played a central role in the formulation of some of our project goals. The sociologist of religion and regular collaborator at CURA, José Casanova, participated in the second of our meetings, providing many important reflections on modern religious change in the Catholic and Muslim worlds. Khaled Abou El Fadl of UCLA provided a paper on the normative grounds in Islamic tradition for democracy that became a key reference material for project participants' discussions. For personal reasons none of these participants was able to prepare a chapter for the present volume, but their role was no less vital.

I also wish to give special thanks to the religion editor at Princeton University Press, Fred Appel. I can think of no other occasion when the editor for a book with which I have been involved has attended a project seminar, offered important intellectual contributions to its proceedings, and been cordial and supportive to boot.

Last but not least I have to thank two people who may be startled to find their names included in the acknowledgments to a book in which they did not directly participate. However, their thoughts and struggles have informed my own effort to understand modern Muslim politics. They are the Iranian thinker Abdolkarim Soroush, whom I had the pleasure to speak with on several occasions during the first phases of this project, when he resided in Boston, and my Indonesian friend and first teacher on civic pluralist Islam, Nurcholish Madjid. My hope is that these two men might hear a faint echo of their own spirit in these pages, without too much, as some say these days, "chatter."

ROBERT W. HEFNER
Boston, January 2004

NOTE ON TRANSLITERATION

THIS BOOK IS INTENDED for a wide readership, nonspecialists as well as specialists. As a result, we have used minimal transliterations of Arabic, Turkish, Persian, and other foreign language terms. No sub- or superscripts have been used, except where an individual author deemed them absolutely necessary. Arabic words have been transliterated and spelled in a manner consistent with national usages rather than an international standard.

CONTRIBUTORS

Bahman Baktiari is professor and director of International Affairs program at the University of Maine. He is the author of, among other works, *Parliamentary Politics in Revolutionary Iran: Institutionalization of Factional Politics* (1997).

Thomas Barfield is Chairman of the Department of Anthropology at Boston University and the author of several books on the history, politics, and culture of Afghanistan and Central Asia, including *The Perilous Frontier: Nomadic Empires and China (1992)*.

John R. Bowen is Dunbar-Van Cleve Professor of Arts and Sciences at Washington University and in Anthropology and Social Thought and Analysis. He has written on religion, politics, and law in Indonesia, most recently in *Islam, Law, and Equality in Indonesia: An Anthropology of Public Reasoning* (2003), and is currently writing on Islam in France.

Dale F. Eickelman is Ralph and Richard Lazarus Professor of Anthropology and Human Relations at Dartmouth College. His most recent book is *New Media in the Muslim World: The Emerging Public Sphere*, coedited with Jon W. Anderson (2003), 2nd edition.

Robert W. Hefner is Professor of Anthropology and Director of the Program on Islam and Civil Democracy at the Institute on Culture, Religion, and World Affairs, Boston University. His recent books include, *Civil Islam: Muslims and Democratization in Indonesia* (2000) and volume 6 of the forthcoming New Cambridge History of Islam, *Muslims and Modernity: Culture and Society since 1800.*

Peter Mandaville teaches in the Department of Public and International Affairs at George Mason University. His publications include *Transnational Muslim Politics: Reimagining the Umma* (2001) and two edited volumes on non-Western and hermeneutic approaches to the study of international relations.

Gwenn Okruhlik is a Visiting Scholar in the Department of Government at the University of Texas at Austin and was a Visiting Researcher/Fulbright Scholar at the King Faisal Center for Research and Islamic Studies in Riyadh during 2002–3. Her research focuses on identity and citizenship,

Islamism, and social movement theory and the political economy of Saudi Arabia.

Michael G. Peletz is W. S. Schupf Professor of Anthropology and Far Eastern Studies at Colgate University. His most recent books are *Islamic Modern: Religious Courts and Cultural Politics in Malaysia* (2002) and *Reason and Passion: Representations of Gender in a Malay Society* (1996); he is currently working on a book on the decline of gender pluralism in Southeast Asia since early modern times (ca. 1500).

Augustus Richard Norton is a professor in the departments of anthropology and international relations at Boston University. He is the editor of *Civil Society in the Middle East*, 2 vols. (1994, 1995), and is now completing a book on 'Ashura in Lebanon.

Diane Singerman is an Associate Professor in the Department of Government, School of Public Affairs at American University. She is the author of *Avenues of Participation: Family, Politics, and Networks in Urban Quarters of Cairo* (1995) and coeditor of *Development, Change, and Gender in Cairo: A View from the Household* (1996).

Jenny B. White is Associate Professor of Anthropology at Boston University. She is the author of *Islamist Mobilization in Turkey: A Study in Vernacular Politics* (2002) and *Money Makes Us Relatives: Women's Labor in Urban Turkey* (1994) and is currently at work on a book about Turkish-German identity.

Muhammad Qasim Zaman is Associate Professor of Religious Studies at Brown University. He is the author of *The Ulama in Contemporary Islam* (2002) and *Religion and Politics under the Early Abbasids* (1997).

Remaking Muslim Politics

Chapter 1

INTRODUCTION: MODERNITY AND THE

REMAKING OF MUSLIM POLITICS

ROBERT W. HEFNER

THE TERRORIST ATTACKS of September 11, 2001, and the subsequent military campaigns in Afghanistan and Iraq placed the question of Islam and Muslim politics squarely in the American public's mind. In bookshops and classrooms, and on radio and television talk shows, Americans were treated to crash courses on the history of Islam, Muslim attitudes toward democracy, the reasons (some) Muslim women veil, and the question of whether the Western and Muslim worlds are indeed fated to a "clash of civilizations."

The impact of this heady media brew was decidedly mixed. In February 2002, a half year after the 9-11 attacks, the liberal-minded leader (*imam*) of one of Washington D.C.'s largest mosques told me that the number of invitations he had received to speak at churches and synagogues had increased twentyfold from the year before, and the number of American citizens whom he had helped to convert to Islam had quadrupled. "Never in my eighteen years of living in the United States have I encountered such an outpouring of interest in Islam, most of it quite sympathetic!" On the other hand, in the months following the 9-11 attacks, there were dozens of unprovoked assaults on Americans of Muslim and Middle Eastern background. Several prominent conservative evangelists blamed the 9-11 attacks not just on individual extremists, but on Islam itself, which they decried as worship of a false god (Cooperman 2003). More alarming yet, surveys conducted by the Pew Forum on Religion and Public life revealed that, two years after the terrorist attacks, growing numbers of Americans believed that Islam encourages violence among its followers (Pew Forum 2003).

In a society as culturally diverse as the United States, it was inevitable that there would be contrary pushes-and-pulls to the post 9-11 reaction. With the passage of time, it was not surprising too that the events of September 11 came to be seen against the backdrop of other events: the U.S. invasion of Afghanistan, the conflict in Chechnya, border skirmishes between India and Pakistan, the war in Iraq, and continuing strife between

Israelis and Palestinians, among others. Other than the fact that, somehow, they all involved Muslims, there was no agreement on the narrative thread with which to tie these events together. What *was* clear was that the question of Muslim politics loomed larger than at any time in modern American history.

As public discussion continued, two broadly opposed positions emerged concerning Islam's compatibility with democracy and civic pluralism,[1] one pessimistic, the other cautiously optimistic. Prominent in the former camp was the distinguished senior historian of the Middle East, Bernard Lewis. Written just prior to the September 11 attacks, Lewis's best-selling *What Went Wrong?* attributed the Muslim world's turbulence to the fact that, in the course of its encounter with Western modernity, "[t]he Muslim attitude was different from that of other civilizations that suffered the impact of the expanding West" (Lewis 2002, 36). In particular, Lewis argued, the premodern history of Muslim confrontation with Europe insured that in the modern era Muslims showed a defensive or even hostile attitude toward things Western. Muslims were "willing enough to accept the products of infidel science in warfare and medicine, where they could make the difference between victory and defeat. . . . However, the underlying philosophy and sociopolitical context of these scientific achievements proved more difficult to accept or even to recognize." This rejection, Lewis concluded, "is one of the more striking differences between the Middle East and other parts of the non-Western world that have in one way or another endured the impact of Western civilization" (Lewis 2002, 81). The difference ensures that it is unlikely that Muslim societies will embrace democracy and pluralism any time soon.

Certainly there is no dearth of *jihadi* militants willing and able to enunciate the starkly anti-Western rhetoric Lewis has in mind.[2] But other observers wonder whether it is fair to take such individuals as representative of Muslim opinion as a whole. There is compelling evidence that many among the world's Muslims endorse no such rejection of modernity and democracy. To take just one example, Ronald Inglehart and Pippa Norris's recent World Values Survey compared opinion in eleven Muslim-majority societies with several Western countries and found in all but one of the Muslim countries (Pakistan) public support for democracy was equal to or even greater than in Western countries (Inglehart and Norris 2003). Where Muslim and Western attitudes diverged was not on matters of democracy, but in relation to "self-expression values" only recently ascendant in the West, such as gay rights and full gender equality.

Recent developments in Turkey, Iran, and Indonesia offer an even more striking indication of Muslim interest in democracy and civic pluralism. On November 3, 2002, voters in Turkey gave their overwhelming support to a new, Islam-oriented party, known as the Justice and Development Party (JDP). The JDP is a reformist party that traces its origins back to a series of Islamist parties banned by secular Turkish authorities in previous decades (White 2002). Despite rumblings from the country's secular-minded Constitutional Court, the JDP managed to escape the wrath of authorities while broadening its appeal among Turkish voters, many of whom had previously been skeptical of Islamic parties. It did so in large part by tapping voter resentment over corruption and the country's continuing economic crisis, while distancing itself from the Islamist rhetoric of its predecessors. More significant yet, as Jenny White explains in chapter 4 in this volume, the party leadership made clear its commitment to principles of human rights, the rule of law, and pluralist democracy. The leadership explained that rather than providing an alternative to democratic institutions, Islam should deepen the values of justice, equality, and human dignity on which those institutions depend.

The terrorist attacks on synagogues and British-owned buildings in Istanbul in November 2003, in which dozens died and more than five hundred were injured (Smith 2003), showed that not all Turkish Muslims agree with Justice and Development's democratic commitments. But the Turkish public's horrified reaction to the bloodshed showed just where most citizens' sympathies lay. In this sense, events in Istanbul were illustrative of a struggle for the hearts and minds of Muslims taking place not just in Turkey but around the world. The contest pits those who believe in the compatibility of Islam with democracy and pluralist freedom against those who insist that such values and institutions are antithetical to Islam.

Events in Iran since 1997 offer a second example of a similar pluralization and contestation of the forms and meanings of Muslim politics. Iran is especially interesting because it is the only country in the Muslim world to have undergone the political metamorphosis from an Islamic revolution to the establishment of an Islamic Republic and, finally, the emergence of a postrevolutionary society (Brumberg 2001; Hooglund 2002). During its first quarter-century, the republic was seen by Islamist activists around the world as proof of their religion's ability to provide an alternative to Western-style democracy. As Bahman Baktiari explains in chapter 5, however, the third, or postrevolutionary, phase of the Islamic Republic's evolution has yielded some surprises. Events since the election of the reform-minded President Khatami in May 1997 show that the youth, women, and professional wings of Iran's new middle class have grown disenchanted with the reigning repressive interpretation of Muslim politics. They seem more interested in the creation of a civil society with genuine pluralism and freedoms than they are the shibboleth of *velayat-e faqih* (lit., "rule by the religiously learned," i.e., clerics; see Arjomand 1988,

148–59). As yet the dream of a democratic spring in Iran remains unfulfilled, and, as in Turkey, the long-term success of efforts to remake Muslim politics is far from guaranteed. But what is clear is that, in Iran as in
Turkey, a growing number of faithful have concluded that there is no contradiction between their great religion and civil-democratic decency.

The Southeast Asian nation of Indonesia offers a third example of a
Muslim politics as plural and contested as its counterparts in Turkey and
Iran. Although often overlooked in discussions of Muslim societies, Indonesia is the largest Muslim-majority country in the world. In the final
years of the Soeharto dictatorship (1966–98), a powerful movement for
a democratic Muslim politics took shape. In alliance with secular Muslims and non-Muslims, the movement succeeded in May 1998 in top-
pling the long-ruling Soeharto. No less remarkable, Muslim participants
in the democracy campaign dedicated themselves to devising religious arguments in support of pluralism, democracy, women's rights, and civil
society (Abdillah 1997; Barton 2002; Hefner 2000). Unfortunately, as I
discuss in chapter 11, in the months following Soeharto's overthrow, Indonesia was rocked by outbreaks of fierce ethnoreligious violence. Some
of the violence showed the telltale signs of ancien regime provocation.
But other acts were linked to independent extremists, including one
group with ties to al-Qa'ida. The violence slowed the reform movement
and put the Muslim community's pluralist experiment in question.

Notwithstanding these and other setbacks, events in Turkey, Iran, and
Indonesia have proved that Muslim politics is not monolithic, and that
there is more to its contemporary ferment than the bleak alternatives of
secularist authoritarianism or extremist violence. Less widely noted but
no less important, there is an effort underway in many countries to give
Muslim politics a civic, pluralist, and even democratic face. In some nations, perhaps the majority, the initiative is still so preliminary or disor-
ganized as to hardly merit the label "movement." Elsewhere, as in Saudi
Arabia (chapter 8), the reformers are not clamoring for full-fledged party
democracy, but greater pluralism and citizen participation. In these and
other Muslim countries, however, there are hints of change in the air, and
hope of better things to come.

The Modern Maelstrom

It was with an eye toward exploring these changes that the Institute on
Culture, Religion, and World Affairs at Boston University, with the generous support of the Pew Charitable Trusts, brought together fourteen
specialists of Muslim politics for three meetings, in May 2002 and in January and September 2003. The meetings were part of an eighteen-month

program of research and analysis on social supports for, and obstacles to, pluralism and democratization in the Muslim world. The project was not intended to address the September 11 violence as such. Having directed a small program on Islam and Civil Society for the previous nine years, I had submitted the project proposal to the Pew Trusts in August 2001, a few weeks prior to the events of September 11. The aim of the "Working Group on Civic-Pluralist Islam," as our project came to be known, was to look at Muslim politics from within, examining the local roots for a pluralist public sphere and a democratic politics. In undertaking this program, we also hoped to bridge the gap between, on one hand, academic scholars and, on the other, policy makers and a general public increasingly concerned about developments in the Muslim world.

The contributors to this volume are first and foremost scholars of Islam and Muslim politics. But all share the conviction that policy-oriented public scholarship is intellectually important in its own right. Some of our colleagues in academia may not share this conviction; even those who do often regard public scholarship as a lesser intellectual genre. What this viewpoint forgets is that most of the great Western social theorists of the nineteenth and early-twentieth century were public intellectuals as well as or even more than they were academics. They understood well the rhetorical demands and intellectual benefits of having to communicate specialized insights to general audiences. What this perspective also overlooks is one of the most impressive aspects of cultural life in the contemporary Muslim world: its proud legacy of public intellectualism (see Abaza 2002, 55–74; Eickelman and Anderson 1999). All this said, the main motive for bringing together the authors who contributed to this volume was our shared conviction that efforts to understand events in the Muslim world can succeed only if we move beyond sound bites and stereotypes and acknowledge the plurality and contest of modern Muslim politics.

To begin to appreciate this variety, and to understand the background to the essays in this volume, we need to look beyond the categories of Western liberal history and recognize several distinctive concerns of Muslim politics. Three are particularly relevant to the chapters that follow. First, far more than is the case in contemporary Western democracies (but not unlike some Western subcultures; see Casanova 1994; Wuthnow 1988, 173–214), Muslim politics is informed by the conviction that religious scholars, the *ulama* (literally, "those who know," sing., *alim*), have the right and duty to make sure that all major developments in politics and society are in conformity with God's commands. Notwithstanding a few radical experiments like revolutionary Iran or Afghanistan's Taliban, this first feature of Muslim politics is not typically understood as an imperative for theocratic rule. Religious scholars do not govern and, again, notwithstanding certain utopian Islamisms to the contrary, real-and-existing Muslim polities are not characterized by a seamless fusion of religion and state or a dictatorship of "clerics" over a supine civil society (see Arjomand 1988, 147–63; Brown 2000; Zubaida 2003). Indeed, in a manner that may at first appear paradoxical, most Muslim societies are marked by deep disagreements over just who is qualified to speak as a religious authority and over just how seriously ordinary Muslims should take the pronouncements of individual scholars.

Rather than an all-powerful theocracy, then, the more general effect of this first principle of Muslim politics is diffusely cultural. The principle makes it difficult for public political deliberation to lapse into laissez-faireism, leaving urgent ethical questions to individual choice or the marketplace of public opinion alone. As Muhammad Qasim Zaman (chapter 3) and John Bowen (chapter 13) illustrate in their discussions of "normativity" in this volume, social and political initiatives are in principle subject to ethical assessment by scholars whose charge is to assure that the developments are consistent with God's commands. The latter are in turn understood in relation to the body of revealed regulations or Islamic "law" known as *shari'a* (lit., "the path," "the way," as in divine regulations or law; see Murata and Chittick 1994, 25–27). In this sense, contemporary Muslim politics operates on two levels: a generalized or mass level driven by the actions and concerns of ordinary Muslims, and a restricted or specialized track involving the efforts of religious scholars to respond to modern problems within the normative horizons of the *shari'a* and Islamic tradition as a whole.[3] Much of the fevered argument of contemporary Muslim politics centers on questions as to how these two tracks are to be harmonized.

Although this first concern informs Muslim political ideals today just as it did during Islam's classical age, its social urgency has varied over time. As occurred with the rise of secular nationalism in the middle decades of the twentieth century, there are times in Muslim history when popular culture drifts away from normative-mindedness, and the public appears less concerned with justifying its political choices with reference to religious ideals. However, when, as in much of the Muslim world after the 1960s, a society experiences a period of deepening Islamization, the concern for religious legitimation will rebound into public awareness, unleashing a torrent of debate on what is and what is not in accord with God's commands.

This social fact points to a second feature of Muslim politics, this one related to contemporary efforts to remake that politics in a pluralist and democratic mold. A key requirement for such a reorientation will be the emergence of public intellectuals backed by mass organizations with the social and discursive resources to convince fellow Muslims of the compatibility of Islam with pluralism and democracy. It goes without saying that the formulation of such religious rationales would have been unnecessary had Muslim societies undergone the process of radical secularization Western theorists had predicted back in the 1950s. But the resurgence of the 1970s and 1980s ensured that contemporary politics in most Muslim societies shows a deep concern with religious powers and discourses.

Viewed from another perspective, this second concern of Muslim politics might seem like a particular example of a general theme in contemporary democratic studies. In recent years "democracy in the vernacular" has been a new and welcome focus of attention in political studies, in large part as a result of efforts to extend that theory's cultural horizons beyond the Atlantic-liberal West (see, for example, Bhargava, Bagchi, and Sudershan 1999; Hansen 1999; Kymlicka 2001). As with Kay Warren's (1998) examination of Mayan activist intellectuals in contemporary Guatemala, or Robert Weller's (1999) study of village temples and women's networks in Taiwan, vernacular approaches emphasize that democratization needs local roots if it is to grow. While recognizing that there are, in the Wittgensteinian sense, "family resemblances" to democratization across cultures, vernacular studies insist that such resemblances are not proof of an end of history or a culturally homogeneous modernity. Notwithstanding certain family resemblances, modernity is multiple in its organizations and meanings (Eisenstadt 2000; Hefner 1998c; Knauft 2002). Democracy and democratization will be as well.

In the case of Muslim societies, there is a distinctive organizational tension to the requirement that pluralism and democratization have vernacular roots. Although Islam has jurists and religious scholars, it has no pope, sacerdotal priesthood, or ecclesiastical hierarchy to coordinate their actions. In most times and places, religious scholars (*ulama*) claimed the main responsibility for fulfilling Islam's prime ethical imperative, "commanding what is right and forbidding what is wrong" (*al-amr bi'l-ma'ruf wa'l-nahy 'an al-munkar;* see Cook 2000). They did so on the grounds that they were most knowledgeable in the sciences of the Qur'an and the traditions of the Prophet.

Even in premodern times, however, just how scholars carried out this duty and who among them was most qualified to do so were questions on which consensus was often difficult. The *ulama* might recognize an informal hierarchy in their ranks, and, in the Shi'a Muslim world in particular, at times the hierarchy's behavior bore a passing resemblance to the ecclesiastical disciplines of Western Christianity (see Arjomand 1988, 177–188; Cole 2002, 189–211). In many countries, however, Muslims recognized more than one school of religious law (*madhhab*). Even where a community adhered to just one school, individual jurists (*fuqaha*) could reach different conclusions on matters of social importance, and the most expert reserved the right to issue opinions of their own. Although they usually shied away from interfering directly in debates on the *shari'a*, rulers, too, did not hesitate to meddle in religious affairs indirectly. They patronized scholars and mystics who voiced opinions on *shari'a* similar to their own. They supported shrines to Sufi saints and sponsored religious festivals that, while avoiding comment on the details of the law, nonetheless enacted a visual model of the way religion, politics, and the social were to be imagined (see Eaton 1984, 334; Hammoudi 1997, 68–80; Woodward 1989, 199–214). Rulers also appointed court jurists to serve as spokespersons before the scholarly community. It is telling, however, that the latter experts were viewed as having "no monopoly of giving *fatwas* [religious opinions], and the practice of consulting private scholars of high reputation has never ceased" (Schacht 1964, 74). Stories of holy men resisting rulers' interference were a classic theme in the popular religious imagination (Messick 1993, 143; Munson 1993, 27). Not the centralized Church of Roman Christendom, religious authority in the Muslim community as a whole tended toward a fissiparous pluricentrism.[4]

As Zaman illustrates in his discussion of modern Pakistan (chapter 3; see also Zaman 2002), in most contemporary Muslim societies the *ulama* still play a role in public ethical discussion. However, modern pressures for pluralism and popular participation are increasingly apparent as well. They can be seen in the fact that the precise influence of *ulama* on public discussion varies widely, as do local understandings of just who is and who is not qualified to provide informed religious opinion. In recent years, then, the long established pluricentrism of religious authority has been compounded by a participatory revolution transforming Muslim culture and politics as a whole.

As Dale F. Eickelman and James Piscatori have observed (1996, 13; cf. Abaza 2002; Esposito and Voll 2001, 3–22), one of the most significant elements in this transformation has been the emergence of "new Muslim intellectuals" across the Muslim world.[5] Although some are graduates of religious schools (*madrasa*) and are familiar with classical commentaries, the majority of new Muslim intellectuals are alumni of national educational systems who acquired their religious knowledge through self-study or participation in small discussion groups (*halaqah*). As recent events in Zaman's Pakistan, White's Turkey, Eickelman's Morocco (chapter 2), and Michael Peletz's Malaysia (chapter 10) all illustrate, one characteristic of their autodidactic education is that the new Muslim intellectuals tend to be more interested than their classical predecessors in linking their religious studies to nontraditional concerns. Some of these are of a loosely populist nature, touching on questions of how to raise one's children, how to live a good life, or how to make household ends meet. At the elite end of the public spectrum, however, others among the new intellectuals grapple with the question of Islam's relation to science, democracy, human rights, and globalization (cf. Abdillah 1997; Eisenstadt 2002; Esposito and Voll 2001; Meeker 1991). Religious conservatives may reject such reflexive extensions of the tradition as "innovations" (bid'a) incompatible with God's law. But other Muslim thinkers, as well as masses of ordinary believers, will beg to differ.

There is an additional organizational feature to these efforts to press public culture and politics into a more participatory mold. The Islamic resurgence took place in the aftermath of a great social and cultural transformation across most of the Muslim world. Urbanization, migration, and growing socioeconomic differentiation combined to undermine received and often village-centered religious disciplines. The state's inability to meet all but a portion of the needs of the new urban masses also created a demand for alternative providers of public services in the fields of health, education, and public security. Finally, mass education, literacy, and a growing network of mosques and Islamic schools combined to strengthen the determination of ordinary Muslims to exercise choice and take charge of their faith (Eickelman 1992). Together, these developments generated a great popular appetite for a more participatory practice of public life and religion. Dale Eickelman and James Piscatori (1996) have rightly seen these events as a potential foundation for a democratic reformation of Muslim politics.

This democratic potential is real enough. However, its realization will depend upon more than the mere fact of heightened popular participation. As events in Europe during the first half of the twentieth century showed all too tragically, mass participation under conditions of ethnoreligious pluralism can generate enormous social tensions, the effects of which may be anything but democratic. As with European fascism and communism, if popular participation and social competition are not embedded in cultures and powers of a civic-pluralist sort, the result may be more polarizing and violent than it is democratic. There is no dearth of such examples in today's world (Brass 2003; Hansen 1999; Hefner 2000; Mamdani 2001). Whether the mass participation that so marks the modern age is democratizing, then, depends on not just participation or associations in civil society, but the higher-level cultures and organizations to which ground-level mobilizations are linked.

In the case of Muslim societies, in particular, the outcome of the new pluralist participation will depend upon a third feature of contemporary Muslim politics: the efforts of rival groupings to "scale up" their influence by strengthening their organizations in society and forging pacts or alliances with influential actors and agencies in the state. Mobilizational initiatives like these usually begin at the local level, with efforts to bring together like-minded actors in associations dedicated to some social, religious, or welfare task. It is activities like these that recent studies of civil society have tended to privilege as the spring from which democratic cultures flow. However, if they are to have a lasting influence in society as a whole, at some point these activities and networks must be drawn into what the sociologist Peter Evans (1996) has described as collaborations "across the state-society divide." As Theda Skocpol has also observed (arguing against Durkheimian portrayals of civil society as entirely independent of the state), civic groups in nineteenth- and early-twentieth-century America were not merely local and not always nonpolitical. Many were linked to translocal organizational networks that sought to forge ties with national leaders and associations so as to influence state policies (Skocpol 1999, 33).[6] There are myriad reasons for civic groups in modern Muslim societies to want to do the same. From the perspective of prodemocracy groupings in particular, it is clear that without some measure of coordinate support from the state and the legal system, democratic elements in society remain vulnerable to attack by uncivil elements in state and society (Hefner 2001; Keane 1996).

It goes without saying, of course, that collaborations across the state-society divide can be put to nondemocratic ends as well. As in Zia ul-Haq's Pakistan (chapter 3), post-Nasser Egypt (chapter 6), modern Saudi Arabia (chapter 8), and post-Soeharto Indonesia (chapter 11), some state officials may conclude that it is in their interest to make common cause with ultraconservative Islamists, rather than Muslim democrats. At other times or in other places, however, ruling elites may choose to lend a hand to the reformist cause. Whatever the political establishment's tack, the prevalence of such mobilizations and alliances in countries across the Islamic world shows that contemporary Muslim politics has changed. It is no longer restricted to a handful of elites, religious dignitaries, and representatives of the privileged classes. The age of mass mobilization has dawned, and with it has come not merely a pluralization of the political field, but a *contestive* pluralization centered on rival interpretations of Muslim politics, and rival efforts to organize in society and across the state-society divide.

In the competitions that ensue, Muslim parties and organizations sometimes enjoy a distinctive advantage over their secular rivals. As Jenny White (2002) has demonstrated for Turkey and Carrie Rosefsky Wickham (2002) in Egypt, some of the most successful of today's Islamic mobilizations owe their success not to formal ideology or top-down party organizations, but to the local networks and relationships from which they draw their membership. Muslim mobilizations often take preexisting religious networks built around neighborhood mosques and religious schools and weave them together into a parallel Islamic sector. As in the Egyptian case (Wickham 2002, 93–118), some Islamic organizations do so by offering educational and health services the state is unable or unwilling to provide. However, the really decisive advantage enjoyed by these mobilizations is their ability to organize their constituencies "on an individual level through known, trusted neighbors, building on sustained, face-to-face relationships, and by situating its political message within the community's cultural codes and norms" (White 2002, 7). While government parties show a preference for a top-down and bureaucratic organization, the new Islamist mobilizations are a politics in the vernacular par excellence.

Again, whether this participation in the vernacular is democratizing is another, more complex question. The contrast between the Egyptian and Turkish examples on this point indicates that the political outcome of the effort can be varied, to say the least. Egypt's Islamists have tended to be conservative on matters of democracy, pluralism, and women's rights, although there are signs this may be changing. Turkey's Islamic parties have tended to look more favorably on democracy and pluralist freedoms. The difference reflects not merely basic cultural differences between these two societies, but, as Richard Norton shows in his chapter, the Egyptian state's unfortunate habit of combining the repression of democracy activists with mobilization of conservative Islamic clients (cf. Sullivan and Abed-Kotob 1999, 126; Wickham 2002, 21–35).

These and other examples illustrate once more that there is no uniform Muslim modernity, nor a monolithic Muslim politics. What Muslim-majority societies do have in common, however, is a new dynamic of popular participation and contestive pluralism. In a growing number of nations, this condition is not merely challenging the old ways of doing things; it is inspiring dreams of a Muslim politics that is civil and democratic.[7]

REMAKING MUSLIM POLITICS

Against the backdrop of these three features of contemporary Muslim politics, it is perhaps easier to understand the distinctive aims and methods of the groups discussed in this volume, most of whom hope to bring about a civic-pluralist reformation of Muslim politics. In light of the first concern of Muslim politics, the concern for religious legitimation, we should not be surprised to see that reformers devote what is, from a Western utilitarian perspective, an inordinate amount of time and energy to coming together to read, write, and formulate the terms for a new practice of Muslim politics. Some reformers do little more than share their reflections with a handful of like-minded intellectuals; others may have access to public platforms in institutions like universities and research institutes. Some, too, may take advantage of new publishing technologies and the Internet to disseminate their writings to larger and more anonymous publics. As Dale F. Eickelman and Peter Mandaville show in their essays on media and transnational Islam (chapters 2 and 12; see also Anderson 2003; Eickelman and Anderson 1999), modern print and electronic media have allowed for the transmission of new ideas even into communities once walled off by established guardians of the faith.[8]

Where conservatives still command a significant mass following, these tentative probes toward pluralist reform may often display a "nonpolitical" guise. As in Diane Singerman's discussion of legal reform in contemporary Egypt (chapter 7) or Gwenn Okruhlik's analysis of pluralism in Saudi Arabia (chapter 8), proponents of reform in such circumstances may choose to focus their efforts not on formal politics, but on educational programs, incremental legal reforms, and public discussions that offer ordinary Muslims an element of choice and participation. Sometimes they also do so because, as Okruhlik makes clear, the reformers are not clamoring for a full-fledged party democracy as much as they are simple pluralist freedoms. Not public spheres of citizen participation in the modern sense of the phrase (see Calhoun 1992; Habermas 1989), the limited-access nature of these activities may also be intended to reduce the risk of conflict with conservative opponents. If and when these "nonpolitical" initiatives begin to make headway, however, the effort almost always goes public, and, as with Singerman's legal activists, is accompanied by attempts to forge alliances with sympathetic actors in state and society.

But going public has its risks. It may only galvanize the ultraconservative opposition and increase the likelihood of confrontation. Committed as they are to a less state-centric practice of their faith, civic-pluralist Muslims may feel torn when confronted by conservative violence and intimidation. Some are willing to, and do, give their lives for the pluralist cause. Recognizing that the success of their efforts depends on long-term changes and the demobilization of "uncivil" groupings, others may quietly retreat to the security of private life and friendships, away from the threat of state repression or public confrontation, praying the storm will pass. Satellite dishes, Internet connections, and the quiet circulation of pamphlets and books may be the only signs of a profession of the faith at odds with those in the commanding heights of religious society.

In the best of circumstances, however, the reformists may succeed at building social coalitions and even creating collaborations across the state-society divide. If and when they achieve the latter, they may get access to the legal and educational resources needed to scale up their influence well beyond the limited-access groupings of society (Eickelman and Anderson 1999, 14; Bowen 2003, 258–68; Hefner 1997). A process of this sort is already underway in countries like Turkey, Iran, Morocco, Malaysia, and Indonesia. In these countries, the movement for a civic-pluralist Islam is no longer just a matter of limited-group discussions, Internet chat groups, or tacit pacts with sympathetic government officials; it has become a powerful stream in public politics and culture. The setbacks that have occurred in several of these countries cannot hide the fact that the struggle to remake Muslim politics is here to stay, and that the circumstances and desires to which it responds are widespread across the Muslim world.

With some 1.3 billion of the world's 6 billion people professing Islam, the outcome of this struggle to reorient Muslim politics is likely to be one of the defining political events of the twenty-first century. As a result of globalization and immigration, the contest will also impact Western societies directly. As John Bowen and Peter Mandaville's essays make especially clear, several Western countries are themselves in the midst of a great Muslim immigration, and their strategies for accommodating the new immigrants vary. Already there are 5 million to 7 million Muslims in the U.S., and no fewer than 30 million in Western Europe, where their numbers are growing more rapidly than the general population (Cesari 1994; Nielsen 1992). As Bowen and Mandaville both show, many among the new population are grappling with the question of what it means to be European or American and Muslim (see AlSayyad and Castells 2002; Ramadan 1999). Although, as Mandaville's essay also illustrates, a few have lent their support to international *jihadi* causes, the more prominent have begun to play a central role in the pluralist stream of transnational Islam (see Mandaville 2001). Their ability to do so effectively over the long run, however, will depend on the willingness of Western societies to accord Muslims full rights of citizenship. This will demonstrate more effectively than any media campaign that there is no clash of civilizations between Islam and the West, but a convergence of interests among people of civil-democratic conviction.

CONDITIONS OF A MODERN POSSIBILITY

There is a broader background to this volume's examination of contemporary efforts to remake Muslim politics. It bears on the question of how we are to understand that politics in relation to processes of participation, pluralization, and democratization seen in other parts of the world. In the late 1980s and early 1990s, the collapse of communism in Eastern Europe and the successful transitions from authoritarianism in Korea and Taiwan inspired optimism about the prospects for transitions of a similar nature in other non-Western societies, including Muslim ones. A host of political scientists, sociologists, and anthropologists threw themselves into the task of determining just why authoritarian regimes collapse and what their fate says about the conditions that might allow for transitions elsewhere.

As is not uncommon in such high-stakes endeavors, the academic community never reached a consensus on most of these questions. Pressed by real-world problems, however, Western policy analysts had no such luxury. They were compelled by force of circumstances to come up with actionable guidelines for democratic transitions. Unlike their obstreperous academic counterparts, then, policy circles soon settled on a few rival models, each with a very different view of the cross-cultural prospects for democracy.

The first model emphasized that the key to democracy and sustainable prosperity lay with the bedrock institutions emphasized by Western Cold Warriors during their half-century of battle with Soviet totalitarianism: free markets and fair elections. In 1993, the historian and policy analyst Francis Fukuyama presented one of the more celebrated versions of this argument. He suggested that the modern world had arrived at "the end of history," in the sense that it was no longer possible for any serious person to believe that there were weighty alternatives to liberal democracy and capitalism. Each time Fukuyama voiced his views, of course, one could hear the sighs of British social democrats, Christian conservatives, deliberative democrats, and American communitarians, all of whom (from different perspectives) lamented what they regarded as a slighting of their recommendations for amendments to liberalism's orthodoxy.

For several years in the early 1990s, however, the Fukuyama formula had an air of commonsense inevitability about it, at least in American policy circles. This was the case not so much because policy makers subscribed to the Hegelian claim that history had ended, but because in anxious circumstances like those of postcommunist Europe, Fukuyama's model was one of the few that seemed to offer a workable guide for the future. The key to sustainable democracy was, simply enough, free elections and "getting markets right."

It was not long, however, before the din of real-world events began to raise questions about the adequacy of the markets-and-elections model. It was not that free elections and equitably competitive markets are not useful things. The problem was that knowing that they are useful is not quite the same as understanding what is required to get them up and running and sustainable. As a series of setbacks in Eastern Europe and Russia during the 1990s showed (Gray 1993), free markets are not "free" in the sense that they are the spontaneous product of unconstrained social exchange. Their free and fair operation depends upon a host of resources in state and society that together "embed" the marketplace (Granovetter

1985; Hefner 1998b; Hollingsworth and Boyer 1997). To build trust, enforce contracts, control crime, and, in a word, make a modern market work, a good deal more is needed than self-interested exchange among so many Robinson Crusoes (Clegg and Redding 1990; Hamilton 1998).

This same qualifying note is all the more relevant when it comes to understanding what is required to make pluralist democracy work. Ethnoreligious violence in Yugoslavia, the genocide in Rwanda, Hindu-Muslim strife in India, racial attacks on immigrants in Germany—these and other developments during the 1990s demonstrated that, at least outside of Washington's Beltway, there were a fair number of people who had yet to learn that history had ended. Indeed, rather than the end of history, outbreaks of communal violence in the 1990s seemed to indicate that, with the Cold War over, "local" histories and cultures had reasserted themselves with a vengeance.

One response to this disturbing realization was to throw up one's hands and conclude that democracy is, above all, a Western institution that depends on Judeo-Christian values; as such, it can take root only in societies of Judeo-Christian background. The most influential statement of this position was that of the Harvard political scientist Samuel P. Huntington, first in a widely read article (Huntington 1993) and then in a later book, *The Clash of Civilizations and the Remaking of World Order* (1996). Whereas Fukuyama had implied that Muslim societies were unlikely to resist the great wave of democratization (Fukuyama 1993, 45–46), Huntington argued that democracy depends on a complex of values and institutions lacking in many non-Western societies, not least of all Muslim ones. The list of requisite values and institutions included "individualism, liberalism, constitutionalism, human rights, equality, liberty, the rule of law, democracy, free markets, the separation of church and state" (Huntington 1993, 40).

Huntington's pessimism represented a departure from his earlier views on the "third wave" of democratization (Huntington 1991). In writings subsequent to his 1993 article, as well as a two-year monthly seminar on cultural globalization at Harvard University that I was invited to attend, he softened the argument somewhat, recognizing that its strict cultural assumptions might be taken as a counsel of relativist despair. European and American policy analysts shared this reservation. In these and other circles, pressure mounted for an alternative to the clash-of-civilizations model.

The alternative was forthcoming soon enough. Setting aside generalizations about civilization and top-down emphases on markets and elections, the new paradigm stressed the importance of grassroots initiatives for building democracy. There were many variations on this model, but perhaps the most influential was Robert Putnam's *Making Democracy*

Work: Civic Institutions in Modern Italy (1993). In this engagingly well written book, Putnam took a page from Alexis de Tocqueville's nineteenth-century *Democracy in America* (1969) and argued that civil society and social capital are "the key to making democracy work" (1993, 185). Drawing on, but also narrowing, a theoretical concept earlier developed by the sociologists Pierre Bourdieu and James Coleman, Putnam defined social capital as "features of social organization, such as trust, norms, and networks, that can improve the efficiency of society by facilitating coordinated actions" (Putnam 1993, 167). Putnam's main thesis was that it was in these voluntary, "horizontal" networks that citizens develop the trust, cooperative skills, and egalitarian attitudes required for democracy. Within these analytic horizons, it was hard to resist Putnam's bold conclusion: "Membership in horizontally ordered groups (like sports clubs, cooperatives, mutual aid societies, cultural associations, and voluntary unions)" is "positively associated with good government," while "membership rates in hierarchically ordered organizations" are "negatively associated with good government" (Putnam 1993, 176). For one brief shining moment, it seemed as if the long-sought recipe for democracy had been found.

The press of real-world events made the concepts of civil society and social capital all the more appealing in policy circles. With several postcommunist states teetering on the edge of collapse, and with the awful evidence that rulers in some countries had deliberately provoked acts of ethnoreligious violence to neutralize rivals, the state in some post–Cold War countries had begun to look like a part of the problem rather than the solution. The idea of civil society provided policy makers with the license they needed to look beyond the halls of state for partners in society.

However beneficial its program impact, the idea of civil society was just not strong enough to stand up under the weight of the theoretical burden it had been assigned. Irrigation associations, small-credit cooperatives, and women's crisis centers are one thing, but what about racially based secret societies, civilian militias, or fundamentalist cults? Sociologically speaking, the latter are all voluntary organizations situated in the space between the family and the state. As such, they qualify for membership in civil society, at least according to the definitions most widely used during the 1990s (see Hall 1995; Hann 1996; Hefner 1998a; Rotberg 2001; Skocpol and Fiorina 1999). However, as with Hindu nationalists in India mobilizing their networks to attack Muslims (Brass 2002, 6; Hansen 1999, 203–14), or Rwandan priests using their leadership capital to goad parishioners to kill Tutsis (Mamdani 2001, 226), the idea that all civil society associations and all social capital are "good" for democracy runs up against one unnerving complication: social capital can be used for all manner of ends, including antidemocratic ones.[9]

All this is to say that associations that are, locationally speaking, part of civil society are not always "civil" in terms of the attitudes they inspire or the political culture they promote (Hefner 2001; Keane 1996, 10). Some forms of social capital and some civic organizations are democracy-friendly, but others—Hutu death squads, the Ku Klux Klan—are not. Robert Putnam's 1993 work attempted to anticipate this objection by emphasizing that it is horizontally organized civic associations that are democracy-friendly, while vertically controlled ones are not. Associations of a horizontal sort, he argued, foster "robust forms of reciprocity" and communicate mutual expectations in "reinforcing encounters," thereby enhancing trust and increasing the flow of communication (1993, 173–4). But many of America's extreme right-wing militias, as well as religious extremists in many parts of the world (Juergensmeyer 2000), show these same robustly reciprocal qualities. And, unfortunately, they do so without producing habits of the democratic heart.

In a subsequent study of social capital in the United States (Putnam 2000), Putnam introduced a useful qualification on his earlier argument, one broadly consistent with the lessons from several essays in this volume. Recognizing that not all social capital is democracy- or pluralism-friendly, Putnam distinguished what he called an exclusive or "bonding" social capital from an inclusive or "bridging" variant. Bonding organizations, he observed, are "inward looking and tend to reinforce exclusive identities and homogeneous groups" (Putnam 2000, 22). By contrast, bridging social capital tends to "generate broader identities and reciprocity" (23). The latter may be well suited for mediating ethnic and religious divisions.

Another way of saying this is that real-and-existing civil societies are always rife with social tensions, not least of all because, rather than being blissfully homogeneous, they are crosscut by divisions of religion, ideology, ethnicity, gender, and class (Hefner 2001; Keane 1996; Stolle and Rochon 2001). Unless counteracted by more encompassing organizations and discourses that extend participatory rights beyond the in-group, these divisions can generate social tensions that are anything but democratic. Moreover, notwithstanding the romantic view of civil society as entirely independent of the state, the development of these stabilizing arrangements depends not only on forces in society, but on symbiotic collaborations across the state-society divide (Evans 1996; Hefner 2001; Skocpol 1999).

Here, then, are a few lessons from recent discussions in democratic theory relevant for understanding events in the Muslim world. They provide important clues as to when the participatory revolution transforming contemporary Muslim politics may be democratizing, and when it may not.

Resurgence and Democratization

As noted above, during the 1970s and 1980s, the Muslim world witnessed a resurgence of piety and public religious activity unprecedented in modern history. The physical signs of this change were ubiquitous: in mosque construction, the proliferation of religious studies circles, crowded Friday worship, pilgrimages to Mecca, bearded men, veiled women, and the growth of Islamic publishing. Earlier, during the heyday of modernization theory in the 1950s, Western analysts had forecast that Muslim societies would inevitably experience the same processes of privatization and decline that, it was assumed (too simplistically), religion in the modern West had undergone. Muslims might be latecomers to the secularization process, the argument went, but they too would succumb to the secularist juggernaut (Lerner 1958). By the time the Islamic revolution swept Iran in 1978–79, this forecast had begun to look jejune. By the early 1990s, it seemed simply absurd.

Ironically, part of the foundation for the resurgence had been laid back in the 1950s and early 1960s not by pious Muslims, but by the secular nationalist leaders who governed most of the newly independent countries of the Muslim world. However meager their achievements in economic policy, the nationalists made headway in the field of general education. Certainly, their record was still modest by comparison with educational programs in East Asia, not least of all because in some Muslim societies women's education lagged significantly behind that of men. In addition, in a few poor countries, like Pakistan, Afghanistan, and the Sudan, rates of education even for males remained stubbornly low (UNDP 2002). Notwithstanding these qualifications, nationalist governments in the majority of countries succeeded in creating the first generation of Muslim youth with general literacy and educational skills (see Eickelman 1992).

During these early years, most among the newly educated applied their skills to more or less secular ends, exactly as nationalist leaders had hoped. From Morocco to Indonesia, socialist and secular nationalist slogans predominated among the educated middle class. With the notable exception of Saudi Arabia, where the state was officially based on *shari'a* law, Islamist issues and parties seemed to have been outflanked by their secular rivals, and seemed marginal to the central currents of postcolonial Muslim politics.

Although their specific views varied from country to country, nationalist ideologues agreed in asserting that folk culture was to blame for the Muslim world's backwardness, and popular culture would have to be aggressively recast if society were to progress. In this regard, the nationalists shared an elite-modernist impulse with Mustafa Kemal, the secularizing founder of modern Turkey (see Berkes 1998). However, with the exception of Kemalist Turkey, nationalist leaders hesitated to launch a too-direct attack on religious institutions. Recognizing Islam's crowd appeal, leaders instead cloaked their secularist programs in a nationalist garb that "retained a modest Islamic façade, incorporating some reference to Islam in their constitutions such as the ruler must be a Muslim or that the *shariah* was a source of law, even when it was not" (Esposito 2000, 2).

Soon, however, the nationalist edifice began to weaken. Having raised popular expectations to such unrealistic heights, the nationalists only insured the population's greater disappointment as it became clear that the state was unable to deliver on its promises. The sense of crisis was exacerbated by a demographic transition taking place across the Muslim world. From 1950 to 1990, the proportion of the population living in urban areas swelled, as a result of rural-to-urban migration and, especially in Africa and the Middle East, some of the world's highest fertility rates. In forty years, urban populations grew 200 to 300 percent, without a corresponding expansion in urban infrastructures. Still predominantly rural in 1950, by 1990 all but a handful of Muslim countries saw 35 to 55 percent of their population residing in cities and towns. There residents suffered the usual ill effects of pollution, crime, unemployment, and poor state services (see Brown 2000, 123–30).

By the early 1970s, then, the secular, socialist, and nationalist stars that had once shone so brightly had begun to lose their luster. Yet the need for some kind of public ethical compass was more compelling than ever. With masses of people from different ethnic and regional backgrounds packed into slums, the old ways of village and town had become obsolescent. The impersonal and often corrupt bureaucracies of state and party inspired even less confidence.

It was during this period, then, that neighborhoods across the Muslim world witnessed a steady expansion in the number of mosques and *madrasas*. Americans familiar with the role played by urban churches in their own country during the late-nineteenth century, when ethnically based congregations helped to integrate foreign immigrants into American society, should find little startling in this phenomenon (Finke and Stark 1992; Wuthnow 1988). Researchers who have examined the wave of Protestant conversion in urban Latin America during the 1970s and 1980s (Martin 1990; Stoll 1990) will also recognize parallels. For the urban poor and lower-middle class, mosques and religious schools offered islands of civility and moral clarity in a turbulent sea. In the face of growing class- and status-differentiation, these institutions provided avenues of participation for believers otherwise consigned to society's margins. As in the late-nineteenth-century United States, the pervasiveness of religious associations gave a deeply religious hue to interactions in civil society. That society was not made up of modern liberalism's individuals freed from ethnoreligious bonds, but individuals and groups bound by crosscutting ties of kinship, ethnicity, and religion.

One telling indicator of the public's heightened interest in religion was the rapid development of a market for inexpensive Islamic books and magazines. The literature provided a means for people who had never had an opportunity to study in religious schools to familiarize themselves with the fundaments of their faith (Gonzalez-Quijano 1998; Eickelman and Anderson 1999). The opportunity also stimulated the emergence of a new class of teachers and preachers, with target audiences different from those of the classically trained *ulama* (Eickelman and Piscatori 1996). Most of the preachers had only a vague familiarity with classical religious scholarship, although, as in Egypt, a few were unemployed graduates of religious colleges (Gaffney 1994). More important yet, the new preachers made their message relevant in ways different from the scholastic preaching of mainstream *ulama,* adapting their topics to the concerns of urban publics. Such were the demands of entrepreneurial success in an increasingly competitive religious market.

Here then was the background to the great religious resurgence seen across the Muslim world in the 1970s and 1980s. Described in the language of modern political theory, the resurgence was primarily an affair of civil society, not the state.[10] Equally important, notwithstanding its impact on rural society, its leading lights and organizations were urban in ethos and organization. The resurgence created a great reservoir of social capital, comprised of networks and solidarities dedicated above all else to public piety and expressions of Islamic identity. As with denominational Christianity in America in the nineteenth century (Finke and Stark 1992; Hatch 1989), the heightened religiosity was accompanied by fierce competition among purveyors of different religious messages. Among the case studies offered in this book, only Afghanistan stood apart from the general pattern of a public Islam redefined by the interests and choices of urban consumers (see Barfield's chapter 9).

Although the cultural temperament of the Islamic resurgence varied from country to country, the process as a whole shared three basic characteristics. The first was that, in scope and density, the resurgence represented a historically unprecedented mobilization of civil society, one that created vast new reserves of social capital—"features of social organization, such as trust, norms, and networks" for "facilitating coordinated actions" (Putnam 1993, 167). In the first instance, the networks and energies of this Islamic social capital were primarily dedicated to public religious activities. Mosques and *madrasas* became the anchors for new forms of public association. The call to prayer marked the rhythms of the day. More women began to veil. Greetings and other everyday commensalities were peppered with Islamic gestures and phrases.

A second observation is equally important, although it is sometimes overlooked in commentaries that overemphasize the politics of the resurgence or, worse yet, confuse it with radical Islamism. In its early years, the resurgence was a profoundly *public* event, but not one that was especially *political* in any formal sense of the term. Most of the newly pious were primarily interested in just what they claimed to be: religious study, heightened public devotion, expressing a Muslim identity, and insuring that public arenas were subject to ethical regulation. The key symbols of the resurgence were similarly pietistic: reciting the Qur'an, keeping the fast, wearing the veil, avoiding alcohol, giving alms. The Muslim world was not alone in witnessing a resurgence of public religion in these years. As José Casanova has noted, a similar "deprivatization" of religion took place among Hindus in India, evangelicals in Africa and the Americas, and in many other countries (Casanova 1994; cf. Berger 1999, Martin 1990; van der Veer 1994). Many of the faithful in these settings were as much concerned with creating islands of civility and piety as they were anything strictly political.

The third feature of the resurgence, however, raises a more sobering question concerning its long-term political impact. In light of its scale and the competition among its promoters, it was inevitable that at some point religious entrepreneurs would move to channel the resurgence's social capital into political ends. The process was made all the more likely in that religious associations were among the few public arenas in which ordinary people could make their voices heard.

Again, however, it is important to emphasize that the range of political ideals voiced varied enormously. Some believers insisted on the compatibility of Islam with pluralism and democracy. Others called for a totalizing transformation of the social order according to an unchanging plan, modeled on an ideal of pristine unity identified with the first generation of Muslim believers (see Voll 1991). Nowhere was the tension between these two visions of Muslim politics more apparent than in matters of women's rights and personal status law. In some countries, conservative Islamists tried to mobilize their membership to reverse legislation on women's rights dating from the earlier nationalist period, on the grounds that it was un-Islamic (Keddie 1991; Kandiyoti 1995). At the same time, developments in education and employment continued to draw growing numbers of women, even from conservative Islamist families, into public life. The result has been an ambiguous and unfinished remaking of women's roles. In all but the most conservative organizations, women today are more prominent than ever in the workforce, public religious life, and even political parties (see Abu-Lughod 1998; White 2002, 52).

At the same time, in many societies conservative Islamists militate in support of polygyny, gender segregation, and mandatory veiling. In short, women's participation in public life has increased in most of the Muslim world. Whether that participation is to take place on the basis of equality and democratic dignity is a question that has yet to be resolved.

Whatever its social ambiguities, the resurgence has clearly acquired a new and, in at least some circles, more political tack. The question now is which among the variety of Muslim politics is to prevail.

AT THE CROSSROADS

To understand why some resurgents would turn to an undemocratic interpretation of Muslim politics, it is helpful to recall that although the radicals' ideas represented a break with mainstream Muslim politics, they did not emerge from a cultural vacuum. Most radical Islamists justify their actions with reference to the ideas of a few seminal thinkers who rose to international prominence in the 1950s and 1960s. The most influential of these are the Egyptian literary critic turned Islamist, Sayyid Qutb (1906–66; see Moussalli 1992), and the Pakistani theorist Mawlana Sayyid Abu'l-A'la Mawdudi (1903–79; see Nasr 1996). Both of these writers were in turn influenced by the earlier, ultraconservative reformism of Ibn Abd al-Wahhab in what is today Saudi Arabia (Voll 1991, 345–52).

A key theme in these writers' works is that God alone has sovereignty (*hakimiyya*) over the world, and that he has provided Muslims with what amounts to a complete (*kaffah*) ethical model for social and political life. This guidance, these authors claim, is contained in a religious law for all times, the *shari'a*. Whereas classically trained scholars regarded the law as complex, subtle, and always in need of expert exegesis (Zubaida 2003, 24–27), modern Islamists tend to insist that the law's meaning is transparent to all willing to submit to its commands. The fact that even radical Islamists cannot agree on the law's myriad details does not diminish this faith in the clarity and singularity of divine command. Inasmuch as God's law is clear, those who refuse its implementation are seen as having allied themselves with the forces of godlessness (*jahiliyya*). Muslims, even the masses of ordinary Muslims, are to be shunned if and when they fall into such error. Through injunctions like these, radical thinkers provide a cultural rationale for a "bonding capital" that is "inward looking and tend[s] to reinforce exclusive identities and homogeneous groups" (Putnam 2000, 22). At the limit, where rulers and publics are deemed in violation of God's command, armed struggle against both may be required.

According to these same writers, a key feature of Islam's comprehensiveness is that Islam does not recognize a separation of religion and state, but demands their unitary fusion in an "Islamic" state. This formula is said to be based on the model of the Prophet and his rightly guided successors. As a number of writers have observed (Brown 2000; Roy 1994; Zubaida 1993), this alleged precedent actually neglects as much as it claims to recall. It forgets that, historically, the great majority of Muslim jurists believed that "the law is God's law, not to be harnessed to the needs and the interests of the state" (Tucker 1998, 37). The conservative formula also fails to recognize that a richly differentiated political landscape took shape even during the Prophet's lifetime, and developed all the more after his death, as the Muslim community evolved from a small charismatic movement to a great world civilization (Lapidus 1975; Zubaida 1993, 2). For it to have been otherwise, for Muslim society and politics to have remained an undifferentiated totality, would have meant the impoverishment and inevitable collapse of Muslim civilization. Muslim societies thrived precisely because their leaders adopted a flexible and differentiated approach in matters of governance, culture, and society.

Rather than fidelity to prophetic precedents, then, the Islamist dream of an all-encompassing religious governance bespeaks a modern bias, one all too familiar in the twentieth-century West. It is the dream of using the leviathan powers of the modern state to push citizens toward a pristine political purity. As the author of an excellent biography of Mawdudi has remarked, there is little in this vision that is specifically Islamic:

> Mawdudi's assimilation of Western ideas in his discourse flowed without interruption. The Islamic state duplicated, assimilated, and reproduced Western political concepts, structures, and operations, producing a theory of statecraft that, save for its name and its use of Islamic terms and symbols, showed little indigenous influence. (Nasr 1996, 90)

Another stream in modern Muslim politics, however, has spoken out against an étatist and essentializing interpretation of politics, calling instead for a pluralistic organization of state and society. Whether with Abdolkarim Soroush and the reformists in postrevolutionary Iran (Soroush 2000), Nurcholish Madjid and the "renewal" (*pembaruan*) movement in Indonesia (Hefner 2000), or Rachid Ghannouchi in Tunisia (Tamimi 2001; cf. Kurzman 1998, 19), a central theme of civil Islam has been the insistence that some degree of separation of state and religious authority is necessary to protect the integrity of Islam itself. The point is not that religion should be a purely private matter, but that its values are more susceptible to corruption if responsibility for religious affairs is surrendered to state elites.

"Religion forbids us from assuming a God-like character," writes the Iranian dissident (and former anti-American militant) Abdolkarim Soroush (Soroush 2000, 64). He goes on: "This is especially true in politics and government where limiting the power of the state, division of powers, and the doctrine of checks and balances are established in order to prevent accumulation of power that might lead to such Godly claims" (64). Like many Muslim reformers, Soroush's formula borrows some of its vocabulary from Western democratic theory. But it also speaks in a movingly evocative vernacular, invoking the example of Islam's great jurists, who protected Islam's ideals by refusing to grant rulers a monopoly over religious truth. Rather than a pristine fusion, then, civil Islamists relocate the center of public religion to the associations and dialogue of civil society, while also pressing for a system of pluralist government subject to effective checks and balances.

Whether the civic-pluralist stream in contemporary Muslim political culture will spread and become the model for a broader, pluralistic reformation of Muslim politics will depend upon more than the cogency of a few intellectuals' arguments. Since September 11, 2001, in particular, Muslim and Western scholars alike have realized that the civil Islamic effort faces a new and unexpected challenge. The September attacks showed that an armed fringe in the radical Islamist community is attempting to overcome its disadvantage in numbers by pressing its one comparative advantage. Groups like the al-Qaʿida and the Jemaʿah Islamiyah in Southeast Asia have taken advantage of globalization to link their finances and military resources to local conflicts to which Muslims are party (see Gunaratna 2002; ICG 2002; see chapter 11 below). Prior to the overthrow of the Taliban in late 2001, the arms, training, and ideological guidance provided at al-Qaʿida camps in Afghanistan added fuel to some of the Muslim world's most flammable conflicts. As Barfield's essay illustrates (chapter 9), the Taliban and al-Qaʿida made an odd couple indeed. Al-Qaʿida is an internationalist organization led by well-heeled dissidents from the ranks of the Muslim upper-middle class, while the Taliban were a ragtag gang of parochial ethnics who emerged from the ruins of the most backward state in the Muslim world.

Unfortunately, as recent attacks in Indonesia, the Philippines, Turkey, Pakistan, and Saudi Arabia have shown, al-Qaʿida and like-minded groupings seem intent on extending odd-couple collaborations like these to other parts of the world. They have made their methods clear. They channel transnational flows of money, arms, and fighters into local conflicts. In so doing, they also portray these conflicts not as local, but as part of a global clash of civilizations pitting Christians, Jews, Hindus, and other "crusaders" against Muslims. Having described the struggle in these Manichaean terms, the radicals provide a moral rationale for attacking the enemies of Islam everywhere they are to be found. For Western readers of the present book, it is essential to realize that the violence is targeted not only at Western interests, but at pluralist and moderate Muslims. The violence aims to polarize local conflicts and, in so doing, destroy the political center.

In a few instances, these tactics have succeeded in giving local *jihadis* an influence greatly out of proportion with their actual numbers in local society (see chapter 11). In all but the most desperate circumstances, however, most Muslim publics have been repelled by these actions. They recognize that the threat to the West posed by the globalization of *jihadi* adventurism is minor compared to the threat such violence poses to Muslims and Islam.

CONCLUSION

The long-term outcome of this struggle for the heart and soul of Muslim politics will depend on not only the clarity of rival visions, but concrete balances of power in state and society. The strengthening of the civil democratic stream in Muslim politics will also depend on a long-term collaborative effort by governmental and nongovernmental agencies in the Muslim and Western worlds.

Owing to, perhaps, an unfamiliarity with the nuances of Muslim politics, as well as regrettably short-term policies, governments in the West have not been as consistent as they should be in their policies toward the Muslim world (Gerges 1999; Hinter 1998). One especially unhelpful factor has been a concern in Western policy circles that if the democratic dam is opened wide, the groups most likely to rush in will be authoritarian Islamists little interested in pluralism or democracy. "One vote, one time," was the phrase that summarized this anxiety in Western circles at the time of the Algerian elections in 1991. The fear led French and American officials to side with the forces of military repression in Algeria, after the electoral triumph of an (admittedly complex) alliance of moderate and militant Islamists (Willis 1996).

It does little good simply to wave this anxiety aside. As in the early-twentieth-century West, there *are* political radicals eager to take advantage of democratic openings so as to pursue undemocratic ends. However, it is helpful to remember that rulers in most Muslim societies have not gone so far as the Algerian authorities to repress moderate opponents and, in so doing, paint the political process into a corner. The essays in this book provide numerous examples of societies in which a vigorous measure of grassroots pluralism is still available for, so to speak, scaling up. Equally important, as noted above, there is a wealth of evidence indicating that most Muslims yearn for democracy and civic decency. They do so not because these ideals were "made in the West," but because they are the most effective and just response to problems of pluralism and participation widespread in our age.

If Muslim governments and their Western friends do not take the steps needed to promote civic pluralism and democracy, the result will likely be only more radicalism and popular disenchantment with the West. The main reason reform must not be delayed is that Muslim societies are already *sociologically* modern. They are modern in the sense that they are well on the way to developing the characteristics distinctive to the condition of modernity: a pluralization of life-worlds, heightened pressures for participation, and a growing popular demand that the script for coordinating roles on the public stage be, in some vernacularized sense, civil and democratic.

This is not to say that democratization is inevitable or that efforts to support Muslim democratization have to be all or nothing. The history of democratization in the modern West shows that the process is enduringly incremental, always incomplete, and, alas, reversible even where it is achieved (Keane 1996). The process typically unfolds in a piecemeal and domain-specific manner, its course specified not just by the brilliance of its ideals, but by concrete balances of power and participatory struggles. The most effective way for Western agencies to support the process in Muslim societies, then, is to invest in those spheres where local actors are already pressing for heightened participation and civic decency. In efforts like these, civil society groupings will be crucial. But programs in civil society will remain vulnerable and incomplete unless complemented by democratic reforms in the state. Democratization is sustainable only when based on leveraged collaborations between state and society that scale up the democratic powers of each.

In light of the centrality of education and public discussion in the Islamic resurgence, investment in general education represents a second and no less critical support for a pluralizing Muslim politics. Skeptics might point out that some of the more violent radicals in recent years have come from the ranks of well-educated youth. The militants who carried out the attacks of September 11, 2001, were not the illiterate offspring of an impoverished underclass. But it is far more noteworthy that some of the most gifted proponents of Muslim pluralism come from the ranks of public intellectuals and religious scholars with a great knowledge of the law, and a habit of enriching its insights by juxtaposing it to other traditions of knowledge (see Abou El Fadl 2001; An-Na'im 1990; Safi 2003). More, not less, education is the key. And education has a greater democratic benefit when it conveys a spirit of intellectual "bridging" rather than exclusive "bonding."

There are two additional reasons for focusing investments in education, including, especially, women's education and higher education. First and most important, this is what the great majority of modern Muslims yearn for. Studies like the recent *Arab Human Development Report 2003* provide vivid demonstrations of the depth of this desire, and the calamity its nonfulfillment has created. The deficit is no more tragically apparent than in the continuing exclusion of women and girls from equal access to education (UNDP 2003, 31).

A second reason for highlighting investment in education is that education is the most paradigmatic of modern cultural institutions. Today no society can compete even in the lower rungs of the global order without a well-run educational system. In its diverse specializations, its encouragement of innovation, its (relative) gender equality, and its culture of civility-in-plurality, higher education is a shimmering example of all that is best about modern freedom and civic decency.

The recent revolutionary experiments in Iran, Sudan, and Afghanistan demonstrate that attempts to use the state to deny modern pluralism, and to implement a totalizing (*kaffah*) practice of the faith, run contrary to the demands of modern education and society as a whole. Again, in sociological fact, Muslim societies are already modern. The growth of the professions, the expansion of the press, the fascination with the Internet, the demand for women's education—these and other pluralizing developments are well under way in all but the poorest Muslim nations. Religious radicals may deny the public's hunger for pluralist fruits. No doubt the Taliban in Afghanistan went to the greatest lengths to deny this interest and press society back toward a pristine, undifferentiated whole. But this only reminds us that Taliban programs bore a more striking resemblance to Pol Pot's Cambodia than they did the model of the Prophet.

Here, then, is the strongest support for democracy and civic decency in the Muslim world. The support is especially significant because it comes from Muslims themselves, not from a West that, unfortunately, has been less than consistent in its attitudes on Islam. The support originates in Muslims' recognition that efforts to impose a repressive homogeneity on a diverse society only damages their faith and consigns believers to backwardness. This latter conclusion will be rejected, of course, by those who insist that Islam has unchanging instructions for everyone and all aspects of social life. Just as was the case with totalitarian schemes in the modern West, efforts to implement such totalizing programs will do great harm to society. Even more serious from believers' perspective, the more radicals press for a fusion of religion and state, the more they remove the checks and balances necessary for maintaining the integrity of not only the political process, but of religion itself. The urge for absolutist union creates the conditions for religion's abuse. Power corrupts; absolute power corrupts absolutely. And nothing more certainly degrades religion than human absolutism in God's name.

These are the lessons that give the civil Islamic project its historic urgency and relevance. Recent events have demonstrated that it is in the best interest of Islam itself that Muslim politics be plural and democratic. In an age of mass participation and powerful states, to do otherwise is to guarantee religion's subordination to the powerful and corrupt. "The modern world has also undermined a right that has always been a source of evil and corruption," writes Abdolkarim Soroush (2000, 64), "that is, the right to act as a God-like potentate with unlimited powers." This is the conviction, so historic and deep, from which civil democratic Islam flows. Originating at the heart of the Muslim experience of modernity, the conviction is becoming more, not less, widespread in our world. Its diffusion ensures that the struggle for a civic-pluralist politics will remain a central stream in Muslim civilization for years to come.

NOTES

1. "Civic pluralism" refers to a public culture and social organization premised on equal rights, tolerance-in-pluralism, and a legally recognized differentiation of state and religious authority (see Eickelman and Piscatori 1996, 158; Hefner 2000, 12). Where such a civic pluralism is in turn linked to a system of free and fair elections, a separation of powers in the state, the rule of law, and human rights we may speak of a civic pluralist *democracy*. As I have discussed elsewhere (Hefner 1998a), the benefit of this phrase is that it makes clear that there are versions of modern democracy other than liberal variants alone. Much like the civic republicanism Charles Taylor has described (1989, 1995), Muslim civic pluralism may well dedicate greater attention to the cultivation of public values, including religious ones, than is deemed appropriate by modern liberal democrats. However, even some of the latter have recently begun to reexamine their heritage's secularist premises. See Rosenblum 2000.
2. For a sample of some of the more radical denunciations, see Parfrey 2001.
3. It goes without saying, of course, that this effort to engage the modern within the horizons of a religiously grounded discourse is by no means unique to Islam. Charles Taylor (1999) and José Casanova (1994) provide compelling reflections on such efforts within modern Catholicism; Tu Wei-ming's (1996) volume provides a richly nuanced sense of the effort in East Asian Confucianism. Thomas Blom Hansen (1999) provides a powerful overview of the politics of the process in contemporary Hinduism.
4. In addition to the varied legal schools, the relative autonomy of religious scholars, the popularity (after the eleventh century) of Sufi mystical orders, and imperial support for shrines and festivals, another institution that served

to pluralize practical religious authority among the community of believers was the institution of philanthropic endowments known as *waqf* (pl. *awqaf*). A *waqf* is a property set aside in perpetuity to provide revenues or resources for the maintenance of institutions such as mosques, religious schools, or charities for the poor. In some precolonial Middle Eastern countries, vast expanses of agricultural land were designated as nonperishable property of this sort. Although rulers might play a role in the management of larger *waqf* properties, religious law set strict limits on the rights of these and other *waqf* stewards. In premodern Muslim societies, the pervasiveness of such lands was an integral economic support for the autonomy of key Islamic institutions and the pluricentrism of religious authority. On *waqf*, see Kahf 1995; on *waqf* and religious authority, see Hoexter 2002.

5. Thomas Barfield's discussion of Afghanistan in chapter 9 offers an example of a starkly conservative society in which new Muslim intellectuals are few in number; war-ravaged Afghanistan is, however, the exception to the modern Muslim rule.

6. Skocpol's conclusion resonates with the non-Durkheimian view of civil society I am emphasizing here: "The story of American voluntarism has been clearly one of symbiosis between state and society—not a story of society apart from, or instead of the state" (Skocpol 1999, 70). This "historically evolved symbiosis of federal democracy and federated voluntary associations," she explains, "created a very special matrix for American citizenship and popular civic participation" (70–71). The synergistic approach to state and society developed in Skocpol and the present chapter implies that democratization is less the result of particularistic trust than it is efforts to build *confidence* in public institutions by, among other things, creating concrete checks and balance among power holders in state, society, and the market. Such leveraged influence can help to pacify and democratize the competition that occurs in all societies. Unlike the romantic characterizations widespread in 1990s literature, real-and-existing civil societies are not calmly consensual, but marked by "organized conflict and *distrust*" (Skocpol and Fiorina 1999, 14; cf. Hefner 2001; Keane 1996).

7. Although the contributors to this book are primarily concerned with its contemporary sociology, the intellectual roots of civic pluralist Islam were laid well before contemporary times. For overviews of these intellectual antecedents see Esposito and Voll 2001; Moussalli 2001; Rahman 1982; and Sachedina 2001. Charles Kurzman's *Liberal Islam* (1998) offers a superb selection of primary materials from some of the most important pioneers.

8. For an analysis of the role of new media in Saudi politics, see Fandy 1999.

9. It is useful to recall that, as originally developed by Pierre Bourdieu and James Coleman, the idea of social capital made no such assumption that the ends to which it is applied are always democratic. Bourdieu defines social capital as "the aggregate of the actual or potential resources which are linked to possession of a durable network of more or less institutionalized relationships of mutual acquaintance and recognition—or in other words, to membership in a group" (Bourdieu and Waquant 1992, 119). In other words, social capital refers to the power and influence created by virtue of membership

in a network or group, and these powers can be applied to all manner of ends. See also Hefner 2000, chap. 2.

10. This generalization would have to be qualified in several countries, where embattled regimes responded to leftist and Islamist oppositions by sponsoring programs of conservative Islamization. Carrie Rosefsky Wickham (2002) provides a brilliant analysis of just such a tactic in Mubarak's Egypt, resonating with Norton's essay in this volume. See also Zaman on Pakistan, Peletz on Malaysia, and my own chapter on Indonesia.

REFERENCES CITED

Abaza, Mona. 2002. *Debates on Islam and Knowledge in Malaysia and Egypt.* London: RoutledgeCurzon.

Abdillah, Masykuri. 1997. *Responses of Indonesian Muslim Intellectuals to the Concept of Democracy (1966–1993).* Hamburg: Abera Verlag Meyer and Co.

Abou El Fadl, Khaled. 2001. *Speaking in God's Name: Islamic Law, Authority, and Women.* Oxford: One World.

Abu-Lughod, Lila, ed. 1998. *Remaking Women: Feminism and Modernity in the Middle East.* Princeton, N.J.: Princeton University Press.

AlSayyad, Nezar, and Manuel Castells. 2002. *Muslim Europe, or Euro-Islam: Politics, Culture, and Citizenship in the Age of Globalization.* Lanham, Md.: Lexington Books.

Anderson, Jon W. 2003. "The Internet and Islam's New Interpreters." In *New Media in the Muslim World: The Emerging Public Sphere,* edited by Dale F. Eickelman and Jon W. Anderson, pp. 45–60.

An-Na'im, Abdullahi Ahmed. 1990. *Toward an Islamic Reformation: Civil Liberties, Human Rights, and International Law.* Syracuse, N.Y.: Syracuse University Press.

Arjomand, Said Amir. 1988. *The Turban for the Crown: The Islamic Revolution in Iran.* New York: Oxford University Press.

Barton, Greg. 2002. *Gus Dur: The Authorized Biography of Abdurrahman Wahid.* Singapore: Equinox Publishing.

Berger, Peter L., ed. 1999. *The Desecularization of the World: Resurgent Religion and World Politics.* Grand Rapids, Mich.: Eerdmans Publishing.

Berkes, Niyazi. 1998. *The Development of Secularism in Turkey.* New York: Routledge.

Bhargava, Rajeev, Amiya Kumar Bagchi, and R. Sudarshan, eds. 1999. *Multiculturalism, Liberalism, and Democracy.* New Delhi: Oxford University Press.

Bourdieu, Pierre, and Loic Waquant. 1992. *Introduction to Reflexive Sociology.* Chicago, Ill.: University of Chicago Press.

Bowen, John R. 2003. *Islam, Law, and Equality in Indonesia: An Anthropology of Public Reasoning.* Cambridge: Cambridge University Press.

Brass, Paul. 2003. *The Production of Hindu-Muslim Violence in Contemporary India.* Seattle and London: University of Washington Press.

Brown, Carl. 2000. *Religion and State: The Muslim Approach to Politics.* New York: Columbia University Press, 2000.

Brumberg, David. 2001. *Reinventing Khomeini: The Struggle for Reform in Iran.* Chicago, Ill.: University of Chicago Press.

Calhoun, Craig, ed. 1992. *Habermas and the Public Sphere.* Cambridge: MIT Press.

Casanova, José. 1994. *Public Religions in the Modern World.* Chicago, Ill.: University of Chicago Press.

Cesari, Jocelyne. 1994. *Être musulman en France: Associations, militants, et mosquées.* Paris: Karthala.

Clegg, S. R., and S. G. Redding, eds. 1990. *Capitalism in Contrasting Cultures.* Berlin: Walter de Gruyter.

Cole, Juan. 2002. *Sacred Space and Holy War: The Politics, Culture, and History of Shi'ite Islam.* London: I. B. Tauris.

Cook, Michael. 2000. *Commanding Right and Forbidding Wrong in Islamic Thought.* Cambridge: Cambridge University Press.

Cooperman, Alan. 2003. "Bush's Remarks about God Assailed." *Washington Post,* November 22, p. A6.

Eaton, Richard M. 1984. "The Political and Religious Authority of the Shrine of Baba Farid." In *Moral Conduct and Authority: The Place of* Adab *in South Asian Islam,* edited by Barbara Daly Metcalf, pp. 333–56. Berkeley and Los Angeles: University of California Press.

Edwards, Bob, and Michael W. Foley. 2001. "Civil Society and Social Capital: A Primer." In *Beyond Tocqueville: Civil Society and the Social Capital Debate in Comparative Perspective,* edited by Bob Edwards, Michael W. Foley, and Mario Diani, pp. 1–14. Hanover, N.H.: University Press of New England.

Eickelman, Dale F. 1992. "Mass Higher Education and the Religious Imagination in Contemporary Arab Societies." *American Ethnologist* 19, no. 4 (November): 1–13.

Eickelman, Dale F., and Jon W. Anderson. 1999. "Redefining Muslim Publics." In *New Media in the Muslim World: The Emerging Public Sphere,* edited by Dale F. Eickelman and Jon W. Anderson, pp. 1-18. Bloomington: Indiana University Press.

Eickelman, Dale F., and James Piscatori. 1996. *Muslim Politics.* Princeton, N.J.: Princeton University Press.

Eisenstadt, Shmuel N. 2000. "Multiple Modernities." *Daedalus* 129, no. 1 (Winter): 1–30.

———. 2002. "Concluding Remarks: Public Sphere, Civil Society, and Political Dynamics in Islamic Societies." In *The Public Sphere in Muslim Societies,* edited by Miriam Hoexter, Shmuel N. Eisenstadt, and Nehemia Levtzion, pp. 139–61. Albany: State University of New York Press.

Esposito, John L. 2000. "Introduction: Islam and Secularism in the Twenty-first Century." In *Islam and Secularism in the Middle East,* edited by John L. Esposito and Azzam Tamimi, pp. 1–12. London: Hurst and Company.

Esposito, John L., and John O. Voll. 2001. *Makers of Contemporary Islam.* New York: Oxford University Press.

Evans, Peter. 1996. "Government Action, Social Capital and Development: Reviewing the Evidence on Synergy." *World Development* 24, no. 6: 1119–32.

Fandy, Mamoun. 1999. *Saudi Arabia and the Politics of Dissent.* New York: Palgrave.

Finke, Roger, and Rodney Stark. 1992. *The Churching of America, 1776–1991: Winners and Losers in our Religious Economy.* New Brunswick, N.J.: Rutgers University Press.

Fukuyama, Francis. 1993. *The End of History and the Last Man.* New York: Free Press.

Gaffney, Patrick D. 1994. *The Prophet's Pulpit: Islamic Preaching in Contemporary Egypt.* Berkeley and Los Angeles: University of California Press.

Gerges, Fawaz A. 1999. *America and Political Islam: Clash of Cultures or Clash of Interests?* Cambridge: Cambridge University Press.

Gonzalez-Quijano, Yves. 1998. *Les Gens du Livre: Édition et champ intellectuel dans l'Égypte Republicaine.* Paris: CNRS Éditions.

Granovetter, Mark. 1985. "Economic Action and Social Structure: The Problem of Embeddedness." *American Journal of Sociology* 91:481–510.

Gray, John. 1993. "From Post-communism to Civil Society: The Reemergence of History and the Decline of the Western Model." In *Liberalism and the Economic Order,* edited by Ellen Frankel Paul, Fred D. Miller, Jr., and Jeffrey Paul, pp. 26–50. Cambridge: Cambridge University Press.

Gunaratna, Rohan. 2002. *Inside Al Qaeda: A Global Network of Terror.* New York: Columbia University Press.

Habermas, Jürgen. 1989 ([1962].) *The Structural Transformation of the Public Sphere: An Inquiry into a Category of Bourgeois Society.* Cambridge: MIT Press.

Hall, John A. 1995. "In Search of Civil Society." In *Civil Society: Theory, History, Comparison,* edited by John Hall, pp. 1–31. Cambridge: Polity Press.

Hamilton, Gary G. 1998. "Culture and Organization in Taiwan's Market Economy." In *Market Cultures: Society and Morality in the New Asian Capitalisms,* edited by Robert W. Hefner, pp. 41–77. Boulder, Colo.: Westview.

Hammoudi, Abdellah. 1997. *Master and Disciple: The Cultural Foundations of Moroccan Authoritarianism.* Chicago, Ill.: University of Chicago Press.

Hann, Chris. 1996. *Civil Society: Challenging Western Models.* London and New York: Routledge.

Hansen, Thomas Blom. 1999. *The Saffron Wave: Democracy and Hindu Nationalism in Modern India.* Princeton, N.J.: Princeton University Press.

Hatch, Nathan O. 1989. *The Democratization of American Christianity.* New Haven, Conn.: Yale University Press.

Hefner, Robert W. 1997. "Islamization and Democratization in Indonesia." In *Islam in an Era of Nation-States: Politics and Religious Renewal in Muslim Southeast Asia,* edited by Robert W. Hefner and Patricia Horvatich, pp. 75–127. Honolulu: University of Hawaii Press.

———. 1998a. "On the History and Cross-Cultural Possibility of a Democratic Ideal." In *Democratic Civility: The History and Cross-Cultural Possibility of a Modern Political Ideal,* edited by Robert W. Hefner, pp. 3–49. New Brunswick, N.J.: Transaction Publishers.

———. 1998b. "Introduction: Society and Morality in the New Asian Capitalisms." In *Market Cultures: Society and Morality in the New Asian Capitalisms,* edited by Robert W. Hefner, pp. 1–38. Boulder, Colo.: Westview.

———. 1998c. "Multiple Modernities: Christianity, Islam, and Hinduism in a Globalizing Age." *Annual Review of Anthropology* 27:83–104.

————. 2000. *Civil Islam: Muslims and Democratization in Indonesia.* Princeton, N.J.: Princeton University Press.

————. 2001. "Introduction: Multiculturalism and Citizenship in Malaysia, Singapore, and Indonesia." In *The Politics of Multiculturalism: Pluralism and Citizenship in Malaysia, Singapore, and Indonesia,* edited by Robert W. Hefner, pp. 1–58. Honolulu: University of Hawaii Press.

Hollingsworth, J. Rogers, and Robert Boyer. 1997. *Contemporary Capitalism: The Embeddedness of Institutions.* Cambridge: Cambridge University Press.

Hooglund, Eric, ed. 2002. *Twenty Years of Islamic Revolution: Political and Social Transition in Iran since 1979.* Syracuse, N.Y.: Syracuse University Press.

Hinter, Shireen T. 1998. *The Future of Islam and the West: Clash of Civilizations or Peaceful Coexistence?* Westport, Conn.: Praeger.

Hoexter, Miriam. 2002. "The Waqf and the Public Sphere." In *The Public Sphere in Muslim Societies,* edited by Miriam Hoexter, Shmuel N. Eisenstadt, and Nehemia Levtzion, pp. 119–38. Albany: State University of New York Press.

Huntington, Samuel P. 1991. *The Third Wave: Democratization in the Late Twentieth Century.* Norman: University of Oklahoma Press.

————. 1993. "The Clash of Civilizations?" *Foreign Affairs* 72, no. 3 (Summer): 14–33.

————. 1996. *The Clash of Civilizations and the Remaking of World Order.* New York: Simon & Schuster.

ICG. 2002. "Al-Qaeda in Southeast Asia: The Case of the 'Ngruki Network' in Indonesia." Brussels, ICG Asia Briefing, August 8.

Inglehart, Ronald, and Pippa Norris. 2003. "The True Clash of Civilizations." In *Foreign Policy,* March/April, 62–70.

Juergensmeyer, Mark. 2000. *Terror in the Mind of God: The Global Rise of Religious Violence.* Berkeley and Los Angeles: University of California Press.

Kahf, Monzer. 1995. "Waqf." In *The Oxford Encyclopedia of the Modern Islamic World,* edited by John. L. Esposito, vol. 4, pp. 312–16. New York: Oxford University Press.

Kandiyoti, Deniz. 1991. "Islam and Patriarchy: A Comparative Perspective." In *Women in Middle Eastern History: Shifting Boundaries in Sex and Gender,* edited by Nikki R. Keddie and Beth Baron, pp. 23–42. New Haven, Conn.: Yale University Press.

Keane, John. 1996. *Reflections on Violence.* London: Verso.

Keddie, Nikkie R. 1991. "Introduction: Deciphering Middle Eastern Women's History." In *Women in Middle Eastern History: Shifting Boundaries in Sex and Gender,* edited by Nikki R. Keddie and Beth Baron, pp. 1–22. New Haven, Conn.: Yale University Press.

Knauft, Bruce M., ed. 2002. *Critically Modern: Alternatives, Alterities, Anthropologies.* Bloomington: Indiana University Press.

Kurzman, Charles, ed. 1998. *Liberal Islam: A Sourcebook.* New York: Oxford University Press.

Kymlicka, Will. 2001. *Politics in the Vernacular: Nationalism, Multiculturalism, and Citizenship.* New York: Oxford University Press.

Lapidus, Ira M. 1975. "The Separation of State and Religion in the Development of Early Islamic Society." *International Journal of Middle East Studies* 6, no. 4 (October): pp. 363–85.

Lerner, Daniel. 1958. *The Passing of Traditional Society: Modernizing the Middle East.* Glencoe, Calif.: Free Press.

Lewis, Bernard. 2002. *What Went Wrong? Western Impact and Middle Eastern Response.* New York: Oxford University Press.

Mamdani, Mahmood. 2001. *When Victims Become Killers: Colonialism, Nativism, and Genocide in Rwanda.* Princeton, N.J.: Princeton University Press.

Mandaville, Peter. 2001. *Transnational Muslim Politics: Reimagining the Umma.* London: Routledge.

Martin, David. 1978. *A General Theory of Secularization.* Oxford: Blackwell.

———. 1990. *Tongues of Fire: The Explosion of Evangelical Christianity in Latin America.* London: Basil Blackwell.

Meeker, Michael E. 1991. "The New Muslim Intellectuals in the Republic of Turkey." In *Islam in Modern Turkey: Religion, Politics, and Literature in a Secular State,* edited by Richard Tapper, pp. 189–219. London: Tauris.

Messick, Brinkley. 1993. *The Calligraphic State: Textual Domination and History in a Muslim Society.* Berkeley and Los Angeles: University of California Press.

Moussalli, Ahmad S. 1992. *Radical Islamic Fundamentalism: The Ideological and Political Discourse of Sayyid Qutb.* Beirut: American University of Beirut.

———. 2001. *The Islamic Quest for Democracy, Pluralism, and Human Rights.* Gainesville: University Press of Florida.

Munson, Henry. 1993. *Religion and Power in Morocco.* New Haven, Conn.: Yale University Press.

Murata, Sachiko, and William C. Chittick. 1994. *The Vision of Islam.* New York: Paragon House.

Nasr, Seyyed Vali Reza. 1996. *Mawdudi and the Making of Islamic Revivalism.* New York: Oxford University Press.

Nielsen, Jorgen. 1992. *Muslims in Western Europe.* Edinburgh: Edinburgh University Press.

O'Donnell, Guillermo, and Philippe C. Schmitter. 1986. *Transitions from Authoritarian Rule: Tentative Conclusions about Uncertain Democracies.* Baltimore, Md.: Johns Hopkins University Press.

Parfrey, Adam. 2001. *Extreme Islam: Anti-American Propaganda of Muslim Fundamentalism.* Los Angeles: Feral House.

Pew Forum on Religion and Public Life. 2003. "Poll: Two Years After 9/11, Growing Number of Americans Link Islam to Violence." Washington D.C.: Pew Forum on Religion and Public Life, September 10 Press Release.

Putnam, Robert D. 1993. *Making Democracy Work: Civic Traditions in Modern Italy.* Princeton, N.J.: Princeton University Press.

———. 2000. *Bowling Alone: The Collapse and Revival of American Community.* New York: Simon and Schuster.

Rahman, Fazlur. 1982. *Islam and Modernity: Transformation of an Intellectual Tradition.* Chicago, Ill.: University of Chicago Press.

Ramadan, Tariq. 1999. *To Be A European Muslim: A Study of Islamic Sources in the European Context.* Leicester, U.K.: The Islamic Foundation.

Rosenblum, Nancy L. ed. 2000. *Obligations of Citizenship and Demands of Faith: Religious Accommodation in Pluralist Democracies.* Princeton, N.J.: Princeton University Press.

Rotberg, Robert I., ed. 2001. *Patterns of Social Capital: Stability and Change in Historical Perspective.* Cambridge: Cambridge University Press.

Roy, Olivier. 1994. *The Failure of Political Islam.* Cambridge: Harvard University Press.

Sachedina, Abdulaziz. 2001. *The Islamic Roots of Democratic Pluralism.* New York: Oxford University Press.

Safi, Omid, ed. 2003. *Progressive Muslims: On Justice, Gender, and Pluralism.* Oxford: One World.

Schacht, Joseph. 1964. *An Introduction to Islamic Law.* Oxford: Clarendon Press.

Singerman, Diane. 1995. *Avenues of Participation: Family, Politics, and Networks in Urban Quarters of Cairo.* Princeton, N.J.: Princeton University Press.

Skocpol, Theda. 1999. "How Americans Became Civic." In *Civic Engagement in American Democracy,* edited by Theda Skocpol and Morris Fiorina, pp. 27–80. Washington, D.C.: Brookings Institution Press.

Skocpol, Theda, and Morris P. Fiorina. 1999. "Making Sense of the Civic Engagement Debate." In *Civic Engagement in American Democracy,* edited by Theda Skocpol and Morris Fiorina, pp. 1–23. Washington, D.C.: Brookings Institution Press.

Smith, Craig S. 2003. "Blast Hits 2 British Sites in Turkey as Bush Visits Blair." *New York Times,* November 21, p. 1.

Soroush, Abdolkarim. 2000. *Reason, Freedom, and Democracy in Islam.* Oxford: Oxford University Press.

Stoll David. 1990. *Is Latin America Turning Protestant? The Politics of Evangelical Growth.* Berkeley and Los Angeles: University of California Press

Stolle, Dietlind, and Thomas R. Rochon. 2001. "Are All Associations Alike? Member Diversity, Associational Type, and the Creation of Social Capital." In *Beyond Tocqueville: Civil Society and the Social Capital Debate in Comparative Perspective,* edited by Bob Edwards, Michael W. Foley, and Mario Diani, pp. 143–56. Hanover, N.H.: University Press of New England.

Sullivan, Denis J., and Sana Abed-Kotob. 1999. *Islam in Contemporary Egypt: Civil Society versus the State.* Boulder, Colo.: Lynne-Rienner Publishers.

Tamimi, Azzam S. 2001. *Rachid Ghannouchi: A Democrat within Islamism.* Oxford: Oxford University Press.

Taylor, Charles. 1989. "Cross-Purposes: The Liberal-Communitarian Debate." In *Liberalism and the Moral Life,* edited by Nancy L. Rosenblum, pp. 159–82. Cambridge, Mass.: Harvard University Press.

———. 1995. "Invoking Civil Society." In *Philosophical Arguments,* pp. 204–24. Cambridge, Mass.: Harvard University Press.

———. 1999. "A Catholic Modernity?" In *A Catholic Modernity? Charles Taylor's Marianist Award Lecture,* edited by James L. Heft, pp. 13–37. New York: Oxford University Press.

Tocqueville, Alexis de. 1969. *Democracy in America.* Translated by George Lawrence. Garden City, N.Y.: Doubleday.

Tu, Wei-ming, ed. 1996. *Confucian Traditions in East Asian Modernity: Moral Education and Economic Culture in Japan and the Four Mini-Dragons.* Cambridge, Mass.: Harvard University Press.

Tucker, Judith E. 1998. *In the House of the Law: Gender and Islamic Law in Ottoman Syria and Palestine.* Berkeley and Los Angeles: University of California Press.

UNDP. 2002. *Arab Human Development Report 2002: Creating Opportunities for Future Generations.* New York: United Nations Development Programme.

———. 2003. *Arab Human Development Report 2003: Building a Knowledge Society.* New York: United Nations Development Programme.

van der Veer, Peter. 1994. *Religious Nationalism: Hindus and Muslims in India.* Berkeley and Los Angeles: University of California Press.

Voll, John O. 1991. "Fundamentalism in the Sunni Arab World: Egypt and the Sudan." In *Fundamentalisms Observed,* edited by Martin E. Marty and R. Scott Appleby, pp. 335–402. Chicago, Ill.: University of Chicago Press.

Warren, Kay. 1998. *Indigenous Movements and Their Critics: Pan-Maya Activism in Guatemala.* Princeton, N.J.: Princeton University Press.

Weller, Robert P. 1999. *Alternate Civilities: Democracy and Culture in China and Taiwan.* Boulder, Colo.: Westview.

White, Jenny B. 2002. *Islamist Mobilization in Turkey: A Study in Vernacular Politics.* Seattle: University of Washington Press.

Wickham, Carrie Rosefsky. 2002. *Mobilizing Islam: Religion, Activism, and Political Change in Egypt.* New York: Columbia University Press.

Willis, Michael. 1996. *The Islamist Challenge in Algeria.* New York: New York University Press.

Woodward, Mark R. 1989. *Islam in Java: Normative Piety and Mysticism in the Sultanate of Yogyakarta.* Tucson: University of Arizona Press.

Wuthnow Robert. 1988. *The Restructuring of American Religion: Society and Faith since the Second World War.* Princeton, N.J.: Princeton University Press

Zaman, Muhammad Qasim. 2002. *The Ulama in Contemporary Islam: Custodians of Change.* Princeton, N.J.: Princeton University Press.

Zubaida, Sami. 1993. *Islam, the People, and The State: Political Ideas and Movements in the Middle East.* London: I. B. Tauris.

———. 2003. *Law and Power in the Islamic World.* London and New York: I. B. Tauris.

Chapter 2

NEW MEDIA IN THE ARAB MIDDLE EAST AND THE EMERGENCE OF OPEN SOCIETIES

Dale F. Eickelman

The New Arab "Street"

The "war in Iraq," as CNN calls it, is the "war against Iraq" or the "aggression against Iraq" in most of the local and international Arabic print media. *Al-Sharq al-Awsat* (London) is the only exception, calling it the "war of Iraq" (*harb al-'Iraq*) in Arabic, but the "war in Iraq" in English. Other newspapers, such as Morocco's *al-Ittihad al-Ishtiraki*, add "No War" in English to the banner of each page of Iraq-oriented news.

For most people, however, newspapers are lagging behind television (and to a much lesser extent radio, at least in cities) as a source for war news. The coalition's military action against Iraq, unlike its 1990–91 predecessor, is fully dominated by television in the Arab Middle East and, for the first time, much of the television coverage is generated by Arab satellite television rather than by European news organizations. Even the quality print media is reduced on many days to using the photographs of televised images. The Arab "street" is fueled by satellite television images and commentaries, and from multiple sources.

I am writing these lines from the *madina*, the old walled city, Fez, Morocco, in April 2003. I arrived in Morocco one day after the beginning of overt hostilities on March 19. Darb Bishara, the neighborhood where I live, is twelve minutes by fast walk to the nearest motor roads and taxi stands, a walk that takes me along Tal'a Sghira, one of the main *madina* thoroughfares, crowded most of the day with donkeys, mules, pushcarts, peddlers, and pedestrians. The larger cafés along the way have television sets and the smaller ones radios. Everyone avidly follows the news reports, but few of the sets are tuned to the Moroccan state media.

State television and radio have lost the battle for eyes and ears except for the countryside, where there is no alternative. Most of the sets are tuned to al-Jazeera Satellite Television or one of the newer Arab satellite channels. Médi 1, the private North African radio station broadcasting from Tangiers with a mix of Arabic and French, dominates the radio sets. Not just among the intelligentsia but also among the shopkeepers and the street peddlers who stop for tea, the state-controlled broadcast media are listened to primarily for the "official story." Its limitations are recognized by virtually its entire audience. Even in the economically "on-the-edge" parts of the old city, such as my quarter, satellite dishes dot the rooftops. Not everyone has satellite TV, but everyone gets exposed to it in the course of the working day.

Although most people do not use the full spectrum of available channels, all major European and Arabic satellite channels can appear on many sets at the press of a button. Everyone compares stories, and there is an understanding of the approaches that different media take. Everyone has been skeptical of the changing U.S. official story of why the "coalition" invaded Iraq. Cheers occasionally were heard up and down the street, as for a soccer match, when Saddam made a live-on-videotape appearance on Iraqi or al-Jazeera Satellite TV. By April 10, there was a general recognition that the "war" had turned against Saddam Husayn. The front page of *al-Sharq al-Awsat* was dominated by a huge photograph of a statue of Mr. Husayn being toppled from its pedestal, with the large-type headline, "and the Regime of Saddam Is Toppled" (*wa-yasqut nizam Saddam*), but the party-sponsored local press confined itself to saying that "obscurity" prevailed in what was happening in Iraq. Satellite television was unambiguous.

There were some street demonstrations through the end of March, culminating in a united call from all Moroccan political parties for mass demonstrations on Sunday, March 30 in the major cities, with the largest taking place in Rabat. After these demonstrations, the relatively minor violence went unreported in the next day's local print and broadcast media—although it was reported (together with a photograph of demonstrators burning an American flag) in the March 31 *al-Sharq al-Awsat*.

After the fall of Baghdad, discussion along this particular Arab "street" in the Fez *madina* was eerily like discussions in the Western press: What happens next? Will America (Britain is scarcely mentioned) bring a better government? What will be the Turkish reaction, especially if Iraq's Kurds are given voice in government? The term "democracy" (*al-dimuqratiya*) is used only by the educated, but a greater number are aware of the restrictions placed on their genuine political participation. Discussion is more animated in private homes. In other words, the Arab "street" is rapidly evolving from the shapeless and manipulable image that it possesses in the West, and there is a more concrete awareness than in the past of the benefits of more open societies.

DISCOVERING OPEN SOCIETIES

The substantial growth in mass education over the last three decades, the proliferation and accessibility of new media and communications, and the increasing ease of travel make it impossible for state and religious authorities to monopolize the tools of literate culture. The ideas, images, and practices of alternative social and political worlds have become a daily occurrence. They enter domestic space through satellite and cable television, and the alternate realities are better understood than in the past. Rapidly rising levels of literacy and familiarity with an educated Arabic formerly restricted to an elite facilitate this better comprehension. They also rehearse viewers to respond to those in authority in the common language of the Arabic of the classroom and the media.

Mass education was important in the development of nationalism in an earlier era (Gellner 1983, 28–29). In recent years, the proliferation of media and means of communication have multiplied the possibilities for creating communities and networks among them, fragmenting religious and political authority, dissolving prior barriers of space and distance, and opening new grounds for interaction and mutual recognition. Combined with mass higher education, the increasing accessibility of the new media facilitates the collaboration of like-minded people across national and regional boundaries. This also facilitates the scaling up of civic-pluralist forces in society.

To be sure, the power of new media to challenge and fragment claims to religious and political authority had become evident at the time of the 1978–79 Iranian revolution. Audiocassettes—easy to smuggle and duplicate—were then the subversive media of choice. Since then, the accessible nature of newer media and rising levels of education have increasingly blurred the boundaries between producers and consumers. Fax machines, desktop publishing, photocopying machines, the Internet, and new uses of older media make communications more participatory and create new audiences. The greater ease of travel—for education, pilgrimage, tourism, labor migration, and emigration—also accelerates the flow of ideas and practices.

More important, some new media seen as innovative in the early 1980s are now almost taken for granted. In countries such as Saudi Arabia, the same fax machines that rapidly disseminate criticisms of the regime from opposition groups abroad are also essential to the conduct of business. The state is powerless to limit their use without disrupting the economy, and attempts to counter "faxed criticisms" in other media—such as the press—by warning readers against disseminating them further merely draws subsequent attention to their existence (for example, "Shaykh Muhammad" 1994).

Elsewhere in the Middle East, since Iran's May 1997 presidential elections, some Iranian intellectuals and Western observers have gone so far as to speak of a new era of "post-Islamism" in the Islamic Republic in particular and the rest of the Muslim world in general due in large part to the rise of educational levels and new forms of communication (Roy 1999). Clearly, this post-Islamism is defined by the widespread awareness of alternatives to existing dominant ideologies and institutional arrangements. Fariba Adelkhah, for example, argues that this transformation is as significant as the original Islamic revolution. It is fueled by the combination of rising levels of education and the coming of age of a new generation of Iranians—now the majority of the population—not even born at the time of the 1978–79 revolution. This new generation, she argues, is creating an Iranian "religious public sphere" (*espace public confessionel*). In spite of resistance from conservatives, many in this generation publicly employ reasoned argument that, even if developed primarily in private or semiprivate settings, also has political repercussions (Adelkhah 2000, 177). Likewise, after many fits and starts in Turkish electoral politics throughout the 1990s, a political party inspired by religious values has persuaded the Turkish electorate—and the military guardians of the secularism enshrined in the Turkish constitution—in 2002 that one can be religiously motivated and adhere to the principle of secularism in the public sphere at the same time (White 2002).

In most Arab states, discussions concerning the nature of just and appropriate governance and the role of religion in politics is not as foregrounded and public as in Iran and Turkey, although debates in newspapers—which reach far fewer people than the broadcast media in the Arab world—are often spirited and hotly contested, even in the Arabian Peninsula. The legitimacy of royal authority and challenges to incumbent rulers are taboo subjects, but on other matters, including legislative reforms influencing the rights of women, the rapidly expanding range of public discourse about politics and religion is quickly outdistancing the pace of change in formal institutions.

A public sphere is emerging throughout the region in which messages and images in face-to-face conversations, newspapers, books, magazines, anonymous leaflets, video- and audiocassettes, and satellite and regular television crisscross, overlap, and build on one another. When censored or suppressed in one medium, such messages recur in another. Images of alternative institutions and practices, once on the periphery of the social imagination of much of the public, are now concrete and foregrounded. Even silence contributes to the public sphere, when some topics are avoided because of real or imagined penalties for direct public expression. Authoritarian limitations on participation in discussions and debate over public issues are resented and increasingly easy to evade. These discussions are not confined to immediate locality but increasingly include attention to wider regional and transnational issues.

Not surprisingly, some critics downplay the emergence of the public sphere in the Arab world. Seymour Martin Lipset (1994, 6), for example, asserts that Muslim, "particularly Arab," notions of political authority are especially hostile to democracy because Islamic political doctrines are "alien" to political freedom. The result is to assume that Muslims, more than the followers of other religions, are guided by religious doctrines that inhibit a shift to democratic rule.

Others argue that the authoritarian "cultural schemas" that pervade expectations of authority throughout the region have hardly changed over centuries. These schemas supposedly privilege hierarchical master-disciple relations in the religious and political spheres, severely limiting alternative political and institutional styles (for example, Hammoudi 1997, 8; Sharabi 1988).

In this respect, Samuel Huntington's (1993, 24–25) crisp "West versus rest" argument that "non-Western civilizations" have increasingly become political actors is as deceptive in its Manichaean simplicity as Daniel Lerner's earlier "Mecca or mechanization" (1964 [1958], 405) and Manfred Halperin's (1963, 129) argument that the Muslim world faces an unpalatable choice: either a "neo-Islamic totalitarianism" intent on "resurrecting the past," or a "reformist Islam" which would open "the sluice gates and [be] swamped by the deluge." This essentializing of civilizational traditions deflects attention from the internal and historical variations among Muslim societies past and present and from the vigorous internal debates that have taken place in the past and that are shaping the present of Muslim-majority societies.

This chapter offers an alternative to such bleak assumptions. It compares the rapidly changing contexts in which political and religious authority and "information" is structured and disseminated in the Arab Middle East. The emphasis is less on formal political institutions—although such institutions as elections play a major *cultural* role—than the commonly shared, often implicit, ideas of what is right, just, or religiously ordained and on which any community or group of individuals form cooperative relations.

THE NEW MEDIA AND MASS HIGHER EDUCATION

Even before the events of September 11, 2001, it was already becoming clear that rapidly increasing levels of education, greater ease of travel, and the rise of new communications media were developing a public sphere in Muslim-majority societies in which large numbers of people—not just an educated, political, and economic elite—expect a say in religion, governance, and public issues. State authorities continue in many ways to be arbitrary and restrict what is said in the press, the broadcast media, and in public, but the methods of avoiding such censorship and control have rapidly proliferated. Today, silence in public no longer implies ignorance, and it is the conjuncture of rising levels of education, new communications media, and increased mobility that have created new forms

Silence, or apparent acquiescence, is often a weapon of the weak. In some countries of the Arabian Peninsula, a "politics of silence" in which audiences applaud tepidly rather than with enthusiasm, is one of the few forms of public protest available, despite the simulacra of democratic forms offered by repressive and authoritarian governments (Waterdrinker 1993). For instance, Tunisia's President Zine el-Abidine Ben Ali was reelected with 99 percent of cast ballots in 1994, but few Tunisians took at face value his response to a French journalist's question that such results, far from being "a bit too good," merely reflected "the profound realities of the Arab-Muslim world," and the vote results "a massive adhesion to a project of national salvation" (Ben Ali 1994). Public silence in Tunisia in the face of such claims does not equal agreement with them.

An exclusive focus on religious extremism deflects attention from the more profound changes taking place throughout Morocco, Egypt, Jordan, and other places in the Arab world which are correlated with mass higher education and the new media, factors that have begun profoundly to affect how people think about authority and responsibility in the domains of religion and politics.

Throughout the Arab world, mass higher education has expanded significantly since the 1960s. As elsewhere in Muslim majority states, mass higher education has reshaped conceptions of self, religion, nation, and politics. It is as significant as the introduction of printed books in sixteenth-century rural France. Ironically, however, we know more about literacy in medieval and premodern Europe than in the contemporary Muslim and Arab worlds. Many scholars have noted linkages between advanced education and religious activism, but the focus on extremism and terrorism deflects attention from conceptual innovations and emerging networks for communication and action (Eickelman 1992).

Religious activism in the political sphere, the claims of its adherents notwithstanding, is a distinctively modern phenomenon, and its supporters are principally the beneficiaries of mass higher education. Mass education may be important in itself, but it also suggests basic transformations in ideas of what people accept as legitimate political authority.

For the most part, mass higher education is a recent phenomenon in the Middle East and North Africa. It began in earnest only in the 1950s, with Egypt's commitment to universal schooling following the 1952 revolution. Fifteen to twenty years later—that is, by the 1970s—after large numbers of students began to complete the advanced educational cycles, its consequences can be more clearly discerned. The timing of educational expansion varies for other parts of the Middle East. Major educational expansion in Morocco began after independence in 1956, accelerated in the 1960s, and today almost matches the rate of population growth. From 1957 to 1992, university enrollment grew from 1,819 to 230,000 students. Fifty times as many women are being educated today in Morocco as in the early 1960s.

A complementary measure of change is the circulation of books and magazines. The Moroccan writer Mohammed Bennis (interview with the author, in Mohammediya, July 16, 1992), recalled his student days in Fes in the 1970s, when the first "little" intellectual journals began to flourish in Arabic, rather than French, which had been the dominant language of the educated elite. In lectures and public meetings, students began to insist that teachers and their classmates express themselves in Arabic and not use French words in Arabic syntax when Arabic words and phrases were available. The shift from French to Arabic and the growing enrollments in higher education significantly increased participation in debates about politics, culture, and society. The intellectual effervescence of the 1970s that Bennis describes saw the emergence of the first cohort of Moroccans to acquire their pervasive "habits of thought" in Arabic, the country's national language (Bourdieu 1988). As elsewhere, pressure from this cohort created a demand for "re-imagining" Islam and politics and produced a significant readership for "quality" books in Arabic. In spite of the rising rate of unemployment among university graduates, reading is for them a means of "appropriating," organizing, and making objective ideas of society, politics, and self (Chartier 1987, 6–11).

As a result, new books and new markets for them have developed, which suggests a sea change in the images and vocabulary that affect the prospects for political thinking. Egypt, one of the few countries where there are figures on readership, provides an excellent case study of the changing market for books and magazines. Although studies of readership in Egypt, as elsewhere in the Arab world, are weak, the few that are available suggest that only 1 to 2 percent of the population read books regularly. But discussions about books—through word of mouth, the broadcast media, or widely read newspapers and magazines (Gonzalez-Quijano 1998, 398–408)—reach much larger segments of the population. Even censors draw attention to books by banning them or attempting to restrict their circulation. The most rapid growth is occurring in publications with religious content: the growth of secular mass education has increased attachment to Islamic culture. As Gonzalez-Quijano (1998, 159–60) explains, during the Nasser era in Egypt, religious books were of marginal importance, at least in terms of official production figures. With the opening of the book market in the 1970s, the relaxation of censorship controls, and subsidies from the oil-rich states, religious books became much more common. In recent years, books have become a part of mass culture in Egypt, and "products" intended for the consumption of a literary elite have become an endangered species.

Especially important is the growth in popularity of "Islamic" books. These are inexpensive, attractively printed texts, accessible to a readership that lacks the literary skills of the educated cadres of an earlier era. The style is often a breezy mix of oral style and colloquial diction. The covers take advantage of modern printing technologies and are designed to be both readily accessible and eye-catching. Thus the cover of Shaykh 'Abd al-Hamid Kishk's *Ayyuha l-Muslimun, ufiqu* (O Muslims, awake) (1989) shows a bearded Muslim (bright blue), seated at a table in front of a red-covered Qur'an, closing his eyes (perhaps in fatigue or distraction) as a serpent (orange and blue) hovering over him prepares to strike. Other covers are reminiscent of pamphlets distributed by the Jehovah's Witnesses. Layla Mabruk's *Rihla ila 'alam al-khulud: 'Adalat yawm al-qiyama* (A trip to eternity: Justice on judgment day) (1989) shows a weakened hand sticking out of a bright red pool, while above the title, encircled by a green garland and oblivious to the scene below, two Muslims pray. A Saudi pamphlet with a curious cover showing a bright red ball plunging into a well in an otherwise parched desert explains that democracy, which is "creeping" (*tatasarrub*) into the Muslim world, is incompatible with Islam because Islam offers governance by the Creator (*al-khaliq*), as understood solely by a properly instructed religious elite, whereas democracy, a non-Arabic term, necessarily implies rule by the created (*al-makhluqin*), in which unbelievers and the ignorant have an equal say in governance and usurp God's rule (Sharif 1992, 16–18). In many parts of the Muslim world, including North Africa, this style of argument—in some respects a mirror image of Huntington's—is regarded with amusement by many, but it also offers a style more accessible than that sustained by Muslim moderates such as Binsa'id (1993), who argue for political pluralism in the mainstream Arab print media.

"Islamic" books seek to capture the religious—and, with increasing explicitness, the political—imagination of a new generation. In these books, readers find echoes of what they already know and have their questions about religion and conduct answered. Conventional intellectuals may accord no legitimacy to the commercial entrepreneurs who benefit from a market that allows Shaykh Sha'rawi to sell 250,000 copies of a book when the sale of 10,000 books is regarded as a success and 50,000 as a best-seller. However, few can fail to recognize the significance of an emerging and distinctive "popular culture" in which the "Islamic" book has become a commodity for a mass audience (Gonzalez-Quijano 1998, 270, 412).

In retrospect, the 1952 Egyptian revolution appears less a break with the past than an intensification of the existing monarchical vision of directing change from above. This notion is visualized by King Farouk's personal bookplate (in Gonzalez-Quijano 1998, 96), which shows a printing press directly under Farouk's name and a crown, with a city and minarets in the background. A learned man in front of the press passes a book to a peasant kneeling next to his plow and oxen. This self-image of the distribution of knowledge was not significantly challenged in the years of the military junta and Nasser's presidency. The real revolution came later, as mass education created a new public for the printed word. In retrospect, the economic reforms set in motion in the 1970s unintentionally created the space for a cultural and intellectual reorientation through "market forces" which favored "Islamization from below"— uncontrolled and uncontrollable by state forces.

The implications of mass higher education and mass communication include (1) a changed sense of authoritative discourse, (2) the emergence of a sense of religion and politics as system and object, and (3) altered conceptions of language and community. First, mass education fosters a sharp break with earlier traditions of authority, with a direct, albeit selective, access to the printed word. With mass education, belief and practice increasingly become expressed publicly without reference to the authority of traditionally educated religious elites and relate more directly to political action than was earlier the case. The rise of this new dominant discourse affects both the expressive forms of the state and its religious and secular opposition. Mass education enables citizens to talk back to state authority, and this changes how the state can represent itself.

Second, mass education and mass communication encourage the conception of religion and politics as self-contained systems that can incorporate features from other systems. Mass education encourages this by treating Islam as one subject among many in the curriculum, even as students learn that "Islam is one" and encompasses all. The successive editions of Sayyid Qutb's Social Justice in Islam, (first edition 1949; seventh edition 1974) show how he refined his view of Islam as "an inwardly consistent and harmonious 'system,' . . . making it possible for it to be at once flexible, comprehensive, and distinctive" (Shepard 1992, 200, 211). Even radical Islam "accepts much that is borrowed from the West" (Shepard 1987, 315; see also Shepard 1989), with the borrowing facilitated by the fact that religion is seen as a "system" (nizam), although such borrowings are often denied or unrecognized. Moderates, as opposed to radicals, are more likely to acknowledge such borrowings, arguing that while Islamic principles are eternal, the way they are implemented can be adjusted to historical context. This point was brought home by a religious activist in the Arab Gulf who explained in 1978 how democracy could never take hold in the Muslim world because it was a concept alien to *shura,* which was Qur'anic and Islamic. In 1990, he asserted that *al-dimuqratiya* was compatible with Islam. When I reminded him of what he said a decade earlier, he replied: "Now we know better. *Shura* is not a major concept in the Qur'an and its few usages there are ambiguous. Democracy can be adapted to Islamic ideals." Likewise, when Islamic activists in Morocco declare that they are engaged in the "Islamization" of their society, they make explicit their sense of one system of ideas and practices—theirs—acting against the system of beliefs and practices held by other members of society.

Finally, the standardized language of mass higher education encourages new senses of community and affinity. In India, the temple-mosque dispute at Ayodhya in December 1992 went from a local matter to a national crisis in Hindu-Muslim relations because of "a massive expansion in the availability of television and the ending of the Indian government's carefully managed news monopoly." The narrative of the BBC World Television reporting of the incident, widely followed by English speakers in India, was a model of balance, but the pictures acted "as recruiting banners for the militants on both sides" (*Economist* 1993). The video clips fed to Oman television by an American network at the time of the massacres in the Sabra/Shatila refugee camps in Beirut in 1982 had a similar effect, as has footage of the Hebron/al-Khalil killings and their aftermath in February 1994, and the live coverage of the 2003 war in Iraq by journalists working for Arab satellite television.

Benedict Anderson (1991) argues that the rise of written vernacular languages in Europe and the spread of print technology have created language communities wider than those of face-to-face interactions yet narrower than the communities created by shared sacred languages. With modifications, this premise can be transposed to the Arab world, in which there has been intensified access to the printed word, and, in terms of the spoken word, to a more standardized Arabic.

One indication of shifts in the religious and political imagination of a younger, educated generation in many parts of the Middle East is the effort of the state to co-opt religious discourse. In Morocco in the 1960s and early 1970s, both the monarchy and its political opposition employed a "developmentalist" idiom in which "religious" issues were separated from "political" ones. By the late 1970s, the public language of the monarchy's supporters was much more religiously oriented, and the monarch asserted that he was developing a cadre of Ministry of the Interior officials trained in administration and Islamic thought, claiming that his actions were modeled on those of the Prophet Muhammad (Hassan II 1984, 162).

SATELLITE TELEVISION CONTENT AND OPEN SOCIETIES

Satellite television has been able to make a strong impact on public space in the Arab Middle East because of the shared "modern standard" Arabic of the classroom and the major broadcast media. This conjuncture becomes especially evident when unimpeded live televised debates are combined with call-in questions and comments. Such uses of the media bring speakers and listeners closer together, allowing authorities to be questioned. Uncensored satellite television in Arabic creates ready and open alternatives to the "official story" promulgated by state-controlled broadcast and print media, challenging other media, obliging them to respond with editorials or rebuttals, and entering many different domains of discussion.

In short, satellite television is contributing to the emergence of a "network" society (Castells 1996). Even if only 10–15 percent of Middle Eastern Arabs regularly watch satellite broadcasts (Alterman 1998, 15), the issues and commentaries on uncensored satellite television increasingly shape regional discussions and debate, linking these discussions to those held among Arab professionals in Europe and North America.

As a contributor to the expanding public sphere, Qatar's al-Jazeera Satellite Channel remains paramount, although it is facing increasing competition from rival transnational satellite channels based in the United Arab Emirates and in Lebanon. There are numerous other Arab satellite channels, but most stick to entertainment because of political constraints. Al-Jazeera began broadcasting in November 1996.

The Al-Jazeera formula resembles the one pioneered by CNN, although its discussion programs are more vigorous and controversial. One example is the weekly program, "al-Ittijah al-Mu'akis" (The Opposite Direction), moderated by Faisal al-Kassim. A Syrian by origin, al-Kassim graduated at the top of his class in English from the University of Damascus in 1983 and won a scholarship for graduate studies in Britain. His doctoral thesis at the University of Hull was on political iconoclasm in modern British drama. He began working part-time for the BBC in 1988 and made the shift from BBC radio to television in 1994, a position that lasted until the collapse of the BBC's Arabic satellite transmissions in May 1996.

In "The Opposite Direction," two guests with contrary views square off in the Qatar studio, although occasionally the program broadcasts from elsewhere in the Arab world. With al-Kassim moderating, the guests talk to one another for about an hour, followed by telephone call-ins. The program is live, including the telephone calls, which are not prescreened or subject to the "time delay" technology common in American broadcasting. The topics and the broadcasts join the central debates of the Arab world—the Arab-Israeli crisis, the state of the economy, Iran and the Gulf, Kuwait-Iraq animosity, polygamy, Turkey-Israel relations, human rights and Islam, Syria's negotiations with Israel over the Golan Heights, and democratization.

Thus a broadcast on Islam and secularism featured a heated discussion between Yusuf al-Qaradawi, a leading religious conservative, and Syria's Sadeq al-Azm, a committed secularist. For many in the audience, al-Azm's presentation was the first time they heard a "secularist" argument. Another program featured a debate on polygamy between Toujan Faysal, the first woman in Jordan's parliament and a secularist, and Safinaz Kazim, a religiously conservative Egyptian. When Faysal said at one point that Qur'anic doctrine was out of date, the Egyptian accused her of blasphemy, ripped off her microphone, and got up to leave. Al-Kassim reminded her that she was on live television. She shot back: "I don't care if we're on Mars. I'm not tolerating this blasphemy," and left the studio. The incident also suggests how satellite television is allowing women to join public religious discussions, albeit cautiously, as "The Opposite Direction" never pairs women with men. In October 1999, a former Algerian prime minister, Reda Malek, unhappy with a particularly sharp telephone question, asked al-Kassim to stop the tape. Al-Kassim replied, "I can't. We broadcast live. You're not in Algeria." Furious, the Algerian cursed on air and stormed out of the studio (author's interview with Faisal al-Kassim, Doha, October 30, 1999).

Al-Jazeera programs also focus on regional issues. Thus Abdallah Nafisi, in a program discussing economics, blurted out an attack against the then head of Saudi Arabia's Supreme Council of Ulama, Shaykh Ibn Baz (1912–99), when he declared:

> I defy Bin Baz to say something about royal corruption in Saudi Arabia. His country is infested with corruption. He can do fatwas on Viagra, but not mention [regime opponents like] Safar al-Hawali, people languishing in prison. We cannot separate politics from money in the Arab Gulf. "The rulers"—he used the insulting phrase, "the shopkeeper rulers" (al-hukkam al-tujjar)—"only care about opening bank accounts in the West." (author's interview with Faisal al-Kassim, March 20, 1999)

Although accused of bias against the Saudis, a Saudi specialist in media studies recently published a program-by-program analysis of "The Opposite Direction," concluding that it showed no political or religious bias (al-Shamri 1998). The publication of such a book in Saudi Arabia itself suggests the rapidly evolving public sphere, as the "craft" of censorship becomes increasingly public.

The contribution of al-Jazeera to the public sphere is manifested in the speed with which videotapes of its programs circulate freely in the shops and private homes in Damascus, Casablanca, Muscat, Amman, Riyadh, and elsewhere, among those without direct access to satellite television. For many viewers, its Arabic news broadcasts have become the standard against which other broadcasters are judged. Given that reliable surveys of viewing habits and trust in the televised media are lacking for the Arab world, the evidence is largely anecdotal. Yet, dependable figures for Gaza and the West Bank place Qatar's al-Jazeera TV as the most reliable source for information (33.7 per cent), followed by other satellite channels (26.0 per cent), with local Palestinian authority (14.0 per cent) and Israeli television (8.9 per cent) lagging far behind, but still ahead of MBC, Egyptian, and Jordanian broadcasts (Jerusalem Media and Communication Center 1999: 9).

Moreover, satellite television tilts the balance of public argument in favor of ideas and practices that can be explained, defended, and fore-grounded. The speed and intensity with which it facilitates the circulation of ideas, images, and practices also distinguishes contemporary public spaces from those of the past. Likewise, journalists and newspaper editors can comment almost simultaneously on events because they can read any of the rapidly growing number of Arabic newspaper Web sites for re-actions to current events. Uncensored satellite television enables a wider public to participate in such discussions.

Arabic language satellite channels, like the other new media, including the Internet, have had profound consequences for the political and religious imagination. First, they create and sustain a new public. Modern mass education means not only more widely spread skills than prior patterns of elite education, but also offers wider, competing repertoires of intellectual techniques and authorities and the erosion of exclusivities that previously defined communities of discourse, extending them also to women and minorities.

Second, viewers can now watch religious and political authorities and commentators explain their views and answer questions more as equals than as distant orators who cannot directly be challenged. Moreover, it is not just religious specialists who debate religion, but other educated persons and public figures. The distance between authorities and their audiences is diminished, and claims to the mantle of authority become more open. Finally, satellite television introduces audiences to new ways of thinking, in favoring effective and reasoned presentations. Satellite television is also immediate. Thus Arab opinion makers and television journalists were almost unanimously opposed to the "coalition" invasion and emphasized Iraqi resistance and civilian casualties. They did not flinch, however, from showing U.S. forces vanquishing the last vestiges of the Saddam Hussein regime, forcing readers and viewers immediately to confront the new situation and the impotence of the Iraqi regime (Morley 2003).

Satellite television thus plays a major role in creating and sustaining a new public sphere and brings to it a new objectivity. Satellite television and other new media contribute to turning anonymous or unknown contemporaries into consociates that share common assumptions of civility and morality. Not everyone can telephone guests on politically and religiously sensitive talk shows, and the number of callers from outside the Arab world still outnumber regional callers. But even this fact reminds people of the limits to expression in the Arab Middle East and North Africa. The viewing public, however, is no longer mass and anonymous, but defined by mutual participation—indeed, by performance. In this sense, which Benedict Anderson (1991, 37–46) refers to as a growing sense of reading together, the public sphere emerges less from associations, more strictly the domain of civil society, than with ways of dealing confidently with others in an expanding social universe of shared communication.

MAKING OPENNESS WORK: MEDIA, AUTHORITY, AND ELECTIONS IN MOROCCO

Although mass education and mass communication are profoundly changing political expectations and ideas of legitimate rule throughout the Middle East, the prospects for democracy vary with the political institutions specific to each country. This is not to say that developments in one country do not have significant repercussions in another. For example, the radicalization of Algerian politics since 1989 led directly to Morocco's October 1992 municipal elections and the June 1993 parliamentary ones. Prior to these elections, the specter of intolerant religious radicalism and equally violent state responses in neighboring Algeria were reported daily in the press and television, and the truth of the violence was confirmed by the many Moroccans with cross-border ties. As in Egypt, assassinations and violent clashes between radical Muslim and state-sponsored hit squads had become commonplace, and the growing Algerian crisis triggered Hassan II's April 1992 decision to hold elections. Although there were reported instances of fraud in both elections, they were generally perceived as "more fair" than preceding ones (International Foundation for Electoral Systems [IFES] 1993, 3; Eickelman 1994). Until the January 1992 military takeover, Algeria followed the "big bang" model of democratization—rapid and direct implementation of decision making on the basis of popular vote. In contrast, Morocco's approach has been incremental, with elections irregularly held since 1963. As was the case for the 1992 municipal elections, the June 1993 parliamentary elections for 222 of the 333 parliamentary seats did not result in a clear victory for any party.

Elections for the remaining 111 indirectly elected parliamentary seats took place on September 17, 1993. On April 26, 1994, "partial" municipal and parliamentary elections—for fourteen seats—were held in the electoral districts where earlier results were invalidated.

The reasons for the large number of invalid votes in the June 1992 elections—13 percent of the 7,153,211 votes cast nationally, with up to 50 percent in some towns, such as Tangier—vary with region, but a high rate of invalid votes can be read as a sign of greater willingness to use the tools of the "system," flawed as it is, and an awareness that the system can be manipulated not only by the government—which acknowledged prior to the September 2002 parliamentary elections that all prior Moroccan elections had been rigged in one way or another—but also by voters. As with the October 1992 municipal elections, some candidates reportedly purchased votes. In some towns, including Casablanca and Khouribga, the "market value" for votes varied between 50 and 100 Moroccan dirhams ($5–$10), roughly the same as for the October 1992 municipal elections. Unfortunately, polling station reports (*taqarir 'an 'amaliyat ihsa' al-aswat*) did not distinguish between empty envelopes and votes invalidated for other causes. However, interviews I conducted with polling station officials and party observers in one locality the day after the 1992 elections suggest that the majority of invalid votes were due to blank envelopes, and a survey of election results in one area where detailed results were accessible suggested a correlation between a high incidence of "null" votes and votes for a candidate—who lost—reputed to have purchased votes (see also IFES 1993). In some areas, such activities were limited because candidates engaged attorneys to monitor the practices of rivals and the efforts by opponents to secure the support of local officials. Rival parties threatened to report illegal practices to local electoral commissions and to other authorities. This response in itself indicated a greater confidence in the "rule of law" and the electors' growing sophistication and awareness of the gap between the rhetoric of the state and its practices.

An exclusive focus on election results deflects attention from major changes taking place beneath the surface. The state needed to make complex arrangements to set the 1992 and 1993 elections in motion and to convince Morocco's political parties that the elections would be fair. The behind-the-scenes negotiations were not secret—the fact that they were taking place was widely known and reported in the national press. Among the issues involved were (1) the creation of national and regional electoral commissions, including procedures for handling instances of fraud and abuse; (2) computerized election registration to reduce the possibility of electoral fraud; (3) lowering the voting age from twenty-one to twenty; and (4) granting political parties access to television for the first time.

Other changes were more subtle. By mid-1992, the activities of human rights groups were regularly reported in the national press. Even when newspapers refrained from publishing details of human rights abuses because of censorship rules, some national newspapers referred to banned books and to the continued concerns of foreign human rights groups. Another innovation followed Hassan II's August 20, 1992, speech from the throne in which he called for a major reexamination of the rights of women and a revision of the *mudawwana,* the *shari'a*-based legal code governing family law administration in Morocco. Even if the results were modest, it set in train conferences and drafting sessions that gave the appearance of improved conditions, especially when coupled with the election of two women to parliament. Finally, press laws were liberalized. The relaxed restrictions culminated in a major scandal in mid-February and March 1993, when Moroccans were treated to daily accounts— a morality play for Ramadan, as it were—of the trial of a senior Casablanca police official for sex crimes involving an estimated fifteen hundred female victims, all of whom he videotaped having forced sex with himself. Although the broadcast media remained silent, the print media covered the trial extensively. For the month of Ramadan, the circulation of Moroccan newspapers soared, as journalists honed their tabloid skills and newspapers regularly sold out (Rocco 1993; Mayer 1993, 93–105). With a total blackout on the subject in the broadcast media, the print media enjoyed a brief renaissance and the event as a morality play was likewise conveyed via audiocassette tapes in Arabic and Berber to wider audiences throughout Morocco (Lakhsassi 1998).

Morocco's September 27, 2002, parliamentary elections offer an interesting contrast to previous ones. They were the first to be held under the rule of Muhammad VI, who assumed the throne after the death of his father in July 2000. On the day before the elections, the prime minister announced that these elections would be a "complete break with the past" and acknowledged that prior ones had been manipulated (cited in Ksikes 2003, 29). In fact, strong efforts were made to eliminate the purchase of votes for cash, the offering by candidates of meals, and other forms of pressure. Prior to the election, the government commissioned television commercials in Arabic and in Berber intended to show illiterates how to vote, and others, featuring a rough-voiced man of authority in a *jallaba,* promising swift and sure punishment for electoral fraud.

With twenty-six political parties and a system of proportional voting for both a national list of candidates for each party and another "local" list, the voters needed all the help that they could get. As a promissory note on the new "transparency" (*shafafiyya*), voters were promised a televised counting of the ballots beginning as soon as the doors shut at the country's thirty-seven thousand polling stations. In the events, only "partial" results were announced after a day's delay, with complete results announced only four days after the elections and an unexplained blackout of the Ministry of the Interior's election Web site (*Le Journal Hebdomadaire* 2003, 13).

The effort at "transparent" elections was a chastening experience for the government, the political parties, and politically aware Moroccans. The government learned that transparency cannot be achieved by top-down orders alone. The complex system of proportional voting proved so complex that local officials hired to tally the votes acknowledged that their cursory training proved inadequate to the task (interviews in Tanger, September 29, 2003; Mohamed Brahimi, cited in Ksikes 2003, 31). Moreover, the tenor of the televised commercials, showing illiterates how to hold a pen and mark ballots for the one of the twenty-six parties of their choice, proved an embarrassment for educated Moroccans. The very effort to communicate such a complex system of voting to Morocco's illiterates—60 percent of the female population and roughly 40 percent of the males—highlighted one of the country's national educational failures. Finally, at the time of the elections and in subsequent published analyses, the government's concern to diminish the "Islamist" vote was evident. Although the breakup of an al-Qaida cell in the summer prior to the elections and the arrest of a religiously motivated criminal in Casablanca in August 2002 were not fabricated incidents (Oberlé 2002), many felt that the government made special efforts to publicize these events and cast Morocco's Islamists in a bad light. Although the followers of Abdesslam Yassine, grouped into a movement known as "al-'Adl wa-l-ihsan" (Justice and Benevolence) are neither recognized as a political party and do not recognize the legitimacy of the elections, another Islamist group, "al-'adl wa-l-dimuqratiya" (PJD, Justice and Democracy) made a strong showing in the circumscriptions where they were allowed to field candidates. The fact that the government had negotiated in advance the numbers of circumscriptions where they were allowed to field candidates was an open secret (Jamaï 2003, 18). The government was afraid that they would make major gains and disrupt the balance of Morocco's recognized, and balkanized, political landscape. The government, allegedly at the instigation of the king, also reserved seats of the national parliamentary list for women, guaranteeing that women would hold at least 30 of parliament's 325 seats.

As in the past, the parties also recognized their limitations in communication. All parties were permitted access to television, but as in prior elections, few possessed the ability to use the medium effectively. Parties also received subsidies for campaign literature and for workers, as in prior campaigns, but these were active only in the days immediately prior to the elections. Most leaflets were confined to showing a candidate's photograph, and the color and symbol allotted to them. Some reports suggested that the Islamist PJD used the pulpits of mosques to get out the vote (Ksikes 2003, 32), but this claim, made only anonymously and after the elections, may have been made only to "explain" the strong turnout for the PJD in contrast to the other political parties.

From the point of view of many voters, the "transparency" of the elections took away from some of the appeal of earlier ones. For many Moroccans who do not understand the electoral process or are not persuaded that they benefit from it, the lack of cash traded for votes may have taken away an incentive to participate in the elections. By 4:00 P.M. on election day, the Ministry of the Interior announced turnout as only 30 percent of the registered voters. By the close of the polls at 7:00 P.M., some 56 percent had voted, one of the lightest turnouts in Morocco's electoral history.

The September elections did not therefore constitute a major transformation for Morocco, although the number of violations of electoral procedures was light compared with prior elections (*Le Journal Hebdomadaire* 2003, 28–29). From the perspective of Tangier, where I observed the elections, the prevalence of cellular telephones by party activists did much to limit opportunities for abuse. Party sympathizers could call headquarters within moments of suspected infractions to report them, so that observers or negotiators could be sent to the scene. Some parties also pooled their efforts to report infractions or problems on a timely basis, and shared information between towns and regions was the norm and not the exception. In past elections, only the government possessed the ability to communicate rapidly, at least between major centers. The government hot line (*numéro verte*) to report violations also functioned, but appeared to function only to record complaints and not to act on them. In the past, such reports might have taken hours or even a day to be communicated.

"Scaling Up" for More Open Societies

Elections such as Morocco's require a conjuncture of "scaling up" and "scaling down." The "scaling up" involves using informal background understandings of trust and cooperation to envisage participation linking persons, localities, and regions to wider society. "Scaling down" entails recognition on the part of the state that elections, like effective plural political participation, require not just a top-down order, but also a recognition of an inevitable trial-and-error as new forms of political organization become part of local background understandings of community and trust. Flaws remain in Morocco's electoral process, but in contrast with past elections, they cannot be imputed exclusively to a grand design from the center. Despite their claims to the contrary, Moroccan political parties unevenly cover the country, and none has a universal appeal. Unlike the situation that existed immediately after independence in 1956, no party has deep roots in all the rural areas, where local candidates with no committed party affiliation other than cooperation with the government, usually in the form of local officials, still prevail. The poor showing of many parties in many regions suggests that Morocco's political parties have only begun to master the techniques needed to secure mass support.

Yet significant political change is taking place. Politically active Moroccans began in 1992 to signal significant long-term political change. As one "opposition" political leader suggested:

> We are seeing the first stage in the breakup of the system of power in Morocco. In the 1970s and 1980s we asked the question, "What is the role which political parties can play in the monarchy?" Now the question has changed to "What is the role of a monarchy in a modern society?" Technically this is a forbidden question, but Hasan knows that this is the issue on everyone's minds. (interview with author, Rabat, June 11, 1992)

Nonetheless, most Moroccans are convinced that the conduct of the current elections breaks with past practices, allowing "democracy" to begin to acquire a specific substance and the "rule of law" to become more than a slogan, in large part because of at least some of the media and the new forms of communication.

Elections cannot be understood or implemented in a cultural vacuum, but take place in a web of significance that includes the background understandings and shared assumptions of a people. In the case of Morocco, as elsewhere in the Arab Middle East, moral authority does not derive from elections alone. In many rural parts of Morocco, voting still takes place along tribal lines. Sometimes this is interpreted as the local manipulation of voters. An equally plausible explanation in many regions is that voters consult with one another and decide collectively prior to elections how they will cast their ballots, although such votes were not always cast along tribal lines.

Linda Layne describes a similar situation for tribal Jordan, where people in tribal areas often voluntarily declare their vote to bystanders because of the cultural sense of dishonor at acting in a covert manner. In the Jordanian tribal context, giving "voice" (*sawt*) to one's vote—the literal meaning of vote in Arabic—meant refusing to separate the role of voter from that of person (Layne 1994, 112–23).

Such background understandings are also evident in the tribal areas of Yemen where, rather than belong to just one political party, most people belong to several even when such political identities are mutually contradictory (Dresch and Haykel 1995). The paradoxical effect is to sustain civil society. Dresch and Haykel argue that understanding the prospects for democracy in the Yemen requires a "local knowledge" that cannot be subsumed by any single, culturally universal instrument such as elections. Elections acquire an importance only when interpreted in context of political understandings derived neither from an overly determined metatheory—"elections are the only means to determine the people's will"—nor from directly "observing the flow of Yemeni social life without the benefit of dialogue with informed Yemenis." Moreover, in the Yemen, as elsewhere, the limits to what are considered "political" are in flux.

Progress toward representative government has been slow in the Arab world, but an awareness of what is lacking has become increasingly evident due to the new media, mass higher education, and the experience of large numbers of people in the region with life elsewhere. During the Cold War years, the United States—to contain the presumed Soviet threat, secure the free flow of oil to the West, and defend Israel's security—systematically opposed popular nationalist leaders, regimes "willing to experiment with political freedom," and those which moved too quickly to replace the old order (Cottam 1993, 20, 32–33). In some cases, these concerns continued after the end of the Cold War—in the case of some oil-rich states, the United States has spoken softly about human rights abuses. Likewise, U.S. concern about promoting democracy was far from prominent when the Algerian military canceled the January 1992 elections.

In the field of the history of science, one major advance has been to break with the assumption that there is a fixed, hierarchical relation between theory, the instruments of perception, and experiment, but rather a wide variety of interactive relations among them (Galison 1988, 208, 210). Setting aside such fixed measures of democracy as proposed by Lipset can offer an ability to understand the complex background understandings needed to make elections work in the different contemporary contexts of the Arab Middle East.

A first step is to learn to elicit the cultural notions of legitimate authority and justice and to recognize the multiple voices of the Muslim and Arab world attuned to these issues. Ideas of just rule, religious or otherwise, are not fixed, even if some radicals claim that they are. Such notions are debated, argued, often fought about, and re-formed in practice. Such debates are occurring throughout the region. Recognizing the contours, obstacles, and false starts, both internal to the different countries of the region and external, to making governance less arbitrary and authoritarian is a needed first step. One observer of Moroccan politics, commenting on the shortcomings of Morocco's September 2002 elections, recently wrote:

> I am no longer interested in transparency as an end in itself, but rather as an instrument of political negotiation to brandish several months prior to [our] local elections. In fact, the [government] communications campaign for these coming elections has already begun. (Ksikes 2003, 29)

"Communication does not necessarily mean credibility," concludes Ksikes. Perhaps not. However, communicating in a common language and being able to confront authority in it, comparing multiple sources of information on other people's experiences with similar issues elsewhere, and possessing rapid means of information and communication held until recently only by state authorities or a political elite have dramatically changed shared understandings of religion and politics throughout the Arab Middle East—and altered the prospects for open societies and democracy. Such challenges are not regional alone, and foreign powers who act in the region to encourage more open societies must now match deeds with words. Successes, like shortcomings, will now become known in real time.

References Cited

Adelkhah, Farbia. 2000. *Being Modern in Iran.* New York: Columbia University Press.
Alterman, Jon B. 1998. *New Media, New Politics? From Satellite Television to the Internet in the Arab World.* Washington, D.C.: Washington Institute for Near East Policy.
Anderson, Benedict. 1991. *Imagined Communities: Reflections on the Origin and Spread of Nationalism.* London: Verso.
Ben Ali, Zine El Abidine. 1994. "L'intégrisme, c'est maintenant votre problème." Interview with Jacques Jacquet-Françillon, *Figaro,* August 2, p. 5.
Binsa'id, Sa'id. 1993. "al-hiwar wa-l-fahm la al-qafl'iyya wa-l-jahl" (Dialogue and understanding, not alienation and ignorance). *al-Sharq al-Awsat* (London), July 7, p. 10.
Bourdieu, Pierre. 1988. *Homo Academicus.* London: Polity Press.
Castells, Manuel. 1996. *The Rise of the Network Society.* Malden, Mass.: Blackwells.
Chartier, Roger. 1987. *The Cultural Uses of Print in Early Modern France.* Translated by L. G. Cochrane. Princeton, N.J.: Princeton University Press.
Cottam, Richard W. 1993. "United States Middle East Policy in the Cold War Era." In *Russia's Muslim Frontiers: New Directions in Cross-Cultural Analysis,* edited by Dale F. Eickelman, pp. 19–37. Bloomington: Indiana University Press.

Dresch, Paul, and Bernard Haykel. 1995. "Stereotypes and Political Styles: Islamists and Tribesfolk in Yemen." *International Journal of Middle East Studies* 27, no. 4 (November): 405–31.

Economist (London). 1993. "Feeding Fundamentalism." August 21, p. 36.

Eickelman, Dale F. 1992. "Mass Higher Education and the Religious Imagination in Contemporary Arab Societies." *American Ethnologist* 19, no. 4 (November): 643–55.

————. 1994. "Re-Imagining Religion and Politics: Moroccan Elections in the 1990s." In *Islamism and Secularism in North Africa*, edited by John Ruedy, pp. 253–73. New York: St. Martin's Press.

Galison, Peter. 1988. "History, Philosophy, and the Central Metaphor." *Science in Context* 2, no. 1 (1988): 197–212.

Gellner, Ernest. 1983. *Nations and Nationalism*. Ithaca, N.Y.: Cornell University Press.

Gonzalez-Quijano, Yves. 1998. *Les Gens du livre: Édition et champ intellectuel dans l'Égypte républicaine*. Paris: CNRS Éditions.

Halperin, Manfred. 1963. *The Politics of Social Change in the Middle East and North Africa*. Princeton, N.J.: Princeton University Press.

Hammoudi, Abdellah. 1997. *Master and Disciple: The Cultural Foundations of Moroccan Authoritarianism*. Chicago, Ill.: University of Chicago Press.

Hassan II. 1984. *Discours et interviews*. Rabat: Ministry of Information.

Huntington, Samuel P. 1993. "The Clash of Civilizations?" *Foreign Affairs* 72, no. 3 (Summer): 22–49.

International Foundation for Electoral Systems. 1993. "Morocco: Direct Legislative Elections." Washington, D.C.: International Foundation for Electoral Systems.

Jamaï, Aboubakr. 2003. "27 septembre 2002: Enquête sur un scrutiny aménagé." *Le Journal Hebdomadaire* (Casablanca), no. 102, April 5–11, p. 10.

Jerusalem Media and Communication Center. 1999. *Palestinian Opinion Pulse* 1, no. 33 (November).

Le Journal Hebdomadaire (Casablanca). 2003. "La Société civile relativise la transparence des elections," no. 106, April 5–11, pp. 28–29.

Kishk, 'Abd al-Hamid. 1989. *Ayyuha l-Muslimun, Ufiqu* (O Muslims, awake!). Cairo: al-Mukhtar al-Islami.

Ksikes, Driss. 2003. "Un Hold-up avorté?" *Tel Quel* 72, April 5–11, pp. 28–37.

Lakhsassi, Abderrahmane. 1998. "Scandale national et chansons populaires." In *Miroirs maghrébins: Itinéraires de soi et paysages de rencontre*, edited by Susan Ossman, pp. 99–109. Paris: CNRS.

Layne, Linda L. 1994. *Home and Homeland: The Dialogics of Tribal and National Identities in Jordan*. Princeton, N.J.: Princeton University Press.

Lerner, Daniel. 1964 [1958]. *The Passing of Traditional Society: Modernizing the Middle East*. New York: Free Press.

Lipset, Seymour Martin. 1994. "The Social Requisites of Democracy Revisited." *American Sociological Review* 59, no. 1 (February): 1–22.

Mabruk, Layla. 1989. *Rihla ila 'alam al-Khulud: 'Adalat Yawm al-Qiyama* [A trip to eternity: justice on judgment day]. Cairo: al-Mukhtar al-Islami.

Mayer, Ann Elizabeth. 1993. "Moroccans—Citizens or Subjects? A People at the Crossroads." *Journal of International Law and Politics* 26, no. 1 (Fall): 63–105.

Morley, Jefferson. 2003. "Arab Media Confront the 'New Rules of the Game.'" *Washington Post,* April 14 (http://www.washingtonpost.com/wp-dyn/articles/A64349-2003Apr9.html)

Oberlé, Thierry. 2002. "Rabat lève le voile sur ses islamistes." *Le Figaro,* September 25, p. 4.

Rocco, Fiammetta. 1993. "The Shame of Casablanca." *The Independent on Sunday* (London), May 9.

Roy, Olivier. 1999. "Le Post-islamisme." *Revue des Mondes Musulmans et de la Méditerranée,* nos. 85/86, pp. 11–30.

Al-Sharif, Muhamad Shakir. 1992 [1412]. *Haqiqat al-Dimuqratiya* (the truth about democracy). Riyadh: Dar al-watan li-l-nashr.

Al-Shamri, Sulayman bin Jazi'. 1998. *Barnamij al-Ittijah al-Mu'akis: Dirasa 'Ilmiyya Akadamiya* (The "Opposite Direction" program: An academic study]. Riyadh: Department of Information, King Saud University.

Sharabi, Hisham. 1988. *Neopatriarchy: A Theory of Distorted Change in Arab Society.* New York: Oxford University Press.

"Shaykh Muhammad." 1994. "Shaykh Muhammad al-Utayman in a Discussion of Incendiary Publications: Whomever Publishes These Leaflets and Pamphlets, Copies Them, or Distributes Them Commits a Major Sin and Bears Responsibility for His Own Crime and for the Crime of All Those Influenced by Them." *al-Sharq al-Awsat* (in Arabic), November 20.

Shepard, William E. 1987. "Islam and Ideology: Towards a Typology." *International Journal of Middle East Studies* 19, no. 3 (August): 307–36.

———. 1989. "Islam as a 'System' in the Later Writings of Sayyid Qutb." *Middle Eastern Studies* 25, no. 1 (January): 31–50.

———. 1992. "The Development of the Thought of Sayyid Qutb as Reflected in Earlier and Later Editions of 'Social Justice in Islam.'" *Die Welt des Islams* 32, no. 2: 196–236.

Waterdrinker, Brigette. 1993. *Genèse et construction d'un état moderne: Le cas du Sultanate d'Oman.* Mémoire de DEA Études Politiques, Institut d'Études Politiques de Paris.

White, Jenny B. 2002. *Islamist Mobilization in Turkey: A Study in Vernacular Politics.* Seattle: University of Washington Press.

Chapter 3

PLURALISM, DEMOCRACY, AND THE 'ULAMA

Muhammad Qasim Zaman

THE QUESTION OF HOW ISLAM AND MUSLIMS view democracy, pluralism, and modern understandings of the rights of human beings has been much discussed, with varying degrees of pessimism and optimism (e.g., Esposito and Voll 1996; Mayer 1999; Humphreys 1999; Hefner 2000; Sachedina 2001). Muslim scholars like Abdulaziz Sachedina (2001) have argued vigorously that a careful reading of the Qur'an *as a whole* provides strong grounds for "democratic pluralism" and for a civil society in which Muslims and non-Muslims enjoy equal rights. Sachedina's argument is premised on a disjunction between the original teachings of the Qur'an and the historical development of juristic and political thought. While the Qur'an, on his reading, is strongly supportive of human rights irrespective of creed, Muslim jurists and rulers of Muslim majority states typically privileged Muslims over non-Muslims, just as they privileged men over women. The challenge faced by the Muslim scholars, the "Muslim religious establishment," is to rethink Islamic law and legal theories on the basis of the Qur'an in the modern world, he says, and he laments that the religious establishment has yet to show any serious engagement with this enterprise.

Others have taken a less severe view of the premodern history of Islamic law and jurisprudence, arguing that even as a sacred law, the shari'ah preserved many crucial elements of flexibility in its norms and that the manner and scope of their implementation could vary considerably at different times and places (see, e.g., Tucker 1998; Hallaq 2001). While underlining certain basic inequalities in the moral universe of the medieval jurists, Baber Johansen has shown that the jurists of the Hanafi school of Sunni law were careful to protect the rights of the individual against the claims of the state (Johansen 1999). The jurists worked with the two overarching categories of the nonnegotiable "rights of God" (such as certain punishments mandated in the Qur'an and in the normative example of the Prophet) and the "rights of man." While the latter were a matter of private negotiation between the parties affected by an infraction, the former—the rights of God—were upheld by the state on behalf of God and of the entire community. But the jurists worried that the state could infringe on the rights of the individual under the guise of protecting God's rights and sought therefore to restrict the laws pertaining to those rights to the barest minimum, even as they extended the scope of the rights of the human being. As one nineteenth-century jurist, Ibn 'Abidin (d. 1836) of Damascus, had put it, "This is not so because we are treating the claims of law [regarding the rights of God] lightly, but because the human being is in need and the law is not" (cited in Johansen 1999, 214).

Such juristic concerns suggest their possible relevance to projects of re-thinking individual rights and civil society in both a modern and an Is-lamic context. Mohammad Fadel has offered another illustration of how there might be unexpected concordance between the concerns of many Muslim "modernists" and the arguments of medieval jurists. In inter-preting Qur'an 2.282, which speaks of the need for *two* female witnesses to replace a single male witness, certain Sunni jurists explained this in-equality in what Fadel characterizes as "sociological" terms: what made a woman's testimony less valuable was the result not of any "natural" de-ficiency (as many others argued), but of the fact that she had less expo-sure to the outside world and thus presumably had less to say about disputes that arose there; in matters of which she might be expected to have a more intimate knowledge, her testimony was not half that of a man, just as in matters of narrating and transmitting religious texts, the authority of her word was no different from a man's. In the presence of such sociological explanations, Fadel concludes:

> one can no longer simply assume that modernist interpretations of Qur'an 2.282 represent a radical break from Islamic law; indeed, from the perspec-tive of *fiqh*, the sociological interpretation . . . is the *only* plausible reading of the verse. . . . [T]his suggests that Muslim modernism in general, and Muslim feminism in particular, might profit from exploiting problems and tensions that have long been recognized to exist within Islamic law. In the long run, this strategy may be more successful than claiming the need for a "new" jurisprudence that is to be derived *ex nihilo* from the original sources of Islamic law. (Fadel 1997, 200)

While Fadel's concern is to recommend this strategy to the modernists, might something similar be considered with reference to the traditionally educated Muslim religious scholars, the 'ulama, as well? Scholars of con-temporary Islam have often seen the 'ulama as a mere relic of the past, as having been entirely co-opted by the ruling elite, as altogether mired in an unchanging view of both Islam and the world and, in any case, as having little of interest or importance to contribute to contemporary Islamic dis-courses. But, as I show elsewhere (Zaman 2002), the 'ulama have not only undergone significant changes in the modern world, they have often also adapted in a variety of ways to the transformations around them and have thereby come to play roles of considerable importance in countries like Pakistan, India, Saudi Arabia, Egypt, Iran, and elsewhere. These roles are varied and, while they can be usefully compared across Muslim societies, they are, in each instance, the product of particular configurations of local, national, and international factors. In each case, moreover, the 'ulama compete for influence and authority with other actors in the public sphere—for instance, with Muslim modernists and Islamists of various stripes.[1] Yet far from marginalizing the 'ulama, it is precisely in the framework of an ongoing public contestation—over religious authority, politics, the proper orientation of their societies, the common good—that many of their new roles and their discourses have often been articulated (Zaman 2004). At the same time, however, it is typically with reference to the Islamic religious and especially the juristic tradition that they have continued to define and express themselves. The prospect of (re)discovering hitherto ignored positions within this tradition should, then, appeal to them more than it does to anyone else.

Whether the shari'ah has the resources at all that can lend themselves to the building or strengthening of a civil, democratic society in the contemporary world is an important and difficult question. And while many scholars deny that such resources exist (cf. An-Na'im 1990), the foregoing illustrations should at least indicate that the question is by no means a settled one and, indeed, that it *can* be answered in the affirmative. Yet this is not the only question worth asking. We also need to ask, as I do in this chapter, whether, in seeking to maintain a continuing link with the premodern juristic tradition, the 'ulama are willing to draw on that tradition's resources *in a way* that might be conducive to a civil, democratic Islam. A common answer to my question is a simple "no" (e.g., Sachedina 2001, 132). There is, indeed, much in the rhetoric and actions of the 'ulama to warrant such a judgment. But as I would argue in this chapter, in focusing on the 'ulama of South Asia and more specifically on those of Pakistan, the answer is in fact much more ambiguous. To appreciate why this is so, we need some understanding of the discourses of the contemporary 'ulama, the ways in which they engage with and build on the premodern Islamic tradition, and the pressures and contradictions of the political context in which these discourses have found expression.

Though they share a colonial legacy, the two nation-states that emerged with the partition of British India in 1947 have evolved along very different paths: India is the largest democracy in the world, whereas Pakistan's experiments with democracy have been interrupted, and marred, by long periods of military or quasi-military rule. The population of India is predominantly Hindu, and Muslims comprise approximately 12 percent of the total population; yet, even this relatively small proportion makes the Muslim population of India larger than that of most predominantly Muslim states (Hasan 1997, 1–3). The population of Pakistan, on the other hand, is overwhelmingly Muslim. And while India is a secular state—although led, since the late 1990s, by a Hindu nationalist government—Pakistan professes to be an "Islamic Republic." All these and other differences notwithstanding, 'ulama and their institutions of learning, the madrasas, have thrived in both postcolonial India and in Pakistan.

Most South Asian Muslims are Sunnis, though there is a substantial Shi'i population in both India and Pakistan (about 15 percent of Pakistan's Muslim population is Shi'i). It was under British colonial rule that the major sectarian orientations within South Asia's Sunni Islam crystallized, in part as a response to the challenges facing the Muslim community with the end of the centuries-long Muslim rule in India, the advent of a colonial power, and the massive economic, social, and technological changes that colonialism brought in its wake. One of the most important of these sectarian orientations is associated with the madrasa of Deoband, which was founded in 1867 in a small north Indian town (Metcalf 1982). The "Deobandis" represent a self-consciously "reformed" Islam, firmly rooted in the foundational texts and in the Hanafi school of Sunni law and defining itself in opposition to "popular" forms of belief and practice they often associate with the veneration of shrines and holy men. The madrasa of Deoband soon had affiliate madrasas, all called "Deobandi," in different parts of South Asia, even as it attracted many students from outside the Indian subcontinent. The "parent" madrasa remained in what became postcolonial India, where numerous other madrasas have emerged since independence. But it is in Pakistan that the madrasas belonging to various sectarian orientations—Barelawi, Ahl-i Hadith, Shi'i and, most notably, Deobandi—have grown most dramatically. Altogether, in 2001, there were 2,715 madrasas in the Punjab alone, the most populous of Pakistan's four provinces; and the number of madrasa students, which was said to be 249,534 in this province in 2001, had multiplied by more than ten since 1960 (Zaman 2002, 2; cf. 126). The products of these madrasas are very unequal in their grounding in the Islamic religious tradition: they range from highly sophisticated scholars of Islamic law and exegetes of the Qur'an and of the traditions of Muhammad (*hadith*) to those barely able to fulfill their functions as prayer leaders and preachers. Yet for all the differences in the stature and credentials of their graduates, it is in these madrasas that those who emerge as "'ulama" *become* 'ulama; and, as I would argue later in this chapter, madrasas are crucial sites for thinking about at least some facets of pluralism and democracy in relation to the Islamic tradition.

The 'Ulama's Islamic Tradition and Muslim Politics

The Muslims of South Asia faced one of the most critical moments in their modern history when, as the end of British colonial rule came in sight, they had to decide how their future as a religious and political community was best secured. One group of Muslim leaders, led by the All-India Muslim League, had come to advocate the creation of a separate homeland for the Muslims, seeing in this the best guarantee for escaping permanent domination by a Hindu majority in postcolonial India. But other Muslim leaders, and these included many prominent Deobandi 'ulama, resolutely opposed the demand for a separate Muslim state. These 'ulama were led by Husayn Ahmad Madani (d. 1957), who argued that Muslims throughout the world constituted a single global community, a community that could not legitimately be carved into separate Muslim nations. Conversely, he held, Muslims living in particular regions—in this case, South Asia—*could* be part of a composite nation with other religious communities in that region. That is, "nations" were based on ethnicity, language, and territory, whereas "communities" were defined by ties of faith. The Muslims of India therefore formed an Indian nation together with the Hindus, even as they remained part of an indivisible, global *umma* (Madani n.d. [1938]).

The position of these "nationalist 'ulama," as represented by Madani, was much derided by its critics for its failure to appreciate the dangers Muslim identity would face in a Hindu-dominated India. Such criticism was not without basis but, irrespective of it, two things are worth noting in the position of Madani and the nationalist 'ulama. First, there are, in fact, important precedents in the premodern juristic discourses on the question of Muslims living in territories governed by non-Muslims. While many jurists were resolutely opposed to such a possibility, others allowed it (Abou El Fadl 1994). And though Madani did not explicitly invoke these debates in defence of his own "nationalist" position, his views unmistakably echo some of these premodern juristic discussions. Second, and no less importantly, he insisted on the "flexibility" of Islam and of the shari'ah in adjusting to different social configurations and in interacting with non-Muslims (Madani n.d. [1938], 39–40, 49–51). To him, there was nothing in Islam that inherently disallowed such interaction, and it is clearly on this understanding of the shari'ah that he, as a leading religious scholar, based his remarkable opposition to the creation of a Muslim (or "Islamic") state in favor of a united, secular nation-state.

Even as the Muslims of postcolonial India profess their allegiance to the secular nation-state, their leaders have continued to debate how best to protect the interests of the community. Sayyid Abu'l-Hasan 'Ali Nadwi (d. 1999), the best known of the Indian 'ulama of the latter half of the twentieth century, argued, for instance, for the need for greater political mobilization by Indian Muslims as a way of safeguarding their religious and cultural identity (Zaman 2002, 160–70). Conversely, 'ulama like Wahid al-din Khan (b.1925) have argued that the interests of India's Muslims are best served by *renouncing* political activism and instead by focusing on building better ties with the non-Muslim majority, while also striving for strengthening the religious foundations of the Muslim community (Khan 1994). Wahid al-din Khan is highly critical of 'ulama like Nadwi, as well as of Islamist ideologues like Abu'l-A'la Mawdudi (d. 1979) of Pakistan for seeking solutions to the contemporary ills of the Muslims in politics (Khan 1996, 163–217, and especially 196–97, 199–207, 210–11). Rather than political activism, he advocates peaceful proselytism at the grass roots of society as the proper path to Islam's reinvigoration (cf. Khan 1986). But unlike Madani, Nadwi, and most other 'ulama, in South Asia or elsewhere, he also advocates a radical critique of the Islamic tradition in the contemporary world (Khan 1996, 31–95). This tradition, he argues, is largely the product of a time when Muslims were politically dominant in the world, with the result that it has little to guide them in drastically changed contexts. Rather than draw their resources from the existing body of premodern juristic debates, he urges Muslims to energetically engage in rethinking Islam to arrive at solutions that are genuinely compatible with the needs of their time. He is not alone among the 'ulama in advocating the need for systematic reflection on the foundational texts for solutions to new legal problems (*ijtihad*) but, unlike many of them, Wahid al-din Khan does not see the premodern juristic tradition as necessarily defining the perimeters within which any further juristic exertion ought properly to be undertaken.

While the minority position of the Indian Muslims led 'ulama like Madani and Wahid al-din Khan to argue for a pluralistic, multifaith society, others outside India have also attended to the question of pluralism *within* the ranks of Muslims themselves. The best known among them is the Qatar-based Egyptian scholar Yusuf al-Qaradawi, one of the most influential of the 'ulama in the contemporary Muslim world (Zaman 2004). Qaradawi invokes the long recognized area of "disagreement" in the premodern juristic discourses to argue that a plurality of views within the Muslim community is no threat to Islam and that it ought to be perfectly acceptable (Qaradawi 2001). Given the long history of juristic disagreements—which often provided the jurists and the judges some space for flexibility in the articulation and implementation of the law—Qaradawi's point is anything but novel. It is significant nonetheless, for invoking this history allows Qaradawi to try to carve out some pluralistic space in *contemporary* Muslim societies. At the same time, it reminds us that, in the culture of the 'ulama, novel or at least present-minded concerns continue to be couched in terms of their tradition.

The foregoing examples tell us something about how the 'ulama have, in their different ways, sought to accommodate Islam to a changing world. Yet none of these illustrations is free of ambiguity. Even as he extols the juristic tradition's tolerance for disagreement, Qaradawi makes a distinction between disagreement that constitutes "variety" and that which he labels "opposition" or "contradiction." The former kind, of which the juristic disagreements on subsidiary matters of the law are the prime instance, is not merely tolerable but a source of the tradition's richness of intellectual resources. But the latter kind of disagreement—by which he presumably means disagreement on the very foundations on which the Muslim society is to rest, or disagreement on whether that society is to rest on Islamic foundations at all—is, for him, intolerable (al-Qaradawi 2001, 210–15). In effect, then, the only sort of "pluralism" that is acceptable to Qaradawi is pluralism within the ranks of those who already agree on the fundamentals of belief and practice in their community. Madani, on the other hand, did clearly envisage a society in which Muslims and non-Muslims would be equal citizens, though he did so, of course, in the context of a state where Muslims were to be a minority. And, as historian Peter Hardy has observed, Madani clearly did not envisage a nation-state in which the Muslim community, qua religious and cultural entity, would altogether merge itself. He appears, rather, to have conceived of a free, united India where Muslims would be autonomous as a cultural entity, to be guided by their own religious leaders, the 'ulama, within the framework of the secular state (Hardy 1971, 38–41). Viewed thus, the significance of Madani's "united nationalism" and its potential for adapting Islam to a pluralistic India is by no means negated, but it does appear less far reaching than it did at first sight. Wahid al-din Khan, for his part, calls for a more vigorous participation of Muslims in weaving India's cultural fabric and in taking seriously the promises of India's secular pluralism. Yet, as noted earlier, his position is articulated on the basis of a thoroughgoing critique of the Islamic intellectual and juristic tradition, one verging on claims of its irrelevance in the modern world, and this exacts a considerable cost in terms of the resonance of his potential appeal for many Muslims, let alone for other 'ulama.

If there are ambiguities in formulations such as the foregoing, there appears to be considerable clarity in the stridency of the *anti*pluralist and *anti*democratic positions that one encounters in the discourses of many contemporary 'ulama. For instance, for all their other disagreements, there is little to distinguish the 'ulama of Pakistan (or of India, for that matter) so far as their attitudes toward the Ahmadi community are concerned. The Ahmadis are anathematized by most other Muslims, and not just in South Asia, for their belief that Mirza Ghulam Ahmad (d. 1908), the founder of their community, was a prophet. This assertion contravenes the fundamental Islamic belief that Muhammad was the last of God's prophets and, under pressure from the 'ulama and the Islamists, the government of Prime Minister Zulfiqar 'Ali Bhutto (1971–77) amended the constitution of Pakistan to expressly declare the Ahmadis as non-Muslims. Many Sunni 'ulama are no less hostile to the Shi'a than they are to the Ahmadis, however, and since the early 1980s, Pakistan has witnessed widespread sectarian conflicts between the Shi'a and the Sunnis (Nasr 2000; Zaman 2002, 111–35). This sectarian militancy has been led by lower-ranking 'ulama, who have tended to combine a humble socio-economic background and madrasa training with, often, military training in Afghanistan in the course of the Afghan struggle against Soviet occupation or during the subsequent civil war. However, many leading figures among the 'ulama of Pakistan and India have also urged the sectarian foot soldiers on, even as their own political influence has been enhanced by the activities of these sectarian militants. There is more to the context of sectarian hostilities in Pakistan than the discourses and activities of the 'ulama, though these do suffice to raise serious questions about the 'ulama's toleration of difference.

Nor do the 'ulama's discourses give solid proof of their commitment to what they often pejoratively refer to as "Western-style democracy" (e.g., 'Uthmani 1993a, 41, 111–16). The most basic of their discomforts on this score lies in what they see as the conflict of such democracy with the immutability of the shari'ah: given that God's law is for all times, no humans—even if they all agree—can have the authority to alter it, let alone to decide whether or not this law ought to be implemented. While Muslims may well debate and disagree on precisely how God's law is to be implemented, for this does admit of many different possibilities, they cannot, by definition, disagree on *whether* it ought to be implemented ('Uthmani 1993a, 49–50). Yet it is precisely the ability to debate the very foundations of a society and polity that a "Western-style democracy" confers on the citizens. So while most of the 'ulama typically endorse such features of a democratic system as regular and free elections and public accountability, they fervently deny that the authority of the elected representatives of the people extends, even in principle, to all areas of public or religious life, just as they deny that democratic inclusiveness can encompass everyone. Thus "heretical" Muslims, let alone those who are not—or are refused recognition as—Muslims, can scarcely be equal citizens with Muslims in an Islamic state.

Even more troubling than a rejection of, or serious limitations on, democratic pluralism is the view, espoused by many 'ulama, that jihad against unbelievers is a continuing obligation. The literature on jihad is voluminous, but I want to briefly take up a single example of the contemporary (but pre–September 11, 2001) discussions on it. This relates to one of the most prominent of Pakistan's contemporary Deobandi 'ulama, Mawlana Muhammad Taqi 'Uthmani, a former judge of the Shari'at Appellate Bench of the Supreme Court of Pakistan and the vice president of the Dar al-'Ulum of Karachi, one of the largest of Pakistan's madrasas. In a written question which, together with his detailed response, was later published in a book by Taqi 'Uthmani, *Islam and Modernism* (1999), he was asked about the legal status of "aggressive" as opposed to "defensive" jihad in the modern world. The questioner himself was of the view that armed struggle by Muslims is only justified in self-defense, and that Muslims are not to open hostilities against any state which has no aggressive designs against them. The proper path for promoting the interests of Islam, the questioner believed, was that of peaceful proselytism, and there could be no justification for aggression against a non-Muslim state that allowed opportunities to Muslims to preach their faith within it. The questioner wanted to know whether Taqi 'Uthmani agreed with this view, or on what basis he disagreed.

In his response, Taqi 'Uthmani disputed the idea that opportunities for peaceful proselytism constituted sufficient grounds for regarding a non-Muslim state as friendly. The crucial issue, he argued, is the "might" (Urdu: *shawkat;* Arabic: *shawka*) of the non-Muslim states, which, being presently greater than that of Muslim states, is by itself an obstacle on the path to proselytism ('Uthmani 1999, 102). Formal permission to preach Islam in such a situation becomes meaningless, he says, for the might of the state so conditions people as to make them incapable of becoming receptive to Islam. It is this might that jihad seeks to undo, Taqi 'Uthmani argues, and he concludes his response with contemptuous disdain for the view that the sort of expansionism aggressive jihad represents has no place in the modern world ('Uthmani 1999, 107–9).

It is impossible to neatly classify the Pakistani 'ulama between the "extremist" and the "moderate," the activist and the quietist, the political and the apolitical. Even many leading figures among them, who have largely devoted their careers to scholarly pursuits, maintain varied links with the radical sectarian militants and benefit from the latter's successes, as noted earlier. Taqi 'Uthmani himself is one of the most prolific of 'ulama—not just in Pakistan but anywhere in the contemporary Muslim world—in terms of his writings on society and politics, his commentaries on classical collections of hadith, and on a range of subjects relating to the interpretation and the implementation of Islamic law. His is far from being the most radical voice among either the Islamists or the 'ulama, and yet, as the foregoing views suggest, it is hard to classify him as a "moderate" in any meaningful sense.

How then do we interpret Taqi 'Uthmani's views on jihad? I would argue that despite the seeming clarity of his position, there is, in fact, considerable ambiguity in it—an ambiguity that sheds some light on the contemporary ʿulama's discourses in general. We should bear in mind that Taqi ʿUthmani's position here is a *theoretical* defense of the idea of jihad, not a call on Muslims to embark upon it. His concern is to safeguard what he sees as Islam's timeless verities—including what the Qur'an or the Prophet's example has to say about jihad—against efforts by Muslim modernists to reinterpret or repackage Islam in light of their liberal values. (Recall that Taqi ʿUthmani's essay on jihad is part of a collection of his essays in a volume entitled "Islam and Modernism.") The real issue here seems to be that of defending jihad *because* it has all along been part of the Islamic juristic and historical tradition. If the Islamic tradition provides the resources on which to conceive of a pluralistic world, as the tentative attempts of Madani and Qaradawi suggest, that tradition equally constrains the possibilities in contemporary discourse. The constraints are not necessarily disabling, however. Indeed, much of the growth and change in premodern Islamic law took place through a careful negotiation between the existing constraints and the available mechanisms for ingenuity and innovation (cf. Jackson 1996; Hallaq 2001); and ʿulama like Taqi ʿUthmani and Qaradawi continue to argue for the possibility of adaptation, growth, and change in that law. Even so, what typically distinguishes the ʿulama from other religious intellectuals in contemporary Muslim societies is precisely their insistence on taking the tradition, or large parts of it, along with them; and it is this concern, more than any other, that underlies Taqi ʿUthmani's alarming, and deceptively unambiguous, defense of jihad.

There is often also a considerable disjunction between the formal discourses of the ʿulama and the range of political and other practices in which they participate. Despite his seeming disdain for the opportunities for proselytism that Western democracies offer to Islam, Taqi ʿUthmani has in fact been a frequent visitor to Europe and North America, and he has published detailed accounts of his travels on these continents (ʿUthmani 1996). Sunni and Shiʿi organizations have engaged in systematic, targeted killings of their rivals, yet their leaders have not been above tactical alliances against what they perceive as common foes. Thus, the leader of the Tahrik-i Jaʿfariyya-i Pakistan, Pakistan's premier Shiʿi political organization, which had been banned alongside radical Sunni organizations by the government of General Pervez Musharraf in January 2002, was part of the alliance of religiopolitical parties in the general elections of October 2002 (*The News,* September 6, 2002). This alliance included factions of the Jamʿiyyat al-ʿUlama-i Islam, the political organization of the Deobandi ʿulama and the parent body of the Sipah-i Sahaba (also banned in January 2002); and it included Pakistan's premier Islamist organization, the Jamaʿat-i Islami, which in the past has often had difficult relations with the 'ulama.[2] The earlier alliance of one faction of the Jam'iyyat al-'Ulama-i Islam with the government of Benazir Bhutto during her second tenure as prime minister (1993–96) offers another instance of the 'ulama's pragmatic politics. This alliance was remarkable in view of the 'ulama's widespread discomfort with the fact that a woman headed the government and that it projected a largely Westernized image. My point here is that irrespective of what many 'ulama would say about secular, liberal regimes, about the Shi'a, about "Western-style democracy," and about proselytism in Western societies, they have seldom allowed their formal discourses to foreclose the range of political options that might be open to them. If the 'ulama's invocation of pluralist ideas continues to have much ambiguity about it, their *rejection* of such ideas is often no less ambiguous.

This ambiguity is important to underscore for at least two reasons. First, it already suggests, of course, that it would be a mistake to characterize the 'ulama as uniformly or irremediably hostile to democratic pluralism. Such a simplistic characterization would not be conducive to an understanding of Muslim politics any more than it would to improving the prospects for a civil, democratic Islam. Second, at least some of the ambiguity we encounter in the world of the 'ulama, in their discourses and practices, is a *studied* ambiguity,[3] one they have often allowed to exist because it facilitates greater maneuverability for them as well as more diverse but simultaneous choices in the public sphere. Yet it is not the 'ulama alone who have allowed the ambiguities and, indeed, the contradictions of their own position, and that of Islam in the public sphere, to exist unremedied. The state itself has played a large role not just in tolerating many of these contradictions but even, in case of Pakistan in particular, in fostering them.

ISLAM AND THE STATE

In an important review of the strategies through which "state-society synergy" might be promoted in the interest of social and institutional development, political sociologist Peter Evans notes the importance of focusing on "positive cases"—instances that indicate how the state and society have, despite meager resources, reinforced each other in helping build institutions rather than those where their mutual suspicions have impeded the cause of social development (Evans 1997, 205; cf. Tendler 1997). Attractive as his proposal is, this section would largely ignore his advice. While Evans is interested, inter alia, in identifying local resources which can be "scaled up" for development through multifaceted forms of interaction between public and private actors, I hope to demonstrate how the

Pakistani state has often provided critical opportunities for scaling up *antidemocratic* and *antipluralist* trends in society. The justification for this line of argument is not to add to the literature on the failings of the state (cf. Evans 1997, 205), but to arrive at a better understanding of the career and contradictions of Islam in Pakistan. Nor does my discussion presume that the Pakistani state is itself necessarily a cohesive or coherent entity. As Robert Hefner has shown with reference to Indonesia, in his chapter in the present volume and elsewhere (Hefner 2000, 65, 142–43), a recognition of the factionalism *within* the ranks of the ruling elite offers considerable insight into the contradictory ways a state might act on particular occasions. Even with such a recognition, however—which I will assume rather than illustrate here—we still need to understand how those who comprise the ruling elite might themselves contribute, in the name and through the instruments of the state, to the scaling up of uncivil norms and practices.

Long before the first of Pakistan's three constitutions (1956, 1962, 1973) was promulgated, the Constituent Assembly of the new state had, in 1949, adopted the Objectives Resolution, which set out the principles on which the state was to be based. The Resolution declared that sovereignty over the entire universe belongs to God, and the people of Pakistan are to exercise this sovereignty as God's legatees. While Pakistan's successive constitutions have often been seen as largely enshrining the vision of a modernist political elite—and some observers of the long debates over Pakistan's first constitution have wondered why the religious groups conceded so much to the worldview of that elite (Binder 1961)—a recognition of the sovereignty of God already gives a decisive rhetorical advantage to those who wish to take that claim seriously. It is hard to imagine that the modernist elite saw this as anything more than an affirmation of the state's overall Muslim identity; and yet the claim remains a very powerful one. Nor was the Objectives Resolution the last instance of the fostering of extravagant expectations about the role of Islam in public life without much accompanying evidence of the state's commitment to live up to those expectations. Nonetheless, such claims and expectations have created an Islamic space where the modernist elite is forced to be constantly on the defensive against the 'ulama and the Islamists.

That Pakistani governments have, more often than not, come to power through undemocratic means reinforces this defensiveness, even as it enhances the temptation to continually put their Islamic commitments on display. The "Islamization" campaign carried out during the eleven-year rule of General Muhammad Zia al-Haqq (r. 1977–88) was by far the most vivid of such displays. Where the Objectives Resolution had previously been a preamble to the constitution, it now became its integral part. The zakat-tax, one of the basic Islamic obligations, was officially enforced by the state; new institutions, such as the Federal Shari'at Court, were created to oversee the implementation of Islamic law; and stringent measures were adopted against an indigenous religious community, the Ahmadis.

The case of the Ahmadis, which we have already touched on, illustrates much more than the range of issues affected by the Islamization campaign; it also reveals how the state has allowed antipluralist tendencies in society to thrive and to be scaled up. The 'ulama, and many others, have actively polemicized against the Ahmadis virtually since the emergence of this community in the late-nineteenth century. Yet Pakistan's first foreign minister, Muhammad Zafrullah Khan, was a member of the Ahmadi community; calls for his dismissal were among the reasons for widespread riots in the Punjab in 1953. Though the rioters had demanded at that time that the Ahmadis be officially declared "non-Muslims," it was not until 1974 that the government of Zulfiqar 'Ali Bhutto brought about a constitutional amendment to meet that demand. Yet, once this battle was won, the assertion of the Ahmadis' otherness took the form of the demand that they be forbidden to use any Islamic symbols whatsoever—such as referring to themselves as "Muslims," or their places of worship as "mosques," or using the call to prayer like other Muslims, and so forth. In 1984, the state obliged again, this time with a presidential ordinance that more or less translated these demands into articles of Pakistan's penal code (Waqar-ul-Haq [1994], 100–101 [Articles 298B&298C of the Pakistan Penal Code]).

Though Shi'i 'ulama had themselves supported demands for the Ahmadis' exclusion from the community, many of the Sunni 'ulama who had honed their skills at agitational politics against the Ahmadis later turned them against the Shi'a themselves. Since the 1980s, Pakistan's radical Sunni organization, the Sipah-i Sahaba, has spearheaded the demand that, like the Ahmadis, the Shi'a too ought to be declared a non-Muslim minority for only then would Pakistan's character as a truly "Islamic state" be affirmed. The state has resisted this demand, though that has not prevented widespread sectarian bloodshed over the past two decades.

One further instance of how the state's own illiberal measures are then scaled up in alarmingly strident directions should suffice here. This concerns the infamous "blasphemy law," which, too, was made part of the Pakistan Penal Code during the reign of General Zia al-Haqq. Under this law, it is a capital offense to "defile" in any way—"by words, either spoken or written, or by visible representation, or by any imputation, innuendo, or insinuation"—the Prophet Muhammad (Waqar-ul-Haq [1994], 99 [Article 295C of the Pakistan Penal Code]). With this law on the books, a number of people, Muslim and non-Muslim, have been accused of "blasphemy," and those so accused have been sentenced to death by Pakistani courts (Dawn, September 10, 1998, March 14, 2001, August

19, 2001; *The News,* July 19, 2002). The capital punishment itself has never been carried out on grounds of blasphemy. Yet the existence of this law (together with extremely fluid conceptions of just what is to count as blasphemy) has led to many acts of vigilantism, and this is aided by the perception that the agencies of the state are themselves less than eager to actually carry out what the law requires of them. The government of General Pervez Musharraf (1999–) attempted to repeal this law, but strong opposition from the religious groups forced it to abandon the effort (Bearak 2001a, 2001b; *The News,* February 19, 2002).

But while many ʿulama have been at the forefront in opposing any change in the law on blasphemy, just as they have been among the most active in calling for the exclusion of particular religious groups from the community of Muslims, it is important to emphasize that the state itself is at least as complicit in carrying through such measures as the ʿulama are in agitating for them. If the ʿulama have made strident demands, particular governments—popularly elected (Zulfiqar ʿAli Bhutto's) or military (Zia al-Haqq's)—have gone along with them; and that, in turn, has provided the ground on which even more stringent demands have been made. If elements within the ruling establishment contribute to the scaling up of an uncivil society, of antipluralist sentiments, it is not difficult to understand the severe constraints the state faces when it seeks to "reform" particular institutions in the interest of creating a "good" civil society.

There is no better illustration of such constraints than official attempts toward the regulation of the ʿulama's institutions of learning, the madrasas. The regulation or reform of madrasas raises questions that pertain to more, however, than the contradictions of governmental policies or the influence of the ʿulama in society. More centrally for our concerns here, they also have some bearing on the problems and prospects of thinking about a civil, democratic Islam in relation to the ʿulama.

Reforming Madrasas in Pakistan

The madrasas of Pakistan have received unprecedented media attention in the aftermath of the September 2001 terrorist attacks. It was in Pakistani madrasas, after all, that many of the Taliban of Afghanistan—including a substantial proportion of their top leadership—were educated (Rashid 2000, 90). As the United States prepared for military action against the Taliban, thousands of Pakistanis, many of them associated with madrasas, decided to go to Afghanistan to fight alongside the Taliban, even as other ʿulama and madrasa students actively sought to rally support against the policies of General Pervez Musharraf. A number of militant Pakistani organizations blamed for terrorist activities both

before and after the September 2001 attacks have likewise been closely
allied to madrasas; and in January 2002, General Musharraf not only
banned these organizations but also declared a new resolve to better
regulate the affairs of the madrasas.

That resolve has remained largely unimplemented so far. While a number of madrasas in Pakistan are large institutions with thousands of students—like Karachi's Dar al-'Ulum, or the Dar al-'Ulum Haqqaniyya in
the North-West Frontier Province, where many of the Taliban had studied—there is no parallel to a central institution like the millennium-old
Azhar University of Egypt. Pakistani madrasas of different sectarian affiliations are affiliated to one another through madrasa boards, but this
connection is at best a loose one. Unlike in Egypt, therefore, it has not
been possible for the government to regulate the religious schools through
a centralized bureaucratic structure, though even in Egypt many dimensions of the religious sphere remain outside of governmental regulation
(Wickham 2002). Madrasas are often largely financed by private donations,
which again makes it difficult to regulate their affairs.[4]

Official committees have periodically been constituted by the government to suggest ways of reforming the madrasas (Zaman 2002, 60–86),
and these have typically been led by bureaucrats. They outnumbered the
'ulama on the madrasa reform committee of 1962 and they were mar-
ginally fewer than the 'ulama on the 1979 committee, though even the
latter was presided over by a Western-educated bureaucrat; the more recent and ongoing initiatives toward madrasa reform are likewise overseen
by bureaucratic officials. To such committees, reforming madrasas has essentially meant the introduction of "useful" subjects (a notion with deep
roots in British colonial discourse) into the curriculum of these institutions—that is, modern science, the English language, and other disciplines that comprise the country's educational "mainstream." Reform
also signifies doing away with the study of the "ancillary" subjects like Islamic philosophy, which for centuries has formed part of the madrasa
curriculum but which the bureaucratic committees do not see as properly
"religious" subjects. The 'ulama, however, not only take a more expansive view of the Islamic tradition than do the modernist ruling elite; to
them governmental initiatives toward integrating madrasas into the educational mainstream are but a thinly veiled effort to undermine their status as bastions of an "unadulterated" Islam in society and polity. As some
of the more strident critics of the effort to reform madrasas have argued,
what would result from "mixed" secular and religious education of the
sort the government has envisaged are "loyal civil servants," not 'ulama
of any significance or stature (Zaman 2002, 79–81; *The News*, July 7,
2002). In the 1990s, when government officials repeatedly pointed to
links between madrasas and sectarian terrorism in Pakistan, the 'ulama

often labeled any effort toward reforming their institutions as an excuse to shut them down altogether. In the aftermath of the September 2001 terrorist attacks, the government's renewed efforts to regulate madrasas came to be seen as the result of international, and especially American, pressure to do so as part of the global War on Terrorism;[5] and while the 'ulama had long equated the defense of the madrasas with the defense of a beleaguered Islam, they now strove—and not without some success— to make that equation more palpable to their audiences.

The contradictions of government policies have, meanwhile, remained unresolved. It is not a little ironic that the government of Benazir Bhutto should have sought to reform madrasas even as elements within the same administration oversaw the rise of the Taliban through Deobandi madrasas in Pakistan. And even members of the government of President Pervez Musharraf have continued to praise the role of madrasas in Pakistan (e.g., *The News*, June 24, 2002b) at the same time as they express their resolve to reform them. But the problem is not merely one of contradictions in governmental rhetoric or even a certain discordance within the ruling elite. Indeed, it extends even beyond the issue of addressing the contradictions of Islam in Pakistan's public life. The issue also relates to the severely limited alternatives that the state itself offers to some of the services the madrasas provide. In a country where almost half of the population is still illiterate, madrasas often provide all the education that many from the poorest segments of the population will ever have. Such education is typically free, as are the food and boarding that madrasas provide to their students. Quite apart from the social mobility that religious learning has often facilitated in many Muslim societies (Edwards 2002, 292), graduates of madrasas are frequently able to earn a livelihood as religious functionaries. Again, in a state with large-scale unemployment, this is not an inconsiderable achievement. It is doubtless such services that government officials have in mind when they acknowledge the "valuable" functions that madrasas serve in society. Yet their aspirations to reform madrasas appear all the more weak in the face of such acknowledgments, and this because such reform proposals offer few credible alternatives to the provision of some of the people's basic needs. The point here is not that madrasas provide most of such needs, or that they provide them well. It is, rather, that in an arena largely left vacant by the inefficiency and perceived corruption of the state, madrasas have, in many cases, offered services that are not otherwise available; and such services may arguably seem the more attractive to at least some segments of the population *because* they are provided in the name of Islam.

Considering their successful resistance against governmental regulation, their independent economic base, their deep roots in local communities, and their engagement with the affairs of society, might we think of

Pakistani madrasas and the 'ulama associated with them as sharing certain features often held to be the basis of a "civil" society? José Casanova has spoken of the roles that "public religions" can play in contemporary Western societies once those religions accept the functional differentiation of spheres in society—that is, once they accommodate themselves to the fact of secularization in this crucial sense (Casanova 1994). The 'ulama typically don't accept secularization in this or most other senses. Yet it is worth noting that they, too, play roles not dissimilar to the kind of roles Casanova envisions for public religions. Reflection on the normative foundations of the polity, on the moral and religious dimensions of public policy, and on the common good as being distinct from merely the aggregate of individual interests (Casanova 1994, 228–29) are to be found in the discourses of the contemporary 'ulama as well (Zaman 2004).

Yet, many Pakistani madrasas often also maintain ties with militant sectarian organizations in the country, as already noted, and the views of the 'ulama on such things as the position of women or on pluralism are often far from being conducive to a democratic society. In and of themselves, however, such illiberal proclivities do not exclude the 'ulama and their madrasas from the landscape of civil society. Rather, they remind us that not all civic associations are *necessarily* committed to democratic civility; some, indeed, help foster a "bad" civil society (Chambers 2002, 100–105; Berman 1997). Though usually not articulated in quite these terms, at least part of what motivates governmental and other modernist criticisms of madrasas is the perception that they retard the growth of a good civil society or that they foster precisely the wrong kind of attitudes in society—attitudes that are xenophobic, antipluralist, antidemocratic. But what governmental initiatives toward madrasa reform also claim is, of course, that even this institution *can* be scaled up in ways that would promote a "good" civil society and the common good; indeed, the very aspiration to reform rather than, say, to shut down madrasas bespeaks such a claim. The 'ulama have, of course, typically seen such statements of intent as a thin veneer for an all-out assault on the integrity of religious education and on the institutions associated for centuries with providing it. Yet it is worth asking whether madrasas can, in fact, be scaled up in ways that might promote a "good" civil society. More specifically, under what conditions might such an effort successfully take place?

Madrasas and a "Good" Civil Society?

Having illustrated earlier in this chapter some of the ways in which the state itself collaborates in scaling up *illiberal* religious trends in society, I will now assume, for purposes of argument, that the ruling elite does in fact have a genuine interest in fostering a "good" civil society and in promoting a tolerant, pluralist, and democratic culture. This is obviously a problematic assumption. It is contested by the historical record of how that elite has conducted itself, as well as by questions about the inner cohesion of that elite (see Hefner, in this volume). Yet my interest in the remaining part of this chapter is not with how to ameliorate the behavior or cohesion of that elite but, rather, with what it would take to reform the 'ulama's institutions. Part of the answer to my question here is, of course, that the institutions of the 'ulama might have better prospects of being scaled up in the direction of democratic pluralism once the polity in which they are located comes itself to be genuinely committed to a democratic culture. But this is only part of the answer, and to highlight other aspects of it, I intend to take this part as a given and to proceed accordingly.

In very broad terms, there are at least two conditions for the scaling up of madrasas to have some reasonable prospects of success: first, the state must act *together with* the 'ulama, in a genuinely synergistic effort, to canalize the madrasas' activities in particular directions; and second, any reform of the madrasas ought to involve a serious grappling with the Islamic tradition of which the 'ulama see themselves as the custodians. It might seem that the various initiatives that have addressed issues of madrasa reform in Pakistan have already fulfilled the first condition. After all, prominent 'ulama have served on the committees entrusted with reform in numbers comparable to or even exceeding those of the government officials. Yet, irrespective of the actual composition of such committees, the initiative has typically rested with the government rather than the 'ulama in all practical respects. Governmental efforts at reform have therefore been seen with great suspicion by many 'ulama, and this even when some have gone along with the governmental recommendations for reform. A genuinely synergistic effort requires that those governmental officials who are concerned with the madrasas—for example, by way of suggesting reforms in them, or in actually overseeing particular facets of a madrasa's activities—be perceived as *at least* not hostile or indifferent to the madrasa's welfare. That the government would have the accounts of madrasas audited, or give special perquisites only to the madrasas which conform to its guidelines, or that it would even create "model," state-sponsored madrasas—all of which is stipulated by the most recent iteration of proposals for madrasa reform (Zaman 2002, 221 n. 75)—can go a long way toward regulating the affairs of the madrasa. But, to many among the 'ulama, these stipulations also easily translate into the efforts of an inefficient, corrupt, and hostile bureaucracy to stifle not just the autonomy of their institutions but their very existence. And it is such suspicions that have often been among major stumbling blocks on the path to reform. If, on the other hand, government functionaries at the local levels work with the 'ulama and madrasas in their communities (that is, with many of the same 'ulama with whom these officials might already interact in their local mosques, or in other ways), it might be possible to create and broaden significant forms of trust between the 'ulama and the representatives of the state. This would be one manner of bridging the much debated state-society divide, whereby the state is able to shape the direction in which institutions of civil society move while remaining responsive to the particular concerns of those institutions (Tendler 1997, 135–65, esp. 146).

The second condition which ought to attend upon any effort to scale up madrasas is that this be done, at least in some measure, by engaging with the resources provided by the Islamic tradition. What does such engagement mean? To the 'ulama, either the invoking of certain isolated passages of the Qur'an in support of a particular argument or even the claim that the Qur'an, "taken as a whole," necessarily supports a certain position is usually less than sufficient justification for that position. Nor do incidental, decontextualized parallels between contemporary and earlier views suffice. To take the tradition seriously is, for them, to engage with the existing record of authoritative juristic or exegetical discourses—which go well beyond the foundational texts—in a way that acknowledges the assumptions and methods informing those discourses, and *then* to show how they bear on the problem at hand. From the perspective of many contemporary 'ulama, such a procedure does not necessarily exclude evolution and change in the law (cf. 'Uthmani 1993b, 85–108 and passim); but it clearly does rule out radical critiques of or departures from the shari'ah just as it rules out ways of approaching the Qur'an that have scant earlier precedent or authority.[6] But taking the tradition seriously also means, to the 'ulama, that *they* be recognized as "experts" in all matters Islamic, on a par with experts in any other area of modern life (Zaman 2002, 99–100). This is a patently exclusionary position, of course, but it becomes the more insidious in that, in the 'ulama's theory at least, "Islam" relates to all facets of life. That the 'ulama have often espoused highly illiberal views on a range of issues does not make this position any more palatable.

Might there be a way, however, to take the tradition seriously—in reforming existing institutions or creating new ones—but to do so while *bypassing* the 'ulama? Though my discussion of madrasas has hitherto been concerned only with Pakistan, it is worth considering a highly interesting proposal put forth by philosopher Akeel Bilgrami regarding the reform of certain Muslim institutions in contemporary India (Bilgrami 1999). Bilgrami seeks to find a path that steers clear of two unsatisfactory approaches to reform: the liberal and the communitarian, as he characterizes them. In the context of contemporary India, the liberal approach refuses to recognize the validity of negotiating with the separate religious communities that constitute the Indian union, or to accept that members of these communities can have valid reasons for resisting certain initiatives which the state sees as essential to a unified nationhood and to the common good. Such initiatives include the necessity for a uniform civil code, which the constitution of India has long promised but which many Muslims have continued to resist because they see it as a challenge to their religious and cultural identity. On the liberal view, the state ought to enact this uniform civil code because it is desirable to do so, and because this measure is resisted only by "reactionary element[s]" within the Muslim community while the "moderate" majority within that community seems to be in its favor (Bilgrami 1999, 199). Opposed to this liberal view is what Bilgrami labels the communitarian position, which also laments the reactionary elements within the Muslim community but remains resolutely opposed to a statist intervention against them. The communitarian position holds that the state should encourage democratization *within* the Muslim community, so that the influence of the reactionary elements is broken; but apart from this facilitating of intracommunity democracy, the state ought not to interfere in telling the community how to behave. Bilgrami, for his part, proposes that the state ought to act by proposing to the community *internal* reasons for reform:

> [T]he state can bring about reform in a way that appeals to (some of) the value-commitments of communities whom it is seeking to reform, in particular by appealing to values which stand in . . . tension with those values and practices which it seeks to reform. In other words it is the *state* which addresses them internally in a way that *they themselves* might have done on intra-community sites. . . . And if the notion of coercion is contrasted with the notion of reason-giving, a state which arrives at secular outcomes in this way need not be seen as any more coercive than the procedures by which these outcomes are delivered on intra-community sites. To see things this way is to see the liberal state as being able to provide a field of force of internal reasons addressing different communitarian perspectives from within their own internal substantive commitments and unsettling them into awareness of their own internal inconsistencies so as to eventually provide for a common secular outcome each on different internal grounds. (Bilgrami 1999, 195; emphasis in the original)

Yet Bilgrami gives *no* example of internal reasons for reform that the state (or anyone else) might proffer. This may well be because he offers his argument at a highly abstract level (Bilgrami 1999, 211). But the lack of specific examples of externally given internal reasons may also underscore the difficulties that arise when the project is predicated on excluding or marginalizing the 'ulama. It is the 'ulama, though not just the 'ulama, that Bilgrami seems to have in mind when he refers to the "reactionary element" whom the government of Prime Minister Rajiv Gandhi had heeded during the Shah Bano Controversy in the mid-1980s (cf. Bilgrami 1999, 199). The issue was whether a destitute divorced woman had the right to be financially supported by her former husband after the expiry of the three-month-long "waiting period" following her divorce. The standard interpretations of the shari'ah held that she had no such right, but the Hindu-dominated Indian Supreme Court had presumed to offer a new interpretation of the Qur'an to argue that the shari'ah's position was not really in accord with the Qur'an itself. While many Muslim modernists applauded the Supreme Court's verdict as upholding the best interests of Muslim women, the Indian 'ulama led what turned out to be a successful mass campaign to have the decision reversed through parliamentary legislation (Engineer 1987; Lawrence 2000, 131–49; Zaman 2002, 167–70; also cf. Nussbaum 2000, 167–240).

There have been occasions, in late-colonial as well as contemporary India, when *internal* reasons were, in fact, given to seek much needed legal reform involving Muslim women (Zaman 2002, 21–31; 2004). But these instances have typically involved internal reasons being given *by* the 'ulama with reference to their juristic tradition, rather than such reasoning taking place on a site that excludes the 'ulama. My point is not, of course, that the 'ulama alone are qualified to offer such reasons. It is, rather, that any appeal to the need for internal reasons would be shallow and unconvincing if it doesn't seriously engage the Islamic religious tradition, and to try to do so means (among other things) being able to converse with those who see themselves as the representatives of that tradition rather than excluding them from any conversation for being "reactionary." As noted at the beginning of this chapter, such a conversation might involve reminding them that *their own* religious tradition is rich enough to allow arguments against some of the views they now hold, that their premodern precursors have held positions that amount to a greater variety of options than the modern 'ulama are often willing to acknowledge, and that even many modern 'ulama have themselves appealed to that variety of options in trying to get out of some particularly difficult situations.

The state does have a role in this effort to find internal reasons for reform, for instance by creating "model" madrasas as proposed by the government of President Pervez Musharraf of Pakistan (*The News,* January 30, 2002; *Dawn,* April 3, 2002). Yet the purpose of governmental reform, and even the logic behind the proposed "model" madrasas, has typically been to introduce modern, Western sciences to the 'ulama, and thereby to integrate their institutions into the educational mainstream (cf. *Dawn,* June 20, 2002; *Dawn,* July 5, 2002; *The News,* July 12, 2002).

While that objective remains worth pursuing, it does not necessarily offer the panacea to the ills that the 'ulama's detractors see them as representing. Reform in this sense has little direct relevance to building resources for democracy and pluralism except inasmuch as it ultimately seeks to remove the 'ulama—Bilgrami's "reactionary element"—from the scene altogether. For all the governmental denials that this might be the purpose behind the reformist project, this at least is how the 'ulama perceive it, which is primarily why they have so vociferously opposed madrasa reform in Pakistan.

Some of the other proposals for sponsoring change in and *through* madrasas seem even less satisfactory insofar as the 'ulama's likely responses to them are concerned. In late 2002, the U.S. Department of Defense briefly contemplated the promotion of favorable views of the United States in certain countries through local religious and other institutions. As reported by the *New York Times,* "[s]uch a program . . . could include efforts to discredit and undermine the influence of mosques and religious schools that have become breeding grounds for Islamic militancy and anti-Americanism across the Middle East, Asia, and Europe. It might even include setting up schools with secret American financing to teach a more moderate Islamic position laced with sympathetic depictions of how the religion is practiced in America" (Shanker and Schmitt 2002; cf. Schmitt 2002). A little less than a year later, a memo from the U.S. Secretary of Defense, Donald H. Rumsfeld, addressed to some of his closest advisers but leaked to the national press, asked if the United States ought to "create a private foundation to entice radical madrassas to a more moderate course" (*Los Angeles Times,* October 23, 2003; also cf. Pincus 2003). That such initiatives would dislodge extreme interpretations of Islam more effectively than they undermine the effort to locate and justify "moderate" ones remains, at best, uncertain.

But a different sort of reform might also be worth considering—a reform for which the state-sponsored "model" madrasas can very well be one possible site. This reform involves, as I have suggested earlier, encouraging the 'ulama to have a more vigorous engagement with facets of their own tradition, and encouraging them to debate among themselves and with others *on these grounds.* The idea of reform in this sense has largely remained foreign to many Muslim modernist intellectuals and policy makers; and the reasons for this are not far to seek. These reasons have much to do with the dim view of the Islamic legal tradition that many of these modernists hold, which in turn is often a product of the limited acquaintance they have with that tradition. As its self-professed legatees and guardians, the 'ulama of the contemporary world have themselves often done little to improve the others' appreciation for, let alone their grounding in, the Islamic tradition. A result of this set of circumstances is for Muslim modernists and policy makers to often begin their reformist arguments by effectively writing off the tradition rather than viewing it as an arena from where (or in which) varied internal reasons for reform might in fact emerge. Yet it is in such internal reasons, with the 'ulama as crucial but scarcely the exclusive interlocutors, that the best prospects for reform might lie—reform that can have very considerable implications for democracy, pluralism, human rights, as well as for a whole range of other pressing issues confronting Muslim societies today.

NOTES

1. In broad terms, I mean by Muslim "modernists" those who have been educated in modern Western (or Westernized) institutions of learning and have sought to rethink or adapt Muslim practices, institutions, and discourses in light both of what they take to be "true" Islam—as opposed to how the Islamic tradition has evolved in history—*and* of how they see the challenges and opportunities of modernity. The "Islamists" share much with the modernists in their intellectual backgrounds and in the novelty of the positions they advocate; but they do not share the modernists' enthusiasm for the need to adapt Islam to the conditions of modernity, just as the modernists don't share theirs for the public implementation of Islamic norms. For a discussion of the modernists, the Islamists, and the 'ulama, and how they might be characterized in terms of their attitudes toward the Islamic discursive tradition, see Zaman 2002: 3–11.
2. This alliance, known as the Muttahida Majlis-i 'Amal (The Unified Association for Action), won 59 out of a total of 342 seats in the National Assembly, the lower house of the Pakistani parliament. In an electoral success unprecedented for the religious parties, the alliance not only emerged as the third largest group in the National Assembly but also won a majority of seats in the legislative assembly of the North-West Frontier Province and was the second largest group in the provincial assembly of Baluchistan. For the results of, and reactions to, the elections to the National and the provincial assemblies, see *Dawn* (Karachi) and *The News* (Islamabad), October 11, 2002, and subsequent days.
3. For other assessments of the ambiguities in the discourses of the 'ulama, though with reference to *premodern* juristic thought, cf. Johansen 1999, 216–18; Kerr 1966, 21–32.
4. A study conducted in 2002 found that private donations to mosques and madrasas amounted to over $1 billion annually, and that an overwhelming proportion (94 percent) of all charity goes to ventures identified as "religious" (*Dawn,* July 29, 2002).
5. For some examples of the resistance along these lines to the government's proposed reform of the madrasas, see *Dawn,* June 23, 2002, June 30, 2002, July 7, 2002, July 19, 2002; *The News,* July 25, 2002, November 22, 2003.
6. The 'ulama's view of tradition can therefore have little room for, say, An-Na'im (1990), who proposes new legal norms derived exclusively from those

verses of the Qur'an that were revealed to Muhammad in Mecca, that is, during the first thirteen years of his prophetical activity, but not during the last decade of his career in Medina. An-Na'im's justification for the outright exclusion of the Medinan materials is that their social and political content, unlike the ethical verities of the Meccan period, have long since lost their utility. It should be clear from my discussion throughout this chapter that no argument developed on the basis of such radical premises can count, for the 'ulama, as valid. Also cf. the comments of Abou El Fadl (2002, 109–10) on Bilgrami 2002.

REFERENCES CITED

Abou El Fadl, Khaled. 1994. "Islamic Law and Muslim Minorities: The Juristic Discourse on Muslim Minorities from the Second/Eighth to the Eleventh/Seventeenth Centuries." *Islamic Law and Society* 1:141–87.
———. 2002. "The Place of Tolerance in Islam" and "Reply." In *The Place of Tolerance in Islam,* edited by Khaled Abou El Fadl, Joshua Cohen, and Ian Lague, pp. 3–23, 93–111. Boston, Mass.: Beacon Press.
An-Na'im, Abdullahi Ahmed. 1990. *Toward an Islamic Reformation: Civil Liberties, Human Rights, and International Law.* Syracuse, N.Y.: Syracuse University Press.
Bearak, Barry. 2001a. "Pakistani Tale of a Drug Addict's Blasphemy." *New York Times,* February 19, A1, A4.
———. 2001b. "Death to Blasphemers: Islam's Grip on Pakistan." *New York Times,* May 12, A3.
Berman, Sheri. 1997. "Civil Society and the Collapse of the Weimar Republic." *World Politics* 49:401–29.
Bilgrami, Akeel. 1999. "Secular Liberalism and the Moral Psychology of Identity." In *Multiculturalism, Liberalism, and Democracy,* edited by Rajeev Bhargava, Amiya Kumar Bagchi, and R. Sudarshan, pp. 164–211. Delhi: Oxford University Press.
———. 2002. "The Importance of Democracy." In *The Place of Tolerance in Islam,* edited by Khaled Abou El Fadl, Joshua Cohen, and Ian Lague, pp. 61–66. Boston, Mass. Beacon Press.
Binder, Leonard. 1961. *Religion and Politics in Pakistan.* Berkeley and Los Angeles: University of California Press.
Casanova, José. 1994. *Public Religions in the Modern World.* Chicago, Ill.: University of Chicago Press.
Chambers, Simone. 2002. "A Critical Theory of Civil Society." In *Alternative Conceptions of Civil Society,* edited by Simone Chambers and Will Kymlicka, pp. 90–110. Princeton, N.J.: Princeton University Press.
Dawn (Karachi). 1998. "Death Penalty under Blasphemy Law," September 10.
———. 2001. "Man Sentenced to Death for Blasphemy," March 14.
———. 2001. "Sentenced to Death for Blasphemy," August 19.
———. 2001. "No Question of Instability in Pakistan: Musharraf," November 9.

———. 2002. "Selected Madaris May be Given University Status," April 3.

———. 2002. "No Help to Madaris without Registration . . ." June 20.

———. 2002. "MMA to Resist Registration of Madressahs," June 23.

———. 2002. "MMA Rejects Law on Madaris, Changes to Constitution," June 30.

———. 2002. "Rs. 14 b[illio]n Project Prepared to Bring Madaris into Mainstream," July 5.

———. 2002. "Villager Stoned to Death on Imam's Call," July 6.

———. 2002. "Gov[ernmen]t Firm on Madaris Law," July 7.

———. 2002. "Seminaries Plan Protest Drive," July 19.

———. 2002. "Madaris, Mosques Collect Rs 70 b[illio]n annually." July 29.

Edwards, David B. 2002. *Before Taliban: Genealogies of the Afghan Jihad.* Berkeley and Los Angeles: University of California Press.

Engineer, Asghar Ali, ed. 1987. *The Shah Bano Controversy.* Bombay: Orient Longman.

Esposito, John L., and John O. Voll. 1996. *Islam and Democracy.* New York: Oxford University Press.

Evans, Peter. 1997. "Government Action, Social Capital, and Development: Reviewing the Evidence on Synergy." In *State-Society Synergy: Government and Social Capital in Development,* edited by Peter Evans, pp. 178–209. Berkeley: International and Area Studies, University of California.

Fadel, Mohammad. 1997. "Two Women, One Man: Knowledge, Power, and Gender in Medieval Sunni Legal Thought." *International Journal of Middle East Studies* 29:185–204.

Hallaq, Wael B. 2001. *Authority, Continuity, and Change in Islamic Law.* Cambridge: Cambridge University Press.

Hardy, Peter. 1971. *Partners in Freedom—and True Muslims: The Political Thought of Some Muslim Scholars in British India, 1912–1947.* Lund: Scandinavian Institute of Asian Studies.

Hasan, Mushirul. 1997. *Legacy of a Divided Nation: India's Muslims since Independence.* Boulder, Colo.: Westview Press.

Hefner, Robert W. 2000. *Civil Islam: Muslims and Democratization in Indonesia.* Princeton, N.J.: Princeton University Press.

Humphreys, R. Stephen. 1999. *Between Memory and Desire: The Middle East in a Troubled Age.* Berkeley and Los Angeles: University of California Press.

Jackson, Sherman. 1996. *Islamic Law and the State: The Constitutional Jurisprudence of Shihab al-Din al-Qarafi.* Leiden: Brill.

Johansen, Baber. 1999. "Secular and Religious Elements in Hanafite Law: Function and Limits of the Absolute Character of Government Authority." In *Contingency in a Sacred Law: Legal and Ethical Norms in the Muslim Fiqh,* edited by Baber Johansen, pp. 189–218. Leiden: Brill.

Kerr, Malcolm H. 1966. *Islamic Reform: The Political and Legal Theories of Muhammad 'Abduh and Rashid Rida.* Berkeley and Los Angeles: University of California Press.

Khan, Wahid al-din. 1986. *Tabligh Movement.* Translated by Farida Khanam. Delhi: Islamic Centre.

———. 1994. *Indian Muslims: The Need for a Positive Outlook.* Translated by Farida Khanam. Delhi: al-Risala Books.

————. 1996. *Fikr-i Islami: Afkar-i islami ki tashrih wa tawdih*. Delhi: al-Risala Books.

————. 1998. *Madamin-i Islam: Islam ke mukhtalif pahlu'on par maqalat*. Delhi: al-Risala Books.

Lawrence, Bruce B. 2000. *Shattering the Myth: Islam beyond Violence*. Karachi: Oxford University Press.

Los Angeles Times. 2003. "Rumsfeld's Memo: 'Are We Winning or Losing the . . . War on Terror?'" October 23, A15.

Madani, Husayn Ahmad. n.d. [1938]. *Muttahida qawmiyyat awr Islam*. Delhi: Qawmi aikta Trust.

Mayer, Ann Elizabeth. 1999. *Islam and Human Rights: Tradition and Politics*. 3rd ed. Boulder, Colo.: Westview Press.

Metcalf, Barbara D. 1982. *Islamic Revival in British India: Deoband, 1860–1900*. Princeton, N.J.: Princeton University Press.

Nasr, S.V.R. 2000. "The Rise of Sunni Militancy in Pakistan: The Changing Role of Islamism and the Ulama in Society and Politics." *Modern Asian Studies* 34:139–80.

News, The (Islamabad). 2002. "Three Model Madaris to be set up," January 30.

————. 2002. "No Plan to Repeal Blasphemy Laws: Gov[ernmen]t," February 19.

————. 2002. "Madaris Rendering Valuable Services," June 24.

————. 2002. "Registration under Draft Madaris Law not Compulsory," June 24.

————. 2002. "Ministers-Ulema Talks on Madaris Fail," July 7.

————. 2002. "Government Serious about New Curriculum for Madaris . . . ," July 12.

————. 2002. "Christian Sentenced to Death for Blasphemy," July 19.

————. 2002. "Religious Bodies Reject Madrassah Ordinance," July 25.

————. 2002. "Provinces Asked to Oust Banned Outfits from Polls," September 6.

————. 2003. "Madaris Pledge to Counter Gov[ernmen]t's Takeover Move," November 22.

Nussbaum, Martha C. 2000. *Women and Human Development: The Capabilities Approach*. Cambridge: Cambridge University Press.

Pincus, Walter. 2003. "Idea of Influencing Schools Echoes '50s." *Washington Post*, November 1, A19.

al-Qaradawi, Yusuf. 2001. *Kayfa nata'amal ma'a'l-turath wa'l-tamadhhub wa'l-ikhtilaf*. Cairo: Maktabat wahba.

Rashid, Ahmed. 2000. *Taliban: Militant Islam, Oil, and Fundamentalism in Central Asia*. New Haven, Conn.: Yale University Press.

Sachedina, Abdulaziz. 2001. *The Islamic Roots of Democratic Pluralism*. New York: Oxford University Press.

Schmitt, Eric. 2002. "White House Plays Down Propaganda by Military." *New York Times*, December 17, A15.

Shanker, Thom, and Eric Schmitt. 2002. "Pentagon Debates Propaganda Push in Allied Nations." *New York Times*, December 16, A1, A14.

Tendler, Judith. 1997. *Good Government in the Tropics*. Baltimore, Md.: Johns Hopkins University Press.

Tucker, Judith. 1998. *In the House of the Law: Gender and Islamic Law in Ottoman Syria and Palestine*. Berkeley and Los Angeles: University of California Press.

'Uthmani, Muhammad Taqi. 1993a. *Nifadh-i shari'at awr us-ke masa'il*. Karachi: Maktaba-i Dar al-'Ulum.

———. 1993b. *Taqlid ki shar'i haythiyyat*. Karachi: Maktaba-i Dar al-'Ulum.

———. 1996. *Jahan-i dida: Bis mulkon ka safar-nama*. Karachi: Idarat al-ma'arif.

———. 1999. *Islam awr jiddat-pasandi*. Karachi: Maktaba-i Dar al-'Ulum.

Waqar-ul-Haq, Mohammed. [1994]. *The Major Acts, with . . . Commentary [on the] Criminal Law (Amendment) Ordinance (Qisas and Diyat Ordinance)*. Lahore: Law Times Publications.

Wickham, Carrie Rosefsky. 2002. *Mobilizing Islam: Religion, Activism, and Political Change in Egypt*. New York: Columbia University Press.

Zaman, Muhammad Qasim. 2002. *The Ulama in Contemporary Islam: Custodians of Change*. Princeton, N.J.: Princeton University Press.

———. 2004 (forthcoming). "The 'Ulama of Contemporary Islam and Their Conceptions of the Common Good." In *Public Islam and the Common Good*, edited by Dale F. Eickelman and Armando Salvatore. Leiden: Brill.

Chapter 4

THE END OF ISLAMISM? TURKEY'S
MUSLIMHOOD MODEL

JENNY B. WHITE

THE RADICAL PERIOD IS OVER, predicted Akıf Beki, Ankara correspondent for the Islamist television station Kanal 7.[1] Islamism has become "religion," relegated to the civil realm, found only in religious communities, no longer in the state. "There has been a civil-ization. Islamism has become Muslimhood." This diagnosis was echoed by Mehmet Aydın, noted Islamic scholar and minister in the new Justice and Development Party (AKP) government. The formerly Islamist AKP won national elections on November 3, 2002, with enough votes to form a government.[2] The party, Aydın insisted, no longer accepts the label "moderate Islamist." Rather, party members consider themselves to be "moderate Muslims" whose religious ethics inspire their public service as individuals but cannot be construed as part of their identities as political actors in the public sphere. "AKP is a political movement and the movement's actors have a very warm, close relationship, primarily as individuals, to . . . religious experience. . . . At the moment, I believe that all the ministers are fasting. . . . We are religious people, but our actions in the public sphere . . . do not have a religious side or theological meaning. Where is there a religious side? There's a link in our values. Just because I've become a politician, I'm not about to leave the values I believe in by the wayside." As parallels, he noted President George W. Bush's personal religiosity and championing of "faith-based programs," as well as the close relationship between church and state in some European countries. He pointed out that the noted Islamist scholar Ali Bulaç had distanced himself entirely from Islamism, saying that it was a period that was now over, as people lived their beliefs within a pluralist framework.

Has Islam become individual, personal practice distinct from the public and political realms, as these voices claim, despite the presence of Islam-inspired devout Muslims in those realms? If so, how does this compare to the vision of the followers of Mustafa Kemal Atatürk, founder of the Turkish Republic, of a pristinely secular, modern public and political realm, with religion relegated to the private sphere? In Turkey, a series of secularist governments, backed by a fiercely Kemalist military, have implemented this model by setting legal curbs on religious expression in public. Religious insignia of all kinds, whether turban or Roman collar, are forbidden on the streets; women's head coverings, while tolerated on the street, are banned in government offices, the civil service, and many university classrooms, and more subtly discouraged in other workplaces and arenas. The state has replaced the *ulema* with a Ministry of Religious Affairs that trains and oversees all religious specialists, vets sermons, supervises mosques and religious schools, and issues advice about how to be a good Muslim that the state feels is compatible with a rational, scientific, secular society. The new AKP government challenges this by agreeing that religion is personal but arguing that, as such, it can be incorporated into the public and political spheres without compromising the secular state system. Kemalists, however, would likely conclude that the secular nature of the state is not safe in the hands of individuals in whose lives religion plays such an important role that they feel the need to fast and pray while doing their public duty (for instance, in the prime ministry).

Thus, the issue that has emerged as a major area of dispute under the new government is the boundaries of the private and the public, the personal, the civil, and the political. The Kemalist model seems to imply that a modern, secular democratic system requires not just certain practices in the public arena, but also a certain kind of person. When a secular person enters the political realm, she becomes secularist; when an Islamic believer enters the political realm, she becomes, by definition, Islamist. The Muslimhood model challenges this by asserting that believing Muslims can be secular politicians, that their qualities of personhood not only do not disqualify them from running the secular governmental machinery, but may even benefit the political realm by inserting personal ethics and a moral stance. On November 3, 2002, Turkey's voters seemed to agree when they elected the Islam-inspired AKP to head the government and threw out the corrupt and ineffectual centrist parties.

What is the evidence for the death of Islamism in Turkey and the rise of a personalized Muslimhood? Can this work as a political formula? If so, can this serve as a more general model for Islamic (or "Muslim") governance, or does it reflect characteristics and circumstances unique to Turkey? Are there alternative trends and actors that might contradict or undercut the personalization and privatization of Islam and the Muslimization of politics and the public sphere?

THE PERSONALIZATION OF ISLAM

Günter Seufert has suggested that Islam in Turkey has become increasingly detached from personal identity and become a means of expression.[3] He linked this to the development since the 1980s of a consumer society in which identity can be demonstrated through purchased goods, and items are advertised by playing on identities. This implies a change in political focus as well. He argued that, whereas in the past, Turks might have asked, "What does an Islamic identity say about national identity?" now they are asking, "What does the nation mean for a Muslim?" "How does democracy fit with Islam?" has become "What does Islam mean for democracy?"

While the Kemalist state has long laid claim to the right to define Islam through its Ministry of Religious Affairs, the new AKP government is challenging this definition, and the market and media are wresting control over defining a "Muslim" away from the state and, perhaps, even away from Islamic groups and movements. Navaro-Yashin (2002) describes the fashion industry that has grown up around a form of veiling, *tesettür*, that has been associated with political Islam. At a *tesettür* fashion show, a woman watching the veiled models striding down the runway told Navaro-Yashin that she welcomed the elaboration of an explicitly middle class form of veiling. She had recently begun to veil, she revealed, and the sales staff in her usual shops no longer recognized her, treating her as if she couldn't afford to shop there. If she wore couture *tesettür*, she reasoned, that wouldn't happen (Navaro-Yashin 2002). The 1990s saw the spread of Islamist gated communities and department stores. During Ramazan in November 2002, the special holiday pages in major newspapers gave advice on such topics as whether or not sushi and lobster were permitted foods and how to take care of the skin while fasting. Subjects generally were approached from a pluralist angle, pointing out different Islamic interpretations and variations by region and country. Scientific explanations were amended to religious ones; for instance, explaining that research by veterinarians had revealed substances harmful to human beings in the flesh of animals like pigs, dogs, and lions. This was true as well for newspapers, like *Zaman*, associated with the Islamic movement. At the mammoth annual Fatih Book Fair, held in the courtyard of the Sultan Ahmet Mosque, people crowded the stands. The book fair is self-consciously Islamic and the patrons dress the part. The book displays, however, sometimes present surprising contrasts, with translations of Dostoyevski, Gogol, Turgenev, and Jack London next to *The Big Islamic Catechism*, and Steinbeck and George Orwell sharing a shelf with *Islam's Smiling Face* and *Army and Commander in Islam*. One stand advertised a sale on Malcolm X, another a computer program for learning prayers in Arabic, a problem for most Turks, who do not understand Arabic. Shoppers, however, often reached over more esoteric offerings and picked up books like *Test Your Child's IQ* and slim, colorful volumes for children about Islam and prayer, including talking books that made the sounds of the Arabic alphabet.

Recently, the Mevlevi, or whirling dervishes, have begun appearing in popular music and video clips and on entertainment shows on television.

This is a radical departure from their previous public performances in which the public was told not to clap, since this was a religious ceremony, not a form of entertainment. On a late-night program on Show TV in November 2002, the female host exchanged light banter with a sexy, blonde Turkish singer, both in low-cut evening gowns, then introduced a small group of young men dressed as (and presented as) dervishes, along with a musician who played Sufi music to accompany them while they whirled for the cameras. One of the dervishes was a young boy of seven, the son of the musician. (Classic Mevlana performances also often included at least one young apprentice dervish.) When the whirling ended, the hostess asked the boy to announce, "Stay tuned. After the commercials, we'll be right back." This was still unusual enough to merit a lightly shocked article on the entertainment page of *Sabah* newspaper, where the journalist Yüksel Aytuğ criticized the show's host for asking the young dervish, "How long have you been turning?" Spinning-tops "turn," he admonished, but dervishes "whirl" and they do so in a ceremony with deep religious and philosophical meaning. They are not dancers or entertainers (November 24, 2002, 30).

Despite unease with the desacralization of religious practices, it appears to be becoming more common. An article in the newspaper *Milliyet* featured a musician that taught children Sufi whirling as a game and planned to put together a show around Sufi whirling and music by a South African singer (November 14, 2002). A more Islamically oriented newspaper advised women to finger prayer beads to reduce stress (*Zaman,* October 28, 2002). Another newspaper showed an actress wearing a *muska,* or amulet, as a fashion accessory over a tight bathing suit. Cultural and musical syncretism is not new in Turkey, but the incorporation of religious practices into such risqué formats would have been thought highly inappropriate until recently and unleashed a negative reaction. As Seufert pointed out, however, over the last four or five years, objects and practices associated with an Islamic identity have come to be dislodged from their religious moorings and become available, primarily via the marketplace and media, to those whose primary identity is not Islamic, but who are interested in demonstrating that they are Muslim. Muslimhood, in other words, has become fashionable.

THE DEATH OF ISLAMISM

What has become of the much-discussed Islamism of the 1980s and 1990s? According to Akif Beki, it is a failed project, a trend that has played itself out. Until the 1970s, he explained, Islam was understood as orthodox religious tradition, not as an ideology, or something that belonged in the political or civic realms. During that decade, influences from India and Egypt made themselves felt with the translation of Mawdudi, Hasan al-Banna and Sayyid Qutb. This brought with it a sense of alienation from and reaction against the West. Their ideas gained a following and began a radical trend that advocated a political project, control over the state so as to set up an Islamic government. By the 1990s, however, this state-centric approach had shown itself to be a dead end in Turkey. It proved impossible to gain control of the state except by political struggle, and radicals were not prepared to wage an armed fight. The final failure was on February 28, 1997, when the National Security Council, the liaison institution between the military and the government, pushed the Islamist prime minister, Necmettin Erbakan (Welfare Party) out of power in what has come to be known as a "soft coup." Erbakan himself, Beki went on, had irritated many in the Muslim community with his confrontational politics, and they were glad to see him go. Islamist ideas, along with the anti-Western "complex," began to be reevaluated and rejected. Another factor was the increasing cultural interaction between Islamist and non-Islamist intellectual circles that led Islamists to be influenced by multicultural approaches. In the 1990s, Beki argued, Islam as ideology was replaced by Islam as religion, centered on the Qur'an.

One of the main arenas for the interaction of Islamists and non-Islamists have been the annual Abant meetings, sponsored by the followers of Fethullah Gülen, an Islamic movement centered on education. These meetings brought together Islamist and secularist intellectuals and politicians from across the ideological spectrum, as well as representatives of Turkey's other major Islamic sect, the Alevi. Since 1998, they have gathered for several days each year in the picturesque mountain town of Abant, halfway between Ankara and Istanbul, to hash out positions on topics like the relation of Islam to laicism (1998), religion and society (1999), state and law (2000), pluralism and social reconciliation (2001), and globalization in light of the "spirit of Abant" (2002). A book of proceedings is published after every meeting and a joint position statement is issued. The platform expresses support for democracy, human rights, and individual freedoms, arguing that these are entirely in accord with Islamic principles. There is no contradiction between religion and rationality: divine inspiration can better be understood in the light shed by the rational accumulation of knowledge. "Religious identity is individual" (*Abant Platformu* 2000, 316–17). It is communal insofar as religion is a component of a person's culture and a source of common values. Mehmet Aydın, one of the organizers, defined the "Abant spirit" as respect for different bodies of knowledge and ideas in Turkey and an attempt to see them represented; respect for the "honor" of knowledge and ideas, even if different, and a willingness to let the discussion go wherever it leads; an open mind and heart, being democratic and courageous; giving importance to the logic of the dialogue; and attempting, at the end of the discussions, to capture a shared common denominator that may not represent everyone's views in their entirety, but enough to recognize their contribution. The Abant meetings are designed to make of this "spirit" of reconciliation a "usable" model (2002, 101–2).

MUSLIM ACTORS: GROUPS

Participants in the Abant meetings comprise organized religious sects or groups as well as individual thinkers who may or may not be associated with particular strains of thought about Islam and its place in the public sphere. Some prominent secularist thinkers also participate. First I will discuss two Muslim groups, the Fethullahcılar and the Alevi, quite different, but well represented in Turkish society and the public sphere and both arguably representative of moderate streams in Turkish Islam. The sponsors of the Abant meetings, the Fethullahcılar, are followers of the retired preacher Fethullah Gülen. Gülen's movement consists of a network of nominally independent organizations in Turkey's major cities united around Gülen's teachings and supporting a publishing and media empire and educational initiative. Gülen's movement is an offshoot of the Nurcu movement, based on the writings of Said Nursi (1877–1960) that argue that there is no contradiction between religion and science. The Nurcu spread in Turkey in the 1950s and held a particular appeal for those educated in the secular school system. Gülen's followers include many teachers, students, businessmen, and educated professionals.

Gülen seeks to "Islamize Turkish nationalism; recreate a legitimate link between state and religion; emphasize democracy and tolerance; and encourage links with Turkish republics" (Aras 1998, 29). He believes that Turks share with Central Asian Turks a knowledge-based, nonpolitical form of Islamic interpretation, influenced by Sufi tradition. He differentiates this "Turkish-Muslim identity" from Arab Islam, arguing that Turkish Muslims are more tolerant and open to dialogue with all parts of society, including other religions and sects. He promotes the seeking of knowledge as a religious value and integration with the Western world, even if that means incorporating Western technology, clothing, and, to some extent, lifestyle. In his writings, he emphasizes that religion is a private matter and its requirements should not be imposed on anyone. Instead, the Fethullahcılar spread their message by sponsoring schools, dormitories, summer camps, and reading circles. Gülen-financed schools can be found in Turkey and abroad, primarily in Central Asia and the Balkans. The Fethullahcılar put on conferences to which they often invite internationally known scholars to discuss themes like Islam, democracy and civil society. They own a popular television station (STV) and a newspaper (*Zaman*) and publish large numbers of books and periodicals.

In the 1980s, the Turkish military and government encouraged a model of nationalist religion, which came to be known as the Turkish-Islamic synthesis, in a bid to counter the appeal of leftist ideologies. Gülen's brand of Turkish Islam, with its emphasis on Islamic education and belief in the compatibility of religious ethics and modern state institutions, seemed ideal and initially was supported. Major politicians accepted invitations to dine and speak with Gülen. However, as Islamist politics grew in popularity through the 1990s, especially at the ballot box, Gülen and his followers were accused of dissembling and, in reality, wishing to turn Turkey into an Islamic state. For the past several years, the frail leader has lived in the United States, where he initially came for medical treatment, unable to return to Turkey under threat of arrest. His movement, however, retains its momentum. It is too early to say whether the AKP government will allow him to return, since the military, the courts, and, to some extent, the police, have acted relatively independently of the government in the past. However, the prime minister in 2002, Abdullah Gül, and other members of his government have attended Abant meetings in the past, and Minister Mehmet Aydın was one of the organizers.

The Alevi are a non-Sunni syncretistic Muslim minority estimated to make up between 20 and 25 percent of the Turkish population. For centuries, they have been marginalized and sometimes persecuted by the Sunni majority for their beliefs, which some consider heretical. They do not subscribe to the Sunni requirements regarding prayer and fasting, and their ceremonies, at which music plays a prominent role, are not gender segregated. Although traditionally socially liberal and politically to the left of center, the Alevi are often overlooked in discussions of moderate Islam in Turkey. This may be due to their association with leftist activities in the turbulent 1960s and 1970s. In the 1980s, however, the Alevis, much like the Fethullahcılar, were perceived to be allies of the state in countering the perceived new threat of Islamism. They were granted permission to reopen their lodges, closed along with other Islamic institutions after the founding of the Republic, and to practice and hold their *cem* ceremonies openly. This has led to what some have called an Alevi revival or repoliticization, including the founding of numerous Alevi associations and foundations and local and national radio stations. In 1989, they issued an "Alevi Manifesto" in which they demanded unconditional acceptance of their religious community and their specific culture by the public and the state, and an end to all discrimination.

That discrimination at times has been severe. The Ministry of Religious Affairs is Sunni-dominated and disproportionately supports Sunni education and activities. As recently as 1995, several people in a café in an Alevi neighborhood were killed in a drive-by shooting, probably by right-wing nationalists. When community residents marched on the police station to protest their inactivity, the police, many of whom are sympathetic to the nationalists, retaliated, killing several residents. The ensuing riots left at least a dozen people dead and over a hundred wounded. That same year, outsiders broke into several university campuses and beat up students eating lunch during Ramazan, the month of fasting. When students protested police inactivity, they were beaten. When a guest on a television entertainment show made a joke that the Alevi have no morals and have group sex during their ceremonies, Alevis tried to set the television station on fire. A former high official at the Ministry of Religious Affairs, himself an Alevi, went on television to calm the situation and reassure the Alevi that they were integrated into Turkish society.

Since the end of the 1980s, however, the Alevis, under the leadership of an educated and politically active Alevi elite, organized in powerful associations, have become a force in Turkish politics and society. The explosion of interest in Alevis by the Turkish media, scholars, and politicians in Turkey and abroad raised Alevi visibility in the public sphere. Participation in Alevi activities increased, particularly in the cities. People were more willing to present themselves as Alevi (Erdemir 2002, 2). These events led to ongoing discussions about what exactly Alevi religion and culture are, particularly among younger, urban, educated Alevis who have lost touch with the inward-looking tribal traditions of traditional religious leaders, the *dede*s (Vorhoff 1997, 56).

Like the Sunni Islamist movement, Alevi presence in the public sphere has taken the form of mass demonstrations, civic organizations, and media publications—books, periodicals, and newspapers. Some of these publications have changed their content to cater to the move in reader interest from socialist politics to cultural commentary about Alevi rituals, music, and personalities (Vorhoff 1997, 57). This has fed a crisis in authority within the Alevi community. The analytical dissection and publicization of Alevi identity and the creation of Alevi civic institutions over the last decade has created a public body of knowledge about Alevi identity that is often at odds with the more esoteric knowledge of the *dede*s and threatens their authority, based on their membership in holy lineages (Massicard 2001). The new public represents what one might call a different market, representing many different interests, including a desire for religious consumption. Unlike the more intimate ceremonies of the past, the new urban *cem*s, held in great, modern halls, may involve hundreds of people, many strangers to one another. Although they provide a welcome opportunity to establish networks that cross village, lineage, and regional ties, some participants are disturbed by their "folkloric" aspect, viewing urban *cem* ceremonies as nothing more than public performances that have lost the authenticity of traditional ceremonies (Erdemir 2002, 9).

Thus, the new Alevi presence in the public sphere is characterized by internal generational, rural/urban, and ethnic divisions, but also by the desacralization of religious ceremonies as Alevi Muslimhood becomes a fashionable identity. What this identity entails will likely be the result of competition in the marketplace of religious consumption, rather than of tradition or politics. Erman and Göker remain skeptical about whether "the recognition of Alevi difference(s) will aid the creation of a more pluralistic political system" (2000, 115). Like Sunni Islamists, Alevis are now riven by social class divisions that may make it impossible to develop an identity politics founded on cultural and religious aspects that address all the needs and interests of a diverse following.

The Justice and Development Party (AKP) seems, at first glance, the most successful manifestation of Islam in the public and political realm. The party is the latest in a series of overtly Islam-inspired parties since the 1960s, each, in turn, closed down by the state (in the 1980s and 1990s, these were the Welfare and Virtue Parties). With each new party, the platform changed and constituency broadened until, by the 2002 election, the AK Party was supported by a spectrum that included peasants and urbanites, poor and wealthy, as well as intellectuals. Its success at the polls was due, in part, to an intensive, personalized method of mobilizing and to an ability to translate its platform of social justice into a local cultural language of neighborliness and mutual obligation (White 2002). Islam as an ideology played a relatively restrained supporting role in Virtue Party mobilization, quite different from the strident Islamism of its predecessor, Erbakan's Welfare Party.

This evolution toward moderate, nonconfrontational Islamic participation was the harbinger of a further receding of Islam into a cultural, ethical stance under the AKP. What caused this moderation and movement from a strident Islam oriented toward changing the state to a model of Muslims doing politics within the state? The chastening effect of continual closings played a role, as did the ability of banned parties to reconstitute themselves to compete again. The decline of other political parties opened the field to competition by a younger generation of politicians. The AK Party is led by the charismatic Recep Tayyip Erdoğan, a former soccer player, businessman, and mayor of Istanbul, who replaced the patronage-based politics of Necmettin Erbakan, leader of the previous Islamist parties, with a more participatory, populist grassroots political style. Market and media created crosscurrents of ideas and practices, uprooting previous meanings.

In the remainder of this essay, I will focus on the special circumstances of Turkish Islamic thinkers that led to a rejection of Arab reformist Islam in favor of what they consider to be a Turkish brand of Islamic philosophy that influences the present government. The movement toward a Turkish Islamic philosophy in some ways parallels the personalization and privatization of Islam and desacralization of Islamic practices discussed above, allowing a fractured new public to position themselves in a variety of ways within an Islamic idiom. In other words, the Muslimhood model does not create a unitary body of thought, goals, or practices, but projects a pluralist vision of an Islamic public sphere that reflects more closely the diverse nature of Islam in Turkey, but also contains within it contradictions that may sow the seed of dissent.

MUSLIM THINKERS: THE REFORMISTS

The annual meetings of intellectuals at Abant and a number of AKP, Alevi, and Gülen sponsored publications, meetings, and educational events have reinforced the Abant model that promotes compatibility with and, indeed, the necessity of pluralism, democracy, and individual rights in a Muslim society. A group of prominent reformist intellectuals, based at Ankara University's School of Theology, has developed a stream of Islamic thought that seeks to develop a new form of interiority of Islamic belief in Turkey—religion as human nature or an internal state, not society's religion or tradition.

This puts them in an ambiguous relationship with some orthodox and overtly political forms of Islamism, but very much in line with the Abant model and the trends of personalization of Islam and Muslimization of the public and political spheres discussed above. In other words, reformist intellectual currents and the effects of market and media seem similarly aligned in encouraging a movement toward personalization of Islam, or Muslimhood, and away from a politicized Islamism.

Some of the main figures among the Reformists (Yenilikçiler), as they call themselves, are Mehmet Aydın, Mehmed Said Hatiboğlu, M. Hayrı Kırbaşoğlu, Ömer Özsoy, Salih Akdemir, Yaşar Nuri Öztürk, and Hidayet Şefkatlı Tuksal, one of the few women prominent in the movement. Mehmet Aydın was born in Elazig in 1943. He graduated from Ankara University's School of Theology in 1966 and the following year, with support from the Turkish Ministry of Education, went to Edinburgh University in England for a doctorate in philosophy. When he returned in 1972, he began teaching in the School of Islamic Sciences at Ankara University and also taught philosophy at Middle East Technical University. In 1984, he moved to Dokuz Eylül University, where he was dean from 1993 to 1999. In fall of 2002, he became a minister in the new AKP government. He is considered to be a modernist and has published ten books on Islam and philosophy, including *Turkish Contribution to Philosophy* (in English, 1985), and *Why?* (in Turkish, 2002), which consists of reflections on September 11. In this collection of his newspaper columns, he suggests that rather than a clash of civilizations, the attacks of September 11 and Muslim responses to it are symptoms of the Muslim world's inability to get its own house in order, understand the West, and explain Islam to the West. This is exacerbated by the Muslim world's lack of understanding of Western languages and, thus, of the West's sociology, social psychology, politics, ideology, and strategic vision. The same, he continues, can be said of the West with regard to the Muslim world.

Many of the Reformists are professors at Ankara University's School of Theology, known as a hotbed of modernism, and most have published extensively. Ömer Özsoy is considered by some to be an Islamic feminist. M. Hayri Kirbaşoğlu, born in Manisa in 1954, specializes in the study and exegesis of *hadith,* the sayings of the Prophet Muhammed as handed down by chains of more or less reliable sources. His "scientific" evaluations of several popular collections of *hadith* have led him to doubt their veracity.

Salih Akdemir represents the less orthodox stream of the Reformists. He does not believe that Islam requires women to cover their heads; he supports gender-mixed student housing and the controversial Muslim practice of temporary marriage. Unlike some of his colleagues, he reportedly does not live an orthodox Islamic lifestyle. He practices an individualistic approach to Islam and argues that Islam is "human nature," not tradition. He is inspired by Jung's notion of collective conscience and he believes that, in this regard, all religions are the same. "Allah is inside all of us. . . . You use a computer, don't you? . . . Allah put inside the angels a diskette; they say whatever is on the diskette; but inside Adam he put a copy of his own hard drive. This potential, this humanity created by Allah, can develop into something like Nietzsche's superior man. The last human being will carry all the godly characteristics. . . . But with . . . our two-faced leaders in Turkey, in America, in Europe, this humanity isn't going anywhere. It's really all slavery. They lift the chains a bit and give them a bit of bread and their eyes widen." The requirements of the Qur'an, he argues, cannot simply be brought into the present. One has to make changes, adapt it to new situations, bring new solutions to bear. He reinterprets Islamic texts by means of semantic analyses. One of his new projects is called the "Transcendental Unity of Semitic Religions."[4] Although *shari'ah* law has been a basic Islamist goal, the Reformers focus on the Qur'an, rather than on the more questionable "Arab" interpretations. Their own analyses draw on eclectic methods and sources. Among Islamist activists, there is no consensus over the meaning of *shari'ah,* with some using it simply as a metaphor for a just society with no change in laws required, while others focus on the legality of marrying four wives.

Another heterodox scholar is Yaşar Nuri Öztürk, born in Bayburt in 1945. He has degrees in law, theology, and Islamic philosophy and, after practicing law for a time, joined the faculty of Marmara University. In 1993, he was appointed dean of the School of Theology at Istanbul University. He is the author of nineteen books and, through his newspaper columns and television appearances, has a broader presence in the public arena than most other Reformists. In the 2002 elections, he was a candidate not for the AK Party, but for the left-of-center and traditionally secularist Republican Peoples' Party (RPP); he is now a member of parliament. His ideas are especially popular with elite secularists. That and his reputation as a gadfly has somewhat tarnished his repute as an Islamic scholar.

Two other names deserve mention here, those of Ismet Özel and Ali Bulaç. representing what some have called Left Islam. (See Meeker 1991 for analyses of their writings and a list of publications.) Their publications and public appearances have been influential among believers and secularists alike. Ismet Özel is a well-known poet and columnist in several radical Islamist newspapers. He teaches French and comparative literature at Bilgi University, an institution known for the left or liberal orientation of its faculty. He was born in 1944 in Kayseri, in central Anatolia, the sixth child of a police official. He studied political science at Ankara University and French literature and language at Hacettepe University. In the 1960s he was well known as a leftist, but by the 1980s had begun to look to Islam instead for solutions. In his first book, *Three Problems: Technique, Civilization, Alienation* (in Turkish), he argues that the central problem for contemporary Muslims is not whether and how "Western science and technology can be integrated with Islamic belief and practice," but rather "the reconstitution of an Islamic way of life, an objective that begins with the individual reconstituting his personal thought and practice" (Meeker 1991, 211). His writings rely heavily on Western philosophers and thinkers. One young theology student admitted to me that he finds Özel's writings "impenetrable."

Ali Bulaç was born in 1951 in Mardin. He spent seven years in a *madrasa* receiving an Islamic education and later studied sociology at Istanbul University. He knows Arabic and is familiar with classical Islamic writers. His first book, *Concepts and Orders of Our Times* (in Turkish), in the late 1970s became what Meeker calls a "kind of manifesto for Muslim intellectuals" (1991, 197–98) and has sold over forty thousand copies. In the book, Bulaç analyzes capitalism, scientific socialism, and fascism as attempts to come to grips with class conflict. At the end of the book, he suggests that Islam provides a means to cope with contemporary conditions by forming the basis of an alternative "moral social order in which property rights are recognized but the rich become the willing guardians of the poor" (Meeker 1991, 200). Bulaç argues that it is not necessary to use Western principles and institutions to confront the Western challenge. The task of the Muslim intellectual "is not to rework Islam so that it takes the form of yet one more modernist construction, but to show how its beliefs and practices remain a sufficient foundation for community in contemporary life" (Meeker 1991, 201). Although Bulaç is heavily involved in Gülen-sponsored publications and the Abant meetings, his and Özel's work represents a distinct stream of Islamic Reformist thought that rejects Western solutions, despite reference to Western authors in making this argument.

As befits a modernist institution, Reformist debates are carried out over the Internet, and some of these intellectuals have personal Web pages. The Reformists also publish a well-respected journal, *Islamiyat,* described as modernist liberal. The journal is the brainchild of Mehmet Aydın and his graduate students. The journal first appeared in 1998. Each issue is centered on a theme; some of the most influential issues have taken up Islam and democracy (1999), increasing worldliness (2001), religion and violence (2002, no. 1), and the Islamic Left (2002, no. 2). The issue on religion and violence included articles about violence in Judaism and Christianity, as well as Islam, with separate evaluations of *jihad* and wife-beating in light of the Qur'an. Writings by Fazlur Rahman appear in several issues, translated from English. *Islamiyat* is linked to a publishing house that issues Turkish-language books by reformists, including translations of contemporary Arab authors like Muhammed Âbid el-Câbirî (*Restructuring Contemporary Arab-Islamic Thought*), Emîn el-Hûlî (*Reformist Approaches to Arab-Islamic Culture*), and Ahmed en-Naîm (*Reform in Islamic Law*). The publication list also includes a book on semantics as a new science of meaning (by F. R. Palmer) and a book on Islamic views on reincarnation. There is little reference to classic Arab Islamic writers. Both Aydın and Özsoy confirmed that the translation of works by Fazlur Rahman in the 1970s "started the ball rolling" and that his remains the decisive imprint on the Reformist movement. Through Rahman, Özsoy explained, "the Turks gained access to Muhammad 'Abduh and other Arab Islamist thinkers."

However, Aydın explained that recent transnational Islamic rethinking had little impact in Turkey "because Turkish Islamic scholars and writers haven't traveled much and many don't speak English or Arabic. . . . Few outsiders understand Turkish. . . . Professor Kirbaşoğlu is known in the Arab world to some extent because he taught in Saudi Arabia. However, for the most part, none of our publications have been translated into other languages. . . . I believe there are significant numbers of people who think along the same lines, but we are not aware of them." As a result of their training at Turkish and European universities, Reformists tend to be fluent in French, English, and other European languages. Aydın, Özsoy and Akdemir told me that they read Arabic. However, their conversations were peppered with examples from the Western canon, ranging from Freud to Heidegger, not Arab sources.

The Reformists' emphasis on Muslim interiority requires them to differentiate between religion and culture. It is here that perceived differences from Arab Islam become most apparent. Özsoy: "Since Islam has been an imperial religion from the beginning, it has the capacity to take on different cultural forms. This allows nations to preserve their characteristics after becoming Muslim. This is, in fact, the result of Islam being a humanistic and realistic religion. Of course, we should not make the mistake of equating ethnic and national character with Islam. In the final analysis, Islam is nothing but the average of what contemporary Muslims are. However, I have always weighed the significance of this. I mean, while reading the Qur'an, to what extent am I facing an Arab reality and to what extent the demands of Allah? We have to distinguish between these."[5]

Arab Islam acts as a foil, highlighting the greater democratic potential of Turkish Islam. Salih Akdemir explained that in the Middle East religion was understood as a relationship of slavery between God and man, so no democracy was possible. Turkish Muslimhood, on the other hand, "is moderate, comfortable," according to Mehmet Aydın. "[We have] a rooted history. . . . If you ask me, religious tolerance was greater in Ottoman times than in the present. . . . It didn't emerge with the Republic; there is an 800 to 900 year history." He gave as an example the acceptance of Jews after the founding of the Republic. "Secondly, Turkish Islam was, of course, culturally influenced to some extent by its Central Asian roots. [For this reason,] in my youth relations between men and women in the villages were extremely comfortable." He suggested that, although one says "Islam" very easily in English, in fact, for Turkey a better word might be "Muslimhood."

Islamiyat is read by other intellectuals and has little currency beyond the circle of theologians and Islamic scholars, yet is one of the most vibrant arenas for new Islamic thinking in Turkey. This begs the question of why we should care about a group with such a limited audience. This is perhaps best answered by pointing to Aydın's new position as minister in the prime minister's inner circle. While disclaiming Islamism, these intellectuals have brought their Muslim approach and Muslimhood model into the government, albeit as individuals. As we shall see below, this does not solve the problem presented by Muslim ideas and practices spilling into public and political space in an entrenched secular (or laicist) system. However, it suggests new possibilities for negotiating these contradictions that would have been impossible with an overtly political Islamism, which would only have been able to resolve the problem by re-placing the secular system with an Islamic one.

Reformist influences have been felt in the most unlikely places in the political sphere. During the election campaign, Deniz Baykal, the leader of the RPP, Turkey's most secular, socialist-oriented party, founded by Ataturk himself, created a media stir when he said, "From Muhammad Iqbal to Sayyid Qutb, Islamic thinkers have been social democrats" (*Sabah*, October 28, 2002). Forced to respond to media outrage that he would put the Egyptian "founder of political Islam" on the same level as Mevlana and Haci Bektaş, Baykal explained that he was not interested in Qutb's political views, but in his ideas about social justice and anticapi-talist views and belief that "social democracy is Islamic." In his response, he referred to the Reformist Yaşar Nuri Öztürk, who had translated Qutb and who was standing as an RPP candidate for parliament. Far from helping the RPP gain votes in the more orthodox countryside, Öztürk may have lost some of those votes by suggesting that the call to prayer be changed from Arabic to Turkish. Nevertheless, the party stood by him as a bearer of enlightened and modern religious knowledge (*Milliyet*, November 12, 2002). Another party member insisted defensively that "[i]n our youth, we didn't just read [Qutb]; we read Marx too!" (*Sabah*, October 28, 2002). After the election, the presence of an Islamic scholar rep-resenting the RPP in parliament presented a slightly humorous benefit when a new independent candidate from the rural east balked at wearing the traditional gold jacket pin given him when he entered parliament. Öztürk was able to reassure him that gold was not *haram*, religiously forbidden (*Milliyet*, November 14, 2002).

The relation of Reformists to Islamic political movements varies. Özsoy takes a critical stance with respect to the conservative Islamist par-ties under Erbakan, but is more favorably inclined toward the AKP, not because it is Islamist, but because it is not. "In Turkey, only a fraction of the so-called Islamists regards [Erbakan's political Islamist] tradition with sympathy. A significant portion has joined other religious commu-nities and the larger body is loyal to the state and regards [the Ministry of] Religious Affairs highly. . . . Just as a party that defends solely the rights of Kurds or a party that promotes the Alevis is not healthy, an Islamist party is [not healthy either]. . . . AK Party [on the other hand] has votes coming from people from different walks of life [and] a diverse body of deputies in the National Assembly. For instance, we have scholars from our faculty [in parliament]. People who are very enlightened; following a reformist interpretation of Islam, and not as a fantasy but as people who have internalized this and know what they are doing. . . . Professor Mehmet Aydın is the most prominent of them. [This is not just] about the AK Party. The people walking down the street have a conception of Islam as well, which is partially influenced by reformist Islam. Islam never stops." Not surprisingly, Reformist ideas have faced criticism from more orthodox Muslims and Islamists, but their influence with AKP inserts their ideas into the mainstream. Their ideas also seem to find support in the general population. A national poll showed that while most Turks considered themselves to be devout Muslims and prayed regularly, most also believed that Islam had no place in politics (Çarkoğu & Toprak 2000).

PUBLIC AND PRIVATE SPHERES

Politics is contestation over what is private and what is public or political. That is, it is an interpretive struggle, not just an issue of control over space. How is that space defined? What are its boundaries? How are the ideas and practices that take place there evaluated? One might consider this a subset of a larger contestation over the place of "tradition" and "modernity," or Islam and secularism. In Turkey, these issues are front and center, as reformist Muslims try to bring their personal Muslimhood onto the public stage in schools, in government, in the streets, and within a laic system. While a secular system requires the separation of matters of church and state, a laic system commands secularism and forbids religion in the public and political spheres and is set up to enforce it. Özsoy describes this form of laicism, as it is practiced by the Turkish state, as a form of atheism, where religion is expected not to exist at all in certain arenas. Islamists and "public Muslims" have come up short against this seemingly immovable barrier. Erdoğan's two daughters study in the United States because they would not be allowed to cover their heads in Turkish schools. Özsoy complained that "this is a faculty of theology [but] our students . . . have to uncover their heads. A large number of our students can't attend classes; others attend wearing wigs. No separation between public and private sphere is left. [The classroom] is defined as public sphere." When it was founded in 2001, the AKP had been warned by the Constitutional Court that it faced closure because six of the party founders wore head scarves; it is illegal for women wearing head scarves to found a political party. Just two weeks after coming to power, the AKP government faced the first major challenge to its Muslimhood model. Protocol required Bülent Arınç, the new speaker of parliament, to see secularist President Ahmet Sezer off at the airport. Since Mrs. Sezer would be there, protocol required that Arınç bring his wife as well. The following day, the photo on the front page of all the major newspapers showed President Sezer shaking hands with a veiled Mrs. Arınç. It did not take long for Sezer to remind the AKP government that this had been an illegal act, not to be repeated. Veiling is not permitted in the political arena, whether in parliament or on the airport runway. Several days later, the heads of the branches of the military paid the new government a routine welcome visit. After spending twenty minutes with the prime minister, they spent exactly two minutes, as timed by waiting journalists, in the office of Mr. Arınç. The message was clear. AKP was not to step over the line again.

This presented an interesting dilemma and occasioned a great deal of public debate in the media and in people's homes about whether and under what circumstances religious symbols like the veil could appear in the public sphere and what exactly constituted the public sphere. Some suggested that a differentiation should be made between those who provide service on behalf of the state (like teachers and members of parliament) and those who receive services (like students and ordinary citizens), with only direct representatives of state service being required to adhere to the restrictions on religious symbolism. This debate has opened a hitherto closed door to redefining the meaning of the public arena by differentiating between society and the state. For many Turks, however, the public is irrevocably political. At present, Kemalist opposition to contracting the parameters of the public sphere retains the upper hand. The Kemalists are concerned to ensure that society remains secular, at least in its public face. The Muslimhood model provides both a challenge and an opportunity to rethink these policies. In so doing, it is useful to point out that the meanings of the concepts of public and private and veiling itself already are contested and have begun to change.

Within the Islamist movement itself, the differentiation between a public and private sphere also has become negotiable and ill-defined. Aggressive marketing has created a middle-class and elite Islamist style that sets itself off against the "unconscious" veiling of the masses. The "new Islamic woman" takes part in previously male-dominated activities in the public sphere, whether political activism or shopping. Veiled political activists from working-class backgrounds also aspire to the well-publicized role of "new Islamic woman," dressing the part as prescribed by advertisements and Islamist magazines aimed at women. Eventually, however, many are forced by economic circumstances to retreat into seclusion within the patriarchal family and the home, an arena set off in Islamist ideology as private in opposition to public. This "private" arena itself has been valorized by the market, resulting in a new bourgeois Islamic home environment marked by certain purchased commodities. This stands in contrast to an Islamic home marked primarily by religiously supported female virtues (like virginity, motherhood, housekeeping, and seclusion). A woman may move between being a "new Islamic woman" and being a secluded housewife, depending on her class and education. Both are legitimated with reference to Islamic doctrine. Veiling itself is a powerful symbol both of Islamist women's right to act in public as well as their duty to remain secluded in the home. Male Islamist activists are more likely than their female colleagues to emphasize the latter over the former. While the veil acts as a visible, unifying political symbol under certain circumstances, the heterogeneity of economic circumstances and motivations of its wearers indicates potential fractures within the movement, particularly along lines of social class and gender, about Islamic definitions of the proper constitution of public and private and women's place within them.

Özsoy believes that "the differentiation of a public and private sphere may be a legal and sociological necessity, but with regard to religion, it is an anachronism. . . . There is a famous story told about the Prophet Muhammed's companion, Omar. . . . It is said that Omar, the Caliph, had two groups of candles. During working hours when he was caliph, he would use the state's candle, but from the moment he thought he had moved to his private life, he used his private candle. Although this doesn't give us a technical way to separate private from public sphere . . . it gives us some clues that can be pursued. [We can find such clues] in the life of the Prophet (PBUH) as well." His point is that Muslims can reconcile themselves to laicism[6] if they understand it as simply a "technology" (which candle do I use where?), rather than as an ideology (am I a laicist or Islamist?). "When laicism is presented as a paradigm against religion it is not possible to say that religious people are at peace with it. However, when it is perceived as a detail, a technique of state formation, in that sense, we don't see that they have a problem together." The question of who will be allowed to use both candles, however, is not addressed.

This functional view of secularism and laicism is echoed by both Tayyip Erdoğan and Mehmet Aydın. "Islam is a religion, and a party is just a political institution," Erdoğan explained. "Secularism is just a style of management. When a person chooses Islam, he becomes Muslim, but he can choose secularism as a style of administration. . . . Secularism is an important part of democracy. [It] establishes the administrative structure of this country" (*Washington Post,* November 10, 2002, B1–2). Aydın agrees that secularism is compatible with democracy in a Muslim society, but insists on defining secular in a nonideological sense as working in conformity with the rule of law in a fully functioning democracy. "I do not want it in other terms. If you say, I will secularize the culture, for instance, [and impose] an educational model in which religious terminology has no place; this doesn't work."

Many people believe that defining public and private by differentiating between service giver and service provider might be a "technical" solution to the seemingly intractable question of whether veiled women may attend schools. Özsoy, however, does not agree. "I do not think this is right in principle because I believe dress is a fundamental right. There are definitely some criteria that will define and limit it. . . . For instance, I must not have the freedom to come here totally naked. . . . This can be called custom, tradition, or moral appropriateness. But it must be regulated by law. [Otherwise,] I believe such restrictions are wrong in principle, whether it be for a service provider or service taker in the public sphere."

Aydın accepts some form of laicism as necessary in a Muslim country to guard the state against a chaos of Islamic interpretation. He believes that laicism is natural to the Turkish interpretation of Islam, because a laic state, for instance, ensures that men and women are equal (as he believes they were in early Central Asian Turkic communities). He argued that the state must be laic because [otherwise] there would be too many people who would claim the right to interpret the law. The result would be a situation like that of "the Vatican and Protestants, or the Reformation and counter-Reformation." For a Muslim country like Turkey, he said, he would advocate laicism "as it is meant in Holland." By this he means a more benign and liberal definition of what is allowed in public space, rather than a redefinition of the space. I suggested the term "secularism," but he didn't like it and suggested "secularity" as something more "natural."

PUBLIC CULTURE

The present debates about what form of clothing and behavior belongs where might well be less a clash of distinct secularist (or laicist) versus Islamist ideologies than the most recent manifestation of a long process of differentiation of personal experience from provincial propriety versus urban mores. As Meeker points out, as a result of continual two-directional urbanization, Turkish citizens, whether in village or city, have been required more and more to differentiate between family space and social space, social and public space, school and work, weekend and weekday, community of origin and community of migration (which could include places as far away as Germany and Saudi Arabia), and to adjust their behaviors and attitudes appropriately (1994, 40). Official Kemalism did not provide many answers to the dilemmas faced by people trying to come up with a moral roadmap for unfamiliar contexts, and left- and right-wing political ideologies of the 1960s and 1970s were suppressed. In the 1980s and 1990s, many Turks focused their hopes on developing civil society; for others, the answers lay in provincial modes of propriety that were common even in cities, unacknowledged by secular nationalist ideology. These norms and patterns of speech and behavior involved, among other things, rituals of cleanliness, distinct ideas of personal status and rights, and a focus on "intimacy, loyalty, interpersonal transparency and affection" and mutual support (Meeker 1994, 37), and were anchored in a local and oral Islamic ethic.

This widespread language and ethic, unacknowledged and even demonized by the Kemalists, served as a powerful foundation for Islamist politics. It is important to note that early Islamic parties, like the National Salvation Party (NSP) in the 1970s, did not do well in elections. Toprak (1981, 101) suggests that this is because religion by itself was not a sufficient factor for mobilization. It was not until the 1990s that an Islamic party began to organize and mobilize people on the basis of what Meeker calls a provincial "Islamic language of being" (1994, 31), rather than on the basis of local interests. (The NSP catered to provincial small businessmen fearful of big business). That change allowed Islamic politics to expand beyond specific interests to attract people across a wide spectrum who perceived in the party a familiar and time-honored strategy for dealing with life's difficulties and change.

These developments have been exacerbated by economic decline and privatization of state industries in the 1980s and 1990s. There is a perceptible nostalgia for traditional strategies and institutions that, in retrospect, seemed to provide solutions. There is a diffuse but discernible nostalgia for a sheltering authority. This can be seen in the recent popularity of films and film series about rural *agha*s who are gruff and demanding, but care about their people, protect them, and meet their needs. The Ottoman Empire, moth-balled since 1923 by the Republic, has been dusted off to provide models for everything from tolerant multiculturalism to veiling styles and architectural models for summer resorts. The Welfare and Virtue Parties that preceded AKP put forward Ottoman-inspired ideas ranging from Bulaç's scheme for *millet*-style religious federalism to charity programs in which wealthy families, in effect, "adopt" poor families. AKP was successful primarily because it organized and mobilized people on the basis of neighborhood networks built around the very characteristics described in Meeker's provincial propriety. The links between neighborhood networks, civic organizations, and political party—a powerful nexus I call vernacular politics (White 2002)—created a broad national movement, flexible enough to incorporate a great variety of people. The masses, in effect, were mobilized on the basis of familiar personal ties and obligations, and their energies and interests channeled into a national political program. Vernacular politics made the line between personal and political, and between local and national, obsolete.

The rehabilitation of provincial modes of propriety as the bases for new urban, modern Muslim identities and national political mobilization became possible with the development of an aggressive media. Television and radio were effectively deregulated in the 1980s as cable and satellite television made it impossible to control. There also was a publication explosion. The Turkish-Islamic synthesis of the 1980s meant that the government allowed a great variety of Islamic ideas and material to be published and broadcast. The newly opened economy of the 1980s brought wealth to conservative and provincial entrepreneurs. The Özal government brought them into the bureaucracy. All of these things led to the development of a new Islamist public culture. Almost immediately, it came into conflict with official public culture. Veiling developed a popular, chic style and began to appear in areas of the city, particularly middle-class areas, formerly the exclusive realm of secularists, and Islamic ideas were debated in the media.

MUSLIMIZATION OF THE PUBLIC

There are, in other words, multiple challenges to the laicist definition of the boundaries and content of the public sphere, from media and market forces, from Muslim intellectuals and politicians, and from ordinary citizens looking for strategies for self-expression. Yet, at the same time, there is widespread concern about the social manifestations of other kinds of difference that seem to be on the rise: an acceptance of lifestyle differences only if they are segregated; a politically unmoored and intolerant Muslimhood that divides people within the same social class, the same neighborhood. A secularist friend worried that AKP's plan to move authority for such things as education and health care from the central state into the hands of local authorities would lead to dangerous differences between, say, school districts, with one allowing head scarves and the other not. He worried it would lead to segregation, "like U.S. blacks," but based on lifestyle. Ayşe Böhürler, the Islamist writer and television personality, complained about Negrofication (zencileştirme).[7] Two relatively new terms, "white Turks" and "black Turks," have come into wide use to refer to urban, secular, left-of-center Turks, on the one hand, and rural (or "reactionary," uncivilized) Islamist conservatives on the other. A middle-aged desk clerk in a touristic hotel who has lived his entire life in Fatih, arguably Istanbul's most religiously conservative neighborhood, described a creeping division between residents who are more devout and those less observant. Whereas in the past, they lived mixed together, he explained, now there is less tolerance. More religiously observant residents are disturbed by the more open clothing and lifestyles of their neighbors. They have, over time, become geographically segregated, so that those living behind the mosque tend to be more observant than those living in front of the mosque.

Is Islamist Politics Dead? Some Questions

Many politicians and intellectuals argue that Islam has ceased to play a direct role in politics, other than inspiring direction. They claim that Islam in both the public and private spheres has become pluralist, multicultural, and modern. The meanings of Islamic symbols and practices seem to be diffusing as they are marketed and popularized. Yet society seems ever more rent by differences that people associate with differing positions with regard to Islamic lifestyle. Also, real forces (the military, the secularist/laicist establishment, beginning with the president and the courts) dispute the presence of what they consider political symbols, like the veil, in public and civic space. That is, they point to a continuation of Islam in politics. Is this simply a matter of definition—Where is the public sphere? Is the veil really a public symbol or just a personal fashion choice? Is Islamic ideology truly dead? —Or is the redefinition of public and private a sleight of hand that makes Muslim values and practices appear to be personal choices even when government ministers are seen to fast and pray together?

The Muslimhood model and Abant model of reconciliation are promising, but without a viable political framework, the problem is not solved. A young urban planner at Middle East Technical University in Ankara compared this to the conundrum of the famed Gordian Knot. Alexander the Great cut the Gordian Knot, which could not be undone, with his sword. "It's a solution," said the urban planner, "but a trivial one. The knot is not undone. In other words, it's not really a solution." This is true whether the army intervenes to keep the government free of Islamic politicians, or whether Muslim politicians bring their ideas and practices into the secular government. To undo the Gordian Knot, he said, one needs democracy. For Özsoy, this does not pose a problem. "Once a fellow citizen asked me if Islam and democracy are compatible. I answered him as follows. . . . If Muslims want it, it is. [This is] because there is no such abstract Islam outside of the way in which Muslims have shaped and brought it to the historical scene." This interpretation reflects both the individualism of the Reformist position and the differentiation of religion from its traditional and cultural historical baggage, separating a Turkish from an Arab Islam. The November 2003 car bombings in Istanbul, apparently planned by Al-Qaeda with the assistance of a local, hitherto unimportant radical Islamist group, can be expected to reinforce this suspicion of Arab Islam and lead AKP to further distance itself from any radical Islamic elements that might still remain within the party.

Can the Muslimhood Model Travel?

The Abant model is seen by many as something that can travel, if only other Muslim countries could overcome their internal barriers (attributed to culture, bad governments, etc.). The Muslimhood model, on the other hand, even though it is based on a universalist conception of human character, is perceived to be more strongly expressed in Turkey because of the characteristics of Turkish Islam (Central Asian Sufism) and Ottoman history. Aydın, however, has a more optimistic view: "If we stay in power another five years . . . there are some things we need to fix in Turkey. . . . Turkish society is religious. If we can put into place the best model of a democratic law state in a religious Muslim society, then it's impossible for Syria and Iraq not to be affected by this. . . . Much radicalism derives from politics, from economic problems. If you have a very narrow definition of nationalism, ethnicity goes up in flames. If you interpret Islam as allowing only this, and all the rest is forbidden, you will have serious problems. In the Islamic world, radicalism derives from fifty years of politicians who have not solved people's economic problems and now try to use religion to clear the way before them. Also, the appearance of radicalism in the Islamic world is linked to Israel's politics, which desperately needs to be solved."

Certain elements present themselves, however, that may be less transferable. Radical Islamism in Turkey as inspired by transnational trends died because of a general realization that a *shari'ah*-based state was not a practicable goal due to state and military resistance, a popular lack of support for Islam in politics, and the recognition that Arab Islam differs from Turkish Islam, which is more individualistic and moderate. There was an all-around moderating effect as representatives of different groups and positions communicated at Abant meetings and in the media. These trends were reflected intellectually by theologian Renewers and politically by AKP. AKP's model of Muslimhood limits Islam in politics to ethical and moral inspiration of individual behavior and individual choice. The party supports democracy because it guarantees freedom of individual belief and expression and, thus, religious expression and its own survival.

Repression of Islamist participation in public life has not led to movement away from a civil sphere to violent radicalism because (1) the repressing mechanisms of state and military enjoy widespread legitimacy and support; the military (in polls ranked the most trusted institution) and the state are both entwined with the heroic nationalist legacy of Ataturk; (2) repressed political figures and parties generally are able to reconfigure and struggle for a new place within a competitive political system. This leads to two questions: (1) whether, in the absence of repression, the other factors mentioned above would have been sufficient to moderate the Islamist impetus; (2) whether the Muslimhood model could survive a system without such repressive mechanisms (an AKP aim). It is conceivable that Muslim ideals might become absorbed and diffused in the secular "technology" of state, or that Muslims might be outflanked by less liberal elements of society.

AKP came to power in part because its message matched religiocultural provincial ethical and behavioral norms that, despite the universalist and individualist claims of the Muslimhood theorists, are not necessarily liberal or based on individualism. Rather, rights in this social paradigm are derived from community membership and obedience to communal norms. While the provincial code protects guests and travelers, it is not particularly conducive to tolerance of behavioral aberration among fellow residents. Due to urbanization and the growth of both Islamic and non-Islamic commercial media, what had been a provincial code has become elaborated into nationally valorized identities, linked in a diffuse way to Islam, with differences among people encoded in symbols like the veil and terminology like black and white Turk. The divisiveness is expressed most obviously in a continuing battle over what constitutes public space (parliament? university classrooms? the street? state occasions?) and who controls what can and cannot appear there. This comes out in such disputes as the permissibility of veiling or, in neighborhoods like Fatih, secular dress in public places, whether women's proper place is in parliament or in the home, and whether or not alcohol sale and consumption should be prohibited in sidewalk restaurants (where nondrinking Muslim passers-by might be offended at the sight).

These dilemmas illustrate an interesting difference between social and political trends. While politics and intellectual discourse on Islam seem to be moving into the realm of democracy, tolerance, and individualism, society is becoming more polarized along the lines of perceived lifestyle differences. Speaker Arınç's protocol dilemma was the first sign of the legally entrenched nature of secularist practices and definition of the public sphere, heedless of the new government's attempts to explain Islamicized practices as individual, rather than public, choices.

NOTES

1. Interview with author, Ankara, November 30, 2002. (Unless otherwise specified, further quotations will refer to the interview first referenced.)
2. Interview with author, Ankara, November 25, 2002.
3. Interview with author, Istanbul, November 23, 2002.
4. Interview with author, Ankara, November 29, 2002.

5. Interview with author, Ankara, November 29, 2002.
6. The Turkish term *laiklik* has been translated as both "laicism" or "secularism."
7. Discussion with author, Istanbul, November 28, 2002.

References Cited

Abant Platformu. 2000. Istanbul: Gazeteciler ve Yazarlar Vakfı Yayınları.

Aras, Bülent. 1998. "Turkish Islam's Moderate Face." *Middle East Quarterly 5,* no. 3: 23–29.

Aydın, Mehmet. 2002. *Niçin?* Istanbul: Zaman Kitap.

————. 1985. *Turkish Contribution to Philosophical Culture.* Istanbul: AKM Yayınevi.

Çarkoğu, Ali, and B. Toprak. 2000. *Türkiye'de Din, Toplum ve Siyaset.* Istanbul: Türkiye Ekonomik ve Sosyal Etüdler Vakfı.

Erman, Tahire, and E. Göker. 2000. "Alevi Politics in Contemporary Turkey." *Middle Eastern Studies* 36, no. 4 (October): 99–118.

Erdemir, Aykan. 2002. "Alternative Modernities? 'Modern' Alevis and Alevi Alternatives." Paper presented at Symposium "Local Modernities: Islamic Cultural Practices as Sites of Agency, Mediation and Change," MIT, Boston, October 5.

Massicard, Elise. 2001. "Local Productions of Alevi Knowledge." *Istanbuler Almanach* no. 5: 70–74.

Meeker, Michael. 1991. "The New Muslim Intellectuals in the Republic of Turkey." In *Islam in Modern Turkey: Religion, Politics and Literature in a Secular State,* edited by Richard Tapper, pp. 189–219. London: I. B. Tauris.

————. 1994. "Oral Culture, Media Culture, and the Islamic Resurgence in Turkey." In *Exploring the Written in Anthropology,* edited by Eduardo P. Archetti, pp. 31–64. Oslo: Scandinavian University Press.

Navaro-Yashin, Yael. 2002. "The Market for Identities: Secularism, Islamism, Commodities." In *The Everyday of Modern Turkey,* edited by Deniz Kandiyoti, pp. 153–221. London: I. B. Tauris.

Toprak, Binnaz. 1981. *Islam and Political Development in Turkey.* Leiden: E. J. Brill.

Vorhoff, Karin. 1997. "Vom Schweigen Zum Schreiben: Alewitische Presse in der Türkei Heute." *Istanbuler Almanach* no. 1: 55–60.

White, Jenny B. 2002. *Islamist Mobilization in Turkey: A Study in Vernacular Politics.* Seattle: University of Washington Press.

Chapter 5

DILEMMAS OF REFORM AND DEMOCRACY

IN THE ISLAMIC REPUBLIC OF IRAN

BAHMAN BAKTIARI

IN MAY 1997, political dark horse Mohammad Khatami surprised his clerical colleagues and international analysts with a landslide win in the presidential race over the establishment candidate, Ali Akbar Nateq-Nouri. Khatami's election signaled Iranians' expectations that their new president would ease the Islamic Republic's restrictions on cultural production and social interaction in the name of religion, execute the rule of law consistently, and strengthen civil society. Four years later, in June 2001, the electorate, skeptical about the pace of these reforms, voted in lower numbers. Nevertheless, Iranians reelected their president by an even wider margin, showing their patience with Khatami, who still confronts intense opposition from the Islamic Republic's conservatives worried about the erosion of clerical supremacy and the advent of secularism.

During both presidential campaigns, Khatami appealed to four constituencies: the middle class chafing under Islamic constraints on social life and frustrated by Iran's international economic isolation; intellectuals objecting to the ruling clergy's violations of human rights; women resisting the clerics' efforts to limit their rights and roles in Iranian society; and youths hungry for cultural and social freedoms and in need of higher education and jobs. These constituencies formed the core of the reformist movement, or Jonbesh-e Dovom-e Khordad, which captured not only the presidency twice but also majorities in the municipal council elections of February 1999 and in parliamentary races a year later. However, reformists in government have not succeeded in fully implementing their platform. They have so far been unable to guarantee freedom of expression (the centerpiece of Khatami's domestic agenda), to repair Iran's broken economy, or to take full advantage of the president's call for a "dialogue of civilization" to normalize relations with the United States.

This stalemate in Iranian politics inspires three questions: Given its victories at the ballot box, why has the reformist movement stalled? How long will Iranians—particularly youths—wait for reforms to have a tangible impact on their lives? And do Khatami's constituents have any alternatives to waiting for the success of reforms?

Arguably, the reformist movement has stumbled over three obstacles: First, the bifurcation of executive power renders gridlock more likely in the Islamic Republic's policy making. Furthermore, President Khatami lacks the personal qualities and skills needed to push reform past conservative opposition; he is a humanist intellectual with a passion for ideas but has sided with the system's preservation in moments of crisis. Thus, in the marathon run toward reform, Khatami's constituents, especially Iranian young people, are out ahead of him. Yet these constituents too have a long way to go before crossing the ever-elusive finish line—formulating policies to delineate the role of religion in public life, to democratize the procedures and substance of Iranian politics, and to engage Iran in a constructive network of foreign relations.

Conceptualizing State-Society Relations in the Islamic Republic of Iran

State and society are important concepts in everyday life as well as in political analysis. But the concepts are elusive and hard to define. One of the most perplexing problems is distinguishing between the two. Where does the state "end" and society "begin," and vice versa? State and society are different, yet they are not entirely separate.

Rather than trying to say that one entity is part of the state and another entity is part of society, a more fruitful approach is to think of arenas in which boundaries, rights, jurisdictions, and power distribution between state and societal agencies are debated, contested, and resolved (at least temporarily). These arenas can be within physical institutions, including those that, structurally speaking, clearly belong to the state—for example, government ministries and militaries. But the arenas can be other institutions, like parliament or universities, entities whose locations in the state structure are ambiguous. Arenas can be groups and organizations not part of a state structure yet in one degree or another are penetrated by state rules and regulations—for example, families, villages, and religious groups. Arenas may also be problems and controversies that are not confined to a particular institution.

In the Iranian case, many questions can be raised about relations between state and society in Iran. A single chapter cannot explore them all. In this chapter I shall concentrate on relations between government authorities and people living within the jurisdiction of that government. In particular, two kinds of questions will be addressed. The first concerns how the political system works: How, if at all, does the state allow or

encourage citizens to be involved in the process of setting and implementing rules and policies of the country? How, if at all, do people in society affect or try to affect what state authorities do? And to what extent
do people abide by what authorities say? The second are normative questions. What should be the relations between state authorities and people
in society? What involvement should the state have in people's economic,
social, cultural, and political affairs? And what involvement should
groups and individuals in society have in state affairs?

In Iran, a current contentious state-society issue is the role of religion
and the *ulema*. The question is whether the *ulema*, as represented now by
an unelected Supreme leader, should have the final word on all matters of
state? Or should the final word rest with elected officials—that is, the
president and the parliament? This question has gained greater significance as Iranian society has undergone significant demographic changes.
More than 60 percent of the population are under twenty-five years old;
they have no memory of the prerevolutionary era, or the first decade of
the revolution. They aspire for greater personal and social freedom, and
demand jobs and a better standard of living.

Sovereignty in the Islamic Republic—Divine or Democratic?

The Islamic Republic's Constitution, as amended in 1989, stipulates a bifurcation of executive power, which is invested in the presidency and the
institution of *velayat-e faqih*. The president is popularly elected for a
term of four years; Iranians sixteen years and older are eligible to vote.
The president's responsibilities include the appointment of a cabinet to
do the nation's business, the proposal and negotiation of a legislative
agenda with the parliament, and the conduct of Iran's foreign policy.

The institution of *velayat-e faqih,* or guardianship of the jurisconsult,
is Ayatollah Ruhollah Khomeini's legacy to Shi'i political theory and
praxis. The jurisconsult, or Supreme Leader, is a highly esteemed cleric
chosen by his peers on the eighty-six-member Assembly of Experts in
recognition of his knowledge of *fiqh,* or Islamic jurisprudence, and his
other religiopolitical credentials. The Supreme Leader's role is to guide
Iranians (and, in theory, other Muslims) toward the just government of
God. His powers are wide ranging. He is the commander-in-chief of
Iran's armed forces, may veto the president's decisions, and is charged
with protecting the government's Islamic character.

After Khomeini's death in 1989 and especially since Khatami's election
in 1997, this dual executive has inspired lively debate over the meaning
and workings of an Islamic republic. Iran's government may be Islamic,
it may be a republic, but can it remain both at the start of the twenty-first

century? The inheritors of Khomeini's ideological legacy have not answered this question definitively, with advocates of opposing perspectives vigorously justifying themselves and, in so doing, pushing open the space for public discourse.

In many ways, the state of political competition in Iran in recent years can be characterized in terms of the complex relationship of the so-called religious intellectuals (Roshanfekraneh Dini) and the ruling clerical establishment (Rouhaniyouneh Hokumati). The religious intellectuals' challenge against the establishment centers on engaging the establishment clerics in debates over doctrinal, political, and sociocultural issues. The most critical component of this debate has had practical consequences on postrevolutionary Iranian polity, because by focusing on the relationship between religion and the state and the role of the clergy, these religious intellectuals seek to strengthen the cause of reform by opening the doors for other intellectuals and defenders of civil society.

Debating the Relationship between Religion and Political Authority

The twentieth century has brought change to the world at a rapid and unprecedented rate. These changes have swept the Muslim world, leading to various responses. The struggle for reform and democracy has been a major component of Islamic resurgence in the twentieth century. As one scholar has stated, "[S]ocial change in our age has drawn great masses of Muslims onto a teeming public stage. . . . As in the nineteenth- and twentieth-century West, one response to these changes has been a call for equality, freedom, and democracy" (Hefner 2000, 8). Like citizens elsewhere, modern Muslims have had to define their relationship to the Islamic past, looking to their religion to provide some answers to the relative values of modernity and authenticity *(asala)*. In this connection, one Western writer has drawn attention to the desire of many Muslim religious intellectuals not to "suffer" modernity but actively accept and foster modernization, and to do so in a religious context that is in harmony with the indigenous culture (Stowasser 1994, 5).

In the last half century, a variety of circumstances have forced this quest for authenticity to the center in many areas in the Islamic world, but nowhere more evidently than in Iran. At the core of the discourses among Iranian intellectuals is the perception of an anxiety-laden dichotomy between a Muslim's individual and social life, influenced on many levels by science, technology, and Western political thought, and what is expressed as the civilization of an almost bygone era, many of whose elements continue to influence Muslim thought.

President Mohammad Khatami provides a good example of this search for cultural autonomy. Khatami considers himself a scholar and thinker. He is a man steeped in the revolution and the clerical establishment. He is related by marriage to the late Ayatollah Khomeini, served as a minister of culture in the 1980s, and was a close associate of Khomeini's son Ahmad until his death in 1995. He is a man of integrity, palpably honest, intelligent, and shrewd, as well as being well read and modest. In his intellectual development (within a Shi'i theological framework) Khatami has signified a new brand of clerical thinking, one that is not averse to acknowledging the importance of civil society, as well as the need for a better understanding of Western civilization. He speaks English, Arabic, and German, and can converse on the works of Alexis de Tocqueville and Immanuel Kant. He has published several books, one of them on Western political thought.

There are three pillars of Khatami's thought: (1) a cosmopolitan Islam, the product of his conviction that Islam must be creatively and at times substantively reinterpreted or reformulated in order to be responsive to the demands of modern life; (2) the belief that Iranian Islam must reflect and respond to a diverse population that includes several ethnic groups; and (3) the conviction that in the postrevolutionary Iranian polity, Islam should not be the state religion but rather an inclusive religious, democratic, pluralistic force. As an ideology of government alone, Islam cannot solve the problems of a world that, for better or for worse, is dominated by the West. In one lecture, Khatami declared bluntly, "We Muslims once had a dominant civilization and were shaping human history in a way that we are no longer capable of today. We want to regain our place in history and, if possible, build a future that is different from our present and even our past, without rejecting those who are different from us, and without ignoring scientific thought and the practical achievement of humanity" (Khatami 1997, 91).

In a recent interview, Khatami stated that Iran is suffering an "identity crisis" brought on by its "failure to understand the freedoms at the heart of Western civilization. . . . The two contradictory attitudes of love and hatred toward the West have blocked us from accurately understanding the West. . . . Our identity crisis can be said to be the most serious predicament in the country in the past 200 years." As a religious thinker, Khatami is fiercely devoted to his faith and Iran, but at the same time, he attempts to realistically appraise both of their places in the modern world. He asks the question posed by so many other Islamic thinkers: How can a society whose identity is religious guarantee freedom, democracy, and social justice?

If the Iranian Revolution of 1979 solely sought a return to an earlier Islamic civilization, a golden age, then it failed because that civilization, in

Khatami's eyes, is an anachronism. It no longer exists in practical terms and, if it did, it could no longer meet the needs of the modern era. In making this argument, Khatami makes a subtle but compelling distinction between Islamic traditionalists, who seek a return to what Islam once had, and Islamic reformists in Iran and elsewhere, who seek to progressively reshape the faith into a viable, modern approach to government and society. The latter, he believes, is the only option, and he envisions it as the true legacy of the revolution:

> Religiosity had always existed, but a religious revolution was something else, and this took place in our time. The essence of the religion which the Imam [Khomeini] spoke about was no different to the essence of the religion which had prevailed since the early days of Islam. . . . However, there was a difference, and this was the factor which led to the revolution. The difference was that this time [with the Islamic revolution], this religious essence—which had been around since the advent of Islam—began to concentrate once again on the realities of society and represent the historical wishes and demands of the nation. It was in this way that this great and magnificent event took place. In their religion and in the face of their Imam, the nation saw the fulfillment of their historical wishes, which could be summed up as independence, freedom and progress. (Khatami 2001a)

In this context, Khatami's vision of Islam is not so different from that of other reformist Muslim thinkers. Abdurrahman Wahid, leader of Indonesia's Nahdatul Ulama (Renaissance of Religious Scholars), has espoused a reformist intellectual synthesis and social agenda that distinguish between unchanging religious doctrines or laws and legitimate accommodation to social change. Like Khatami, Wahid is among a generation of Muslim reformists who advocate a progressive Islam, one that is democratic, pluralistic, and tolerant. In contrast to those who have advocated the Islamization of Indonesian society, Wahid emphasizes the Indonesianization, indigenization, or contextualization of Islam (Hefner 2000, 31–36; Barton 1996, 213–14; Brumberg 2001).

Khatami and other reformist thinkers have also emphasized indigenization. In one passage, Khatami argues that "dismantling aspects of tradition must be based on indigenous models, not imported and artificial. Indeed, Westerners at the dawn of modernity were awakened by delving deeply into their tradition. Thinkers revisited the artistic tradition of the Greeks and the social traditions of Rome. Religious believers returned to what they considered to be the most authentic aspects of Christianity, and hence the Reformation. And these returns to tradition and reappraisals ushered in the new epoch" (Khatami 1998, 33).

Hence, one does not need to opt for a solution that calls for a break with the past, accepting a secular world that rejects any constructive role for religion. The challenge is to create a balanced vision that incorporates one's past without ignoring the complexities of modern existence: "Democracy is a vital need of today's mankind, including Iran. In my opinion, democracy has only one alternative. That is, seeking self-interests. And no one would choose seeking self-interests over democracy. If I were to summarize the roots and essence of the people's reformist movement for the past 100 years, I would say that the movement is aimed at the establishment of democracy" (Khatami 2001c).

Khatami is a skillful politician. He recognizes that he is venturing into uncharted territory, issuing calls for religious reform and democracy that could only come from a cleric who speaks the language of the educated clergy. Often he uses selective quotes from Khomeini to bolster his position. In one passage, Khomeini asserts that in Islamic government "there should always be room for revision. Our revolutionary system demands that various, even opposing viewpoints be allowed to surface. . . . It is here that traditional religious leadership prevalent in our seminaries will not suffice" (Khatami 1998, 39). In one speech, Khatami asserted that "if we limit ourselves to the appearances of and have a narrow view of religion, then the concept of 'Islamic Republic' itself will mean separation from Islam. Where did you ever have anything called a republic in Islam? Where in Islam—the beginnings of Islam—do you find anything called a parliament?" (Khatami 1999)

At a forum convened in June 2001 by the pro-reform Islamic Iran Participation Party (IIPP) entitled "Imam Khomeini's Reforms and the Concept of Republicanism," parliamentary deputy Elahe Koulahi commenced the deliberations: "The situation in the past was such that experienced pro-reform individuals did not dare to talk about reforms. . . . The late Imam Khomeini paid due attention to the gap between the people and the government, believing that the latter's legitimacy depends on its relation with the people and on the good trust they have in each other" (Baktiari and Vaziri 2002, 18).

Significantly, Ayatollah Khamene'i disagrees with Khatami's understanding of the Islamic Republic's essence and objectives. Commemorating the twelfth anniversary of the passing of the "father of the Islamic Revolution and Founder of the Islamic Republic, the late Imam Khomeini," the Supreme Leader claimed that his mentor was

the symbol of Islam and the people, because by relying on Islamic sovereignty and power, he founded an Islamic society on the basis of spirituality and justice. . . . Like any person who is acquainted with Islam, the late Imam believed, as we continue to today, that it is Islam and Islamic principles that ensure the happiness, welfare, freedom and dignity of a nation. It is Islam that ensures that justice is upheld in society. Reliance upon the people, in the true sense of the world, is made possible only in the context of up-holding Islam and Islamic principles. (Khatami 2001b)

As different as these two interpretations are, they offer a greater insight in that they speak to the prestige Ayatollah Khomeini still commands in postrevolutionary Iran. Yet, to create the flexibility in theology pursued by reformers like Khatami means to break the clergy's monopoly on religious interpretation—a right held by the *ulema* in Shi'i Iran to a far greater extent than by their Sunni counterparts elsewhere in the Muslim world. Despite their theological disputes, the Shi'i clergy have historically considered themselves the spiritual guardians of the community; their spiritual prestige was the foundation on which Khomeini built the Islamic state. Khatami and other reformist thinkers see a danger in that same prestige, the prospect of a single, infallible interpretation, made even more formal when it becomes an ideology of government. Nevertheless, both Shi'i and Sunni *ulema* have faced challenges by new Muslim intellectuals whose work and activities appeal to a broader public audience. These Muslim intellectuals engage in a discourse that presents their faith in quasi-ideological terms, as a source of practical knowledge (Antoun 1989).

The Iranian thinker Abdol Karim Soroush is an example of this sort of new Muslim intellectual. He is the most senior intellectual identified with the reform movement, having raised many of the questions mentioned by Khatami years before the elections of 1997. Soroush has been one of the most vocal critics of what he calls "the insular dogmatism of the clergy." His argument is essentially simple, but devastating. It starts by distinguishing Islam as a religion from those who interpret it, and claims that much of what has been handed down through the generations and articulated as the faith is in fact little more than human interpretation, and therefore subject to human fallibilities (Soroush 1994, 414). In a lecture entitled "What the University Expects from the *Hawzeh*" (religious seminaries), Soroush criticized the *ulema* for reproducing ideological positions to justify their political power. He called on the seminaries to "abandon the habit of stealth and concealment in matters of religious knowledge; desist from treating questions as scandalous; and refrain from expedient speech and action that subserves political power" (Soroush 2000, 174). In another work, Soroush makes the point that the association of religious scholarship with political and economic power is bound to affect that scholarship and could not be considered in the best interests of theological and philosophical investigation. He goes on to argue that "religion is greater than the *ulema,* that Islam as a faith is greater than jurisprudence *(fiqh)."* He adds that the *ulema* could not in any case be considered universally worthy of respect, because "the truth is that among the *ulema* (or those who call themselves *ulema*) those who are impious, poorly educated . . . are not few" (Soroush 1997, 27). In a more direct attack on the clerics who serve in positions of power, Soroush states that "the matter of religion is too great an issue to be exclusively entrusted to the clergy. A clergy that supports itself through religion will gradually be converted to a body whose work will be aimed at preserving itself. When a person's livelihood depends on confirming and supporting the organization of clergy, how can he think freely?"(Soroush 1995, 26).

Soroush's project is a familiar one to those acquainted with Jamal al-Din al-Afghani, or more recently, Ali Shari'ati. Islam to both of these thinkers was foremost a belief in the transcendence of God and in reason. *Ijtihad* (independent judgment, interpretation) was a necessity, and the duty of man was to apply the principles of the Qur'an to the problems of the time. If society does not do this it will stagnate or merely imitate (authorities), and imitation corrupts society. The problem then, as Khatami and Soroush have emphasized, is a static society, one that can no longer meet the psychological, material, and social needs of the people but, more dangerous, obstinately refuses to acknowledge its failings. Iran, Khatami has suggested, falls into that category, and the dangers posed by it could undo the vision of a religious society. In another address, Khatami urges people not to follow the dictates of the clergy blindly, pointing out that even Khomeini himself was not infallible. Again and again, he remarks on the danger posed by "unenlightened religious dogma," and, in a way, puts forth his own eclectic education, one both religious and secular, as a model. "A moral person who is a moving encyclopedia but lives outside his time," he said, "for whom the most pressing problems are for example the second and third Islamic centuries, cannot solve even the smallest of today's problems, for today's problems do not interest him." Interestingly, Khatami praises Ali Shari'ati, an influential Iranian sociologist who tried to synthesize socialism with traditional Shi'ism and adapt the theories of Marx, Fanon, and others to a prerevolutionary Iranian environment. Shari'ati, who died in 1977 at the age of forty-three, was criticized by some clergy who suggested he had a poor grounding in Islamic thought and accused him of propagating anticlerical views (Mortimer 1982, 335–46). In hindsight, aspects of Shari'ati's thought have an obvious overlap with Khatami (a cleric) and Soroush.

In making their arguments for a more pluralistic interpretation of Islam, Soroush and Khatami are joined by other thinkers from important theological centers—clerics like Mohsen Kadivar and Ayatollah Mohammad Mojtahed Shabestari. Both of these clerics are very popular among students and the educated class in Iran. These reformist thinkers do not want to do away with religion in civic and political life. They are not against the idea of an Islamic Republic. But they want to blend it with democracy, individual freedom, civil society, and tolerance. By the late 1990s they had drawn many of the revolution's staunchest defenders to their ranks. As stated eloquently by Shabestari:

> The conclusion I would like to make is that if we are supposed not to take the approach suggesting that the values of democracy are something that exists in religious texts, there will remain another option and that is the true meaning of religious democracy. In this case, we will look at the issue of religious democracy from an angle which is different from the others. From this angle, Muslims living in a religious society will ask themselves, "Are our lives under a democratic system of government more compatible with our religion than our lives under a totalitarian or despotic regime?" Here we are not going to change the meaning and content of democracy or accept it from a position of noncompliance with religion. In other words, we, as committed Muslims should ask this question, "If we accept these values on a contractual basis, establish a form of democratic system of government and live with it, will this be more compatible with our Islamic faith than other methods?" (Shabastari 2002)

For Mohsen Kadivar, a popular professor and a middle-ranking cleric who was sentenced to eighteen months of prison in April 1999, "the political and cultural struggle between proponents of religious democracy and those of religious autocracy has become the most important battle in Iran" (Kian-Thiébaut 1997, 14). According to Kadivar, the dominance of the authoritarian tendency in the early stages of the revolution can be attributed to a number of factors. However, the most important was a tendency toward authoritarianism among the *ulema* who found themselves in powerful positions in the government, because not long prior to the revolution, these same *ulema* were staunch pillars of the monarchy (Kadivar 1999, 200).

As if this statement was not enough to draw the wrath of his opponents, Kadivar follows it up by saying that in the eyes of many people who had fought in the revolution for the right to make their own decisions and control their own destinies, there was little difference in their experience of the monarchical regime and that of the Islamic Republic. It was, he noted, "as if it were an Islamic monarchy." Then, to clerics who justify their involvement in the government by saying it is their "Islamic duty to serve the people," Kadivar poses the question, "[I]f Islam as an ideology is the only solution to a nation's problems, political, economic, social, and of course, moral, who is to blame when the same ideology brings misery?" (Kadivar 1999, 210).

The establishment *ulema* have countered these arguments by accusing religious intellectuals of "sloganeering." They maintain that these intellectuals have little understanding of their aims and ambitions, or the consequences of their words. Ayatollah Taqi Mesbah-Yazdi, a member of the Assembly of Experts and a lecturer in the holy city of Qom, has responded that "the prophets of God did not believe in pluralism. They believed that only one idea was right." He goes on to say that "the prophets believed that the right idea must be identified and promoted. . . . And opposing ideas must be rejected through logic. However, if the opponents of the right idea were to decide to impose their own ideas to rule, then tolerance would become meaningless and they must be confronted" (Mesbah-Yazdi 2002).

Mesbah-Yazdi has been the most vocal defender of the clerics' involvement in politics, and has not shied away even from encouraging acts of violence against religious intellectuals. In one passage he directs his comments to Khatami and the latter's assertion that Ayatollah Khomeini supported popular sovereignty, stating that "the Imam [Khomeini] used to say that he was concerned about Islam's future. And we see that today the old slogan of 'independence, freedom and Islamic Republic' is replaced with 'independence, freedom and progress.' That is, the name of Islam is gradually removed from our slogans. . . . The slogan of 'independence, freedom and progress' is a distortion of history and it is a lie. It is regrettable that the passage of time has made some people so presumptuous that they dare forget the fundamental principles of the state" (Mesbah-Yazdi 2002).

Other conservative personalities have accused the religious intellectuals of being "intoxicated with Western liberal ideas," and simply interested in "imitating Western concepts." Mahmaud Fathali, a midranking cleric who teaches in Qom, uses the term "pseudo-intellectuals" when referring to people like Soroush:

> In my opinion, these gentlemen do not have correct and transparent bases and swallow what they get from the West without digesting it. This is due to the hunger they have for the West. Therefore they have no reform thought to put forward in the Islamic sense of the word. The tolerant ideology is very pleasant to some youths who are in the grips of emotions and physical desires and are very attractive to the liberals and the supporters of liberal thought. They think they can take advantage of the situation, but for the masses of the people, who are at one with Islam, it is very hard to accept this kind of talk and it seems that the ideology of tolerance—the way they want it—will never be established in Iran. (Fathali 2000)

If elections results are any indicator, the majority of eligible Iranian voters agree with the president's emphasis on the republican quality of the Islamic Republic, yet during every election since 1997, the conservatives have done their best to skew the process and outcomes. The Council of Guardians disqualified prominent reformists, especially women, from the parliamentary and presidential races, and the conservatives demanded recounts of votes in localities where they lost by narrow margins. These measures seemed counterproductive, because the parliamentary contest of February 2000 gave the reformists some two-thirds of the seats.

However, if reformists have the heart and mind of most Iranians, conservatives control all the important instruments and levers of power. When the newly elected reformist deputies sought to amend restrictions on the press passed by the previous parliament, the conservatives flexed their muscle. Reformist legislators wanted to revoke a law preventing once banned publications from reopening under new names and barring the reemployment of journalists from such publications. As the reformist majority passed a bill repealing these stipulations, the conservative minority appealed to the Supreme Leader, who took the unprecedented step of intervening in the legislative process. Ayatollah Khamene'i vetoed the more liberal press law on the grounds that its text contradicted the precepts of Islam. The parliamentary majority and the popular will were trumped by the appeal to divine sovereignty. According to one scholar, these actions demonstrate that contrary to the revisionist approach of the reformists, the founding fathers of the Islamic Republic had rejected democracy. "Radical Islamists (some of whom have turned reformists today) in the early 1980s argued that there were two kinds of state, i.e., ideological and non-ideological, and placed the Islamic Republic in the former category, together with the Soviet Union. And in their political writings, the supporters of the Iranian regime argued that the main difference between democracies and the Islamic Republic is that the former laws are made by the people, whereas in the latter they were provided by God" (Chehabi 2001, 51).

During the Persian calendar year 1379 (March 2000–March 2001), as Khatami's first term was ending, Iranians witnessed a campaign of repression unprecedented since Khomeini's death eleven years earlier. Conservative leader Ayatollah Mesbah-Yazdi went as far as to preach that recourse to violence is "obligatory" if the Islamic Republic cannot otherwise defend itself, "even if thousands of people must perish." Devout Muslims must "kill on the spot" anyone who "insults Islam or the Prophet" (Mesbah-Yazdi 2002). Ayatollah Khamene'i also declared unequivocally that violence was a legitimate tactic to oppose the flouting of Islamic precepts.

The press stood at the front lines of the conservative assault against the reformists. During ten days in April 2000, the judiciary, headed by Ayatollah Hashemi Shahrudi, closed sixteen reformist newspapers without any hearings. Conservatives forced all the pro-press officials out of the Ministry of Islamic Guidance and Culture, with the result that requests for publications were increasingly refused. Between April 2000 and March 2001, roughly two thousand requests to publish were filed with the Press Supervision Council; only sixty-two publications received licenses. In March 2000, Iran's newspapers had a total daily circulation of approximately 3.12 million, which dropped to 1.75 million a year later—a 45 percent decline.

While readers watched pro-reform newspapers disappear, other members of Iran's fledgling civil society also faced the conservatives' wrath. Academics, journalists, lawyers, liberal clerics, publishers, student leaders, and even some midlevel officials were arrested. Charged with seditious activities, some were sentenced to lengthy jail time following public or closed-door trials, while others, not yet tried, are still held in secret confinement, their whereabouts unknown to their attorneys or families.

Among those arrested was eminent theologian Hassan Yussefi-Eshkevari, for the crime of apostasy; he defended the principle of separation between mosque and state, and contended that Islam does not require women to veil. Although he was condemned to death in a closed-door trial, the Court of Appeals overturned Yussefi-Eshkevari's sentence. Mashallah Shamsolvaezin, the bold editor-in-chief of several banned dailies, is now serving a thirty-month prison term for publishing an article urging the death penalty's abolition in the name of Islam. In April 2001, the judiciary accused and jailed some forty nationalists for conspiring to overthrow the Islamic Republic, including Ezzatollah Sahabi—in his eighties and in frail health, a former member of Khomeini's Revolutionary Council, a member of the Freedom Movement (Nezat-e Azaadi), and editor of the weekly *Iran-e Farda*.

When the parliamentary majority argued that Ayatollah Shahrudi had violated the Islamic Republic's laws and, even worse, the constitution, he rejoined that only clerics are entitled to interpret these texts. What he meant was that only his colleagues, mostly clerics from the Haqqani theological school in Qom, were qualified to do so. Once a prestigious institution led by relatively enlightened ayatollahs, the school has more recently become a hotbed of reactionaries, scorned as "the Iranian Taliban" by other clerics.

Reformists questioned Shahrudi's loyalty to Iran, because he was born in Iraq and was a founding member of the Supreme Council of the Islamic Revolution in Iraq (SCIRI) opposing the Ba'athist government in Baghdad. The daily *Hambastegi* proclaimed, "The founder of the Islamic Republic and the Commander of the Revolution (i.e., Khomeini) was opposed to the idea of employing 'returnees' (those of Iranian origin expelled from Iraq) in positions and areas of government responsibility." *Hambastegi* was then shut down.

During this wave of repression, President Khatami was reduced to voicing his disapproval, since the reformers were powerless to protect those whom they had urged to speak freely. Khatami could only weakly protest: "Three and a half years, and still one has not enough authority for the accomplishment of such a grave responsibility!" Without sufficient authority to redress violations of the constitution, some of Khatami's aides suggested that he may not run for reelection. "As long as the president does not have the power to carry out what he is supposed to do, he will have real reservations about contesting the elections" (*Iran Daily*, December 21, 2001).

Youths Politicized — Resentment, Rebellion, and Revelry

As the presidential race of 2001 neared, reformists worried about the impact of this repression on voters. With more than two-thirds of Iranians under thirty, young people form the largest voting bloc. Youths under thirty comprise 52 percent and those fifteen to twenty comprise 22 percent of eligible voters, respectively. Most young people have little if any memory of the Islamic revolution, did not participate in the referendum establishing the Islamic Republic, and did not vote to ratify its constitution in 1979. However they have long had to deal with the consequences of these events, which their parents' generation celebrated at least initially.

Iranians sixteen years and older have numerous reasons for being skeptical of Khatami in particular and resenting the Islamic Republic more generally. Not forgotten is the campus rioting of July 1999, sparked when police and vigilantes attacked a Tehran University dormitory as students protested the closure of a pro-reform campus newspaper. One student was killed and at least twenty were injured, igniting the most significant unrest in Tehran and other cities since the revolution in 1978–79.

Students around the country chanted pro-Khatami slogans, but the president cautioned that violence would not expedite reform, which must come slowly and deliberately. Although at first caught off guard by the students' demands, the ruling clerics quickly closed ranks. Khamene'i and Khatami authorized the suppression and arrest of student rebels while assuring the nation that the entire episode, including police misconduct and vigilantism, would be investigated. Many young people initially felt betrayed as Khatami sided with the preservation of clerical supremacy. Meanwhile, students have not shied away from politics, joining Islamist and reformist organizations. The largest student group, the pro-reform Office to Foster Unity, is some 500,000 strong.

Even without joining such organizations, however, the under-thirty generation is marked by its political consciousness. Practically every aspect of a young Iranian's daily existence is political and politicized. Youths lead a double life in Iran. Publicly, they must obey the ruling clergy's prohibitions against socializing with the opposite sex, listening to pop music, consuming alcoholic beverages, men wearing shorts, women using cosmetics, and so forth. In the privacy of their own homes, they pursue intimate relationships with the opposite sex, enjoy parties where alcoholic drinks flow and Iranian and Western pop music plays, experiment with dress and cosmetics as a form of self-expression, and the like. However, youths consistently fear being caught even behind closed doors.

Young Iranians aspiring to a university education must endure a grueling entrance examination, knowing that their prospects for matriculation are slim. Out of 1.5 million high school seniors who took this exam in 2001, the university system accepted a mere 150,000. University graduates then struggle to find employment. For every twenty-three graduates, there is one job; 85 percent of Iranians under twenty-five are unemployed. Without earning steady income, young people literally cannot afford to marry, despite the cultural value invested in matrimony.

Arguably, these bleak prospects for economic stability, self-actualization, and companionship have intensified other social maladies among youths. Psychiatrists have seen cases of depression, schizophrenia, and substance abuse multiply. Mohammad-Ali Zam, director of the Tehran Municipality Cultural and Art Organization, disclosed that roughly 5,000 kilograms of narcotics are used in Tehran daily, and that drug addiction has now even afflicted the schoolchildren. Zam also indicated that prostitution is on the rise, with the average age of a prostitute dropping from twenty-seven to twenty.

In the absence of better alternatives and still hopeful that Khatami could improve their lives, two years after the student rebellion young Iranians are still the most vocal about how Iran is governed—not just systemically, but on a daily basis. Watching Iran's promise thwarted by widespread corruption, high unemployment, global isolation, and repression, youths have demanded accountability and, ultimately, democracy from the reformists. During campaign rallies a week before the 2001 presidential race, students carried placards with such slogans as: "Khatami the hero, the hope of the young," "Freedom of thought, always, always," "We will make the crisis-makers despair by voting for Khatami again," "Human beings must be allowed to ask questions," and "We have come to renew our allegiance to reform" (Khatami 2001c).

Khatami's reelection, while hailed by young Iranians, provoked some conservatives' ire. Upon the order of judiciary chief Ayatollah Shahrudi, security forces launched a wave of public floggings targeting youths. During August–September 2001, more than four hundred people, most under twenty-five, were flogged publicly, accused of "consuming alcohol, having illicit sex, or harassing women." Outraged, Khatami warned that in a "society where discrimination, poverty and graft abound, one cannot expect youngsters not to break the law. . . . With tough punishments, you cannot remove social corruption." Foreign Minister Kamal Kharrazi also denounced the floggings, concerned about harm to the Islamic Republic's international image.

However, conservative clerics applauded this type of punishment. Chief Justice Ayatollah Mohammad Mohammadi-Gilani even claimed that the Supreme Leader had approved the floggings, insisting that the offenders "should be beaten to the point where the whip breaks the skin and scars the flesh underneath." Conservatives cared little about the Islamic Republic's image abroad; nor would they cave in to domestic critics of the beatings. They believe that flogging is a deterrent against un-Islamic behavior and rising crime rates. Defending this form of punishment, Ayatollah Shahrudi stated, "All should be sensitive toward the issue of the promotion of corrupt means and fight against the enemies' efforts to deprave our children" (Baktiari and Vaziri 2002, 18).

The wave of floggings heightened tensions on the streets of Iran's major cities, where youths have pushed the limits of those cultural and social freedoms that have increased during the Khatami years, despite the conservative backlash. During October–November 2001, boisterous soccer fans, mostly young men, poured into the streets, particularly in Tehran, to celebrate victories and lament losses by Iran's national football team as it struggled to qualify for the World Cup. When young women joined the men in reacting to their team's fluctuating fortunes and some revelers became rioters, the ruling clerics called on security forces to patrol the streets. The lack of occasions for young people to be simply who they should be—carefree and joyful when they are not at school or at work—creates frustration. One twenty year old reveler's comments about the ruling clerics' restrictions captured the sentiments of Iran's youths: "If they had taught us from the beginning how we can have fun, maybe it would turn out to be more constructive than breaking windows. When we only have one time every four years where we can go out and express our happiness, riots happen" (Nelson 2001).

After two of the games, fans rioted, breaking windows and shouting antigovernment slogans, mostly directed at the Supreme Leader, Ayatollah Khamene'i. The security forces responded by arresting some twelve hundred youths in Tehran alone, most of them under eighteen. The mounting frustration of youths is eroding not merely the conservatives' credibility, but also the legitimacy of the theocracy as a whole. The soccer-spectatorship-turned-protest provoked the daily *Nowruz* to sound an editorial on October 8, 2001, warning: "If we are not intent in deceiving ourselves, if we do not wish to reduce the protests of the young generation to the plots of the enemies inspired and guided from the other side of our borders, we must admit that the gulf between the desire for social freedoms and the restrictions and limitations imposed by the government has been turned into the most active form of social conflict. The generation between 15 and 25, which was born and brought up after the Islamic Revolution, is dissatisfied with the limitations and prohibitions that have been imposed on it, not on the basis of the Constitution, but rather on the basis of the wishes and demands of a small minority, and is resisting these pressures and compulsions."

Prominent pro-reform personalities have urged Khatami to change his strategy toward the conservatives, demanding that the president be more assertive or resign. Perhaps the most significant protest to Khatami's passivity was Ayatollah Jalaleddin Taheri's resignation from his post as Isfahan's Friday prayer leader in July 2002. The Ayatollah lamented watching "the flowers of virtue being crushed, and values and spirituality on the decline" among Iranians. In a scathing resignation letter, Taheri condemned the ruling clerics' corruption and greed: "[W]hen I hear that some of the privileged progeny [aqazadeh] . . . some of whom don cloaks and turbans, are competing among themselves to amass the most wealth and to achieve their own ends, I recall that there are many dervish's cloaks that are best thrown into a fire" (Taheri 2002).

Reformist officials had hoped that Taheri's resignation would spark sustained demonstrations by their sympathizers. Yet after two days of rioting in Isfahan, the judiciary forbade the press from reporting any news about Taheri's letter or the rioting. When Nowruz printed the cleric's letter in full, the daily was shut down. Khatami's quiet during this controversy prompted the newspaper Etemad (July 21, 2002) to ask, "[A]mid all this, we are wondering: Where is Khatami? We are all amazed at Khatami's absence . . . from the [political] scene. Clearly, a silent Khatami is a Khatami who serves the conservatives' interests."

Emboldened by Taheri's resignation, Iran's main pro-reform party threatened to quit the Islamic Republic unless the conservatives stopped undermining the elected administration. Mohammad-Reza Khatami, the president's younger brother and the Islamic Iran Participation Party (IIPP) chief warned: "We want to work towards agreement. . . . But if [the conservatives] do not heed the people's demands . . . then we can only withdraw the reformist presence—that it is to say the legitimate elected representation—from the regime" (Etemad, July 21, 2002).

As clerical factionalism intensified, President Khatami proposed two controversial pieces of legislation in September 2002. Directly challenging the conservatives' power, one bill would enhance the president's ability to take on officials who violate the Islamic Republic's Constitution, and the other would curb the Council of Guardians' role in vetting candidates for elections. With a reformist majority in parliament, these bills will probably become law by the end of 2002 or in 2003, increasing Khatami's prerogatives, at least on paper.

Soon after the submissions of the bills, conservative elements attacked Khatami for "attempting to change the constitution." Even prominent reformists doubt the initiative will bring about any significant change in the balance of power. Tehran MP Ali Reza Nouri said he expected the Council of Guardians to reject both Khatami bills. Others echoed his view. "Khamene'i may pay some lip service, but I have not heard any public statement in favour of the president," stated another reformist MP. "Nothing is going to change" (Mesbah-Yazdi 2002).

Even if the bills are enacted, conservative officials are unlikely to pay more than lip service to these laws. More than the reformists, conservatives enjoy control over the coercive arms of the state—the judiciary and various security forces—and are willing to resort to force when they perceive their interests are at stake. Khatami is a lame duck whose presidency will end with the 2005 election. His legislative proposals will benefit his successor, but Khatami may have to resign himself to the pattern of one step forward toward reform, and two steps back as conservatives have persisted in thwarting any moves toward pluralism.

Conclusion—From Revolution to Reform and Back Again?

Observers cannot deny that Iran's politics, and particularly the ruling clergy's interaction with society, are complex but also fascinating. The Islamic Republic is a case study of a revolutionary government attempting to reform itself in the face of increased popular appeals for participation in the country's cultural, political, and socioeconomic development.

As a reformist journalist, Hamid Reza Jalalipour remarked, "We are witnessing the decline of the fundamentalist movement in Iran. Two decades ago, we had our fundamentalist experience, and we saw the outcome. Fundamentalism is good for protest, good for revolution and good for war, but not so good for development. No country can organize its society on fundamentalism." Iranians, especially youths, may not wish to forsake religion altogether. Arguably, they hope to see religion returned to private realm, where one can worship and experience his/her relationship to God without compulsion—not necessarily a post-Islamic Iran, but rather an Iran where the citizens may decide freely what role faith plays in their lives.

However, the future of the reformist movement and its goals remain unclear and even debatable due to the interaction of structural, societal, and human factors. Structurally, the Islamic Republic is for now more Islamic than republican. The constitution enshrines both democratic and theocratic elements, but gives the latter dominance in the management of the state. The exercise of divine sovereignty has so far obstructed the democratic will. Revisions to the constitution are required to reverse this trend, and the conservatives would surely fight this suggestion.

Within society, President Khatami still enjoys support, despite weariness with the pace of reform. Even after their disappointment with the outcome of the 1999 student revolt, youths returned to Khatami, praising him in heroic terms. Yet young people, including the student movement, lack a coherent leadership and a common strategy. They belong to numerous pro-reform parties and organizations but have not come together to forge a conscious majority. Youths have engaged the conservatives in a cat-and-mouse game, because they are still not capable of orchestrating a sustained campaign for the cultural and social freedoms they desire. Young Iranians may have to endure more painful confrontations with conservative clerics on the judiciary in order to gain the experience and will needed for such a campaign.

Nevertheless, youths as well as Khatami's other constituents have gone beyond their president in their conception of reform. In a precarious position vis-à-vis his conservative rivals, the president has tried to ensure his own political survival as well as that of the Islamic Republic. He is thus more the spokesman rather than the leader of the reformist movement. A humanist intellectual with a passion for theology and philosophy, he entered the upper echelons of Iran's political arena with some reluctance and little personal ambition. In this sense, Ayatollah Khamene'i was perhaps correct when, exasperated by "illusions fostered abroad," he recently explained that Iran is not the former Soviet Union and that Khatami is not its Gorbachev.

Under President Khatami, Iran's international image has improved greatly. Iran's foreign policy has in recent years been focusing on dismantling the wall of isolation that has been built around it. However, repeated setbacks for the reformists have led to alienation and hopelessness today as pro-reform constituents outpace their president in seeking reform. Khatami may eventually have little choice but to rise to the occasion in a moment of crisis and reckoning with the conservatives. If the president does not seize the moment and conservatives continue to resist change, Iranian citizens themselves will grow increasingly impatient. Whatever the fortunes of particular government officials, Iranians have come to view reform—indeed, even democratization—as inevitable, and they no longer ask "Why reform" or "What kind of reform?" but "How?" and "When?" In a way, Iran is on a long journey of learning how to develop democratic institutions and pluralism based on its own culture, religious and historical traditions.

REFERENCES CITED

Antoun, Richard T. 1989. *Muslim Preacher in the Modern World: A Jordanian Case Study in Comparative Perspective.* Princeton, N.J.: Princeton University Press.

Baktiari, Bahman, and Haleh Vaziri. 2002. "Iran's Liberal Revolution." *Current History,* January 2002, 17–21.

Barton, Greg. 1996. "The Liberal, Progressive Roots of Wahid's Thought." In *Nahdlatl Ulama; Traditional Islam and Modernity in Indonesia,* edited by Greg Fealy and Greg Barton, pp. 191–223. Clayton, Australia: Monash Asia Institute.

Brumberg, Daniel. 2001. "Dissonant Politics in Iran and Indonesia." *Political Science Quarterly* 116 (Fall 2001): 381–411.

Chehabi, H. E. 2001. "The Political Regime of the Islamic Republic of Iran in Comparative Perspective." *Government and Opposition* 36, no. 1 (Winter 2001): 48–70

Etemad (Tehran). 2002. July 21.

Fathali, Mahmaud. 2000. "Ideology of Tolerance and Acceptance in Islam." *Foreign Broadcasting Information Service* (FBIS) South Asia, December 4.

Hambastegi (Tehran). 2001.

Hefner, Robert. 2000. *Civil Islam: Muslims and Democratization in Indonesia.* Princeton, N.J.: Princeton University Press.

Iran Daily. December 21, 2001.

Kadivar, Mohsen. 1999. *Baha'ye Azadi* (The price of freedom). Tehran: Ghazal Publishers.

Khatami, Mohammad. 1997. *Hope and Challenge: The Iranian President Speaks.* Binghamton, N.Y.: Institute of Global Cultural Studies.

——. 1998. *Islam, Liberty and Development.* Binghamton, N.Y.: Institute of Global Cultural Studies.

——. 1999. "Khatami on Religious Thought Renewal." *Iran Daily,* June 21.

——. 2000. *Religion and Intellect Trapped in Tyranny.* Tehran: Tarhe Nou Press.

——. 2001a. "Speech by Mohammad Khatami to Mark the Anniversary of the Islamic Revolution." *Islamic Republic News Agency* (IRNA), Tehran, February 10. Translated by *Foreign Broadcasting Information Service* (FBIS), Near East/South Asia.

——. 2001b. "Speech at the Mausoleum of Ayatollah Khomeini." *Vision and Voice of the Islamic Republic,* Tehran, June 5. Translated by the *Foreign Broadcasting Information Service* (FBIS).

——. 2001c. "Speech Delivered at the Annual Meeting with University Students." *Islamic Republic News Agency* (IRNA), Tehran, December 23.

Kian-Thiébaut, Azadeh. 1999. "Political and Social Transformations in Post-Islamist Iran." *Middle East Report* 212, vol. 29, no. 3 (Fall): 12–16.

Mesbah-Yazdi, Mohammad. 2002. "Speech before the Friday Prayer Gathering in Tehran." *Islamic Republic News Agency* (IRNA), Tehran, October 25.

Mortimer, Edward. 1982. *Faith and Power: The Politics of Islam.* New York: Vintage Press.

Nelson, Soraya S. 2001. "Mild Conflict Marks Street Celebration of Iran's Soccer Victory." *Los Angeles Times,* November 1.

Nowruz (Tehran). 2001. October 8.

Shabestari, Mohammad Mojtahid. 2002. "Religious Democracy: From Which Angle?" *Nowruz* (Tehran) 2, no. 350 (June 18).

Soroush, Abdol Karim. 1994. *Qisse-yi Arbab-e ma'rifat* (The story of Master Thinker). Tehran: Mu'ssasih-yi Farhangi-yi Sirat.

———. 1995. "Freedom and Clergy." Tehran: *Kiyan* (Tehran) 3, no. 24 (August–September): 23–29.

———. 1997. "Saqhf Mashiat bar Sotoun Shariat." (The roof of livelihood on the pillars of religion). *Kiyan* (Tehran) 5, no. 26 (August–September): 133–42.

———. 2000. "What the University Expects from the *Hawzeh.*" In *Reason, Freedom and Democracy in Islam: Essential Writings of Abdolkarim Soroush,* translated and edited by M. Sadri and A. Sadri, pp. 171–83 Oxford: Oxford University Press.

Stowasser, Barbara F. 1994. *Women in the Quran, Traditions, and Interpretation.* New York: Oxford University Press.

Taheri, Jalaledin. 2002. "Resignation Letter." *Nowruz* (Tehran), July 10.

Chapter 6

THWARTED POLITICS:

THE CASE OF EGYPT'S HIZB AL-WASAT

AUGUSTUS RICHARD NORTON

WHAT HAPPENS WHEN ISLAMISTS go against the grain, and declare their commitment to pluralism and their acceptance, if not endorsement, of secular political principles? This is a study of exactly such a party, the Hizb al-Wasat, or Center Party, a remarkable attempt by a group of moderately oriented Islamists to play by democratic rules of the game in Egypt. The initiative was not the product of Western-designed projects of reform; to the contrary, it grew from debates within the Islamic *tayyar,* or current. This is a case in point for the reflexivity in ideology that one encounters routinely in Egypt and in the broader Muslim world.[1] The impediments that are routinely placed in the path of nonviolent oppositional voices are also illuminated. Finally, while the purpose of the study is not primarily prescriptive, the realms for potential reformation become obvious as the story unfolds.

Despite its failure to gain legal status, Hizb al-Wasat is noteworthy for its embrace of religious toleration and its rejection of a privileged interpretation of religion. Hizb al-Wasat was not only opposed staunchly by the Egyptian government, but the official suppression of the fledgling party was emphatically endorsed by Egypt's venerable Islamist organization, the Ikhwan al-Muslimun (the Muslim Brethren). The Ikhwan's own efforts to lawfully participate in politics have been frequently sabotaged over the past two decades by the same government apparatus. Many of the proponents of the fledgling party had roots in the Ikhwan, but, quoting a cofounder, the party was an attempt "to go beyond the slogan 'Islam is the solution'" (Murphy 2002). The motives of the Ikhwan in joining in the suppression of the party prove quite mundane—namely, to eliminate a potential political competitor. Thus, this is a spectacle of a new generation attempting to play by new rules but being held at bay by an old guard that will only retire in the grave.

In encounters with the middle-aged professionals in Egypt, it is common to hear complaints about the domination of the political system by septuagenarians and even octogenarians. The legal opposition parties, the Wafd and Tagammu, are obvious examples. In both cases, the emerging younger elites are in their seventies. Hizb al-Wasat illustrates a quest of thirty- and forty-somethings for a hand in the game, and as one supporter said, "[I]t's about time that this middle generation carries the flag and does its duty for the nation." He is not alone. A leading regime intellectual recalled a metaphor used by Mustafa Fikhi to observe that he was part of the "mezzanine generation," sitting just above the ground floor filled with surging young people intent on a place in the system, but closed out of the cohort that wields power on the floors above (author's interview with 'Usama al-Ghazali Harb, November 7, 1999). Mustafa Bakri, the editor of al-'Usbu', an independent weekly, remarked somewhat wistfully in 1998, "I think it is natural that any political party demanding that the president of the republic shouldn't be allowed more than two terms in office should also do the same in its own party" (Schemm and Apiku 1998).

The plan of this chapter is to offer an overview of Egyptian politics that addresses patterns of control that the state has used to regulate dissent in recent years, followed by a discussion of the attempt to register Hizb al-Wasat as a lawful party. Then the reader is introduced to a collection of Egyptian personalities who either played key roles in the Hizb al-Wasat episode or offer uncommonly valuable insights on the case. These personalities include a former chief justice of Egypt's Constitutional Court, an Islamist engineer and cofounder of the party, a Christian intellectual and cofounder of the party, the Ikhwan's Supreme Guide, and a key political adviser and one of the most powerful men in Egypt. These materials are based on interviews conducted by the author in Egypt from 1995 to 2003. Concluding comments highlight the implications of this case study and suggest a few broader lessons that may be relevant in a period when major attention has been focused upon the challenge of political reform in the Middle East.

BACKGROUND

Since 1928, the quintessential Islamist movement in Egypt has been the Ikhwan al-Muslimun. After a period of phenomenal growth in the 1930s and 1940s, the Muslim Brethren seemed to be on the threshold of seizing power from the decrepit Egyptian monarchy. Indeed, embassy reports in the late 1940s anticipated the end of the monarchy and the emergence of the Ikhwan as the dominant political force in Egypt. In contrast to the army, the Ikhwan distinguished itself in the Arab-Israeli war of 1948–49. Indeed, years earlier the army had been described as "a decrepit thing" by none other than the Commander of the Army. As a group of unlikely young officers (led by the son of a village postmaster, Gamal Abdel Nasser) plotted to topple the monarchy, they worked hand-in-glove with the Ikhwan. Anwar Sadat, the future president, was the Free Officers' liaison to the Ikhwan, with whom he enjoyed amiable relations (Sadat 1957). Sayyid Qutb, later to pen arguably the most accessible and most influential Islamist polemic, collaborated closely with the officers and emerged as a functionary in the new regime in 1952.

Within two years of the coup the erstwhile allies flew apart. It is striking that many educated Egyptians pointedly refer to the 1952 event as an *inqilab* (coup), not a *thawrah* (revolution). Even President Husni Mubarak's closest political adviser emphasizes the former terminology (author's interview with Osama al-Baz, November 11, 1999). Lieutenant Colonel Nasser remained in the shadows, deferring to General Muhammad Naguib, who was recruited to serve as nominal head of the revolutionary government. Naguib was gradually nudged aside, and then placed quietly under house arrest as Nasser emerged from the shadows to lead Egypt (Neguib 1955). Meanwhile, the Ikhwan felt its claim to power slipping away and attempted to assassinate Nasser in 1954, during a visit to Alexandria. Sadat's friend and Ikhwan-member Abdul Monein Abdul Raouf was implicated, and the Ikhwan was outlawed.

Until Nasser's death in 1970, the Ikhwan remained a constant target for state repression. Nasser's conception of the state was organic-corporatist and modernist, and the Ikhwan posed a threat to the state's hegemony. As a result, the record of the 1950s and 1960s, the Nasser years, is a disgraceful chronicle of horrendous prison camps where the Ikhwan honed their opposition to the state. The full history of this period remains to be written, but one legacy of the period is the work of Sayyid Qutb (hanged 1964), especially the lucid and polemical *Ma'alim fi al-Tariq* (Milestones; Qutb 1988). *Jahiliyyah,* the core concept of Qutb's prison-written tract, lies at the very heart of the ideological construction of 'Usama bin Laden. (Cf. *Du'aa La Qadat* or "Preachers not judges" by Hassan al-Hodeibi, the Ikhwan's contemporaneous rejoinder to Qutb). Muhammad Qutb, the brother of the hanged writer, later taught 'Usama bin Laden. If bin Laden later used the notion of *jahiliyyah* to refer to Western powers, and especially the United States, this was certainly not Qutb's primary intent. Though Qutb was contemptuous of the United States (he was disillusioned by his exposure to the United States in the late 1940s, not least because of racial discrimination and sexual permissiveness), he very much had contemporary Egypt in mind when he honed the concept, which he borrowed from the work of Mawlana Sayyid Abul A'la Mawdudi, the Muslim thinker and founder of Pakistan's Jama'at-I Islami.

Nasser's successor, Anwar Sadat, calculated that he needed a counterweight to the Arab socialist and nationalist bedrock that extolled the late president and abhorred Sadat. His fateful decision was to build his legitimacy formula on the right, reflecting his own ties to the Ikhwan in the 1940s. The outrageous repression of the Ikhwan ended, and the Islamists moved from the shadows to the open spaces of the university and the public arena. In particular, the 1970s witnessed a rapid growth in Islamic groups (*jama'aat*) on the university campuses, and the *jama'aat* were the seedbed for the generation of Islamists that sought to create al-Wasat. Eventually, Sadat grew apprehensive of the growing criticism of his power and attempted to reverse the mobilization of dissent. However, it was too late to stem the tide, and in 1981 Sadat died in a hail of bullets provoked in significant measure by the repression born of his second thoughts.

Husni Mubarak (1981–) has long surpassed Nasser (1954–70) as the longest-serving president in the history of the Egyptian republic. Following the assassination of President Sadat in 1981, Mubarak conceded political space to the Islamists and experimented with the controlled inclusion of mainstream Islamist opposition forces in parliament. Although the Ikhwan have had no legal standing in Egypt for the past half century, Islamist candidates were permitted to use secular parties as ships of convenience in 1984 and in 1987, thereby winning an impressive number of seats in parliament.

By the early 1990s, the experiment had run its course, much to the regret of many members of the intellectual elite in Egypt, who argued that the experiment was succeeding. As one respected insider noted in a 1995 interview, "political pluralism can exist without changing the basic power structure" (author's interview with 'Ali al-Din Hillal Dessouki, July 9, 1995). The government was intent to maintain the upper hand, and even in the elections of 1984 and 1987, which were relatively free, there was never any doubt that the progovernment candidates would maintain a dominant voice in the People's Assembly (the lower house of the parliament; the upper house, or Shura Council, is composed of 140 appointed members). Thus, in the May 1984 balloting, the regime's National Democratic Party won 72.9 percent of vote and 87 percent of the seats (389 out of 448 seats). In a distant second place, the resurrected Wafd Party, running in alliance with the Ikhwan, captured 15 percent of votes and 13 percent of seats (59 seats, of which 8 were Ikhwanis) (Ayubi 1991).

In the April 1987 elections, the high point for the opposition parties in parliament, 30 percent of the voters cast their vote for the opposition candidates, and 17 percent of all votes went to the tripartite alliance of the Liberal (al-Ahrar) and Labor Parties with the Ikhwan. The coalition won 60 seats, including 36 Ikhwan and 4 Islamist independents. The Wafd captured slightly fewer than 11 percent of all votes, or thirty-five seats. Considering the extensive scope for electoral manipulation by the government, and the extremely low participation rates in middle-class urban districts where cynicism about elections runs deep, the opposition success offered a stunning riposte to one-party rule in Egypt (Ayubi 1991).

The parliamentary elections of 1990 were the beginning of the end to Mubarak's experiment in inclusionary electoral politics. The 1990 elections were mandated by Egypt's high court, which ruled that the 1986 electoral law discriminated against independent candidates and thus violated the constitution (Auda 1991). Although the Egyptian judiciary remains a bastion of independent thinking, it obviously lacks the power to implement its mandate. Heavy gerrymandering and the state's refusal to accept judicial oversight of the elections prompted the major opposition parties, including the Islamic Alliance and the New Wafd party, to conclude that despite major changes of the election law the electoral system still grossly disadvantaged the opposition. As a result, the major opposition parties boycotted the election. When the elections were conducted, there were customary cases of fraud and intimidation, but the balloting was also marked by an unprecedented level of violence, leading to opposition claims that the 1990 election was "the worst in Egyptian history" (Farag 1991).

The dominant position of the NDP in the parliament should not be allowed to mask an essential weakness of the party, its fundamental lack of grassroots support. As one close observer noted, the ruling party is fictitious. It is a façade. Its structure is weak. The government has not succeeded in creating a strong party. This is one reason that the government is afraid of elections. Only with a strong progovernment party can the government permit a strong opposition (author's interview with 'Ali al-Din Hillal Dessouki, July 9, 1995).

If there was any hope that 1990 was an aberration in a process of democratization, the hope was dashed in the November 1995 elections, when the opposition parties won only 14 seats in all. Opposition poll watchers were routinely harassed and detained; candidates, especially Islamists, were arrested; and ballot boxes were crammed filled to overflowing with bogus ballots. Although the government was able to engineer a sweeping electoral victory, it did not succeed in masking its extensive manipulation of the results. Though ominous attempts were made to dissuade them, three prominent secular activists, Said al-Naggar, Saad Eddin Ibrahim, and Milad Hanna, still succeeded in mounting a major monitoring effort to report on the widespread irregularities in the election. Their unofficial report highlighted electoral irregularities that discredited the government's "victory" and led to yet another judicial overturning of an election.

At no time during Mubarak's presidency was there any doubt that the ruling party would maintain control of parliament capable of passing virtually any law that it wished. What appeared in the 1980s to be an effective process of controlled inclusion later became an engine for cynicism and contempt as the regime became increasingly intolerant of dissent, reflecting what many Egyptians refer to as its sclerosis. In the 2000 elections, the Ikhwan managed to gain 17 seats compared to NDP's 388, making it the largest opposition block in parliament. Notably, the Ikhwan was careful to calibrate the candidacies of its members to avoid posing too wide a challenge to the regime.

THE BATTLE FOR THE SYNDICATES

More impressive than the limited electoral success of Islamist candidates were the inroads that they made in the professional syndicates (*niqabat*), which have been mainstays of the regime since the Nasser period. As the syndicates fell to Islamist control, Mubarak and company sensed that the hegemony of the regime was being challenged.

In Nasserite Egypt the syndicates were expected to be obedient appendages to the state. In contrast, the syndicates in recent years have been an arena for political debates. Unlike the associations and groups that fell under the heavy hand of the Ministry of Social Affairs and the stringent dictates of infamous Law 32 (the law of associations), the syndicates usually enjoyed considerable freedom of action and have been less subject to manipulation by the government than political parties and other overtly political organizations.

There are twenty-one professional syndicates, encompassing about 2.5 million members (Zaki 1995). The largest are the teachers and graduates of faculties of commerce, both of which tend to be supportive of government policy. The signal success was in the Medical Association, where in 1986 Islamists secured a majority of seats on the executive board of the association. In 1988 they built on their success to win in a landslide, capturing all seats except the chair, which was preserved for the NDP candidate—a calculated sop to the government. The same pattern persisted in the 1990 elections. Even in the Pharmacists' syndicate the Islamists captured all but three executive board seats, as well as the chair, despite the fact that the majority of the syndicate's members are Coptic Christians.

The Muslim Brotherhood was concurrently building a strong base in the Engineers' syndicate and among university professors, but the development that reportedly stunned Mubarak was the result of the 1992 executive board elections in the venerable Bar Association. The Islamists captured 75 percent of the seats in an election in which only 10 percent of the association membership participated.

The Islamists successes reflect the changing sociology of the syndicates, their relative autonomy of the government, and the voting behavior of their members. Perhaps most important, the youthful profile of the syndicates implies that rank-and-file members are deeply affected by the arduous economic struggle that confronts most Egyptians. In contrast to the older and established syndicate members who often benefit significantly from their connections to the state, the younger members must eke out their own economic solutions. Reliable observers estimate that about 35 percent of the members are less than thirty-five years of age. Since little was done by established syndicate members to assist their younger colleagues, there was a considerable resentment, which was exploited by the Muslim Brotherhood (Ibrahim 1996).

At the same time, only a small number of syndicate members participated in syndicate affairs, including elections. Thus, fewer than one-quarter of all members participated in the four Medical Association elections from 1980 to 1990, and, as noted above, only 10 percent of the Bar Association membership voted in the fateful 1992 elections. Islamist members of the syndicates were able to capitalize on the low turnout by mobilizing their members, some of whom were unemployed and were able to join their occupational syndicate only with financial help from the Ikhwan. Where the turnout was higher, as in the Journalists' Syndicate and the Union of Social Professions, the Islamists did not fare nearly as well.

The government responded to the Islamist foothold in the syndicates by quickly pushing a new law through the parliament in February 1993. Elections within professional syndicates would now require a quorum of 50 percent of all registered members for the first ballot, and a quorum of 30 percent of all registered members for a subsequent election to be held two weeks after the first ballot. If no quorum could be produced, then the syndicate was to be run by an appointed council of senior members, chaired by a judge. As though the government's intention was to thwart the achievement of a quorum, elections were banned on weekends or official holidays (Ibn Khaldun Center 1993; al-Sayyid 1995).

As the authoritarian state attempted to loosen the influence of the Ikhwan in the syndicates, the Islamists continued to build support on Egypt's campuses. By the early 1990s many university faculty clubs were under Islamist domination, and the Ikhwan appeared poised to extend its influence to the leadership of major universities. The state responded on May 30, 1994, with an amendment to the Universities Law that provided for an end to the practice of electing deans, despite the loud clamor of dissent from the professorate.

If the controlled opening of the 1980s offered some hope that the state would grant more political space, the evidence of the 1990s offered a different lesson. The response of Egyptians was mixed. On the one hand, resentment of the arrogant exercise of power by the state was rampant. On the other hand, extremist Islamist groups (Jihad and the Gam'at Islamiyya) embarked on a campaign of violence and terrorism, designed, in part, to interdict the tourist trade and weaken the state financially. Many Egyptians found these tactics opprobrious and supported a vicious state response. While the curtailment of the experiments in controlled inclusion and the government's autocratic riposte to the Islamists' successes in the syndicates did not seem to augur well for a new experiment in peaceful participation, this is precisely what a number of younger Islamists were pondering in the mid-1990s, both within and on the periphery of the Ikhwan.

Hizb al-Wasat

In April 1995, the Ikhwan signaled a major departure from the teachings of its founder, Hasan al-Banna (assassinated 1949) when it declared its acceptance of a multiparty politics.[2] The Imam, as al-Banna is often called, railed against *hizbiyya* ("partyism") with the argument that political parties breed divisiveness (Commins 1994). (In this sense, al-Banna's perspective is consistent with the organic-corporatist bias of today's regime, which refuses to countenance a serious challenge to effective monopolization of politics by the ruling party.) Nonetheless, his successors in the Ikhwan leadership issued an important document in April 1995, which embraced parties as instruments of *shura* (consultation), while reiterating that power may not be taken by the sword (al-Hudeibi 2000). The statement was intended to be a clear signal of the Ikhwan's willingness to play by democratic rules, but the rejoinder from the regime was studied silence. The political climate of the mid-1990s was one in which a number of efforts were underway to find entrée into the political system, especially since the regime was moving aggressively to tighten its control of the political system.

Liberal reformers, such as the respected economist Dr. Said al-Naggar, president of the Civic Forum, worked energetically to promote a "civic compact" (*mithaq madani*) in 1995. The compact emphasized many of the values embraced the following year by the Hizb al-Wasat, including freedom of belief, democratic participation, and women's rights. This writer (along with Farhad Kazemi) happened to be meeting with the late 'Adil Hussein (died 2001), a leading figure in the Labor Party, an ally of the Ikhwan, on July 11, 1995, when al-Naggar visited party headquarters on Port Said Street to seek Labor's endorsement of the compact.[3] The Labor Party, now suppressed by the government, has veered from left to right, and by the 1990s enjoyed an Islamist ambience, yet faded signs from the 1970s testified that these were the offices of the *Socialist* Labor Party. Hussein excused himself to join the negotiations, and upon return revealed that he wanted to sign the civil compact along with other members of his party. His view was that the Ikhwan "would lose, if they did not sign it." In the end, the Ikhwan refused to sign because the document did not declare that the *shari'ah* was the sole basis of law.

This was also a period of calibrated government persecution aimed precisely at the Ikhwan, the most potent opposition group. In 1995, the middle-level leadership was savaged by arrests. In all, fifty-four were arrested and sentenced to three-to-five year terms, including many of the rising young *'amirs* ("princes"), such as 'Issam al-'Iryan. Among other motives, the government sought to eliminate many of the most credible candidates for parliament, thereby sabotaging any attempt by the Ikhwan to repeat their electoral successes of the 1980s. Intimidation at balloting sites was widespread as well.

Among younger members of the Ikhwan, many of whom were actively involved in public and professional life, especially in the syndicates of doctors, engineers, and other professions, these discussions were a culmination of many dialogues (Wickham 1996). These dialogues were part of a centrist trend that is sometimes referred to as *al-wasatiyya* (Baker 1997) or *'jil al-sab'inaat* (the seventies generation), as reflected in recent debates within the Ikhwan (Hamzawy 2003). It is also common to hear references to the renewal trend (*al-tayyar al-tajdidi*).

Against this backdrop of repression, political foment and debate, a large group broke away from the Ikhwan to form Hizb al-Wasat in late 1995. The name serves a dual purpose. Not only does it emphasize the role the party seeks to place as a mediatory element in society, but it is instantly recognizable to many Muslims because it invokes Qur'anic injunction to be an *'umma wasat* (a justly balanced community). "Thus have We made of you a justly balanced community. That ye might be witnesses over the nations" (Qur'an 2:143). The name implies the project of mediation by a younger generation intent to emphasize a connection to society and to Islam in a modern civilizational context. Of the seventy-four original founding members of al-Wasat, sixty-two came from the ranks of the Brotherhood (Stacher 2002). Many of the founding members had been active in the professional syndicates where they honed political skills and developed a taste for political struggle. By January 1996, they presented an application for legal party status to the governmental Political Parties Committee.

Mustafa Mashur (1919–2002), then newly ascended to the post of Supreme Guide (*murshid*) of the Ikhwan, and his associates reacted swiftly and furiously to al-Wasat's display of independence. Mashur, by profession a meteorologist at Egypt's National Weather Forecasting Center, joined the Ikhwan in 1938. Like many of his colleagues, Mashur had paid his dues—in his instance, eighteen years in prison. In an April 1996 interview, he simply observed that al-Wasat did not display a "pure image of Islam" (Murphy 2002). Behind the scenes, the Ikhwan moved quickly to quell the rebellion in its ranks.

Many members of the founding cohort left the new party under threat and returned to the Ikhwan's fold. In May, the government committee rejected the party's petition on the procedural grounds that they lacked the requisite fifty members to constitute a party (under the terms of Law 40/1977). For its part, the government believed that the party initiative was a scheme by the Ikhwan to find a side door into legitimate party status. Three founding members along with nine others were then arrested for attempting to reorganize the Ikhwan and for plotting against the government; the al-Wasat members were released three months later without being tried or even charged.

What followed was extraordinary. The Hizb al-Wasat filed an appeal, and in 1997 the Ikhwan openly opposed the application during formal hearings (Shadid 2001). Abu al-'Ala Madi, a founder member of al-Wasat, complained to a newspaper:

> This small group of people waged a war on us that we did not expect. We expected them to say we disagree with you or we have nothing to do with this project. But waging a comprehensive war against us on all levels was a big shock that took some time to absorb. . . . Their attack was even worse than what the government did with us. (Murphy 2002)

The following May, the Political Parties Tribunal rejected the application on familiar grounds. Under the terms of Law 40/1977, a new party must fulfill a legitimate purpose not met by an existing party. Since the ruling National Democratic Party claimed to do all and more that Egypt requires, the standard is virtually impossible to fulfill. The al-Wasat is one of at least thirty-two parties that have failed to meet the standard.[4]

Among leading independent Muslim thinkers, the Ikhwan's riposte to al-Wasat was described as heavy-handed and unfortunate. For instance, Shaikh Yusif al-Qaradawi, one of the leading reformist thinkers, argued that al-Wasat was a way to break the isolation that the government imposed on the Islamic movement. "I fear that the Islamic movement constrains the liberal thinkers among its children and closes windows of renewal (*tajdid*), interpretation (*ijtihad*), and stands on one side of ideas and thought while not accepting the other point of view or those holding different opinions about objectives or the means to accomplish them." Others, such as Tawfiq al-Shawi, endorsed al-Qaradawi's criticism and urged that rather than stifling dissent, initiatives like al-Wasat should be encouraged.[5] There is an intellectual link joining both al-Shawi and al-Qaradawi to Sheikh Hassan al-Ashmawi, who died in 1972 in Kuwait. Al-Ashmawi had been the Ikhwan's major link to the Free Officers, but he is remembered as an influential reformist thinker who rejected in principle the idea of religious government.

Following its first failure, the aspiring party was reorganized as the Hizb al-Wasat al-Masri (i.e., the Egyptian Center Party). Over ninety members were listed in the "new" party's petition, of which only twenty-four were former members of the Ikhwan. The founding men and women include a number of younger professionals, teachers, students, and tradesmen. There were nineteen women listed, and a total of three Christians ('Abd al-Karim 1998). In September 1998, this attempt to register also failed on the grounds that the new party did not contribute anything new. By June 1999, the second round of appeals ran their course.

Two years earlier, the party had filed an application with the Ministry of Culture to start a newspaper, *al-Mustaqbal* (The future), but the application simply disappeared into the bowels of the ministry. There has been no response whatsoever to the application.

The al-Wasat program has been published in two versions.[6] The first was authored by a leading Protestant intellectual (Habib 1996a) and the second by a former Brother and professor of aeronautical engineering at Cairo University ('Abd al-Karim 1998). Both versions of the program are strikingly free of jargon. The program urges a modernist interpretation of Islamic law and argues that the *shari'ah* should be interpreted and applied in a way that does not hinder progress. Indeed, *shari'ah* is conceived as a valuable collection of flexible principles, whereas the implementation of those principles requires the crafting of laws by people. There are several novel elements of the published program. While secularism (*al-'ilmaniyya*) is rejected on principle, the thrust of the program is decidedly complementary to toleration, diversity, and pluralism (*ta'addudiya*). In particular, pluralism is understood to correspond to a society in which religion remains a fundamental component, but religious practice as well as political orientation vary as a matter of course. "National unity and religion as one unit are of extreme importance whereby each Muslim and Christian, through their own religion, would comprise this national unity. Religion is one of the strongest sources of moral commitment" (Habib 1996a, 32):

> Islamic scholarship affirms that too much religion on its own does not insure justice and not enough religion does not prevent acquiring what is just. Invoking what is just in the political arena or exercising authority on behalf of a particular religious faction in a religious pluralistic country is a claim that has no judicial base. The *'ulama* emphasize that the objective of life and political participation does not come about by having too much religion but through the proper and civil behavior in order to achieve the goals and interests of the nation. With that, we emphasize that the Copts enjoy the

rights of citizenship and nationality. This is an issue that is both legally and functionally decided and agreed upon without a disagreement among the nation in that regard.

The unity of religion and state is a dogmatic truth for many Islamic movements, but reformist thinkers increasingly shift from the concept of *din wa dawla* and emphasize that Islam is marked by *din wa 'ummah* (religion and community). This is very much the focus of the al-Wasat program. In this sense, the usual Salafi focus on the period of al-Rashidun as an exemplar for contemporary Muslim societies is rejected. Thinkers such as the octogenarian Gamal al-Banna, the younger brother of the late Hasan al-Banna, are part of the *tayyar*. Al-Banna argues that the unity of *din wa dawla* was unique to the Golden Era in Islam and may not be recreated. Instead, the appropriate focus is to foster the promotion of religion and community (al-Banna 2002). What then becomes problematic is the definition of community. In the instance of al-Wasat, the community is defined inclusively so as to encompass Muslims and Christians. While secular reformers such as al-Naggar judged the party to be a significant initiative, at least a point of departure for discussion, concern remains that rather than embracing an Islamic ethos, the *shari'ah* remains central in the party's ideology (Stacher's interview with Said al-Naggar, December 19, 1999, in Stacher 2001).

The second version of the program by 'Abd al-Karim adds material on pluralism and representation. While substantial sections of the first program are rewritten or condensed (some general comments on freedom and human rights are omitted), the substance of the two documents is consistent. Both versions deal with widely discussed questions such as corruption and violence and both urge adherence to the constitution, free elections, and an effective parliament, concerns that link al-Wasat to a variety of opposition groups across the political spectrum. There is equal, if not greater emphasis on social justice and reducing economic inequality (during a period when the gap is actually widening). "One of the worst problems associated with unemployment is the feeling of injustice and lack of opportunity that cause depression, resentment, anger, hatred, lack of loyalty or belonging. The extravagant life lived by a certain class provokes the negative feelings of the poor and the unemployed" ('Abd al-Karim 1998). This signals a need to encourage charity (*zakat*) as a means of reducing the disparity, as well as a normative commitment to social justice that contrasts with the indifference of the government.

It is noteworthy that the role of women in society receives significant attention, and the idea that women may fill any role in the political system is remarkable by Egyptian standards. "The party emphasized the women's equal right and equal commitment in civil and political matters.

It is therefore her right to hold any position, to vote or get elected or become a member of the parliament and to perform all public and professional functions. She is also required to commit to her participation the work force" (Habib 1996a, 58; 'Abd al-Karim 1998, 29).

In April 2000, the government tacitly defined the boundaries of permissible opposition by permitting the establishment of an NGO (nongovernmental organization) in which many of the al-Wasat organizers were key participants. Under the terms of Law 153, since overturned, an NGO would be deemed licensed in sixty days absent an explicit disapproval by the Ministry of Social Affairs. Hence, the government permitted Misr: Lil-Thiqafa wa Hiwar (Egypt: For culture and dialogue) to emerge. A deal with the government was widely suspected, and there is certainly no reason to take seriously Muhammad Salim al-'Awa's claims that there is no connection between Wasat and the creation of the NGO. The new society aims to "support the culture of dialogue in a society in which violence prevails" (*Cairo Times* 2000). The major participants are a who's who of respected independents, including liberals such as Atif al-Banna, editor of *al-Ahram Center Strategic Report;* Wahid 'Abd al-Majid from *al-Ahram;* and Amani Qandil, a sui generis NGO guru and also a woman. Other members of the society include Engineers' Syndicate member Salah 'Abd al-Karim; author of the first al-Wasat program, Rafiq Habib; attorney 'Issam Sultan (and, initially, chairman of the NGO); publisher Muhammad Abd al-Latif; and Abu al-'Ala Madi. Muhammad Salim al-'Awa, a constant intellectual presence in al-Wasat, was elected chair of the new NGO's board at the first annual conference in May 2001 (al-'Awa's wife Fatima, herself a lawyer, was a founding member of al-Wasat).

Although Madi periodically declares that al-Wasat will once again apply for legal recognition, his energies and those of his colleagues appear to be largely focused on holding seminars on themes such as Islam and the West, the Islamic movement and education, or, perhaps most revealingly, "Professor al-Banna: Fifty Years after His Martyrdom What Remains of His Call?"

The unsuccessful attempt by Madi and his collaborators to break new political ground with al-Wasat is further unpacked in the interview vignettes that follow, each revealing a different perspective on the episode.

THE JUDGE

Now retired, this distinguished attorney was the chief justice of the Constitutional Court, one of two bulwarks against arbitrary rule by the state. The other is the Court of Cassation. On two recent occasions, in 1987 and 1995, the Constitutional Court ended the tenure of the parliament

due to electoral irregularities or unconstitutional electoral procedures
and mandated new elections.

The comments here are a composite of two interviews lasting more
than four hours, one conducted in September 1999 and the other in February 2003. The judge is a contemplative and humble man. His office has
none of the trappings of accumulated adulation that people of accomplishment tend to collect. His broad desk is piled high with reference
works, an Egyptian text on civil society, a book on the U.S. Constitution,
titles in French on free speech and assembly. He is reading a book on U.S.
constitutional law, specifically First Amendment law and the right of assembly. This man loves the dignity of the law fairly administered, and he
does not hide his contempt of "rubbish judges" who seek only to toe the
government's line.

One topic among many we discuss is the legal standard for the creation
of political parties in Egypt. The judge's reasoning is lucid and to the
point. The people are permitted under the constitution to form associations. A political party is an association, and there is no language in the
constitution that can be construed to authorize or require resort to a Political Parties Committee or Tribunal. In other words, the process that al-
Wasat has had to navigate is questionable on constitutional grounds.

As for the requirement that an aspiring party must meet a legitimate
need unfulfilled by extant political parties, the judge reflects, "If a marketplace of ideas is a right, then what is the logic for this restriction? Plus,
there are many different ways to reach the same aims." To his regret, the
Constitutional Court has considered this requirement to be valid. As a result, "political life is paralyzed." Although the judge notes his conviction
that the constitution protects the right of assembly, in practice the law allows any party to be barred from forming. The state imposes "undue restrictions" on political life by restricting the formation of new parties.

Legally speaking, people may gather together for political purposes
even if they are not constituted in a legal party. The right to form political associations derives from the right of assembly, the judge emphasizes.
Nonetheless, this is an issue that has been adjudicated on appeal by the
Supreme Administrative Court in the case of Hizb al-Wasat, yet the court
refused to see the clear logic of the constitution.

Before I can fully articulate the question, he anticipates it. "Why doesn't
the government open up?" "Sometimes people are haunted by fear not by
hopes." He argues that Mubarak is popular and would win a competitive
election, but he is afraid of something. Mubarak believes that the answer
is to be in control, to control everything. The government restricts political activity out of insecurity. "Measures are taken to tame the tiger, even
though there is no tiger in Egypt." As result, Egypt loses the opportunity
to strengthen its power through democracy. "If democracy and civil society were stronger in the Middle East, the governments would be more

powerful to face the USA." This from the lips of a man who knows America well, has traveled to Washington as a VIP guest of the U.S. government, but who is pained by America's then looming invasion of Iraq. His prime despair is reserved for his own government, which he both fears and despises. "I don't know why some people feel safe, and we do not have that simple right. I don't feel safe talking to you. I do not know what to do."

THE ENGINEER

Al-Qasr al-Aini is a long, bustling Cairo avenue with one menagerie after another of shops, peddlers, offices, government agenices, and apartments. This is commercial Cairo, perfumed less by the scent of food and the stink of urban waste than the acrid scent of automobile exhausts. The engineer's office is nearby a well-known pharmacy, in an apartment building that has been converted to office space. The suite is labeled "*al-markaz al-dawli lildaraasat*" (the International Center for Studies) and the bustle of half a dozen clerks and assistants greets the visitor in February 2003. His is the generic office of the middle class professional. A pair of facing overstuffed chairs and a low table for water and coffee are placed in front of a desk large enough to signal that this is a man with a title, in this case, *muhandis*—engineer. We sit, exchange greetings, and efficiently elide into the familiar ritual of interview.

Abu al-'Ala Madi was a university student in the 1970s in Minya, one of the upper Egyptian towns that has been a seedbed for Islamist recruitment. Like other students at Minya University, he participated in a campus Islamist group, one of many that owed their existence to Sadat's flirtation with the Islamic right. He joined the Ikhwan in 1979, and as the Ikhwan moved into the syndicates in the 1980s, he became one of the leaders of the Engineers' Syndicate, rising to assistant secretary general.

In one interview, Madi bluntly emphasized that his connection to the Ikhwan followed his engagement in campus politics, which had little to do with the Ikhwan either operationally or ideologically:

> In order to describe the correct situation you have to know that we had an Islamic vision before we entered the Muslim brotherhood. And this point is very important. Before we were silent about this, out of courtesy and respect to the brotherhood. We remained silent when some claimed that the brotherhood were the ones who established the Islamic students' movement in the 70s, we were silent out of respect because we later became members of the brotherhood. And the truth was that the brotherhood was completely far away and distant from this student movement. And after the Islamic factions [*kawaadir*] joined the brotherhood, a blending of thought took place.

And we accepted some of those ideas inside the brotherhood and rejected others. And this reaction persisted in a quiet manner but those leaderships were faced with a severe shock when we discovered the real condition of the brotherhood where we found out that the big picture we imagined the brotherhood to be was not true. And this shock kept reacting until we left the brotherhood (Madi ca. 1999)

As for the Ikhwan, there is a reform current, but the conservatives still hold sway in the leadership. While Madi claims to have very good relations with the middle leadership, where he has "secret support," relations between him and the old guard are bad. He was taken aback by the counterattack of the old guard, which he argues is out of step with changing times. He has, of course, quit the Ikhwan.

Madi distinguishes between Hasan al-Banna's two legacies: the school and the organization: "As for the organization, it is in its worst shape due to the change in the behavioral understanding and moralities established by al-Banna. Due to the absence of freedom of expression and a freeze in the movement's intellect at the time when individual thinking and the concept of hear and obey without questioning hindered us from changing some of the teachings of al-Banna to suit our time" (Labib 1998).

He emphasizes his own links to a variety of non-Islamist intellectuals, including the lawyer 'Atif al-Banna, and several independent Muslim intellectuals, especially Muhammad Salim al-'Awa, whose wife was a founding member of the party, and Hasan Hanafi, who like al-'Awa is a respected professor at Cairo University. For the aged generation of *tajdidi* intellectuals, men like Gamal al-Banna, al-'Awa's name evokes enthusiasm. ("He is one of the best ones," al-Banna remarked in February 2003.) Hanafi enjoys a worldwide reputation for his prolific writings and his modernist orientation in the tradition of Muhammad 'Abduh, but his influence on al-Wasat was immanent, not strategic. In contrast, al-'Awa has lent a strong hand to the party. The party platforms are certainly consistent with his own ideas, and it is easy to imagine that he played a role in drafting al-Wasat's programmatic documents. Al-'Awa's perspective is nicely summarized in the following comment: "the problem of government resides upon two primary, complementary tenets: the belief in Divine existence and faith in individual freedom. Individual freedom must assert itself before the challenges of both the metaphysical and tangible worlds" (al-'Awa 1999).

Secularly oriented skeptics, as well as leading government officials, argue that Madi and his colleagues are simply masking their real views, namely their aim to seize power and establish a system of Islamist rule ('Abd al-Karim 1998; Abdel-Latif 1999). "We are not using *taqiya*," Madi insists. "We are not seeking to establish a religious party per se. We are talking about a civil party with an Islamic frame of reference. . . . We know that the hardest choice is moderation, and the easiest choice is extremism. . . . We form part of Egypt's political landscape in the coming century."

While Nasser horribly repressed the Ikhwan, Madi, like many of his generation, reveals a wistful nostalgia for the equalitarian elements of Nasser's programs. "The positive aspects of the Nasser era cannot be denied. Social reforms, free education and medical care allowed a new elite to emerge, one rooted in the humblest social classes" (Labidi 2002).

Simultaneously, Madi has a nuanced appreciation of the West, and like many Muslim intellectuals he was deeply impressed by the antiwar demonstrations that preceded America's invasion of Iraq. The antiwar demonstrations in 2003 prompted him to reflect that the West is not America, and the U.S. public is not the U.S. government. He reasons that this means there must be dialogue at all levels. Madi underlines that Egypt's relations with the United States discourage reforms, because reform would contradict U.S. interests, yet serious efforts by the United States to broker reform would be well received, he argues.

THE PARTY INTELLECTUAL

The son of a revered Protestant minister, the late Samuel Habib, Rafiq is one of the intellectual architects of Hizb al-Wasat, one of a handful of Christians who became founding members. His books are well known in Egypt and he has written on faith and politics, history's legacies in Egypt, and democracy (Habib 1996b, 1996c, 1998). His office is in the headquarters of the Coptic Evangelical Organization, in al-Nuzha al-Jadida, an obscure suburb of Cairo where this interview took place on November 9, 1999. After a few moments of shared reminiscences about Reverend Habib, we launch directly into the substance of the interview.

The political problem lies with the administrative and military origins of the state. Over time there has been a decrease in the quality of political figures in the system. The country is led by a military administrator, and there is no site for real politics. The army is the source of the problem. Mubarak's only fear is that the army is not with him. He does not understand the language of reform. Habib reflects that the problem is like trying to talk about engineering to someone who only knows administration. Technical issues are reduced to management problems, which means that you never get to the root of the problem at hand:

> So Egypt is left with a political system without real politics. Political space is depoliticized. After 1992 [when the Algerian Islamic Salvation Front won a sweeping electoral victory and stood on the threshold of power only to be

denied by a coup], Mubarak became afraid of everything. There is no serious political thought and the government has had no real success against the opposition. Mubarak's attitude is that the Islamic parties are a threat, just as in Algeria. Thus, the Islamic movement has been suppressed and political life is frozen.

Since 1995, no new parties have been allowed, though many parties effectively exist. In fact, Islamic thinking is in flux. Hizb al-Wasat has new ideas; so does the Ikhwan. But the Ikhwan cannot deal with the emergence of the Wasat movement, so things have slowed down. In time, the fear will decline (and the old men will die) and an optimistic vision of the future would see the "silent *ummah*" take power from the government in a context of passive resistance. Habib argues that the successful Ikhwan businessmen, who have large constituencies, will lend their hefty weight to politics. The mentality of business is practical and the liberal wing of the business community wants a political party. Others, who are linked to the state sector, will not be enthusiastic, but an optimistic vision would point to more influence for the chambers of commerce and the power of private capital.

As for "the system," all the eggs have been put in one—reform—basket, namely, reform only within the context of state control. Habib is alluding to the discussions about Hizb al-Mustaqbal, a failed initiative to create a new party under the leadership of Gamal Mubarak, the president's son. Mubarak closed the door on this venture in 1999, perhaps after he sensed negative views emanating from the army. (Since then, Gamal Mubarak has been ensconced as chair of the NDP policy committee, and he has been warmly received on three official visits to Washington, D.C., as though he is the anointed successor to his father.)

On his role forming the Hizb al-Wasat, Habib notes that he was isolated by the move among Copts, whereas he expected to be joined by others. They need to reach more people, he notes. He observes that the first rejection noted that the party was not different from other extant parties. As for the second effort to gain recognition, which culminated in an appeals ruling on June 5, 1999, Habib argues this was handled illegally by the government. There were new ideas. Al-Wasat proposed a different government system, including two councils—one for politics, another for constitutional matters. The representatives in the council would be agents of the *'ummah* not representative of the people. The government said these were old ideas, derived from outside Egypt. They even asserted, inexplicably, that the ideas stemmed from "*iqta*" (feudalism).

In one of his books, *al-Muqadas wa-al-Hurriyah* (The sacred and freedom), Habib argues that the nation is defined by its sacred consciousness (*al-muqadas*) and its fixed principles (*al-thawabet*). The problem arises when the *sulta* (or authority, by which he means the government) seeks to impose beliefs (namely, secularism) by force and law. In doing so, the people's freedom is taken away in the interests of foreign values. This leads to a situation in which groups become convinced that the only way to preserve *al-muqadasat* and *al-thawabet* is to acquire power. While people are free not to believe, not to accept the sacred truths, they may not destroy the nation and its beliefs. What is needed, he argues, is a re-discovery of the sacred and the renewal of the principles that underlie the nation. This must be done peacefully, as through parties like al-Wasat, because if it is done violently, the nation will only be weakened and will only be more vulnerable to Western interference. Egypt is a conservative society and Habib's argument resonates with many Egyptians, whether Christian or Muslim (Habib 1998).

THE GUIDE

Islamic circles (*nadwas*) in Cairo intersect and intertwine. The interlocutor was a venerable independent thinker in Cairo, a man known for his criticism of the Ikhwan; but, knowing that an appointment with the Supreme Guide was desired, he set it up in a few hours' time. His assistant 'Adil, described warmly as a man "with one foot inside the Ikhwan and another outside it," serves as a friendly escort. The meeting is with Muhammad Ma'amoun Hudeibi, an eighty-one-year-old former judge. He has been the Ikhwan's *murshid* (Guide) for less than a year, though his rise to this post has been a foregone conclusion for a decade. The session is in a shabby apartment building in al-Manya, a very ordinary Cairo neighborhood. There is no doorman or policeman in sight, just a peasant woman who looks on beseechingly as we pass. Then I recall an interlude in Upper Egypt, years before in an Assiut police station, where a cast of informants, a profile of everyday Egypt, sat on narrow benches waiting to be paid. A policeman opened a desk drawer to reveal a fat pile of bank notes. Then again, this may just be an old woman.

One removes his shoes on entering the headquarters, not out of piety but respect for the premises, a common practice in old Cairo. We are ushered in to see Hudeibi almost immediately. The *murshid* has the physique of a snowman and the friendly smile of a grandfather.

The Guide begins by noting that Islam is belief and ritual plus *shari'ah*. "My religion orders me to insist that I be governed by *shari'ah*." But Hudeibi is intent to note that while personal status matters (such as inheritance) are fixed, and while relations between men and women are defined clearly, there are many areas where there are differences (*ikhtilaf*) within the Qur'an and the Sunna.

We have to be creative. "There is a difference between two hundred years ago and today." He notes that at the time of the founding of the Ikhwan only 7 percent of men were literate, and even fewer women:

> Hasan al-Banna was only forty-two years old when he was martyred and he did not see his daughters grow up. We believe that women have a right to work, and to education, but they may not be forced to work. When they are married, this is an issue that is settled within the family. We recommend that children have the attention of their parents but, in fact, many women work.

"I find that eighty percent of Ikhwan are married to women who have finished their education." Citing his own family, Hudeibi noted he had four children, all of whom are doctors. In one case, the daughter (married to an engineer) is still practicing medicine. In the other, the daughter has given up her professional work (her husband is also a doctor). "This is a family choice," he comments.

Hudeibi notes that the husband is the head (*ra'is*) of the family, but when I question him on this, noting that the man might be nominal head while the wife has extensive influence, he responds with what he calls a pre-Islamic proverb from Arabia: "*'awana ammat lahu yakun 'abdan laki*" (if you are a slave for him, he will be a slave for you).

With regard to elections, "we encourage women to vote and we depend on their votes." He stresses that "women have the right to run for election." Hudeibi complains that were it not for the manipulation of the government in Alexandria during the 2000 elections, a sister named Jihan Khalifawi would have won a seat.

As for contemporary questions of governance for society, he emphasizes the import of *shura* and *'ijma,* and recalls that the first *khalifa,* Abu Bakr, did not force himself upon the community but was widely accepted as head of state. Applied to modern times, when literacy is much more widespread, representation requires free elections. Thus, people have the right to select the government. Principles and values determine how people vote. In contrast to questions of family law, which are more or less fixed, *ijtihad* suggests elections. As far back as 1936, Hassan al-Banna approved representation, but "we live in different times," Hudeibi declares. Not only was the public less well educated, but al-Banna's time was marked by occupation and monarchy.

The position that Hudeibi describes is an important departure from the fixed positions that prevailed for half a century until the 1980s. Hudeibi declares that "one party means dictatorship." The hard-won lesson of the Ikhwan is that there must be a multiparty system with a turnover of representatives ("three or four year terms") and "the will of the majority must be respected, including the peaceful transfer of power."

The discussion then shifts to the case of al-Wasat. He listens calmly as I outline the events, more or less as summarized in this chapter. Then he responds directly: "[A]ll of the information that you have is wrong in terms of the role of the Muslim Brethren."

> The decision to form the [al-Wasat] party was not approved beforehand. As long ago as 1986 we decided to have a party. We felt that all leadership in the party should be known. We know that giving a license for a party is the will of one person [President Mubarak]. All procedures leading up to the president's decision are just for the sake of appearance.
>
> We knew that the president would not allow a party to be formed. Mubarak has said, "even if the Constitutional Court allows a party, I will not allow it." We would not try to form a party because the decision would seem to be rational and fair, whereas it is the decision of one man. It leaves the deceptive impression that it is possible to form a party.
>
> We are a political party in reality. We have our structures, we have announced policies and we are the largest party in parliament. . . . No one said we were unethical. Hence, the issue is just applying the law to reality.

Hudeibi observes that it is natural that others will oppose the Ikhwan. "We want Muslims to have the right to practice *shari'ah*." Hudeibi recalls the parliamentary elections of 1995, when 165 Ikhwanis ran for election and not a single one won. "This event shook our confidence." In the same year, the government was arresting brothers and sentencing them to jail terms. "People were astonished. They did not know what to do."

"The people in al-Wasat were accused by the government of representing the Ikhwan. Some people decided to embarrass the government by claiming a party was being formed." At the same time, he acknowledges that "within the ranks of the Ikhwan, a number of people started to ask to create a party." He notes that there was a modified program being developed, one that kept the core values of Islam. "Always, when we see people who are enthusiastic, why not? They are our sons."

> Unfortunately, when they wrote the program we did not approve it. They took an unethical position. They communicated with other members and told people that they were acting on behalf of the Ikhwan. The *murshid* asked for the al-Wasat people to appear. They refused to come to the office. They went to the home of the *murshid* and told him that they had already written the program and submitted it to the Political Parties Committee, which [we knew] would then transmit it to intelligence. We sought to avoid guile. The *murshid* was shocked that seventy-five Muslim Brothers were aligned with al-Wasat. When the issue came up, especially the participation of Ikhwan, I was shocked. If you really work in politics, if you really are a politician then you have to be more professional, not amateurish. It was

only by coincidence that I found out about it just before the program was submitted. If reporters had come, I would know nothing. [Hudeibi handled press relations at that time.] I took a decision to put an end to this embarrassing decision, to announce that this is a group outside the Ikhwan.

As for the al-Wasat people, Hudeibi told them:

You, if you are asked, your answer will be limited to your program, and you are not from the Ikhwan. Of course, I knew there would be talk about internal divisions. We did not want to have media looking at divisions. Unfortunately, they did talk about the Ikhwan in the press. After that, most brothers who had supported it returned to the Ikhwan when they discovered the leadership did not approve.

Reliable reports indicate that serious pressure was applied to convince al-Wasat supporters to return to the Ikhwan. "They objected to the use of their names and refused further participation. They said we are ready to do whatever you wish. We then decided to go to the Political Party Tribunal and say that the Muslim Brothers do not approve of any party. In any case, we were one hundred percent sure that the party would not be approved." Hudeibi urged al-Wasat not to pursue an appeal. In front of the world, it would be the court that would vote against the party, whereas, in reality, it was Mubarak who vetoed the party. After the initial application was disapproved, "we were surprised to find that they had filed an appeal with the tribunal."

"Since the people who had given names now refused, their lawyer should have said that he is representing five people." Instead, "the lawyer said that he was representing all of the people on the list. Therefore, other people [viz, the Ikhwan] had to present their own papers."

"We did not stand with the government. We just objected that seventy people would have their names used. We are not against any party. They were unethical."

THE ADVISER

Dr. Osama al-Baz is a thin man with a somewhat nasal voice and great power. In November 1999, I am meeting him for the third time. The interview begins punctually in the Foreign Ministry building. The spacious corner office befits one of the two or three most powerful men in Egypt. The opening comments focus on modernist trends in Islam and Al-Baz volunteers that he read *al-Kitaab wa al-Qur'an* (The book and the Qu'ran) by the Syrian engineer Muhammad Shahrour, which he notes was excellent. Shahrour's rationalism appeals to established educated professionals, but few of the Islamists seem to have read Shahrour. They prefer work that is more focused on the problematics of contemporary society and politics than Shahrour's tedious but modernist *tafsir.*

The conversation turns to Samuel Huntington's "clash of civilizations" thesis. Al-Baz likes Huntington's book. He especially appreciates "the acceptance of diversity," the idea that globalization is not going to erase cultural dissimilarities. He has not read the original article it seems, only the more nuanced book.

After the interruption of a phone call, marked by the use of short generic phrases intended to signal the caller that a visitor may be listening, the discussion continues and turns to Egypt. He talks about widespread complaints about deepening government corruption, even from people who are not shrill critics of the regime. He picks up on the question of decorum, not corruption. "Yes, this is very important. People must be respectable." Even as we are speaking the government is pursuing the persecution of several figures in the Islamist-aligned Labor Party, including Magdi Hussein, the editor of *al-Sha'b,* the party newspaper that has been doggedly attacking the then Minister of Agriculture Yusif Wali for corruption, malfeasance, and contacts with Israel. (The Labor Party has since been dismantled by the government.)

People were looking for new faces in government, but the government announced following Mubarak's reelection in September 1999 is packed with familiar faces. Al-Baz acknowledges that people feel frustrated, but he says the problem is that they themselves raised unreasonable expectations. "They were making lists of all the people they expected to see removed from the cabinet. Of course, this did not occur." What they do not realize is that some of the people they condemned were constrained in the last government. People don't realize that the ministers were often blocked. In any case, "just wait for three months," he says. "There will be very important improvement."

Although he does not mention the name of Saad Eddin Ibrahim, the activist think-tank head who created a tempest of debate by writing about discrimination against Coptic Christians, it is clear that he has Ibrahim in mind when he complains about people making broad charges of systemic discrimination. The Copts did suffer discrimination, al-Baz acknowledges, "especially in the first years following the 1952 revolution. These injustices should and must be corrected." As for NGOs, the answer is not to engage in sweeping accusations. In his eyes, the problem lies largely with foreign-funded human rights organizations. If there are problems, he complains, these groups should identify them and they will be dealt with. Given Egypt's dependence on U.S. assistance ($2 billion annually), it is easy to imagine that questions about Christian mistreatment would jeopardize Egypt's standing on Capitol Hill. There is little question, based on al-Baz's comments, that he would like to see Egyptian NGOs brought to heel. The following year, in fact, the government closed Saad Eddin Ibrahim's Ibn Khaldun Center, and jailed Ibrahim and a score of his associates. The crackdown followed months of character assassination in the press, including accusations that Ibrahim was a spy. Only in early 2003 was Ibrahim freed from jail, after his case was overturned on appeal to the Constitutional Court, where the appeal was argued by Dr. 'Awad al-Murr, a former president of the court.

As for the Islamists, "they want power. That is their goal." Al-Baz recalls the earthquake of October 1992. (The earthquake killed more than 550 Cairenes.) He was in Turkey when it happened. "When there was a small earthquake here, the Islamists responded very quickly, but the government agencies were slow to react. Not surprisingly, the people said, 'fuck the government.' They did not do this out of the goodness of their hearts; they did it to convince people to support them so they can seek power. That is their goal." He cites the case of Iran where the mullahs were only one of the groups that toppled the Shah, but they took over. "They want to take over." In short, this is a zero-sum game.

As for the idea that the Islamists can form a legal party, "No way. . . . I will speak to them as individuals, as I will speak to anyone, but we will not recognize them as an organization." He gives the example of a recent funeral where he was approached by several of them, and he was willing to talk to them as individuals. On the specific case of the Hizb al-Wasat, al-Baz responds that this is just a front for the Ikhwan.

Only months before we met, there was discussion of a new party, the Hizb al-Mustaqbal, or the party of the future. Gamal Mubarak was mentioned as prospective head and al-Baz a leading member, but the possibility was squashed by no less than the president. Al-Baz dismisses these reports as rumors and emphasizes that he had nothing to do with the party. He goes on to argue that the president needs a constituency, and any new party would weaken his constituency. If President Mubarak is weakened, "what will his base be?" "I will tell you," and he points at his shoulders, and crosses his fingers as though tracing the crossed rifles of officers' military insignia. Even now, a half century after Lieutenant Colonel Nasser and the Free Officers rose to power, the power of the army retains a trump card. This leaves little real room for maneuver. The result is that no opposition political parties can be allowed to evolve, Islamist or otherwise.

By Way of a Conclusion

On the face of it, Hizb al-Wasat is a case study in failure that illustrates that arduous path that any aspiring opposition group must confront in Egypt, or in many of the other authoritarian states in the Middle East.

The zero-sum mentality that often informs ruling circles permits little scope for other than decorative and tame opposition groups with narrow political bases. What is missing, alas, is reflexivity in the regime. Though some bright regime intellectuals would dearly like to see change, few new ideas bubble to the upper reaches of the regime. When new ideas do surface they are merely melded into regime rhetoric, as in 1999 when Mubarak's embrace of "institutions" spawned momentary hope of serious reform but was quickly forgotten.

Nor is zero-sum thinking unique to those in power, as the example of the Ikhwan's reaction to al-Wasat illustrated. In an important sense, reform needs to begin at home—namely, within the long-entrenched opposition elites who fear the dissipation of their authority and privileges.

Certainly, there has been little external pressure on the Egyptian government to embrace reform. One is left to wonder whether a well-placed nudge in 1996 might have eased the path for al-Wasat, but the focus in Western capitals at that time, and certainly in Washington, embraced static stability, not reform (Indyk 2002). Now the mood seems to have changed dramatically, spurred significantly by the horrific events of September 2001. In November 2003, President George Bush eloquently embraced the project of democratic reform in the Middle East and pointedly rejected the longstanding penchant of the U.S. government for supporting stable autocracies:

> Sixty years of Western nations excusing and accommodating the lack of freedom in the Middle East did nothing to make us safe—because in the long run, stability cannot be purchased at the expense of liberty. As long as the Middle East remains a place where freedom does not flourish, it will remain a place of stagnation, resentment, and violence ready for export. (Bush 2003)

One wonders whether the embrace of democracy extends to self-consciously Islamic groups such as al-Wasat. Important policy statements by Bush and others seem to envisage a secular model of political parties that might not only exclude the Ikhwan, but even parties like al-Wasat emphasizing the *shari'ah* as a collection of principles (Powell 2002). In high profile presentations U.S. officials note warily that democratic elections will bring greater power to "parties with an Islamic character" (Haass 2003). Yet, the al-Wasat example illustrates that "parties with an Islamic character" may well invoke creative political ideas and pragmatic principles. These are parties that deserve to be embraced and encouraged, not marginalized and feared.

Al-Wasat was not a shot out of the blue, but a culmination of tajdidi trends that have been developing dramatically since the 1980s (al-Mawla 2000; Norton 2002). It is a modern manifestation of liberal Islam, but its commitment to interpret *shari'ah* flexibly flows also naturally from the modernism of Muhammad 'Abduh, almost a century ago. When he created the Ikhwan in 1928, Hassan al-Banna was more comfortable with Rashid Rida's conservative Salafism than with 'Abduh's modernism. Now the paths are recrossing, as reflected even in the comments by the Supreme Guide. The emergence of al-Wasat does not mark a new azimuth as much as a new context and a new era in Islamist politics. In this sense, it is an instructive sample of modern political parties that will appear with increasing regularity throughout the Muslim world.

NOTES

1. These trends are described in a lecture broadcast on WBUR (Norton 2002a), and the contending perspectives on these trends in Islamic thinking are the subject of a Ford Foundation–funded project on *Tajdid* (or renewal) that the author cochaired with Bahman Baktiari in 2001. The project will resume in 2004.
2. Four authors provide informative accounts of Hizb al-Wasat. Joshua Stacher (2001, 2002) has done yeoman service by putting together a valuable collection of factual material, as well as offering his own insights. Caryle Murphy (2002) reflects on her contemporaneous reportage of the Hizb al-Wasat and contextualizes the party in the broader Islamic debate over reform. Anthony Shadid (2001) offers crisp and thoughtful reportage, and Sa'ud al-Mawla (2000) successfully analyzes the case (in Arabic) in the broader historical context of the Ikhwan.
3. Professor Farhad Kazemi and I collaborated on several research projects during this period, notably the Civil Society in the Middle East project at New York University, which we directed together. My conclusions from the mid-1990s reflect fieldwork that Kazemi and I conducted together, and I could not have developed some of these ideas without his inspiration.
4. Three years after al-Wasat filed its first application, two more Islamist parties were proposed, but they had a very different pedigree from al-Wasat's. The two, respectively, were drawn from the Gama'at Islamiyya and al-Jihad, both notorious for antigovernment violence and acts of terrorism. Kamal Habib's Reform Party (al-Islah) and the Islamic Law Party (Hizb al-shari'ah) were both denied legal status in 1999 (Murphy 2002).
5. See Islam on Line (in Arabic): http://www.islamonline.net/Arabic/contemporary/politic/2000/article30S.shtml. The author is indebted to Maha 'Eid, who located some of these materials.
6. Amani Abu-Shakra's assistance in translating the program was indispensable, especially in those sections that stymied my ability in Arabic.

REFERENCES CITED

'Abd al-Karim, D. S., ed. 1998. *Awraq Hizb al-Wasat al-Masri*. Cairo: n.p.
Abdel-Latif, Omayma. 1999. "The Hardest Choice Is Moderation." *Al-Ahram Weekly* (Cairo), December 16–22. (http://weekly.ahram.org.eg/1999/460/ramadan2.htm)

Auda, Gehad. 1991. "Egypt's Uneasy Party Politics." *Journal of Democracy* 2, no. 2: 70–78.

al-'Awa, Muhammad Salim. 1999. "A Return to the Centre." *Al-Ahram Weekly* (Cairo), December 9–15.

Ayubi, Nazih N. 1991. *The State and Public Policies in Egypt since Sadat.* Reading, Mass.: Ithaca Press.

Baker, Raymond William. 1997. "Invidious Comparisons: Realism, Postmodern Globalism, and Centrist Islamic Movements in Egypt." In *Political Islam: Revolution, Radicalism, or Reform?* edited by John L. Esposito, pp. 115–33. Boulder, Colo.: Lynne Rienner.

al-Banna, Gamal. 2002. *al-Islam din wa Ammah wa lisa Dinan wa Dawlah.* Cairo: Dar al-Fakir al-Islami.

Bush, George. 2003. *Remarks at the 20th Anniversary of the National Endowment for Democracy.* Washington, D.C.

Cairo Times. 2000. "The Little NGO that Could: Members of the Would-Be Wasat Party Get a License to Form a Society." April 13–19 (http://cairotimes.com/news/wasat.html).

Commins, David Dean. 1994. "Hasan al-Banna." In *Pioneers of Islamic Revival,* edited by Ali Rahnema, pp. 125–53. London: Zed Press.

Fandy, Mamoun. 1994. "Egypt's Islamic Group: Regional Revenge?" *Middle East Journal* 48, no. 4: 607–25.

Farag, Iman. 1991. "Le politique a l'egyptienne: Lecture des elections legislatives." *Monde Arabe Maghreb-Machrek* 133: 19–33.

Haass, Richard. 2002. *Towards Greater Democracy in the Muslim World.* Washington, D.C.: Council on Foreign Relations.

Habib, Rafiq, ed. 1996a. *Awraq Hizb al-Wasat al-Masri.* Cairo: n.p.

———. 1996b. *Misr al-Qadimah: Bayna al-taghrib wa-al-takfir.* Cairo: Dar al-Sharuq.

———. 1996c. *Tafkik al-Dimuqratiah.* Cairo: Dar al-Sharuq.

———. 1998. *al-Muqadas wa al-hurriyah.* Cairo: Dar al-Sharuq.

Hamzawy, A. 2003. "Exploring Theoretical and Programmatic Changes in Contemporary Islamist Discourse: The Journal *al-Manar al-Jadid.*" In *Transnational Political Islam,* edited by A. Karam, pp. 132–54. London: Pluto Press.

al-Hudeibi, Muhammad Ma'amoun. 2000. *The Principles of Politics in Islam.* Cairo: Islamic, Inc.

Ibn Khaldun Center. 1993. "Qanun al-niqabat al-Muhania al-Muhid: Yathir zuba'a fi Fanajan." *al-Mujtama' al-Madani,* March 4–8.

Ibrahim, Saad Eddin. 1996. *Egypt, Islam, and Democracy: Twelve Critical Essays.* Cairo: American University of Cairo Press.

Indyk, Martin. 2002. "Back to the Bazaar." *Foreign Affairs* 81, no. 1 (January–February): 75–88.

Labib, Hani. 1998. "Interview: Abu al-'Ela Mady." *Civil Society: Democratization in the Arab World,* 7, no. 82.

Labidi, Kamel. 2002. "Egypt's Squandered Hopes." *Le Monde Diplomatique,* July 11 (http://mondediplo.com/2002/07/11nasser).

Madi, Abu al-'Ala. c. [1999]. "[Interview] la yujud lada al-ikwan rawiah siyasiah nadajah." *Al-Ahram al-'Arabi* 18.

al-Mawla, Sa'ud. 2000. *Min Hasan al-Banna illa Hizb al-Wasat.* Beirut: Mu'assasa al-'Ula.

Murphy, Caryle. 2002. *Passion for Islam: Shaping the Modern Middle East. The Egyptian Experience.* New York: Scribner.

Neguib, M. 1955. *Egypt's Destiny.* London: Victor Gollancz.

Norton, Augustus R. 2002a. "Who Speaks for Islam: A Sampling of Reformist Thinking." *Boston University World of Ideas* (radio), April 10, 2002 (*http:// www.buwi.org/*).

———. 2002b. "Islamic Activism and Reformism," *Current History,* November, 377–81.

Powell, Colin L. 2002. "The U.S.–Middle East Partnership Initiative: Building Hope for the Years Ahead." December 12. Washington, D.C.: Heritage Foundation.

Qutb, Sayyid. 1988. *Ma'alim fi al-Tariq.* Cairo: Dar al-Shuruq.

Sadat, Anwar. 1957. *Revolt on the Nile.* New York: John Day Co.

al-Sayyid, Mustapha Kemal. 1995. "A Civil Society in Egypt?" In *Civil Society in the Middle East,* edited by A. R. Norton, pp. 269–93. Leiden: Brill.

Schemm, Paul, and Simon Apiku. 1998. "The Battle of the Generations in Egypt's Opposition." *Middle East Times,* August 23 (http://www.metimes.com/issue98-34/eg/the_battle_of.htm).

Shadid, Anthony. 2001. *Legacy of the Prophet: Despots, Democrats, and the New Politics of Islam.* Boulder, Colo.: Westview Press.

Stacher, Joshua A. 2001. "Moderate Political Islamism as a Possible New Social Movement: The Case of Egypt's Wasat (Center) Party." MA thesis in Political Science, American University in Cairo.

———. 2002. "Post Islamist Rumblings in Egypt: The Emergence of the Wasat Party." *Middle East Journal* 56, no. 2: 415–32.

Sullivan, Denis J., and Sana Abed-Kotob. 1999. *Islam in Contemporary Egypt: Civil Society versus the State.* Boulder, Colo.: Lynne Rienner.

United Nations Development Program (UNDP). 2002. *Arab Human Development Report.* New York: UNDP Regional Bureau for Arab States (RBAS).

Wickham, Carrie R. 1996. "Political Mobilization under Authoritarian Rule: Explaining Islamic Activism in Mubarak's Egypt." Ph.D. dissertation in Political Science and Near Eastern Studies, Princeton University.

Zaki, Moheb. 1995. *Civil Society and Democratization in Egypt, 1981–1994.* Cairo: Konrad Adenauer Stiftung and Ibn Khaldun Center.

Chapter 7

REWRITING DIVORCE IN EGYPT:

RECLAIMING ISLAM, LEGAL ACTIVISM,

AND COALITION POLITICS

Diane Singerman

> The New Marriage Contract Initiative adopted a strat-
> egy of engaging religious discourse, based on the women's
> reading of their rights under the principles of Sharia.
> We reclaimed for the first time our right to redefine our
> cultural heritage, as Muslim women under the principles
> of Sharia. It was evident that we could not rely on mod-
> ern constitutional rights of equality before the law, as
> these did not equally apply under Family Law, which
> claimed to be based on the principles of Sharia. We
> could not afford to shy away from the challenge and
> continue using solely a strategy based on constitutional
> and human rights. We had to prove that the religious
> discourse could also be used by women to defend their
> cause.
>
> —Mona Zulficar, *The Islamist Marriage*
> *Contract in Egypt*

In January 2000, after a month-long period of controversial, often vitri-
olic debate and media attention, the Egyptian parliament passed "The
Law on Reorganization of Certain Terms and Procedures of Litigation in
Personal Status Matters" (Law No. 1, 2000). Personal Status Law (PSL)
regulates marriage, divorce, child custody, and inheritance issues, but this
law only ushered in procedural changes rather than basic changes in PSL
law itself. In short, this legislation was controversial because it provided a
woman with the right to initiate a "no-fault" divorce against her husband,
in return for giving up her financial claims upon him, including the deferred part of the dower, or *mu'akhar saddaq*.[1] This type of divorce is
known as *khul'* and is religiously legitimated because of fears that a
woman will not be able to "keep within the limits of the law" if she finds

her husband so repulsive or incompatible. Thus, a Qur'anic verse (*Surah* 2:29) allows her to "give something up to her husband [the deferred dower] in exchange for her freedom" (Awde 2000, 25). Procedural changes also consolidated all disputes associated with divorce in a new Family Court system, while disallowing further appeal in *khul'* divorces (reducing the period of litigation associated with divorce). The legislation also created a *Sanduq al-Usr,* or "Family Fund" to provide child support for impoverished families, giving authority to the government to garnish the wages of recalcitrant husbands who renege on alimony and child support. Finally, another important revision in the law provided more flexible criteria to facilitate divorce in *urfi* or unregistered marriages, as well as procedures for proving paternity for their offspring (Allam 2000; Shahine 1998; Ezzat 2000).

This legislation was the culmination of a fifteen-year campaign to facilitate divorce for women, orchestrated by a coalition of activists, lawyers, government officials, civic leaders, legislators, and scholars. It was but the most recent chapter of a century-long battle by women and sympathetic men to reform personal status law. The quote above, by one of the key activists in the Personal Status Law coalition, Mona Zulficar, reveals the self-conscious and strategic thinking innovative leaders developed to provide women with access to divorce. While leadership was absolutely key to the ultimate passage of Law No. 1 in 2000, along the way hundreds of meetings, interviews, conferences, strategy sessions, phone calls, lobbying efforts, and studies generated enough support across diverse constituencies for the bill to succeed.

More importantly, this coalition represented a convergence of several innovative projects within the contemporary Middle East that deserve far more attention because of the way in which they are creating new political alliances and possibilities, legitimated by an Islamic, indigenous, religious frame. These initiatives, deliberately and militantly rooted in the rule of law and sound legislative practices, may gradually be leading to the further institutionalization of democracy, while widening the spectrum of what "Islam" means to various constituencies engaged in collective action. The embrace of Islam by the PSL coalition leaves some women activists and leaders ambivalent or critical, however, because they are skeptical of the inegalitarian or patriarchal aspects of Islam. Some of these activists promote secular ideals as a solution while others promote a more progressive Islam that rearticulates fundamental concepts of belief and traditions (see Safi 2003; Ali 2003). Yet a growing number of activists in Egyptian civil society, and beyond, are making convincing popular arguments that Islam is a source of positive social and political change.

In this coalition, a divergent group of postcolonial scholars of history, law, sociology, religion, and philosophy, motivated by their professional identities and training, challenged the predominant religious discourse on women, as well as the historical record of women in the Islamic and pre-colonial era. They are part of a larger movement of postcolonial scholars who are reclaiming subjugated knowledge, buried and disguised or disqualified and marginalized over the centuries (Bond and Giliam 1994, 8; Foucault 1980, 78–109).

While these women are themselves the demographic and political product of an independent postcolonial Egypt that increased public education and professional opportunities for women, granted them suffrage, and encouraged them to contribute to Egypt's development, they are nevertheless still constrained in their daily and professional lives. Women could become ambassadors, deans of Islamic philosophy, international corporate lawyers, wealthy businesswomen, leaders of organizations, scholars, and politicians, yet they still feared divorce, financial ruin, and losing the custody of their children if they worked, wanted to further their education, or traveled without the permission of their husband. Personal Status Law still allows a man to claim his wife has been "disobedient" and if she works, seeks education, or travels without his approval, he is not obligated to support her after a divorce. Thus, although much of the international and national direction of the women's movement has been to promote female education, political rights, and equality for women, the Egyptian women's movement and others across the Muslim world also understand the need to change the balance of power within marriage, through legal change, if they are truly to benefit from these other changes (see Sonbol 2003).

Gerda Lerner argues that although women have been enduring patriarchy for millennia, at certain moments in time the "contradiction between women's centrality and active role in creating society and their marginality in the meaning-giving process of interpretation and explanation" encourages women to perceive deprivations that they wish to change. This "coming-into-consciousness . . . becomes the dialectical force moving them into action to change their condition and to enter a new relationship to male-dominated society" (Lerner 1986, 5). The women and their male supporters in the PSL coalition not only tried to overcome the contradictions of their daily and professional lives through this campaign, but in the process they became part of a new transnational movement of Muslim intellectuals and activists that are reimagining the past and the Islamic canon, contesting dominant frames legitimated by religious authorities who often have indirect or direct ties with the more conservative Islamist groups (see Bowen; Baktiari; and Peletz in this volume).

This said, the work of the PSL coalition demonstrates that more than scholarship and ideas are needed to win a hotly contested battle where powerful constituencies have every reason to maintain the status quo. Coalitions need powerful supporters, resources, and tactical innovations to succeed, as social movement theorists remind us. "Movement entrepreneurs" not only need to motivate diverse groups to work together, but they must cast unpopular ideas in a more acceptable light, exploit political opportunities, and enlist some sector of the elite in their project (see McCarthy and Zald 1977; Tarrow 1994). This new coalition was ultimately successful because it scaled across to that part of the religious establishment that would concur with their religiously framed policies, it scaled up with political elites in the executive branch, legislators and officials in the ruling National Democratic Party, and high Ministry of Justice Officials, and it also scaled down to gain support from a variety of organizations in civil society and their memberships (see Hefner 2000, and in this volume).

This chapter tells part of the story of this coalition by exploring the innovative strategies utilized by the women's movement in Egypt to guide the passage of important new procedural guidelines for Personal Status Law. In particular, I will highlight the prominent role of largely female lawyers, who rallied broad elite support across a number of important NGOs, the religious community, and within the government, and utilized a relatively new strategy of legal activism in the realm of administrative law to realize their objectives. A commitment to the rule of law and sound legislative practices directed the coalition to eventually take up the challenge of engineering legislative reforms of Personal Status Law through the Egyptian parliament. The unintentional consequences of this legislative initiative, which was very controversial and contested by legislators, strengthened the links and the relevance of parliament to civil society. But this case also demonstrates that working within civil society is not enough. Coalition members succeeded because they realized that they needed to play with the "big boys," and enlist the president, the law, parliament and, most importantly, religious authorities in their campaign. We need to recognize, as Jenny White argues about the Turkish case in this volume, that meaningful change can proceed only if activists have begun to assert themselves in national politics and in legitimate arenas of political contestation. In Egypt, activists are beginning to take legislatures more seriously. They are lobbying, holding legislators accountable, and building constituent politics. Although Parliament has been constrained by authoritarian politics, the domination of the National Democratic Party, and questionable electoral practices, it is an increasingly important arena of contestation and an architect of public policy.

The coalition developed new lobbying strategies so that the legislative campaign represented a learning curve for the women's movement in democratic and representative politics. The case also provides valuable lessons for others working for social change within the Islamic context. Of special interest is the manner in which the activists in the PSL coalition turned religion into an *asset,* rather than a liability, beating the religious traditionalists at their own game while engaging in civil, legal, rightful collective action that was acceptable within the constrained space of illiberal rule in Egypt. It was a campaign that could not have been successful without its Islamic frame.

DIVORCE: THE EGYPTIAN CONTEXT

In Egypt, men have a unilateral right to divorce that they can exercise without being obliged to enter into a court proceeding. A woman has traditionally only been able to seek a divorce in court (*tatliiq* or *tatfriiq*) by presenting proof that her husband has "harmed" her in specific ways that qualify as grounds for divorce (desertion, imprisonment, sterility, sexual deviance, lack of financial support, "harm" due to a husband taking a second wife).[2] Most divorce cases initiated by women have languished in the courts, taking as long as eight to ten years to resolve, and husbands have had many legal and indirect ways to prolong the process, causing great anguish for the wife and often the family. Each divorce case, one study suggested, produces at least five other cases in different courts over child custody, *nafaqa* (financial support/alimony), obedience (*ta'a*), the marital abode, and dispersion of the couple's assets and property (Zulficar and El-Sadda 1996, 251). In addition, due to the appeals process in Egyptian courts, some women have finalized their divorces only to have the decision reversed years later, after they have already remarried and had children. Such a reversal effectively renders the women bigamists, making them legally vulnerable in multiple ways.

Quite apart from the social costs of protracted lawsuits, the judiciary and international business interests have long expressed concern about the situation, since divorce cases and personal status disputes overwhelm the court system in Egypt's already extremely litigious society. While caseload statistics on divorce vary, one source suggests that 1.5 million divorce cases are filed each year in a population of 64 million (Shah 2000; Hammond 2000). A quarter of a million Egyptian women visit the courts annually (Tadros 2000a; Sakr and Hakim 2001) producing a huge caseload of approximately 5 million cases before the Egyptian courts (Soliman and Saleh el-Diin 2002). One estimate suggested that in 1997,

14 million lawsuits were in the court system and only four thousand judges were available to review them.[3] Another source claimed that 12 million new cases were brought before various Egyptian courts each year, or that the number of new court cases a year approaches one per household! (Brown 1997, 189–90) The judiciary is paralyzed by these cases and the backlog they produce, and political forces have been disappointed by the lack of "judicial reform" in Egypt, which they see as an essential precondition for and component of Egypt's growing involvement in the global economic order.

Even with the presence of these concerns, large-scale changes to personal status laws have been slow in coming. While Personal Status Law has been codified since 1929 (though a law of procedure was codified earlier, in 1897), modest reforms were achieved in 1979 and 1985 after popular controversy and vigorous debate (Brown 1996; al-Atraqchi 2002). The legal and historical dimensions of this debate are complicated and fascinating; new scholarship continues to emerge to explain the changing nature and context of this body of law and practice (see Sonbol 1996; Brown 1997; Afifi 1996; Zilfi 1997; Abu-Odeh 2002, n.d.; Ali 2003). These historical debates will barely be discussed here, but it is critical to understand that debates on personal status law since the nineteenth century have been framed around Islam, the religious community, and Westernization. At the same time, as Moors explains, family law is "central to the reproduction of the social and cultural order: it arranges for the transfer of material resources from one generation to the next (succession), it organizes the care for and socialization of the next generation (custody and guardianship), and it regulates sexual relations (marriage and its effects)" (2003, forthcoming).

The inroads of centralizing Ottoman codes and colonial, Western, secular law made religious authorities and indigenous political elites guard even more jealously the terrain of Personal Status law. While criminal and civil codes were greatly influenced by European codes, despite the abolishment of separate Personal Status courts in 1955 after the Free Officers Revolution, *shari'a* remained the source of law for Personal Status issues. "Bits and pieces of Western law" and interpretations from various *madhahib* (schools of law) were merged together to create "a new system" bundled into a "legitimate Islamic package" (Sonbol 1996, 277). This link between personal status law and religious legitimacy made changing these laws particularly difficult. And while female employment, education, and economic activity gradually improved, personal status laws remained discriminatory toward women. Furthermore, when women challenged those laws they were derided as secular, westernized, or immoral (see al-Ali 2000; Badran 1995).

A STRATEGY EMERGES

It was against this complex backdrop that a broad coalition formed to usher Law No. 1 of 2000 through the Egyptian parliament. From the outset, key activists recognized the importance of the challenge presented by the overtly religious basis for Personal Status Law. It was understood that if women were to change the laws, they had to formulate their legal and ideological challenge on Islamic grounds as well. Each Egyptian man, according to one key activist, walks around with a little pyramid inside of him, thinking and acting as if he is a pharaoh, and Islamic law can restore the balance in the Egyptian family that has been unfairly tipped toward patriarchy. Their position was simple: in Egypt, tradition and custom are stronger than religion, and a patriarchal Islamic tradition has deprived women of the protections and rights that Islamic law is supposed to give them. The coalition argued that Personal Status Law has already been distorted by secular, customary, Western, and Ottoman influences, and that Muslim women should reexamine the historical record of this body of law and restore the rights that Islam really affords them. Husn Shah, whose film *Uridu Halan* (I want a solution) brought the legal limbo of divorced women "out of the closet" and provoked widespread public debate in the 1970s, argued more recently in an interview that "people act like they understand Islam or they act like they don't, but *people don't know Islam;* they say we must do this and that, but really they are very selective in what they identify as Islamic." The coalition thought they might as well turn the selective interpretation of Islam to their own advantage.

The dual need to base a strategy for change on legal and religious grounds, incorporating a subtle critique of Western colonial or imperial Ottoman influences on national traditions, places this coalition within a much broader international movement of activists "reclaiming Islam." Like many of their counterparts in Morocco, Iran, Palestine, Bangladesh, India, Pakistan, or Malaysia, this coalition continued to promote a "rights discourse" but veered away from the liberal, individualistic, secular framework of feminism associated with the West and women's "liberation" (see Peletz in this volume on the efforts of Sisters in Islam in Malaysia). Rather, they utilized the sacred texts of the Qur'an, the *hadith* (the "sayings" of the Prophet), and Islamic jurisprudence to legitimize their actions. "Re-imagining foundational narratives" lies at the center of what Cooke calls Islamic feminism (Cooke 2001, xxv). Joining a transnational movement of women who are reinterpreting Islamic texts and traditions (Carroll and Kapoor 1996), Egyptian women have begun to legitimize their activism by studying the Prophet Muhammad's life and the women around him who were important figures in Islamic history;

engaging directly in Qur'anic textual analysis, adopting a historicist perspective to critique patriarchal trends that negatively influenced Islamic traditions and texts, and reconsidering the appropriate application of the Qur'an to the contemporary situation; and finally, and most radically, engaging in *ijtihad* (relying on independent reasoning on issues which are not clear from the text) (Cooke 2001, 62; Abou El Fadl 2001).

Zainab Redwan, the dean of the College of Philosophy at Cairo University, Fayoum branch, member of the Shura Council (upper body of the Egyptian parliament), and scholar of Islamic philosophy, was a critically important and publicly prominent member of this coalition. As she explained, women realized that if they sought change from a religious foundation, based on religious principles, the change could not be refused. This new idea and new strategy became the grounds for a reform movement that was legitimate and far more popular, or acceptable, than earlier approaches of the women's movement (Redwan 2000). Another activist in this coalition outlined the strategy this way: "Many female elites used the rhetoric and language of *fiqh* discourse (the Islamic canon) in their defense of *khul'*, as a way of preventing objections to the bill. They did this to give people 'no excuse to object' to the new law." While one can debate whether this "strategic move" was only tactical and instrumental or whether it represented a deeper commitment to Islamic tenets and values by these activists, it was indisputably a successful strategy. Hoda El-Sadda, a key activist in the coalition, professor of English literature at Cairo University and daughter of a professor of Islamic law, emphasized in her account of this coalition that she and others recognized there is a "Big Middle" of practicing Muslims in Egypt who are the majority. These women and men are ordinary, faithful people who want freedom, but they get lost between two radical poles. This silent majority, she and others believed, would welcome further freedom and opportunities for women (and men) if they were religiously legitimate.

The Personal Status Law coalition used both Qur'anic texts and *hadith* to legitimize the new law. *Khul'* is referred to in *hadith* collections in the story of Gamila, the wife of Thaabit ibn Qais, who went to the Prophet and explained that she simply hated her husband and could not fulfill her [sexual] obligations to him, although he was not an immoral or horrible person. The Prophet, in accordance with the Qur'anic verse, asked her to return her dower of a garden to her husband and she was divorced (Awde 2000, 25).

The coalition activists commissioned studies of the historical record of *shari'a* courts, marriage contracts, and divorce disputes in Egypt and other Muslim countries to understand how earlier periods had afforded women more rights, or at least more room to contest their situations, than were currently available and/or socially acceptable. Scholars met in international conferences and exchanged ideas and research, making alliances while refining and articulating their theory so it could emerge as "praxis." By presenting the historical record of women's greater access to divorce and the courts' greater flexibility and more sympathetic tolerance for the dissolution of marriages in earlier historical periods, they questioned common perceptions of Egyptian "progress" and "development" over the last century (Sonbol 1996, 1995; Hanna 1995). Furthermore, they demonstrated that the historical record was diverse and complex, and argued that if women may have fared better centuries ago, then surely there was not a single, fixed, essentialist religious or legal "position" on Personal Status issues. At the very least, there was room to reinterpret their own traditions to restore the rights that women had enjoyed in earlier period of Islamic history.

LEGAL ACTIVISM

Before moving to a specific discussion of the substance of changes under Law No. 1, 2000, it is important to note that this coalition could not have succeeded without the participation of trained lawyers (both women and men) and an explicit strategy of legal activism. This strategy is becoming more important as a political weapon throughout the Middle East as tentative experiences with illiberal democracy gradually yield a modicum of political space (Kienle 2001). As with many other women's movements around the globe, the Egyptian movement faced a hostile public in a nation where women are politically and economically underrepresented. Even in this environment, the passage of the Personal Status Legislation demonstrates that "legal activism" can produce substantial change.

Useful comparisons can be made with American women and African Americans in the 1960s, and gays and lesbians in the 1970s and 1980s, who also faced overwhelming institutional, legal, and cultural discrimination and held little electoral power. With only a small elite of highly successful, experienced, professionals (particularly lawyers) to wage their battle, activists were able to effect radical change through a civil campaign that used the courts to end discriminatory laws and practices, eventually forcing legislators to enact new laws (O'Connor 1980; Mueller 1997).

In Egypt, parliamentary politics has remained very constrained by executive influence over the dominant party, the National Democratic Party (NDP). Yet despite the record of authoritarian politics in Egypt and political repression stoked by the challenge of radical Islamists, Makram-Ebeid argued recently that "the judiciary has replaced the opposition." It has been the judiciary that has issued a spate of court rulings enhancing democratization, as its decisions have reigned in executive authority and protected legislative and bureaucratic authority and procedure (2001, 7). It was the judiciary that the PSL strategically incorporated into its coalition.

The coalition's activities showed the efficacy of a legal challenge as a "rightful" form of resistance, within the bounds of law, articulated by some of the most respected members of the local legal community and state bureaucracy (O'Brien 1996). Legal challenges have been used in a variety of fashions by a wide range of political movements, from contemporary challenges to centralized communist party elites from rural Chinese villages, to the Charter 77 movement in Czechoslovakia, which demanded that the communist government in the 1980s follow its own laws. In Egypt, ironically, the success of Islamist lawyers in promoting their cause through controversial and sensationalist court cases inspired lawyers in the PSL coalition to try a similar strategy of legal activism. Resisting political authority on its own terms and grounds can offer greater protection and legitimacy to political activists, particularly in contexts where many varieties of "normal" politics are constrained by authoritarian policies and violence. It is also difficult for the government to strike out against respected members of the judiciary who may have issued decisions that the government dislikes because these same lawyers also often work on behalf of the government to mediate political conflict or represent the government before various international bodies.

O'Connor's discussion of amicus curiae (friend of the court) litigation seems to most closely resemble the strategy used by Egyptian women activists and lawyers in the PSL coalition. In this strategy, experts submit extensive and well-reasoned amicus curiae briefs to fully inform the court of the legal challenge's implications and validity (1980, 3). The PSL coalition's particular legal strategy was to operate not just through the courts, but to work together in a coalition with government sympathizers and the Ministry of Justice to rewrite administrative law and personal status law. The presentation of historical, religious, and strategic arguments and evidence convinced government insiders to join their effort. This strategy of organizing "talking shows" and *nadwat* (seminars and conferences) encourages informal networking, politicking, and alliance-formation (al-Ali 2000). The state regulates the establishment, finances, and activities of associations very strictly in Egypt, so that forming fluid, ad hoc, temporary "single-issue" coalitions is more appropriate and less risky (see Norton in this volume). The Group of Seven, which published a booklet in 1988 outlining women's rights in Egypt and promoted the initial marriage contract project, is a great example of an ad hoc coalition that circumvented the lengthy, bureaucratic, and politically delicate task of building a new organization, since the main players already had a well-established associational or professional base. The negative side of "conference politics" is that discussions can alienate potential coalition members, personality and leadership conflicts can worsen, and the coalition actors may not contribute sufficient financial and organizational resources from their groups to the coalition's goal (al-Ali 2000, 171–72; Costain and Costain 1983).

The PSL coalition began this new tack after Law No. 44 of 1979 was declared unconstitutional in 1984 due to procedural irregularities, and a largely hostile parliament refused to reinstate the controversial articles in the new Law No. 100 of 1985. In an interview, Mona Zulficar described her disappointment when the 1979 reforms were abrogated, recognizing that Egyptian men continued to benefit from a long patriarchal tradition where they simply had more control over women. Women's advocacy and organizations needed to *break* that control. However, in 1984, the gains of the recent past were suddenly and easily obliterated on "procedural" grounds that were difficult to contest (and in fact, many supporters of the 1979 reforms were themselves distressed by Sadat's abuse of executive authority). Zulficar realized that advocates could no longer take shortcuts and that they had to be "consistent" and make sound laws that could withstand legal challenges.

The women's movement learned in the 1980s that their plans for reform were not only thwarted by traditional *'ulama* (religious scholars and jurists) from Al-Azhar university but also from what Zhegal has called "peripheral" *'ulama,* who were critical of Anwar Sadat's supposed commitment to reconcile Egyptian law with the *shari'a* and who had become increasingly allied with various popular Islamist movements in Egypt. By the time the Supreme Constitutional Court declared the 1979 reforms unconstitutional after Sadat's assassination in 1981, Islamists had gained more ground in the parliament; in an alliance with the Wafd Party, they were able to weaken the provisions of the substitute 1985 reforms.

A New Strategy: The Marriage Contract Project

With neither a presence in parliament nor popular support for reforms, several women activists hatched a new approach that concentrated on legal and bureaucratic changes, circumventing the parliamentary process in order to avoid the vocal Islamist element. In 1985, a small group of women decided to pursue the idea of drafting a new marriage contract that would allow room for a couple to "check-off" certain voluntary stipulations. This new marriage contract, they reasoned, would replace the standard contract (unchanged since 1931) that each couple signs before the *ma'zun* (marriage registrar). Because the Ministry of Justice issues the standard contract (*aqd al-jawaz*), the coalition soon began to work with the Ministry of Justice, particularly a high-ranking official who is currently chief justice of the Supreme Constitutional Court, Fathi Naguib (see Zulficar 1999, 9). He is recognized by many activists in the coalition as one of its prime "architects" and strategists, who for a variety of reasons that are both professionally and personally motivated, believed that women should have greater access to divorce and that Personal Status Law needed substantial reform on a variety of fronts. Naguib argued:

> When we assess the benefit of the law we have to consider the position of those women who were trapped either in a miserable marriage or in the vicious circle of court procedures over the years, before and after the new law. *Khul'* cannot be assessed through the eyes of those who suffer no problems and yet disapprove of its use by the ones who are suffering. All this results from the culture that regards women as inferior to men and not entitled to the same rights. This same culture blocked the legalisation of *khul'* for a long time although it is compatible with Shari'a. Islam is fair and balanced in the rights and duties it stipulates. (Sakr and Hakim 2001)

The marriage contract "project," as it was referred to by its proponents, was designed as a consciousness-raising tool. The idea was not only to educate women about rights that they were already entitled to, but also to encourage them to insert new stipulations in the contract that enhanced their power in the marriage. Activists hoped that a discussion before the marriage of each partner's expectations and registration of them in the contract would avoid problems farther down the road, and if divorce ensued, this new contract would allow women to easily extricate themselves from the marriage and avoid complicated, costly legal battles.

A small group of women, already linked by professional, political, family, educational, and economic networks, published a pamphlet in 1988 entitled the "Legal Rights of Egyptian Women in Theory and Practice." The document discussed the status of women in Egypt and the problems they faced, and made a series of recommendations, including the proposed new marriage contract. Social historians and legal historians had laid the groundwork for this endeavor by engaging in archival studies of the courts and the evolution of Personal Status Law (see Sonbol 1995, 1996; Zulficar 1999; Zilfi 1997; Hanna 1995). They then networked with other activists, academics, and lawyers to ensure that their efforts would not be summarily rejected by their traditional antagonists: the religious establishment, Islamist groups, and a government that abhorred public controversy.

The religious justification for the project was clear: throughout Islamic history, from its very beginning, women have included conditions in their marriage contracts that have been widely recognized as legitimate, if at times uncommon. The most famous historical example is the marriage contract of Sakina, the daughter of Hussein ibn 'Ali Talib, who stipulated conditions in her marriage contract that her husband could not restrict her freedom, could not marry another woman, and could not prohibit her from attending poetry and literary salons (Zulficar and El-Sadda 1996).

The new draft marriage contract included a "recommended" list of conditions that would be part of the contract and simply "checked" if mutually agreed upon. These recommendations included the couple's agreement on the possession of the furniture in case of divorce, and the inclusion of the bride's rights to education, to work, and to travel without her husband's permission. The bride could also stipulate that she retained the right to divorce herself in her "hand" ('isma bi-iidiha). One study suggested that only 325,000 women out of 18 million women of marriageable age in Egypt had included this right to divorce in their marriage contracts (Ezzat 2000, 43). If a woman stipulates this right in her marriage contract, it does not cancel the man's right to unilateral divorce, but only facilitates the divorce procedures for wives since it alleviates the wife from the burden of proving legal "harm" before a court (Zulficar and El-Sadda 1996, 253). The second relevant clause in the list of recommendations that had a central role in the PSL coalition's eventual, and successful, legislative strategy, was khul' divorce. Many other Arab and Muslim countries have historically allowed khul' and 'ibraa' divorces, but these have necessitated gaining the consent of the husband (Welchman 2000; Moors 1995; Haeri 1990; and Mir-Hosseini 1999, 1993).

While activists worked closely with religious authorities, lawyers, professors of Islamic law and philosophy and government officials to promote this new marriage contract, the project itself was eventually postponed, for three reasons. First, activists realized that even if these conditions were legally accessible to any woman, social convention still prevented women from using them. These new conditions in the marriage contract were only *voluntary,* and if it was scandalous actually to utilize them, then immense political capital and strategic efforts would be wasted on only a few women. The vast majority of Egyptian men would never accept these conditions, and even if a groom might consider them, their families (who are intimately involved with, if not orchestrating, their marriages) would not allow it, since they invest huge financial resources in a marriage.[4] As one *ma'zun* working in Imbaba (a poor area of Cairo) argued, "No man who deserves to be called a man can accept this: a woman to decide for him or to divorce him" (Ezzat 2000, 43).

Second, many women's groups and activists objected to including a right of work, education, and travel for women in the marriage contract, because they believed they were already protected under the Egyptian constitution's protection of equality and they did not want to be party to weakening their claim to formal legal authority under national and international law, particularly the U.N. Convention on Eliminating Discrimination Against Women (CEDAW), which Egypt signed in 1981.

The third reason that the coalition abandoned the Marriage Contract initiative was the largely negative nature of the public discourse surrounding it, particularly from conservative religious forces. By 1991, the Ministry of Justice and Fathi Naguib had already become deeply involved in the project and revised the recommendations for the new contract. Supporters of the project had received tentative positive responses to the basic model of the new marriage contract from some religious authorities; the Grand Mufti, Shaykh Mohamed Sayed El-Tantawi, approved the third draft of the marriage contract. Despite his approval, others criticized it, and some who approved of the religious legitimation for the new contract still opposed it on other grounds. For example, after fierce attacks by more conservative 'ulama both inside and outside of Al-Azhar, the Shaykh al-Azhar, Gad al-Haqq, rejected the marriage contract idea—not on religious or legal grounds, but because he argued it would discourage marriage between young people and cause social problems (Zulficar 1999, 9).[5] The support for the project was waning as opposition to it arose from various quarters.

SCALING UP: A TURN TOWARD THE LEGISLATIVE AND EXECUTIVE BRANCHES

By 1993, preparations were already under way for the 1994 U.N. Conference on Population and Development (ICPD) to be held in Cairo. In Egypt, Aziza Hussein, a longtime activist, sociologist, and head of the Family Planning Association (and also a relative of Mona Zulficar's) was chosen to head the National Preparatory Committee for NGOs for the ICPD. Informants suggest that she ran the forum in a very inclusive manner, encouraging activists and their organizations to cooperate and strategize cooperatively about promoting their agenda before the ICPD and the Egyptian government.

The Egyptian government was pleased to have Cairo chosen as the site of the ICPD and saw this conference as an opportunity to play a leadership role in the international community. At the same time, it wanted to counter the image in the West that Egyptian women were oppressed. The forum created a Gender Equality Committee, which organized symposiums and commissioned a number of legal and social studies, eventually embracing the new marriage contract as its own. One study demonstrated that most men and women were not aware that including stipulations in the marriage contract was legitimate under *shari'a* principles

(Zulficar and El-Sadda 1996, 255–59). It is at this juncture that the "social imaginations" designed for the marriage draft law project were appropriated for a larger, more ambitious project (Zakaria 2002). As one activist explained, "Women thought law—wow! We should target the Personal Status Law itself, but that was too big of a project and perhaps we should begin with something small, with which we had some experience, and it was here that the procedures surrounding Personal Status Law were targeted. We really needed something that was 'doable.' Just to succeed in *anything* would be great, but we needed some achievable goal, some success, something concrete." A focus on procedural changes in Personal Status Law involved only administrative changes, rather than changes in the basic law, and could be "marketed" as such. It was doable, it could be historically and religiously legitimated, and at the same time, the debate and discussion that the new law would provoke could be useful as "consciousness raising."

Although the new marriage contract project was not abandoned (and many of its provisions were eventually included in the new marriage contract issued by the Ministry of Justice in June 2000), the focus of the coalition turned toward rewriting the procedural regulations for Personal Status issues (Leila 2000). New support came from a very important quarter: Suzanne Mubarak, Egypt's First Lady. Partially as a response to the renewed attention on women and development sparked by the ICPD, as well as her own commitments to gender equality and development, the National Commission for Women, originally established in 1978, was revitalized in 1993 under the leadership of Suzanne Mubarak. A series of well-publicized national conferences were held in succeeding years, and this new commission embraced the procedural law changes and the new marriage contract.

This support from the First Lady was critical to the PSL coalition, providing protection and an indirect message to all other government actors that the president was behind the reform effort, and thus the campaign could now move to the parliamentary realm. Some activists critiqued the PSL coalition for being too close to the government and even condemned activists for "selling out." While it is clear that the coalition had the personal support of Suzanne Mubarak and probably the president, the First Lady remained discreetly behind the scenes. The more visible role of mobilizing supporters for the initiative was played by prominent and well-respected lawyers such as Mona Zulficar, Tehani El-Gebali, Fathi Naguib, former parliamentarian Fawziyya Abdel-Sattar, and Amira Bahieldin, as well as leaders such as Aziza Hussein and Iman Bibars, and academics such as Zainab Redwan and Hoda El-Sadda. The "liberal" Islam promoted by the PSL coalition strengthened the government's centrist position and even demonstrated to its critics in civil society that gradual change was possible if groups would only agree to work with the government, rather than against it. Yet, the organized and activist conservative religious forces had not yet finished their attack.

The Parliamentary Surge

The ability of this coalition to weave Law No. 1 of 2000 through parliament, I would argue, represents not only a significant legislative victory but also an important learning process for women's rights activists and NGO leaders. While the coalition's gradualist approach might have frustrated many of its supporters, it carefully laid the groundwork for success by outmaneuvering and anticipating its opponents' moves and enlisting the support of the leadership of the People's Assembly and National Democratic Party. The coalition benefited particularly from Dr. Fawziyya Abdel-Sattar's leadership, since she was a respected professor of law at Cairo University, had served in the People's Assembly from 1990 to 1995, and was the first female chair of its legislative committee. This gave her essential experience and the respect of her colleagues in parliament—key attributes that the coalition was able to utilize. Abdel-Sattar argued that women, who had first entered parliament in 1975, were now becoming experienced enough to attempt such initiatives even though their members were still small and only 7 women deputies (out of 444) had won office in the last national election (Elbendary 2000a, 2000b). Most of the women in parliament remained silent on this issue, maintaining, as another activist put it, their status as "decor." But since she was no longer in parliament, Dr. Abdel-Sattar was probably more valuable to the coalition, since she could plan parliamentary maneuvers and run interference for the coalition with her former colleagues.

The bill was presented on January 16 to an unusually packed house with 70 percent of the representatives in attendance. The session was opened by Justice Minister Farouq Seif al-Nasr, who declared that "marriage should not be a prison for women, but a blessing" (Abdel Hamid 2000, 10). The Grand Imam of Al-Azhar, Shaykh Mohammed Sayed El-Tantawi, was also present; he reminded the Assembly that the bill had been thoroughly examined by the Academy for Islamic Research and that it had been approved by thirty-five of the Academy's forty members (Atiya 2000). Despite these efforts to publicly demonstrate the 'ulama's support of the bill, opposition to the legislation was intense and came from a wide array of legislators. While the controlling National Democratic Party was supposed to support the legislation, most members of the party still fought it in the People's Assembly. This legislation, according to one source, represented only the second time that the NDP seriously opposed government policy, but in the end, party discipline won the day and the bill passed by a majority. A newspaper that presents the Islamist perspective complained that "only a few members were allowed to criticize the law while the majority had to stick to the government's position while voting" (Khalil 2002). At one point, the Wafd Party, objecting to the NDP's attempt to limit and cut off debate and force a vote, walked out of the parliament. Since it has been increasingly aligned with Islamists, the Wafd stated it would not take part in this "crime against Egyptian society," arguing that the legislation was contrary to *shari'a*, and that it would only help rich women who could afford to give up their financial claims in a divorce (al-Abd 2000). The leader of the Wafd party, Isma'il Serag El-Din, accused the government of lying about how many members of the Academy of Islamic Research in Al-Azhar had approved the draft legislation (the government said thirty-five out of forty had; he suggested it was only twenty-three and thus not a majority) and accused the government of following improper procedures when the upper house of parliament, the Shura Council, vetted the legislation (al-Abd 2000). One column in the Wafd Party's newspaper argued that "it is strange that the government ignored the *'ulama* and the legislators and left the task of reform to a female Egyptian lawyer," clearly a negative reference to Mona Zulficar (al-Hayawaan 2000). In general, and along with other legislators opposing the bill, the Wafd objected to the haste with which the government guided the bill through parliament. (This is a typical ruse of the government to avoid public contestation and the limited maneuverability that the small opposition forces have at their disposal.) One member of parliament accused the Minister of Justice of implementing the law, interfering in the domain of the parliament, but of course the Minister of Justice denied the charge (Fikry 2002). The Nasserists and the Left were silent in parliament, though they ultimately supported the bill. One impassioned newspaper columnist criticized the parliament for its double standards—despite their demands to impose the *shari'a* and give religious authorities more political power, these same MPs attacked this legislation even though it had been vetted by the Shaykh al-Azhar and the Academy for Islamic Research. He suggested, "I fear that some of those opposed to *khul'* are the ones who walked the ways of corruption and escaped with what they had earned illegally [*haram*] and are therefore afraid that their wives would take it and go" (Hammouda 2000).

The nature of the debate was quite misogynist in tone, revealing the fear, if not terror, that many men associate with women's rights. Constant references to the fickle, impressionable, emotional nature of women, and women as betrayers (*kha'iina*) were made, which derided their ability to make as important a decision as filing for divorce, according to Hoda Zakaria's analysis of the legislative sessions. For example, even Dr. Aisha

Rateb, the former Minister of Insurance and Social Affairs and one of the few women to reach Cabinet rank in the government, questioned the legislation, stating, "Some might say that this gives women from a certain class the right to change their husbands the same way they change their dresses. We have to make sure that this is going to benefit a lot of middle class women, and even the lower class" (Abdel Kader 2000, 3). In addition, legislators were alarmed by a provision in the bill to allow women to travel abroad without the approval of a male guardian. Resistance to this clause was so intense that it was ultimately sacrificed for the sake of compromise and the bill's passage. One member of parliament from Upper Egypt, a traditionally more conservative part of Egypt, said that male and female equality was like ignoring the differences between a turkey and a chicken. Ali Nasr, a member of parliament from Beni Suef in Upper Egypt, objected to the draft law, asserting the supremacy of men over women and citing an example from the animal world: "A rooster can have 40 hens and a lion marries more than four wives, but it has never happened that a hen married two roosters" (Tadros 2000b). Saad Eddin Ibrahim suggested that "the fears of the Sheikhs [and parliamentarians] is nothing but classical authoritarian Masculine fear from the partial equality that is advocated by the new law" (2000). Fayda Kamel was one of few women parliamentarians who spoke up on behalf of women. She reminded her male colleagues about the vital roles that women played at the birth of Islam, when they served in battle, yet their position had deteriorated since then and change was needed.

Fathi Surour used the derisive descriptions of women as an excuse to halt debate on the bill, arguing that parliament should not be in the business of "punishing" women. Closing off debate certainly enhanced the bill's chances to survive a vote. As another concession to mollify the bill's critics, a clause was written into the procedural law that mandated a two-month period to reconcile the couple with the aid of court-appointed social workers and family representatives. If the couple had children, mediation would be mandated for a four-month period. While divorce would not be immediate, Law No. 1 did not allow any appeal for *khul'* divorce.

Clearly, the most vociferous attacks still came from diverse groups inside and outside the religious establishment, despite the long history of Al-Azhar's involvement with this project and coalition. Members of parliament looked to their allies among the *'ulama* to sanction their critiques and tried unsuccessfully to send back the legislation to the Academy of Islamic Research, an official body within Al-Azhar University, for further study. Although information about some of the details is contradictory in the press, the publication of a "Manifesto" by "High Ranking *'Ulama* from Al-Azhar" laid out a complex rationale to reject the draft law. It was published as a letter to President Mubarak and suggested that the government was rushing through the legislation; it claimed that *"khul'* is not supported by evidence from God's book, from the *sunna* or from the Islamic schools of law"; it argued that the irrevocable nature of *khul'* divorce and the lack of appeal was contrary to *shari'a;* that the law canceled the husband's will and ignored his "guardianship" over women; and that *khul'* necessitated the husband's consent and could not be a unilateral act by the wife. Finally, the "Manifesto" linked the current Personal Status Laws to the colonial era, suggesting that this reform was similar to earlier Western manipulation of *shari'a* law, even if it was done in the name of religion (*Al-Usbu'a* 2000). One of the scholars who signed the plea, Yehya Halboush, argued that the Shaykh of Al-Azhar did not adequately discuss the law with Islamic scholars, "especially when many of the forty members of the Academy [for Islamic Research] are not *shari'a* experts" (Tadros 2000b). The authors of this Manifesto have a long history of critiquing both the government's commitment to Islam and leaders among the religious establishment who have close ties to the government and are not as radical as they are (see El-Nahhas 2002; Moustafa 2000, 16; and Zeghal 1999).

There are clearly multiple claimants for religious authority in Egypt, though they do battle with vastly different war chests, supporters, and alliances. As Zaman notes, "[A]mbiguities about the place of Islam in the polity have . . . contributed to strengthening the *'ulama'*s public roles" even though both the state and the *'ulama* "regularly fail to live up to the logic of their own premises" (Zaman 2002, 151; and in this volume). The PSL coalition and its project of reinterpretation of the Islamic canon is a new claimant to religious authority, but this approach can only work hand-in-hand with more traditional authorities while treading very carefully. There are others in the women's movement who are still very skeptical of this approach, fearing it will only give more power to religious authorities. As Nadia Wassef, an Egyptian women's activist and anthropologist argued, "You can play their game, but you'll never win, because it's their game" (Gauch 1998 as quoted in Pavalko 2002).

Civil Islam in the Public Interest?

A final and more general consequence of the coalition's activity was that women activists and some NGOs began to take parliament, legal activism, and rightful resistance more seriously. While many women's organizations and activists felt that this law did not go nearly far enough and worried that the women's movement had wasted precious political capital on so marginal a return, other organizations realized the potential of engaging the parliament and sympathetic legislators. Iman Bibars, director of the Association for the Development and Enhancement of Women (ADEWS), praised Mona Zulficar's efforts to direct organizations, like her own, to lobby some legislators who were sitting on the fence. Their efforts had an effect as, eventually, more legislators supported the law, perhaps as a result of pressure from the NDP or due to these modest lobbying efforts. Iman Bibars emphasized that the experience in lobbying for Law No. 1 in 2000 was a model for successive legislative initiatives, particularly in support of the Citizenship Law that would give Egyptian citizenship to the children of Egyptian women married to foreign men. In this other struggle, which is currently winding its way in a positive fashion through the government and parliamentary arenas, ADEWS and other NGOs orchestrated a full-scale lobbying effort, sending literature, films, and constituent letters to members of parliament. They also began organizing constituents to lobby their parliamentary representatives directly, which was also a fairly new development. While it would be excessive to read too much into these parliamentary initiatives, since Egypt remains tightly controlled by its executive and its political life is still highly constrained, they remain credible examples of the possibilities for legal activism and coalition politics in Egypt. In other countries of the Islamic world, such as Jordan, it is already possible to perceive a demonstration effect from the Egyptian PSL coalition as other legislative initiatives use Law No. 1 and its provisions for *khul'* as their model (Sonbol 2003).

As in all political coalitions that mobilize a considerable array of interests behind them, this campaign took advantage of a particular time in Egypt's political, social, and demographic history. Here, it is important to recognize the fruits of the Nasserist revolution, which greatly increased public educational opportunities for all, but particularly for women. While female illiteracy rates remain almost twice as high as male illiteracy (50 percent female illiteracy, 29 percent male) younger urban women are drawing much closer to their male counterparts and 45 percent of all university graduates from nine disciplines in 1996–97 were women (Shafey 1999, 11). The push for public education in the 1950s and 1960s, as well as the opportunities for more lucrative international networking and business opportunities after Egypt opened up its economy in the 1970s and 1980s, have produced a generation of highly successful, prominent, middle-class and wealthy female leaders. Many of these women, including activists from the PSL coalition, were invited by the government and its chair, Suzanne Mubarak, to join the National Council of Women, established by Presidential Decree 90, shortly after the passage of Law No. 1 in 2000.

Tehani El-Gebali, one of the lawyers involved in the coalition, notes that 23 percent of all lawyers in Egypt are women, and some of them hold high positions in the government and the judiciary, in corporate law practices, in the media, in human rights organizations, and in civil society. A new generation of female lawyers, concerned with development and women, she argued, want to work on concrete solutions and are available as allies to the women's movement, working from both within government and civil society. As one obvious manifestation of this trend, young lawyers can now volunteer in legal literacy programs sponsored by a range of institutions or help produce pamphlets on legal literacy, such as the one on *khul'* in the "The A, B, [Cs] of Law" series from the Egyptian Center for Women's Rights (Mohsen and Abu al-Komsan 2000; al-Ali 2000, 166). The role of prominent female lawyers in the PSL coalition is critical to the women's movement's growing ability to engage in legal activism through the courts and political activism in the legislature.

While women schooled in Islamic sciences are far less numerous in the coalition and among leading women activists, their knowledge of Islamic law and tradition means that they are nevertheless essential players in the coalition. They provide the expertise to argue about the space within Islam for women's rights and can, more importantly, defend their rationale in front of the well-organized and more traditional conservative religious forces and political groups who use their notion of Islam for quite different ends. Very slowly, women are also entering the ranks of Al-Azhar jurists and have begun to participate in councils such as the Dar al-Ifta' which issues *fatwas*, or religious opinions (Abou Bakr 2002).

The same forces represented in the PSL coalition are now attempting to push the envelope of legal reforms and administrative changes in other ways in Egypt. Another provision of Law No. 1 in 2000 was to consolidate all cases related to divorce and place them in a new Family Court. While the court has yet to be established as of early 2003, activists had suggested that this might be the first court where female judges would be appointed. There were no female judges in Egypt, though they preside over courts in many other Arab and Muslim countries. In January 2003, however, Tehani El-Gebali became the first female judge, appointed not to the Family Court but to the highest court in Egypt, the Supreme Constitutional Court, where her PSL coalition ally Fathi Naguib serves as the Chief Judge (Leila 2003). Their interaction in the coalition was no doubt germane to El-Gebali's appointment, which was warmly welcomed by the government, the women's movement, and international human rights and women's organizations.

Despite this appointment, the courts still remain a somewhat hostile environment for women seeking a *khul'* divorce. Recent studies of the implementation and consequences of Law No. 1 are disquieting, since they describe the sexism and bias of many judges toward women. In some courts, particularly in rural areas, judges have put pressure on women to withdraw their *khul'* cases by suggesting that they will have to give their husbands the deferred dower, return their *shabka,* generally increasing their financial losses beyond the intention of the law (Soliman and Saleh el-Diin 2002).

Social movement theorists underscore the importance of the link between identity and activism (Melucci 1995). They note that submerged networks of people from different communities can utilize "weak ties" to build a new sense of identity as well as their own capabilities to enact change. It is always easier to build movements among people who know each other as long as they bring their communities and networks into the mix. Knowing someone engaged in activism is the clearest route to involvement (see McAdam 1988; McAdam and Paulsen 1997; and Melucci 1995). At the same time, activists' commitments are reinforced by their own sense of self, and in the case of the PSL coalition, it is largely the professional commitments of activists that motivate them. In other words, there is a strong link between their professional identity and their role as activists. They are only doing what they have been trained to do: moving into higher and higher ranks of law, development, the academy, and parliament, for example. This coalition thrived on these weak ties, reinforced by the commitments of the scholars to public education, by the historians' motivation to set the historical record straight, by the philosophers' need to reaffirm the equity and equality of Islam, and by the lawyers' commitment to the rule of law and its transformative potential. Islamist politicians use the slogan "*Islam, huwwa haal*" (Islam is the solution) for their political agenda in elections, and the PSL coalition seems to have been inspired by it, as they used Islam as a solution to their problems. The lessons of politics that direct activists to seize new opportunities and imagine a different order can be drawn from anywhere, but within the Islamic world, Egypt and the PSL coalition may serve as a successful model, whose modest aims and innovative legitimating strategy to improve the power and position of women finally prevailed.

NOTES

This research is based on fieldwork in Egypt that included elite interviews and the collection of primary and secondary source materials in English and Arabic during October 2002. I am greatly indebted to the following people for their candid and insightful analysis: Dr. Fawziyya Abdel-Sattar, Nehad Abu al-Komsan, Dr. Iman Bibars, Tehani El-Gebali, Heba Raouf Ezzat, Mohammed Hakim, Dr. Mona Makram-Ebeid, Dr. Mustapha Kamel al-Sayed, Dr. Maye Kassem, Dr. Zainab Redwan, Dr. Hoda El Sada, Atef Shahat Sayed, Husn Shah, Azza Soliman, Dr. Hoda Zakariyya, and Mona Zulficar. In addition, I am deeply appreciative of the research assistance of Dina Bishara from the American University in Cairo, Seda Demiralp and Nida al-Ahmad at American University in Washington, D.C., and

Shimaa' Hatab from Cairo University, as well as to Leila al-Atraqchi for generously sharing information with me. Finally, I would like to acknowledge my collaboration with Dr. Barbara Ibrahim and support of MEAwards from the Population Council in Cairo for a related project on the costs of marriage in Egypt and the support and comments of Robert Hefner and other participants in the "Civic Pluralist Islam: Prospects and Policies for a Changing Muslim World" project, funded by the Pew Charitable Trusts.

1. Typically, a divorced woman is entitled to whatever property she brought into the marriage as well as the *mu'akhar saddaq,* or the deferred part of the dower that is stipulated as a payment to the wife in the advent of divorce or death of the husband (Welchman 2000, 247).
2. According to the 1979 Personal Status Law reforms, orchestrated through a coalition of women and the leadership of Jihan Sadat, a wife would have the automatic right to divorce when her husband informed her of his intent to marry a second woman. However, Law No. 100 in 1985 forced a wife to prove "harm" before a court from the second marriage in order to gain a divorce (Al-Atraqchi 2002).
3. Interview with Atef Shahat Sayed, American University in Cairo, October 2002.
4. The national cost of marriage in Egypt, according to a 1999 survey, equals four and a half times per capita GNP (gross national product) or $5,957 (Singerman and Ibrahim 2001, 92).
5. The Shaykh al-Azhar, Gad al-Haqq, had by this time grown more critical of the President's policies and the Egyptian government's position at the United Nations' International Conference on Population and Development. He had allied himself with some of the more activist radical *'ulama* and against the Mufti, Shaykh El-Tantawi, whose *fatwas* legitimated controversial government policies. The former Mufti is now the Shaykh al-Azhar himself, which has ushered in warmer relations between the government and Al-Azhar, thereby setting the ground for the passage of Law No. 1 in 2000 (Zeghal 1999, 388; Moustafa 2000, 13).

References Cited

al-Abd, Sharif. 2000. "Munāqashāt fii Jalsa Maglis al-Sha'b" (Conversation in the parliamentary session). *Al-Ahram,* January 26.

Abdel Hamid, Mohammed. 2000. "Preliminary Approval for Personal Status Draft." *Cairo Times,* January 20–26: 3.

Abdel Kader, Sayed. 2000. "Qānūn al-Ahwaal al-Shakhsiya al-Jādūd Bayn al-Mar'at wal-Rajul" (The new personal status law between women and men). *Akbar Al-Yom,* January 17, 3.

Abou Bakr, Omaima. 2002. "Gender and Islamic Texts." Paper presented at the Annual Meeting of Middle East Studies Association, Washington D.C., November 25.

Abou El Fadl, Khaled. 2001. *Speaking in God's Name.* Oxford: OneWorld Publications.

Abu-Odeh, Lama. n.d. "Egyptian Feminism: Trapped in the Identity Debate." Manuscript.

———. 2002. "Legislating the Family in the Arab World." Paper presented at the Annual Meeting of Middle East Studies Association, Washington D.C., November 24.

Afifi, Mohamad. 1996. "Reflections on the Personal Laws of Egyptian Copts." In *Women, the Family, and Divorce Laws in Islamic History,* edited by Amira El Azhary Sonbol, pp. 202–18. Syracuse, N.Y.: Syracuse University Press.

Ali, Kecia. 2003. "Progressive Muslims and Islamic Jurisprudence: The Necessity for Critical Engagement with Marriage and Divorce Law." In *Progressive Muslims: On Justice, Gender, and Pluralism,* edited by Omid Safi, pp. 163–89. Oxford: OneWorld Publications.

al-Ali, Nadje. 2000. *Secularism, Gender, and the State in the Middle East: The Egyptian Women's Movement.* Cambridge: Cambridge University Press.

Al-Atraqchi, Leila. 2002. "The Women's Movement and the Mobilization for Legal Change in Egypt: A Century of Personal Status Law Reform." Ph.D. dissertation. Department of Humanities. Concordia University, Montreal, October.

Allam, Abeer. 2000. "Urfi Delivers the Goods, at Half Price." *Middle East Times,* February 18.

Atiya, Ahmed. 2000. "Arba'īn Min 'Ulama' Al-Azhar Yu'akidūnn al-Khul' Qunbila Mawqūta Tuhadid Binhiyar al-Buyūt" (Forty Al-Azhar scholars confirm: *Khul'* is a time bomb, which threatens the destruction of homes). *Ahrar,* January 28.

Awde, Nicholas, ed. 2000. *Women in Islam: An Anthology from the Quran and Hadiths.* New York: St. Martin's Press.

Badran, Margot. 1995. *Feminists, Islam, and Nation: Gender and the Making of Modern Egypt.* Princeton, N.J.: Princeton University Press.

Bond, George C., and Angela Giliam, eds. 1994. "Introduction." In *Social Construction of the Past,* edited by George C. Bond and Angela Giliam, pp. 1–22. New York: Routledge.

Brown, Nathan J. 1997. *The Rule of Law in the Arab World: Courts in Egypt and the Gulf.* Cambridge: Cambridge University Press.

———. 1996. *Women and Law in the Arab World.* Unpublished paper (http://www.geocities.com/nathanbrown1/WomenLaw.htm) (visited May 1, 2003).

Carroll, Lucy, and Harsh Kapoor. 1996. "Talaq-i-Tafwid: The Muslim Woman's Contractual Access to Divorce. An Information Kit." Women Living under Muslim Laws, London.

Cooke, Miriam. 2001. *Women Claim Islam: Creating Islamic Feminism through Literature.* New York: Routledge.

Costain, Anne, and Douglas Costain. 1983. "The Women's Lobby: Impact of a Movement on Congress." In *Interest Group Politics,* edited by Allan Cigler and Burdett, pp. 191–217. Washington D.C.: Congressional Quarterly Press.

Elbendary, Amina. 2000a. "A Voice of Their Own." *Al-Ahram Weekly,* October 19–25 (http://www.ahram.org.eg/weekly/2000/504/el2.htm) (visited December 3, 2001).

———. 2000b. "The Meaning of Success." *Al-Ahram Weekly,* November 23–29 (http://www.ahram.org.eg/weekly/2000/509/eg4.htm) (visited December 3, 2001).

Ezzat, Dina. 2000. "Sacred Knots and Unholy Deals: The Road towards Pro-Women Legal Reform in Egypt." In *No Paradise Yet,* edited by Judith Mirsky and Marty Radlett, pp. 39–60. London: Panos/Zed Press.

Fikry, Zakariyah. 2002. "'Udwa Bi Majlis al-Sha'b Yatahim Wizārat al-'Adl Bi Tabakh Qānūn al-Khul' wal-Wizara Tatabara'" (A member of Parliament accuses the Minister of Justice of Passing the *Khul'* Law: The Minister declares his innocence). *Al-Wafd,* April 23.

Foucault, Michel. 1980. "Two Lectures." In *Power/Knowledge: Selected Interviews and Other Writings, 1972–1977,* edited Colin Gordon, pp. 78–108. New York: Pantheon Books.

Gauch, Sarah. 1998. "New Views of Islamic Law Elevate Women: Cairo." In "Where Women Stand (Part 5): Around the World, Women Find Very Different Roads to Wider Rights," by Linda Feldmann, *Christian Science Monitor,* July 22, 1–9.

Haeri, Shahla. 1990. "Divorce in Contemporary Iran: A Male Prerogative in Self-Will." In *Islamic Family Law,* edited by Chibli Mallat and Jane Connors, pp. 55–69. London: Graham & Trotman.

Hammond, Andrew. 2000. "Personal Status Law Not a Personal Choice." *Middle East Times,* January 21 (http://metimes.com/2K/issue2000-3/eg/personal_status_law.htm) (visited November 18, 2002).

Hammouda, Adel. 2000. "Al-Khul' Qānūn Li Tahrir al-Rajul Aydhan" [*Khul'* is a law for the emancipation of the men too]. *Al-Ahram,* January 8.

Hanna, Nelly. 1995. "Marriage and Family in Seventeenth-Century Cairo." In *Histoire Economique et Sociale de l'Empire Ottoman et de la Turquie (1326–1960): Actes du Sixieme Congres International tenu a Aix-en-Provence du 1er au 4 Juillet 1992,* edited by Daniel Panczac, pp. 349–58. Paris: Peeters.

al-Hayawaan, Muhammad. 2000. "Kalimat Hub" (A word of love). *Al-Wafd,* January 24.

Hefner, Robert. 2000. *Civil Islam: Muslims and Democratization in Indonesia.* Princeton, N.J.: Princeton University Press.

Ibrahim, Saad Eddin. 2000. "The Masculine Mentality and the Personal Status Law." *Civil Society: Democratization in the Arab World* 9 (February).

Khalil, Ashraf. 2000. "Majlis al-Sha'b Yabsum 'Ala Ta'dīlat al-Hukūma Lil Qānūn Mutajāhilan Tahdhīrat Mukhālafatahuw Lil Shari'a Wa 'Adham Dustūriyatahu" (The People's Assembly rubber-stamps the government's revisions to the law, ignoring warnings of its violation of Shari'a and its unconstitutionality]. *Al-Shaab,* January 14.

Kienle, Eberhard. 2001. *A Grand Delusion: Democracy and Economic Reform in Egypt.* London: I. B. Taurus.

Leila, Reem. 2000. "The Terms of Engagement." *Al-Ahram Weekly* 484, June 1–7.

———. 2003. "A Family Affair." *Al-Ahram Weekly* 621, January 16–22 (http://weekly.ahram.org.eg/print/2003/621/fe1.htm) (visited January 18, 2003).

Lerner, Gerda. 1986. *The Creation of Patriarchy.* New York: Oxford University Press.

Makram-Ebeid, Mona. 2001. "Egypt's 2000 Parliamentary Elections." *Middle East Policy,* June, 41.

McAdam, Doug. 1988. *Freedom Summer.* New York: Oxford University Press.

McAdam, Doug, and Ronnelle Paulsen. 1997. "Specifying the Relationship between Social Ties and Activism." In *Social Movements: Readings on Their Emergence, Mobilization, and Dynamics,* edited by Doug McAdam and David A. Snow, pp. 145–58. Los Angeles: Roxbury Publishing.

McCarthy, John, and Mayer Zald. 1977. "Resource Mobilization and Social Movements." *American Journal of Sociology* 82:1212–41.

Melucci, Alberto. 1995. "The Process of Collective Identity." In *Social Movements and Culture,* edited by Hank Johnston and Bert Klandermans, pp. 41–63. Minneapolis: University of Minnesota Press.

Mir-Hosseini, Ziba. 1993. *Marriage on Trial: A Study of Islamic Family Law. Iran and Morocco Compared.* London: I. B. Tauris.

———. 1999. *Islam and Gender: The Religious Debate in Contemporary Iran.* Princeton, N.J.: Princeton University Press.

Mohsen, Ahmed, and Nehad Abu al-Komsan. 2000. *Al-Khul' Wa Ahkām Ukhrā (Khul'* and other rulings). Egyptian Center for Women's Rights A B Law Series. Cairo: Egyptian Center for Women's Rights.

Moors, Annelies. 1995. *Women, Property, and Islam: Palestinian Experiences, 1920–1990.* Cambridge University Press.

———. 2003 (forthcoming). "Public Debates on Family Law Reform: Participants, Positions, and Styles of Argumentation in the 1990s." *Journal of Islamic Law and Culture.*

Moustafa, Tamir. 2000. "Conflict and Cooperation between the State and Religious Institutions in Egypt." *International Journal of Middle East Studies* 32:3–22.

Mueller, Carol. 1997. "Conflict Networks and the Origins of Women's Liberation." In *Social Movements: Readings on Their Emergence, Mobilization, and Dynamics,* edited by Doug McAdam and David A. Snow, pp. 158–71. Los Angeles: Roxbury Publishing.

El-Nahhas, Mona. 2002. "Defying Al-Azhar." *Al-Ahram Weekly,* August 29–September 4 (http://www.ahram.org.eg/weekly/2002/601/eg3.htm) (visited September 5, 2002).

O'Brien, Kevin J. 1996. "Rightful Resistance." *World Politics* 49:31–55.

O'Connor, Karen. 1980. *Women's Organizations' Use of the Courts.* Washington, D.C.: D.C. Heath and Company.

Pavalko, Rima. 2002. "Within Borders: Transnationalism and Women's Rights in the Middle East." Paper presented at the Annual Meeting of Middle East Studies Association, Washington D.C., November 24.

Redwan, Zainib. 2000. "The Islamic Treatment of Problems in Marital Life." In *Personal Status in Egypt: A Study of the Legal and Social Dimension of the Procedures of Personal Status Law,* edited by Leila Abdel Gouad and Muhammed Hakim, pp. 111–14. Cairo: National Center For Sociological and Criminological Studies.

Safi, Omid, ed. 2003. *Progressive Muslims: On Justice, Gender, and Pluralism.* Oxford: OneWorld Publications.

Sakr, Hala, and Mohamed Hakim. 2001. "One Law for All." *Al-Ahram Weekly* 523, March 1–7 (http://www.ahram.org.eg/weekly/2001/523/sc1k.htm) (visited January 5, 2003).

Shafey, Halla, ed. 1999. "Gender and Development 2—Gender Statistics." Vol. 2.
    In *Gender and Development: An Information Kit for Egypt,* 5 vols. Cairo:
    DAG Sub-Group for Gender and Development.
Shah, Hosn. 2000. "Sī Al Sayed Ya'tarid Alā Al-Qānūn Al-Jadīd" ('Si El Sayed'
    . . . Objects to the new law!). *Akhbar Al-Yom,* January 9.
Shahine, Gihan. 1998. "The Double Bind." *Al-Ahram Weekly* 397, October 1–7.
Singerman, Diane, and Barbara Ibrahim. 2001. "The Costs of Marriage in Egypt:
    A Hidden Dimension in the New Arab Demography." In "The New Arab Fam-
    ily," edited by Nicholas Hopkins, *Cairo Papers in the Social Sciences,* (Spring/
    Summer): 80–117. Cairo: American University in Cairo Press.
Soliman, Azza, and Azza Saleh el-Diin. 2002. "Critical View from the Inside of
    the Law on *Khul'.*" Paper presented at the conference "Reaping What You
    Sow: Two Years after *Khul',* " Center For Egyptian Women's Legal Assistance,
    Cairo, October 22.
Sonbol, Amira El Azhary. 1995. "Modernity, Standardization, and Marriage
    Contracts in Nineteenth-Century Egypt." In *Histoire Economique et Sociale de
    l'Empire Ottoman et de la Turquie (1326–1960): Actes du Sixieme Congres In-
    ternational tenu a Aix-en-Provence du 1er au 4 Juillet 1992,* edited by Daniel
    Panczac, pp. 485–96. Paris: Peeters.
———. 2003. *Women of Jordan: Islam, Labor, and the Law.* Syracuse: Syracuse
    University Press.
———, ed. 1996. *Women, the Family, and Divorce Laws in Islamic History.*
    Syracuse, N.Y.: Syracuse University Press.
Tadros, Mariz. 2000a. "One Step Forward, a Hundred to Go." *Al-Ahram
    Weekly* 464, January 13–19 (www.ahram.org.eg/weekly/2000/464/spec1.htm)
    (visited December 3, 2001).
———. 2000b. "Roosters' Wrath." *Al-Ahram Weekly* 465, January 20–26
    (www.weekly.ahram.org.eg/2000/465/eg4.htm) (visited January 5, 2003).
Tarrow, Sidney. 1994. *Power in Movement: Social Movements, Collective Action,
    and Politics.* New York: Cambridge University Press.
Al-Usbu'a (Egypt). 2003. "A Manifesto by High Ranking 'Ulama from Al-Azhar:
    The Law Does Not Comply with Sharia and We Ask President Mubarak to
    Postpone Its Issuing." January 17.
Welchman, Lynn. 2000. *Beyond the Code: Muslim Family Law and the Shari'a
    Judiciary in the Palestinian West Bank.* The Hague: Kluwer Law International.
Zakaria, Hoda. 2002. "*Khul':* Its Legal and Social Dimensions." Paper presented
    at the conference "Reaping What You Sow: Two Years after *Khul',* " Center
    For Egyptian Women's Legal Assistance, Cairo, October 22.
Zaman, Muhammad Qasim. 2002. *The Ulama in Contemporary Islam: Custodi-
    ans of Change.* Princeton, N.J.: Princeton University Press.
Zeghal, Malika. 1999. "Religion and Politics in Egypt: Al-Azhar, Radical Islam,
    and the State." *International Journal of Middle East Studies* 31:371–99.
Zilfi, Madeline C. 1997. "We Don't Get Along: Women and Hul Divorce in the
    Eighteenth Century." In *Women in the Ottoman Empire: Middle Eastern
    Women in the Early Modern Era,* edited by Madeline Zilfi, pp. 264–96. Lei-
    den: Brill.

Zulficar, Mona. 1999. "The Islamic Marriage Contract in Egypt." Paper pre-
    sented at the International Conference on the Islamic Marriage Contract, Har-
    vard Law School: Islamic Legal Studies Program, Cambridge, January 29–31.
Zulficar, Mona, and Hoda El-Sadda. 1996. "Hawl Mashru' Tatawiir Namuzhij
    Aqd al-Jawaz" (About the project to develop models of marriage contracts).
    Hagar: On Women's Issues 3–4:251–59.

Chapter 8

EMPOWERING CIVILITY THROUGH NATIONALISM:

REFORMIST ISLAM AND BELONGING

IN SAUDI ARABIA

GWENN OKRUHLIK

A MOMENT OF OPPORTUNITY: FINDING CIVILITY IN CRISIS

The politics of Islam and reform in Saudi Arabia generate enormous interest. Though its internal landscape is rich with nuance, one would think otherwise when viewed through the lens of the mainstream narrative within the United States in the aftermath of September 11, 2001. This narrative has not always been helpful because much of it merely skims along the surface of Saudi Arabia's political waters, which is a mistake. Internal contests are not simply about a choice between revolutionary theocracy and royal absolutism. Political struggles are more complex than that, reflecting a large and diverse population. My purpose here is to look more deeply at the internal context of Saudi Arabian politics to better understand the roots and repercussions of Islamist dissent there.

It is a time of serious ferment in Saudi Arabia. This has been a turbulent year of petitions presented to the Crown Prince, shootouts throughout the country, protests in the streets of Riyadh, a new dialogue of tolerance among people who usually do not even acknowledge one another, massive arrests, and the discovery of arsenals of weapons in every nook and cranny of the country. Political, economic, and social problems in the country have provided a fertile field for dissent; it can no longer be "managed" from above. If problems are addressed in a meaningful manner, the attraction of the radical flank of Islamists is likely to diminish in the presence of credible alternatives. If serious structural reforms are not implemented, the call from the most radical flank will almost certainly find an audience among the population. This is a defining moment, and the task is not an easy one. It is incumbent upon the al-Saud to accept political expression that is critical and vibrant in order to provide an alternative to the militants. In this time of ferment, political space and voice must be given to social forces that are reformist in nature.

Many Saudi Arabians hope that the tragedy of September 11 accelerates meaningful and difficult domestic reforms. The country faces formidable challenges, all of which have been further complicated by the war in Iraq. Internally, the country must implement serious reforms in politics, economics, and social relations, reforms that have been studiously avoided for two decades. Grievances include authoritarianism, maldistribution, and exclusion. Externally, Saudi Arabia also faces challenges from the United States and United Kingdom for allegedly funding terrorism, from global capital interests to throw open its economy, and from transnational groups that seek to promote human rights.

More than anything, the attacks on the World Trade Center and the Pentagon prompted a period of intense and critical self-scrutiny in the kingdom, with Saudi Arabians confronting the harsh reality that many of the hijackers came from within their own borders. As ordinary Saudis and prominent spokespeople alike turn their attentions inward, this is an opportunity to redefine the contours of what it means to be a good Muslim in Saudi Arabia. This is a "moment" for believers in civil, tolerant Islam to assert their positions in national debates. It is, after all, the Islam of millions of Saudis.

PROMOTING REFORM WITHOUT BACKLASH

Contentious social and political voices resonate in Saudi Arabia because the exclusionary structure of governance does not reflect the reality of a diverse population. From above, the sprawling religious and political bureaucracies do not represent the heterogeneity of ordinary Saudis, but the hegemony of an empowered minority. From below, there is precious little room for social forces to organize, debate, or contest the state. In between, the old social contracts that implicitly linked ruling family to citizenry are now deemed irrelevant. All of this is further complicated by demographic, economic, and social problems. For two decades, there has not existed a safe political space for civil Islam to assert itself or selves.

Crown Prince Abdullah, the de facto ruler of the country, must contain the radical religious right as he simultaneously institutes reform. This is key. He must move quickly enough to satisfy the many disgruntled elements in the country, yet with enough sensitivity to prevent a far-right backlash and thereby enhance the power of the religious extremists. This is no easy task given that the al-Saud historically based their right to rule largely on Islamic legitimacy. Indeed, the al-Saud walk a fine line: pushing the religious right too far may destabilize the regime, but not pushing at all will surely do so.[1] Even a hereditary monarch must respond to the contests among different domestic constituencies that seek to influence national policy. But Abdullah also has competitors within the ruling family who seek to stave off reform, cater to the religious right, and contain his power.

The social carriers and the cultural resources that could promote civil Islam permeate the country. The problem is that civil Islam is not politically empowered. The carriers must be politically and institutionally empowered. A fruitful way to do this is to thoroughly integrate civil Islam into the debate over "who we are" so that civility is part of the newly emerging, but still embryonic, national identity that is taking shape. I address this opportunity for "scaling up and across" in the conclusion to this chapter. First, however, I explain the relationship between religion and state, and how a very narrow practice of Islam became empowered in the first place. Political debates must be understood within their fuller context.

THE MYTH OF HOMOGENEITY

The central developmental challenge in Saudi Arabia is that the exclusionary structure of governance does not incorporate the diversity of the population. Contrary to popular images, Saudi Arabia is not a homogeneous country in religion, ethnicity, or class. Saudis are not all tribal, Najdi, rich, male, and "Wahhabi."[2]

Religious Practice

The vast majority of the Saudi population is Sunni Muslim. But the plurality of Sunni religious practice, while long denied, is rich, including mainstream Hanbali, Wahhabi orthodoxy, Maliki, Hanafi, and Shafi'i. There are Sufi communities throughout the Hejaz. The largest Shi'a community is in the Eastern Province, but there are other Shi'a communities in Mecca and Medina. The southern region of Najran is overwhelmingly Ismaili. The challenge is not, as many Westerners believe, to promote tolerance for Christianity in Saudi Arabia. The first challenge is to promote tolerance for non-Wahhabi Muslims in Saudi Arabia. The problem is that only Wahhabis have been rewarded with institutional and bureaucratic positions of authority. This very narrow, and often intolerant, practice of Islam dominates the public discourse even as private practice is diverse. Islam will continue to be a part of private and public life in Saudi Arabia. The key to reform is an emphasis on a more tolerant, plural Islam. Wahhabi doctrine will continue to be important among parts of the population, but if alternative political space grows, Wahhabism may return to private socioreligious expression rather than the explicitly political manifestations of recent years.

Ethnicity

Despite increasing internal mobility, the different regions of Saudi Arabia
are still characterized by ethnic distinctions among local populations.
The population and economy of the Eastern Province have for centuries
been related to merchant activities, and later to the oil industry, as families from Iran, Bahrain, and India migrated to the east with work. Con-
comitant with this, Shi'i religious affiliation is prominent in the east,
unlike in the rest of the Sunni affiliated country. In the west, the Hejaz is
noted for a multiplicity of ethnic identities for two reasons: a long history
as the center of commerce and as the site of the annual religious pilgrimage, the *hajj*. Families that came to the region to perform religious rituals
stayed over and established thriving businesses. Some of the most prominent Hejazi families are from Persia, Indonesia, India, or other Arab
states. In addition, there is a notable and fairly cohesive Hadrami community in the Hejaz, originally derived from the Hadramawt region of
Yemen. In the southwest of the country, the Asir region shares more in
common culturally, ethnically, geographically, and architecturally with
the neighboring state of Yemen than with others parts of Saudi Arabia.
Finally, the central region, the Najd, is home to many indigenous tribes.
It was less common for foreign families to settle in the heartland than in
the coastal regions and as such, the Najd remained insulated from migration flows for a longer period of time. This rich ethnic diversity is per-
meated as well by distinctions and barriers between people of tribal and
nontribal lineage. Of course, approximately one-third of Saudi Arabia's
total population is foreign labor, made up of people from diverse ethnic
and national backgrounds.

Class

There are also new class distinctions among the Saudi population. Historically, class lines were clearly demarcated—between citizen and foreigner. The underclass was composed of the millions of foreign laborers
imported to staff the oil-driven economy. Today, however, there is poverty
among Saudi citizens. Crown Prince Abdullah's now famous walk through
impoverished slums of Riyadh in November 2002 was the first public ac-
knowledgment of the breadth of the problem. This poverty is coupled
with significant cuts in state subsidies for many basic goods, subsidies
upon which Saudis rely. Unemployment is high and sustained.

This complex diversity of people must be incorporated into governance.
This means that men and women, rural and urban, rich and poor, bureaucrats and shop owners, Shi'a and Sunni (of all practices), and people
from all the regions of the country must be represented in government, in

the economy, and in the sprawling religious bureaucracy. The regime in Saudi Arabia must respond to multiple domestic constituencies—Islamists, women, the unemployed, intellectuals, nationalists, and business people, many of whom have competing interests. How did such a richly diverse country come to empower a very narrow strand of religion?

CONTEXTUALIZING ISLAM: POWER, RELIGION, AND STATE

The foundation on which contemporary political contests rest did not form suddenly. The al-Saud base their contemporary claim to legitimacy on the success of military conquests in the 1920s and 1930s and on their alliance with religious authorities. They rule in an uneasy symbiosis with the clergy. This relationship dates back to the 1744 "alliance" between Muhammad ibn 'Abd al-Wahhab and Muhammad ibn Saud, a sort of merger of religious legitimacy and military might that has been lionized in the country's civic mythology. The descendants of al-Wahhab, now known as the al-Shaykh family, still dominate the official religious institutions of the state. But Islam remains a double-edged sword for the al-Saud. It grants them legitimacy as protectors of the faith, yet it constrains their behavior to that which is compatible with religious law. When members of the family deviate from that straight path, they are open to criticism, since the regime's "right to rule" rests largely on the alliance with the al-Wahhab family.

Today, the "alliance" between the regime and official clergy is much contested by dissidents because the parties no longer serve as "checks" on each other. The official clergy are said to be dependent upon the al-Saud for their existence. They regularly issue *fatwas* (religious judicial opinions) that justify the policies of the al-Saud in Islamic vocabulary, even when such policies are deplored by the people. Although the ruling family still needs the legitimation conferred by the clergy, the clergy have become subservient and bureaucratized in the last twenty-five years.

Resentment of abuse of state authority has long simmered just beneath the surface in Saudi Arabia, but the regime has historically been denounced only in private conversation, with criticism rarely erupting into public confrontation. But two important historic moments of opposition provide striking parallels with today's Islamist opposition movement: the 1929 Ikhwan rebellion and the 1979 seizure of the great mosque in Mecca. In both instances, the Islamic legitimacy of the al-Saud family was seriously challenged by movements that emanated from the heartland of their traditional support, the Najd. This meant that both movements were composed of "Wahhabis," who follow a particularly austere and puritanical belief system.[3] In both uprisings, opposition was justified because the regime deviated from the straight path of the Qur'an and Sunna. Corruption was a common theme, as was dependence on the West.

During the conquests of the peninsula in the early part of the twentieth century, the founder of Saudi Arabia, Abdulaziz, depended on the formidable fighting force of the Ikhwan, tribal *muwahhidun* warriors, to extend the borders of his kingdom. When the strength on which he had depended turned against his leadership, Abdulaziz crushed the Ikhwan as a military force at the Battle of Sabalah in 1930. Nearly fifty years later, in 1979, Juhaiman al-Utaibi and his followers forcibly took control of the sacred mosque in Mecca in an effort to topple the ruling family. He was the grandson of an Ikhwan warrior; his charges against King Fahd of corruption, deviation, and dependence on the West echoed his grandfather's charges against Abdulaziz. Al-Utaibi did not garner much popular support because he chose a holy venue rather than a palace, but the incident exposed the vulnerability of the regime. It took several weeks and the assistance of French special units to root the rebels from the mosque.

RESISTANCE AND THE EMPOWERMENT OF THE RELIGIOUS RIGHT

There are deep historic roots to the empowerment of the religious right, but the contemporary turning point was 1979. The takeover of the Great Mosque was coupled with other tumultuous events. The Islamic Revolution in Iran had just toppled the shah's government and initiated new institutions in the country. The long-oppressed Shi'a minority in the Eastern Province of Saudi Arabia organized open demonstrations (known as the intifada, or uprising) in the streets of several towns. The confluence of these three important developments led to greater surveillance over the populations, more power for the *mutawwa* (a sort of "police" responsible for enforcing public virtue), new constraints on mobility and expression, and simultaneous promises of reform.

The panicked response of the regime produced two decades of political paralysis in the country. The regime responded first by executing the rebels and then by instituting ever-tighter controls over social and political life in the country. Since they had been accused of deviating from Islam, the regime sought to justify itself by allowing the religious right ever more maneuver in Saudi life. Rather than confronting the religious right, King Fahd wrapped himself ever more securely in the mantle of official Islam, changing his title from Your Majesty King Fahd to Custodian of the Two Holy Cities, King Fahd. He sought to bolster the legitimacy of the ruling family by appropriating the power of Islam. Religious educational institutions were funded throughout the country, even during the oil bust of the mid-eighties when other projects were scaled back. There were new restrictions on women's mobility and employment. Women covered more, ventured forth less, and were prohibited from appearing in newspapers or on television. Gender segregation was profound and enforced in public. There were "men" and "family" sections established in restaurants and parks. The black paint that had covered the windows of girls' school buses had been removed in the mid-seventies, but the windows were repainted after 1979. Women were barred from their old jobs in shops and salons. Scholarships for women to study abroad were severely cut back. The *mutawwa* were granted more leeway in their oversight of behavior in the public realm. Tiny shops and fancy malls closed tightly several times a day for prayer. Music could be played only in the privacy of homes. The heavily censored media became a mouthpiece for the government. Always and everywhere, the *mutawwa* were ubiquitous. A narrow and intolerant interpretation of Islam dominated the national discourse. Sulaiman al-Hattlan explained: "Different groups ended up competing with fundamentalists over who can appear more conservative in the public eye." After 1979, only one very particular practice of Islam was empowered. Excluded from public discourse were the many Sufi, mainstream Sunni, and Shi'i populations.

During the 1980s, an expanded Islamic education system fostered a new generation of sheikhs, professors, and students. The regime sought to legitimate itself during hard times by binding religion and state institutionally. Imam Mohamed bin Saud University in Riyadh, the Islamic University in Medina, and Umm Al Qura University in Mecca continued to grow even as other programs were cut back. By 1986, over 16,000 of the kingdom's 100,000 students were pursuing Islamic Studies. By the early 1990s, one-fourth of all university students were enrolled in religious institutions. They had ideas and resources: intellectuals, computers, fax machines, libraries and everything necessary for mobilization. This generation of students serves as bureaucrats, policemen, *mutawwa, shari'ah* (religious law) judges, or preachers in some of the twenty thousand mosques in the country.

An Islamic resurgence swept the country during the 1980s. It was not about politics nor was it directed against the regime. This resurgence was about private belief systems and the comprehensive message of Islam. Several nonviolent, nonpolitical Islamist groups took root during this time. The embrace of Islam that they advocated was about a spiritual awakening. They were not formal organizations but they did inculcate a sense of group identity. What began as small closed circles grew gradually into large loose underground groups. The resurgence was also propagated by the newly returned Arab Afghan *mujahidin* (holy warriors). About twelve thousand young men from Saudi Arabia went to Afghanistan to fight the Soviets; perhaps five thousand were properly trained and saw combat. At the time, no one ever thought the *mujahidin* would fight their own regime; the state had supported them. All of this cultivated a fertile field for political dissent into which Islamism effectively tapped. Empowered during the 1980s, the religious right was further transformed with the Gulf War.

ISLAM AND THE GULF WAR

These developments culminated in the rise of an Islamist opposition movement during the Gulf War (Okruhlik 2003). The 1990s were a difficult decade in Saudi Arabia. Festering anger suddenly exploded with the stationing of U.S. troops in the country. Opposition groups organized domestically and abroad, most under the rubric of Islamism. For decades, there had been sporadic resistance, but with the war it changed to continuous resistance. Individuals emerged as symbols of resistance to the corruption of the al-Saud. The resistance accelerated the debates that were long under way in private. A new generation of clerics voiced strident political opinion in sermons, calling for the removal of U.S. troops and the overthrow of the ruling family. Friday sermons became an occasion for political criticism. Tapes of sermons and underground leaflets were circulated in the streets, schools, and mosques. Opposition to the presence of U.S. military bases reached a fever pitch.

Several prominent preachers were jailed. Salman al-Awdah, an influential leader in Buraydah, was arrested by police for criticism of government policy. He was forbidden to deliver sermons. In Riyadh, a popular preacher, 'Aidh al-Qarni, was detained for criticizing the foreign military presence. Safr al-Hawali, an intellectual from Imam Mohamad bin Saud University, was harassed and eventually jailed for publicly arguing that the al-Saud had deviated from the straight path of the Qur'an and *sunna*. During this turmoil, Islamists charged King Fahd with deviation from the straight path of Islam. He was criticized for his personal behavior, methods of governance, domestic and foreign policies, and, of course, his decision to allow the stationing of American troops. Such criticisms echo the historic predecessors of 1929 and 1979.

Popular *imam*s offered *fatwa*s that effectively countered the *fatwa*s of the official clergy. For example, when the official, state-appointed clergy issued a *fatwa* that justified the presence of U.S. troops in Islamic vocabulary, the popular clergy responded with *fatwa*s that condemned the presence of U.S. troops, also grounded in Islamic vocabulary and reasoning. The popular opinions often carried more credibility than did the official opinions. The alternative clergy decried waste and imprudence in government expenditures; it highlighted the absence of a capable military despite massive expenditures on weaponry. This charge resonated among the population.

Several petitions were presented to King Fahd that demanded structural reforms in the kingdom. The very dialogue of political intercourse changed. Before the war, criticism could be offered only in private and on a one-to-one verbal basis. Now it was transformed into a public discussion—much of it written, signed, and documented. The most influential petitions were from opposition Sunni clergy. In spring 1991, religious scholars, judges, and university professors issued a petition that in strong and direct language called for a restoration of Islamic values. The petition asked for twelve political reforms, focused on the judiciary, foreign policy, a redistribution of wealth, an end to corruption, and above all, the primacy of religious law.

In September 1992, 107 religious scholars signed a "memorandum of advice (*muzakharat al-nasiha*) to King Fahd. He refused at first to receive the forty-six-page document. It was even bolder and more defiant than the petition drafted the previous year. Its tone was straightforward; its charges, specific. The petitioners deplored the "total chaos in the economy and society . . . widespread bribery, favoritism, and the extreme feebleness of the courts"; criticized virtually every aspect of domestic and foreign policy; and demanded a more rigorous application of Islamic law. The government was shaken because the people thought to be its pillar of support had endorsed such sweeping changes. The ruling family was concerned not only by the petition's content, but also by the very public way in which it was circulated, making the rounds of schools and mosques before the king saw it. Because it abrogated the norm for privacy in political discussion, the Supreme Council of Scholars, the elite of the official clergy, condemned the publication and circulation of the petition (but not its substance).

Pressures for reform were not limited to Sunni Islamists. Representatives of the Shi'a Reform Movement (an umbrella organization of several Shi'a opposition groups that press for the rights of the minority Shi'a community) continued to call for a consultative council that included representatives of their community. The business community submitted a so-called liberal petition that demanded structural reforms. Forty-seven women kicked their foreign male drivers out of their cars and drove through the streets of Riyadh.

FROM WAHHABISM TO NEO-WAHHABISM: THE SOCIORELIGIOUS BECOMES POLITICAL

By 1993, numerous organizations had been formed to disseminate the opposition message. Demonstrations—largely unheard of under this authoritarian regime—erupted to demand the release of the imprisoned sheikhs, the most significant occurring in Buraydah in September 1994, the very heartland of the ruling family's support. The al-Saud regime simultaneously denied the existence of an opposition movement, co-opted semiloyalists, and initiated a massive crackdown on dissent.

Though the universities closed for much of the Gulf War, the mosques became centers of sermons, ideological debate, and political opposition. Mosques and private homes served as safe havens for opposition activists during this turmoil. In their sanctuary, people wove narratives that provided them with a vocabulary to utilize in distilling their discontent. The dominant history and prevailing ideology could be questioned in these safe spaces, and oppositional alternatives could be constructed. Social intercourse and sermons provided alternative historic narratives that made sense to people and empowered them.

Although Islam has often been used by the ruling family to bolster the prevailing order, it can also be used to oppose that order. During the Gulf War, the call to Islam was especially vibrant and empowered sympathizers. Islamists are by far more coherent, powerful, and organized than any other social force in Saudi Arabia, including those based on nationalism, liberalism, regional identity, or business activity. Islamism provided the vocabulary, symbols, and historic reference points that resonated with the population. A coherent set of ideas provides the populace with common scripts and symbols to utilize when confronting the overwhelming power of state and social institutions (Swidler 1995). Only Islamism did so in Saudi Arabia. It is the only movement able to cut across multiple cleavages there.

With the stationing of U.S. troops during and after the Gulf War, what had been an inchoate resurgence of Islam was transformed into an organized and explicitly political movement. In short, many Wahhabi believers became neo-Wahhabi activists.[4] The resurgence of Wahhabism in the previous decade was largely private, inwardly focused, and concerned with the purity of religious practice and social norms. Believers were identified by short *thobe*s (the customary dress for men), beards, and the lack of an *agal* (rope) to hold their *ghutra* (head cloth) in place. The women of their families likely covered more and were strictly segregated, often even within the home. Now the private became public; the spiritual became political; the intrafamilial norms became enforced on others; and the individual became organized. What was an inward focus on the just believer became an outward vision of the just state and just society. The Wahhabi *da'wa* (call) that had been social and religious became political with the Gulf War.

The social origins of radical Islamists remains a sensitive topic within Saudi Arabia. The subject is avoided as it is potentially explosive. Some liberal intellectuals suggest privately that the members of Najdi religious groups are primarily from a nontribal (non-*asil* or *khadiri*) background.

Thus, they cannot demand things through a tribal identity, as so many others are able. But they can demand things through Islam. Islam is a protective umbrella and an equalizing force that allows them to compete with the tribes in Saudi Arabia. An observer explained: "Buraydah has too many sheikhs. So I asked myself, Where do all these sheikhs come from? These are men who needed Islam as a power base. They are *khadiri*. Unsure of their social roots, they seek authority and respect through Islam. Politicizing Islam gave them influence. Radical Islam has become a tribe for the tribeless."

POSSIBILITIES FOR PLURALISM

Believers in a civil and tolerant Islam can take advantage of the existence of multiple clergies, socioeconomic distress, and the convergence of dissent to position themselves as the voice(s) of the wide middle ground, and the future, of Saudi Arabia.

Multiple Clergies

Historically, the king dealt primarily with the official clergy (ulama). During the Gulf War, the state-appointed official clergy were supplemented by an empowered popular-level alternative clergy that was vocal and articulate. A dissident explained: "The previous al-Saud regimes had legitimacy conferred on them by one religious establishment [the state appointed]. The regime [of Fahd], though, has two religious establishments to contend with." It is even more complicated now as Crown Prince Abdullah has the official clergy and multiple layers of alternative clergy with which to contend. The multiple clergy complicates governance for the al-Saud. The divide between official Islamic authorities and popular Islamic leaders is great. The dissident continued: "The old clergy believe that the ruler is the vice-regent of God on earth. Advice can only be given in private and in confidence. The new clergy reject the idea of vice-regency. Rather, it is the duty of the clergy to criticize the ruler and work for change." Popular *fatwa*s that counter the official *fatwa*s are a means to do so.

Many Islamists argue that the official clergy should be abolished or that it should include representatives of all Muslim practice in Saudi Arabia. They advocate the existence of contending clerical voices in the country. They argue that debate would be healthy and that each believer could choose to abide by the clergy he or she considers most legitimate. The point is that the ruling family would not control the clergy through the appointment of a single nonrepresentative official voice.

The rhetoric of *jihadis* and of *salafis* does fall on sympathetic ears. Nevertheless, though zealots exist, most people long for leaders who offer them hope for the future, that have an impact on their everyday lives. It is a hope devoid of both royal and religious authoritarianism.

Social and Economic Distress

Islamism taps into an already distressed social and economic environment. Demographic problems are well documented: high and sustained unemployment, a very high birth rate, a youth bulge, the exclusion of women, dependence on foreign labor, and declining per capita income. The economy is still overwhelmingly dependent on oil, foreign labor, and state support. It must be made more diverse, local, and private. Since the heyday of the oil boom, per capita income has plummeted by two-thirds, from about $18,800 in 1981 to $6,700 in 1995. For a long time, the birth rate was a very high 3–3.5 percent, though it is said to be declining now. There is an age bulge, with the majority of the population under fifteen. These young adults will register their demands for education, jobs, and housing at the same time. But the kingdom's once fabulous infrastructure, constructed during the boom, is now crumbling. This is especially true in schools, hospitals, and municipal services, things that touch the everyday life of people. Unemployment in the general male population hovers around 10 percent, but it soars to around 30 percent among recent male college graduates. Yet Saudi Arabia remains utterly dependent on foreign workers, who constitute perhaps 90 percent of the private sector and 70 percent of the public sector labor force. Social norms militate against the participation of local women in many economic activities; women constitute over half of the local population. While there is a glut of university graduates, only 49 percent of the appropriate school age population enrolls at the high school level. Despite an extensive, impressive, and free public education system, 37 percent of the population was illiterate in 1995. There are reports of new social problems such as guns, drugs, and crime. Also troublesome is the apparent alienation or anomie that many young Saudis feel, made evident in rampages after football games, roaming street thugs after *eid* celebrations, and women being heckled at shopping malls. Civil Islamists can position themselves as problem solvers, and creators of a moral economy, an attractive option in an oil economy.

Convergence of Dissent

Despite their very significant differences in ultimate agenda, many social sources of dissent now converge on three central points: calls for the redistribution of wealth, procedural social justice, and regime accountability—

in essence, the rule of law. Thus, the state can no longer resort to its time-honored strategy of playing one group against another and thereby avoid all reform. This convergence cuts across cleavages of region, gender, class, school of Islam, ethnicity, ideology, and rural-urban settings. Private businessmen and public bureaucrats, industrialists and mom-and-pop shop owners, Islamists and secularists, Sunnis and Shi'as, men and women share core grievances. People are weary of ad hoc and arbitrary personal rule. There is a pervasive sense of frustration.

The incremental response of King Fahd to popular dissent satisfied no one. In 1992, he appointed a nonlegislative consultative council and gave more power to provincial governments, where other family members ruled. These "reforms" disappointed some and angered others. They had the effect of consolidating the ruling family's centrality to political life, rather than broadening meaningful participation. Civil Islamists can champion meaningful and enduring reform.

SOCIAL OPPONENTS AND STRUCTURAL OBSTACLES TO CIVIL ISLAM

The obstacles to civil society and representative governance in Saudi Arabia are many. Of course, most obvious is the rise of the *jihadi* movement, or the radical religious right, in the country. There are other problems as well.

First and foremost is the entrenchment of the religious right in institutional positions throughout the country. From low to high bureaucracy, from education to the judiciary to the *mutawwa,* the religious right is overrepresented. Certainly, the idea of having a single state-appointed *'ulama* that is granted vast authority (the official *'ulama*) stifles social and religious debate. The many layers of alternative clergy must be heard.

Second, a potential obstacle to civil Islam are power struggles within the al-Saud. The country is fortunate that Abdullah is a strong nationalist. He is also relatively unblemished by charges of deviation, and is thus able to confront, theoretically at least, the religious right. Abdullah has the personal legitimacy to reign in the radicals and initiate reform that will empower civil Islam. He has such instincts, but for now, he lacks the capability. He is hemmed in by less-reformist members of the al-Saud (such as Prince Nayef), who use the religious right to solidify their own power base in governance, and that of their sons. The intolerant right may be solidified in future succession struggles that empower less-reformist members of the al-Saud family.

Third, though the ongoing domestic debate indicates that there is indeed an important opening in Saudi Arabia, the reforms are not yet institutionalized. In the end, this new leniency is dependent upon the person and leadership of Abdullah. He is cognizant of the importance of national development. He is also one person and is elderly. As a Saudi remarked, "We are capable of identifying the problems. But solving them will require more than a reform minded sovereign. It will require an army of reformers." If reforms are to endure beyond Abdullah and if they are to survive extremist backlashes, then they must be given institutional grounding. Otherwise, the effort may backfire.

But institutional grounding will backfire if not accompanied by normative foundations. In short, norms must accompany forms. Norms of tolerance must be the foundation for various forms of social and political organizations. Too often, the inculcation of norms is left behind in the rush to create organizational form. For example, the current *majlis al-shura* (consultative assembly) is not broadly representative, and it has no legislative power. The *majlis* is indicative of organizational form without a foundational norm of pluralism. In Saudi Arabia, norms of tolerance for diversity are central to the civil society project because otherwise it cannot be sustained when challenged. Diversity is the reality of the Saudi Arabia population. It must be appreciated as a strength of the nation-state rather than perceived as a threat to it.

Fourth, international imbroglios deflect attention away from pressing domestic concerns and particularly from the empowerment of civil Islam. Such things as Israeli aggression against Palestinians, the U.S.-led war in Iraq, and the incessant Saudi-bashing in the United States tend to divert energies from reform of politics, economics, and society in Saudi Arabia. Instead, such actions fuel anger and humiliation, a dangerous combination that propels young people to the *jihadist* cause.

Fifth, a backlash from the religious right will immediately inflict damage in two realms: the status of women and in education. Women are especially vulnerable during times of crisis, as evidenced in both 1979 and 1991. Each time there is a serious domestic or international crisis, the position of women deteriorates. Women are symbolic markers of much larger political issues in Saudi Arabia. Also, the intense international pressure for reform of the education system in the wake of September 11 (sometimes misguided) first resulted in the affirmation of the health of the current national educational system rather than renewed efforts to evaluate it.

Sixth, the unyielding pressure to join the World Trade Organization is not helpful to the development of a strong local economy at this time. The local private sector, composed primarily of small- and medium-sized businesses, will be eaten alive should unfettered foreign investment be welcomed in Saudi Arabia. They simply are not yet competitive, though vital to a vibrant civil society.

Seventh, and importantly, the religious right has an organizational base that liberals lack. Even if it is fluid, the right has leadership and organizations that allow it to promote an agenda. Their social connections, through mosque and family networks, are also stronger than the social connections of liberal reformists. The assertiveness of the religious right was long matched by the hesitancy of the liberals. Only now are the liberals beginning to coalesce and construct leadership.

Finally, a further complicating variable in the reformist movement in Saudi Arabia is that—even if they attain success in implementing social, political and economic reforms for Saudi citizens—the peculiar nature of an oil-based rentier economy means that about one-third of the total population is still left out of such reforms. The massive population of foreign laborers will remain largely unaffected by such reforms in the short term.

Prospects for a Civil Society

The prospects for a vibrant civil society in Saudi Arabia are quite good, though it is not likely to "fit" the standard definition. Civil society is often defined in terms of voluntary associations, business organizations, labor unions, and other entities that are located between the household and the apparatus of the state. In Saudi Arabia, familial and religious networks are part and parcel of civil society and will not wither as more formal organizations take root. The rich cultural resources of Saudi Arabia—what may be called social capital—must be harnessed to nurture civil society. This means using the fluidity and strength of family and religion to construct a strong civil society, and thus a strong nation-state. Though highly patriarchal, family and religion are otherwise quite civil and tolerant.

Civil society exists in homes, mosques, and *suq*s (traditional markets), and increasingly in professional associations of lawyers and journalists, chambers of commerce, philanthropic organizations, universities, and the media. Many observers of the developing world believe that religious and familial (or tribal) identities threaten civil society. Such identities do not necessarily do so in Saudi Arabia because they will continue to coexist alongside newer affiliations rather than be supplanted by them. If religion and family were ever threatened in Saudi Arabia by more anonymous organizations, the backlash would be swift and sure. Some liberal Saudis report a fear of joining civil associations after the experience of Saad Eddin Ibrahim in Egypt (see the essay by Richard Norton in this volume). Whether his release emboldens people remains to be seen.

Saudi Arabia has long been an intensely private society in which behavior is severely circumscribed in order to protect the ideals of consensus and familial loyalty. Newly emerging is a small but broadening public sphere in which ideas can be traded and people can simply talk without threatening the integrity of the family unit or state. The very idea of a public space or public culture is a welcome and radical innovation in Saudi Arabia.

The Internet may ultimately be a transformational tool in Saudi Arabia but for now, it is both liberating and limited. Activists and intellectuals regularly disseminate information on a number of popular Web sites and participate in discussion groups. Chat rooms are quite popular, especially among the young. In general however, it is not distributed widely enough and it is censored, although code-breaking is a lucrative job. Users remain solitary and anonymous; many are automatically suspicious of political Web sites. The print and broadcast media, however, create a community of public discourse—citizens who share a common image or word. It may be more powerful in the near term as editors and writers continue to take risks in their work. Satellite television has clearly reinforced a pan-Arab identity among viewers and promoted a larger community of discourse. This new opening is not a direct consequence of September 11. While that may have accelerated the pace, a process of critical self-examination began unfolding in Saudi Arabia in late 1998, once Abdullah found his footing.

PUBLIC CARRIERS AND SOCIOPOLITICAL SUPPORTS OF CIVIL ISLAM

In order to promote a healthy civil society, the social carriers of civility that already exist must be empowered in institutions so they gain the confidence necessary to challenge the entrenched religious right. The social carriers of civility are already there, including outspoken journalists, women, large and small business owners who are tired of politics as usual, artists, and writers who continually push the envelope, academics who test the waters, mothers and fathers who recognize that the world of their teenagers is quite different from their own historic memory, and civil sheikhs. The key is whether the social carriers who value the norms of tolerance, criticism, and inclusion are rewarded. They also need the religio-normative backing of clergy, whether dissenting or official, to lend them social weight so they may speak out consistently and without retribution.

Clergy

Interestingly, the clerics called "radical" before September 11 turned out to be "reformists" after September 11. For example, Sheikh Salman al-Awdah, a fiery opposition preacher who spent five years in a Riyadh prison after the Gulf War turmoil, denounced the attacks and admonished Saudi youths against heeding calls for *jihad*. Rather than calling for the overthrow of the al-Saud, he now calls for "more avenues for people to express their opinions, and more opportunities available . . . to engage in fruitful and constructive dialogue." Sheikh Safar al-Hawali, out of jail for three years, also now speaks of reforming the system rather than overthrowing it. He also released a six-page, single-spaced "Open Letter to President Bush" in October 2001. To be fair, many Saudis charge that some of the former radicals turned reformists have come full circle, and are now simply co-opted by the government and have become a tool of the regime. Because some individuals appear to be opportunists, it is unclear what role they will play in Saudi political development.

The Gulf War *sahwaeen*[5] were bypassed by a more radical, fiery group of *jihadi* sheikhs including Nasser al Fahd, Ali al Khodair, and Ahmad al Khalidi, whose fatwas inspired many young people to violence. In the wake of terror, the government instituted a program to rationalize and professionalize the *mutawwa* and removed hundreds of sheikhs from the mosques. The government now allows the reformists in Saudi Arabia to speak with relative freedom in the media (direct criticism of the ruling family is still off limits). The al-Saud realized, too late, that exclusion promotes radicalization; inclusion may moderate political positions. For meaningful reform to blunt the call of the radical flank, it requires that the regime allow a vibrant political space to grow, a space that can be filled by tolerance.

There is much discussion about limiting the power and scope of the religious authorities in Saudi Arabia. There are people who call themselves secularists, but secular humanism, however compelling, remains for now on the fringe of the discussion. Clergy, even if circumscribed and disempowered in some activities, will continue to play an influential role in Saudi life. They cannot be ignored, as they have followers and influence. The debate over the future of Saudi Arabia is not about whether or not Islam is an important part of the country. That is an artificial argument that plays into the fears of everybody and empowers the religious right, and is disseminated by them for that purpose. There are many sheikhs and thoughtful Islamists who are not *jihadi*, neo-Wahhabi, or *sahwaeen*. The rich array of civil Islamists must be a part of the new dialogue in Saudi Arabia. The National Dialogue Forum, a state-sponsored meeting of Moslem leaders, was a first step toward tolerance, but participation must be expanded further to encompass civil Moslems who are openly critical of authoritarianism.

Educators

Curricular reform will occur. Contrary to the wishes of some strident foreign observers, the government cannot (and should not) simply delete Islamic subjects from the curriculum. It can, however, mandate inclusion of the richness and diversity of Islam in order to promote greater social

tolerance. It is also critical, in my view, that the formal curriculum be re-
formed so that Islam is not positioned as antithetical to the nurturing of
national pride. Further, in the emphasis on curricular reform, other pressing issues are overlooked: teaching pedagogy, dropout rates, teacher attitudes, and an inadequate infrastructure. They are at least as important.
Children are still taught by rote memorization and repetition rather than
problem solving and creative analysis.

Women

Changing stringent social norms that mandate gender segregation, the
covering of women, and sometimes their seclusion in the domestic realm
will require sensitivity and time. Abdullah, a champion of women's rights
in the Saudi context, has moved cautiously to grant women a bit more
mobility and a few more rights while avoiding a backlash from the religious right. After the tragic fire in a girl's school that claimed fifteen
young lives, a cleric was sacked and educational bureaucracies were reorganized so that the same authority now administers both male and female education. Control over girls' education was one of the last bastions
of unfettered religious authority. It may be that this incident was so
heinous and indefensible that it actually provided Abdullah the space to
rein in the religious right. It remains to be seen if any substantive changes
follow the administrative reorganization.

Importantly, the issues that matter to Saudi Arabian women are less
about covering and segregation (though still important to some) and
more about equal resources in education and employment; training the
next generation of girls; reining in the religious police because they de-
grade and humiliate women; equality in legal proceedings (e.g., appoint-
ing women attorneys to represent women clients); mandatory premarital
genetic testing and counseling; and abolishing the requirement that businesswomen have a male representative (*wakeel*) to conduct business.
Women who seek empowerment now utilize the traditional philanthropic
associations (which can be quite untraditional); stipulations to marriage
contracts to protect themselves; computers to bypass concerns about
physical interaction; and the women's sections of chambers of commerce
to network among themselves.

Business

The mega-issues of the WTO and foreign investment opportunities do
not insure a sustainable future for Saudi Arabia. More important is an
emphasis on building a local private sector that is competitive. More of
the economy is composed of small- and medium-size firms (70–80 per-

cent of trading, services, and industry). They are not well represented in the chambers of commerce nor in discussion with the World Trade Organization. There are no linkages between the multisectoral megaconglomerates and the plethora of smaller businesses that are the reality of the economy. Small and medium businesses need new resources in management, technology, marketing, and financing. As is, they will be severely hit when globalization hits full force, as they are unable to withstand rigorous competition without linkages. Yet small and medium business networks are vital for building a civil society.

Further, though the fact that the chambers of commerce do not really represent "the little guy in the *suq*," they are the site of the only proto-democratic elections in the country. For several years, part of each board of directors has been elected by secret ballot after contested campaigns. "Parties" declare themselves with agendas and followers. These elections are the closest that Saudi Arabia comes to the common expectations of democracy. Though friends tend to conglomerate together and the positions of some groupings are not in conflict, these bodies may represent an embryonic democratic form in an authoritarian state. Unfortunately, electoral activities were circumscribed recently.

Intellectuals and Media

There are many Saudi journalists and writers who take risks each week to push the boundaries of permissible expression ever further. Writing from a variety of perspectives, there are many critical voices of civility and reform during a time of crisis including Mohamed al Salahudin, Jamal al-Khashoggi, Khaled Batarfi, Hussein al Shobokshi, Mansur al Nugaidan, Nawal al Yousef, Mishari Zaydi, Abdelaziz al Gassem, Jameel al Farsi, Sulaiman al-Hattlan, and Alia al Fraid. At universities, there are fewer brave voices today to speak up for civil rights because earlier they were severely reprimanded when they spoke out. If there is any silver lining to the tragedies of September 11 and the war in Iraq, it is that many Saudi scholars now also write strong articles in the local newspapers (e.g., Matrook al-Faleh, Turki al-Hamad, Fowzia Abu Khaled). There is more crossover between the universities and the media than previously. Of course, it is "safer" to speak about Palestine, the U.S., or Iraq than about local politics.

Nevertheless, in January 2003, 104 Saudis, representing different regions, occupations, and ideologies, signed a petition to Crown Prince Abdullah that sought liberalizing domestic political reforms. Within the year, the National Reform Document was followed by four other petitions to Abdullah, each seeking reform. There are new human rights groups and regionally based political groups that demand the rule of law in Saudi Arabia. Among Islamist scholars and activists, it is imperative to allow and reward the voice of tolerant, plural, reformist Islam. There must be a countervailing force to the weight of intolerant extremism that has become entrenched in institutions.

NEGOTIATING A SOCIAL CONTRACT

An Irrelevant Triad

The al-Saud have historically based their "right to rule" on a triad of legitimizing factors: victory in military conquests (coercion), Wahhabism, and, much later, the distribution of oil revenues. In retrospect, we understand today that conquest bred resentment, Wahhabism never reflected the diversity of the population, and oil revenues shrank as the population mushroomed.

Likewise, the traditional social contracts (or political pacts) that Saudis refer to in conversation have lost their relevance. These are the agreements made between Abdulaziz, the founder of modern Saudi Arabia, and the Hejazi notables; between Abdulaziz and the *'ulama* of the Najd; and between Abdulaziz and representatives of major families, sects, and tribes in the eastern and southern regions. These pacts were thought to define the relationship between religion, state, and society. They protected private citizens and clergy from the reach of the state by providing a separate space for them. In the eyes of many Saudis, all three pacts have been violated. Later in the country's development, a fourth "pact" was added to the mix, an implicit understanding that the ruling family would administer and distribute oil revenues in return for political acquiescence (though this pact was always more important to foreign theorists than to ordinary Saudis). The old triad and the old pacts are no longer sufficient to govern a complex, smart, and diverse population.

At this time, a pacted transition to civility and pluralism cannot simply be assumed. The radical religious right has far more organization and ideological attraction than any other social force. At this writing, they are the only viable alternative to the al-Saud (though the emerging coalition of reformists is gaining ground). The reverberations of the war in Iraq will surely affect the domestic struggles. If there is a pacted transition to civility, participation, and pluralism, then the radical right will diminish in its magnetism. If there is no pacted transition, then Saudi Arabians are left in the unenviable position of either an unacceptable status quo (an authoritarian ruling family) or the triumph of the radical right. The middle ground must be empowered.

A healthy civil society will have a direct and positive effect on the prospects for more representative governance. Some analysts contend that a strong civil society would oust the al-Saud family. For now, it is more likely that the al-Saud will continue in some positions of authority, but their authoritarian tendencies will be countered. Their ostentatious behavior will almost certainly be curtailed. The ruling family may continue to rule but increasingly make compromises with the demands of social forces. If the al-Saud are to retain their power, the government must become more representative and inclusive of the diversity of the population. Simply put, if the al-Saud wish to retain power, they must relinquish power. The conundrum is that if the al-Saud do allow greater diversity, the far right backlash will be difficult to counter. It is, indeed, a difficult period in national development.

While the al-Saud will likely continue as primary decision makers for quite a while, they must now bargain with civil forces over the nature and degree of representative governance. Eventually the family as a unit may serve to symbolize the unity of the nation-state while individual family members still function in government alongside other citizens. It is ironic that liberals who used to stridently criticize the ruling family (and even call for their ouster) now begrudgingly acknowledge their position, in fear of the ascent of the religious right. And it is the al-Saud who empowered the religious right!

Absent upheaval (a big assumption), the al-Saud are not going away, though they must answer to the full population in ways they have not been expected to previously. That is, if civil Islam is empowered, we should expect a transition from subjects to citizens in the coming years. It is in this transition that the voices of civil Islam can have the greatest impact. The pull of radical Islam would likely diminish in the presence of meaningful participation and reform. It is not yet clear whether the ruling family has the skill or desire to empower civil Islam in the same way that it empowered the religious right after the tumultuous events of 1979.

What Many Saudis Want

It is not that the majority of Saudis are clamoring for full-fledged, party-based competitive electoral democracy. They are, however, clamoring for freedom of expression, freedom of assembly, and representation. They resent the exclusionary nature of governance. Toward this end, political institutions and religious bureaucracies must be reformed to incorporate different regions, ethnicities, religious branches, and both genders in order to cultivate the wide middle ground between the extremes of radical Islam and royal authoritarianism. Neither extreme reflects the aspirations of most Saudis. Ordinary Saudis want to participate in the development of their country, particularly in meeting the needs of a young, booming population for education, housing, and employment.

The turbulent debate that unfolds is over the proper relationship between state, ruling family, clergy, and citizen. This is a struggle to constitute a social contract in Saudi Arabia. What many ordinary Saudis want are a negotiation of the social contract and a definition of the rules of the game. The process is just beginning. It is a contest over the terms of "belonging" to the nation-state. The contest over the terms of the emerging social contract is mediated by region, sect, gender, age, class, and principled beliefs. The terms of the contract would be written differently by, for example, clergy, liberals, *jihadis,* or princes.

The new pact will require that the al-Saud broaden the basis of their "right to rule" by ensuring at least four things: the representation of divergent social forces, some form of meaningful participation, regularity and predictability in the conduct of business and politics, and the guarantee of new civil rights such as mobility, expression, and assembly. In exchange, the al-Saud retain their roles as representatives of the unity of the nation and the unity of the Islamic community (*umma*). The al-Saud are not irrelevant in the new pact by any stretch of the imagination. In the longer term, the contract will delineate the proper relations between religion and state, a hotly debated subject. I expect it to be more inclusive of non-Wahhabi Muslims.

CONCLUSION—SCALING UP AND ACROSS CULTURAL RESOURCES:
A NATIONAL CONVERSATION ABOUT IDENTITY AND CITIZENSHIP

Any sense of national identity in Saudi Arabia is embryonic. People have always identified themselves by other, multiple layers of identity based on region, religion, and family. With the oil boom and the influx of foreign workers in the 1970s and 1980s, "being Saudi" became defined by *what it was not* (a foreign laborer). Thus, identity and citizenship had a negative referent. There is now an effort to define "being Saudi" in terms of *what it is,* or by a positive referent.

Today—after the turmoil of 1979, the rise of the radical right in the 1980s, the politicization of Wahhabism with the Gulf War, the events of September 2001, and the war in Iraq—Saudis from all regions and walks of life are actively engaged in debate about their future. The larger debates in Saudi Arabia today are about the construction of meaning as a nation. People are talking about the terms and content of their belonging together, and about the right to talk about such sensitive topics. The contemporary debate is about what it means to "be Saudi," that is, the meaning of citizenship. What does it mean, if anything, to belong to this nation-state called Saudi Arabia? What do we share in common; why are we together? What is our relationship to the larger Arab and Islamic world? The tremendous political ferment that exists in Saudi Arabia today is part of an effort to define the proper relations between religion, state, ruling family, and citizenry.

Social forces are vibrant and engaged in Saudi Arabia. People talk passionately about religion and politics, corruption, the economy, their children not working, and the future of their daughters. It was the Islamists who began this national conversation about what it means to belong and about the relationship of ruling family, state, citizen, and religion. This is no small accomplishment in Saudi Arabia, where only a decade ago, the most controversial criticism that could be published in the papers were parental complaints about school lunches. But this conversation must occur on multiple levels between different kinds of people. There must be collaborations between state and social forces for the rich cultural resources of Saudi Arabia to be harnessed. Civility and tolerance must be "scaled up" to bridge state and society and included in any construction of citizenship and belonging to the nation-state. The Saudi Arabian case is further complicated because civility and tolerance must simultaneously be "scaled across" populations that historically do not interact much— across genders, regions, sects, tribal and nontribal, and across principled beliefs.

From this critical self-examination and debate will likely emerge a new sense of national identity. The manner in which Saudi civil Islamists assert themselves (or do not) and the coalitions they forge (or do not) will help shape the contours of this new identity. If they gain political voice and space, then the national identity is more likely to be Islamic, tolerant, plural, and representative. Though it may not be exactly democratic, it can be increasingly capable of fostering pluralist and democratic ideas. The new social contract will define the relationship between religion, state, ruling family, and citizenry.

NOTES

1. The term "religious right" incorporates two groups in Saudi Arabia; the radical, violent *jihadists* and the traditional state-appointed *ulama* (religious authorities), the very conservative men who have written many social absurdities into law and routinely write *fatwas* that further restrict social life. Both are religious right, and both are problematical, but they are very different.

2. A linguistic note: "Wahhabi" seems to have taken on a hegemonic meaning in the international press that does not accurately reflect its usage in Saudi Arabia prior to September 11. Believers would never refer to themselves as Wahhabi, as that implies worshiping someone, Muhammad ibn 'Abd al-Wahhab, other than God. They prefer instead to call themselves *muwahhidun* or *ahl al-tawhid,* to emphasize the centrality of monotheism, or Salafi,

to emphasize the purity of their beliefs based on the precedent of the Prophet. Usually, Salafi is a broader category than Wahhabi, and the latter implies less tolerance of diversity than the former. The term "Wahhabi" was used by "liberals" in a derogatory manner, but it now appears that the word *Wahhabi* is entering the Saudi Arabian vocabulary and press in fairly regular usage. It does not necessarily imply links to al-Qaeda, as is often implied in Western media. It is a confusing state of affairs, as the term means different things to different people. It may be useful to think of three meanings of Wahhabism: as a religious practice grounded in time and place; as a set of social norms dominant in the Najd; and as broader political aspirations directed against the hegemony of the West.

3. Wahhabism has existed in Saudi Arabia for centuries and is most prevalent in the Najd, the central region of the country. It is an offshoot of the Sunni Hanbali school of Islam that assumed a local specificity. Muhammad ibn 'Abd al-Wahhab (d. 1792) drew his inspiration from Hanbali scholars Ibn Tamiyya (d. 1328) and his disciple, Ibn al-Qayyim (d. 1350). Monotheism is carefully defined by what it is not, i.e., there is an emphasis on what actions are prohibited (*haram*) or *bid'a* (innovations). Wahhabism is opposed to extreme Sufism, saint worship, and folk religious traditions. It is exclusionary, carefully delineating boundaries that distinguish believers from others. Believers reject sectarian divisions and perceive Wahhabism as the one, true Islam.

4. Contemporary political activists who draw inspiration from Wahhabi traditions are often referred to as either neo-Wahhabi or neo-Salafi to capture their explicitly political orientation.

5. The *sahwaeen* are those sheikhs who "awoke" at the time of the Gulf War and became openly critical of the regime (e.g., al Awdah, al Hawali).

References Cited

Okruhlik, Gwenn. 2003. "Making Conversation Permissible: Islamism and Reform in Saudi Arabia." In *Islamic Activism: A Social Movement Theory Approach*, edited by Quintan Wiktorowicz, pp. 354–84. Bloomington: Indiana University Press.

Swidler, Ann. 1995. "Cultural Power and Social Movement." In *Social Movements and Culture*, edited by Hank Johnston and Bert Klandermans, pp. 25–50. Minneapolis: University of Minnesota Press.

Chapter 9

AN ISLAMIC STATE IS A STATE RUN BY GOOD MUSLIMS: RELIGION AS A WAY OF LIFE AND NOT AN IDEOLOGY IN AFGHANISTAN

THOMAS BARFIELD

FEW PLACES IN THE MUSLIM WORLD present more paradoxes than Afghanistan. The country has one of the most thoroughly Islamic societies in the world, but has no significant institutions of Islamic learning. It has experienced failed governments driven both by radical socialists and puritanical Islamists and yet has a population that has never been moved by ideologies of any sort. It is place where the concept of Islamic politics is little debated, but only because its people assume there can be no other type. It was home for many years to Osama bin Laden's al-Qaeda training camps, yet almost no native-born Afghans ever participated in the movement's terrorist actions abroad. It is a country that fought a ten-year *jihad* to expel the Soviet Union but then deserted the Islamic Taliban within weeks to support an American invasion.

One explanation for this is that Afghanistan represents an older form of Islamic society in which religion is not considered a form of ideology but remains an all-encompassing way of life. Issues that spark debate in other Islamic countries that originated in experiences of their colonial pasts, mass education, urbanization, rapid economic changes, and mass mobilization through explicitly political parties had little resonance in Afghanistan. Afghanistan was never a colony, has low levels of literacy, has an economy that is still overwhelmingly rural, and is a country where kinship and ethnic ties have always trumped political relations based on ideologies.

In this context a pluralist Islam is not likely to emerge in Afghanistan as part of a formal political structure or through an intellectual debate. It may emerge through negotiation among all the different regional and ethnic groups that are currently seeking to share power in a new government. Since each has its own variety of Islam, and the government lacks the power to define or enforce a single set of beliefs, then pluralism will be a natural by-product. On the other hand this will not be a secularized civil society in which religion is compartmentalized and accepted as an individual's voluntary choice. Liberalism in the immediate Afghan context will be the acceptance and noninterference among the different types of Islam in the country. It will not go as far as allowing individuals to choose non-Muslim faiths or atheism, forms of apostasy that will remain criminal offenses.

Background: Geography and Economy

Afghanistan is a mountainous semiarid country in Central Asia about the size of France, divided north and south by the Hindu Kush and Pamir mountain ranges. Before the Soviet invasion of 1979 it had an estimated population of 16 million people, almost exclusively Muslim, about 85 percent of whom were Sunni. The vast majority of the population was rural, engaged in subsistence agriculture and pastoralism, and there was historically poor integration between local and national institutions. The capital, Kabul, was (and remains) home to the largest urban population and the center of national politics. Other important cities such as Herat in the west, Kandahar in the south, and Mazar-i-sharif in the north were given little autonomy until recently but now have become centers of regional power.

Afghanistan's lack of integration was in part the result of geographic obstacles. Its mountain ranges bisect the middle of the country, and much of the south is desert. The country's transportation system consists of little more than a single two-lane all-seasons paved road that links most major towns, but it was not completed until the mid-1960s and now lies in partial ruin. The country has never had a rail system and has only minimal air transport facilities. Being landlocked, it has no ports, although a few ferry landings and a bridge cross the Amu Darya north to Tajikistan and Uzbekistan. Its social structure has been resistant to political integration because no overarching national identity or ideology has ever supplanted regional tribal and ethnic identities.

Cultural, Religious, and Ethnic Factors

Few peoples in the world, particularly the third world, have maintained such a strong and unproblematic sense of themselves and their culture as the Afghans. In abstract terms all foreigners, particularly non-Muslims, are viewed as inferior to Afghans. Although the great powers might be militarily, technologically and economically stronger, as nonbelievers and infidels, their values and way of life are naturally suspect. Afghanistan's

Muslim neighbors, however, fare only slightly better in Afghan eyes. The Uzbeks must have been asleep to allow the Russians to occupy Central Asia for more than a century; Pakistan is a land of recent Muslim converts from Hinduism that never should have become a nation; and Iran is a nest of Shi'ite heretics who speak Persian with a ludicrous accent. This sense of commonality against the outside world is leavened by the fact that Afghanistan is itself divided among a large number of different ethnic, religious, and regional groups.

Ethnic Groups

The most important ethnic groups in Afghanistan are the Pashtuns, Tajiks, Hazaras, Uzbeks, and Turkmen, although a number of smaller ethnic groups have regionally important roles (most notably the Nuristani and Baluch). However, the range of diversity at the local level, where social organization is based on smaller kinship groups or regional communities, reduces the utility of the major national ethnic labels as clear units of political analysis because these large groups do not act in a unitary fashion.

The country's Pashtuns, about 40 percent of the population, historically inhabit the area south of the Hindu Kush. Some were later resettled (or deported) north of the Hindu Kush Mountains to increase Pashtun representation in border areas of Afghan Turkestan. The imposition of the so-called Durand Line divided the Pashtuns between British India and Afghanistan in the late-nineteenth century, and so a larger number of ethnic Pashtuns probably reside in Pakistan in the Northwest Frontier Province and Baluchistan. The Pashtuns are tribally organized, all claiming descent from a common ancestor, but they are divided into a large number of clans and lineages. The largest division among Pashtuns in Afghanistan is between the Ghilzai, who straddle the Pakistan border, and the Durrani, who are settled between Kandahar and Herat. Although the Ghilzais have historically been the larger group, for most of the country's history the Durrranis have been politically preeminent. They maintained an exclusive hold on political leadership through the Muhammadzai dynasty that was only displaced by the communist coup of 1978. Even at that time, however, power remained primarily in the hands of the Ghilzai Pashtun faction of the Afghan communist party. With few exceptions Pashtuns are exclusively Sunni Muslims. In rural areas, however, there is such melding of their tribal law (the *Pashtunwali*) with Islamic religious law that the two are often viewed as inseparable and mutually supportive. Local charismatic religious leaders, known as *pirs*, played important roles in politics historically because they and their disciples crossed tribal lines and could act as counterweights to the landowning tribal khans who dominated Pashtun clans and lineages.

The Tajiks are Persian speaking Sunni Muslims who make up about 30 percent of Afghanistan's population. They do not have a tribal organization and identify themselves by locality. They make up the bulk of Kabul's urban population and dominate the mountainous regions of the northeast, where their co-ethnics inhabit Tajikistan and parts of Uzbekistan. Persian speakers also dominate western Afghanistan, but they have closer cultural and economic links to Iran. The Afghan Tajiks were particularly important as a group historically because Persian was both the lingua franca of Afghanistan and the language of government. If the Pashtuns dominated the leadership positions, it was the Tajiks who ran the bureaucracy. As a more urbanized and literate population, they were also more strongly represented in the ranks of the *ulama* who received state stipends or held state positions. They also tended to dominate the ranks of clergy who had received advanced religious training.

Uzbeks and Turkmen of northern Afghanistan are the two major Turkish-speaking groups in Afghanistan. They are extensions of ethnic groups that now dominate the adjacent Central Asian states of Turkmenistan and Uzbekistan. The Turkmen, like the Pashtuns, are tribally organized and maintain elaborate genealogies that divide them into a series of named clans. The Uzbeks, by contrast, have a weaker tribal organization with less political significance. Both groups are Sunni Muslims but were influenced by the Sufi orders of Central Asia, such as the Naqshbandiyah. Before the Soviet war these Turkish populations had little visibility nationally.

Non-Sunni populations inhabit very mountainous regions of central Afghanistan and urban enclaves in major cities, particularly Kabul and Mazar-i-sharif. The largest are the Shi'i Hazaras, but there are some Ismailis as well. Although Persian speaking, they claim descent from the Mongol armies that invaded the region in the thirteenth century and now constitute perhaps 15 percent of Afghanistan's total population. Before 1978 they made up about one-third of Kabul's population. They traditionally had hostile relations with the Pashtuns and faced considerable discrimination from Pashtun-dominated governments. Iran developed close ties to the Hazaras during the Soviet period and has retained considerable influence among some groups there. A small population of Ismaili Muslims inhabit a series of valleys in the remote Pamir regions of northeastern Afghanistan. Often referred to in the Russian literature as "mountain Tajiks," in fact they speak a number of old Iranian languages, not Persian. Through the leadership of the Aga Khan they have more links to the outside world and neighboring communities in northern Pakistan and Tajikistan than one would normally expect for people living in such isolated locations.

Religion in Government

Sunni Muslims have led all of Afghanistan's governments, and the Hanafi legal tradition set the country's legal framework (Kamali 1985). The religious establishment consisted of orthodox clerics who served on the government payroll as *qazis* (judges) or were supported by religious foundations (*waqf*) and less orthodox Sufi *pirs* who were supported by donations to their orders or individual Sufi saints. Historically clerics who wished to receive advanced religious training went abroad to study in madrasas in Delhi, Bukhara, or Cairo. Afghanistan itself had no traditional centers of advanced learning. This is not surprising since the country was the borderland that separated Central Asia and India, places that had long been centers of Islamic higher learning. Shi'i clerics usually studied in Iran but were generally excluded from Sunni government posts. Village mullahs, the bulk of the religious class, were supported and recruited by local communities and had a relatively low social status and poor religious educations.

Attempts to bring the *'ulama* under tight state control began with Amir Abdur Rahman (1890–1901), who created the modern Afghan state. The most powerful tool at his disposal was financial. He nationalized the formerly independent *waqf*s and administered them himself. This undercut the autonomy of the clergy and allowed the Afghan government to decide who would get support. He also put the *qazis* on the state payroll as a means of controlling them and their decisions. He was at odds with the Sufi saints because they remained beyond his direct control, and he saw them as instigators of opposition against government policies and even fomenters of revolt (Kakar 1979). It was Sufi orders and their saintly leaders who were most independent of Afghan governments and who often wielded considerable political influence. They were particularly popular in rural regions, but some of the established saintly lines had many urban followers (Olesen 1995). One reason for their political importance was their ability to transcend tribal boundaries, particularly among the Pashtuns.

Historically Islam was used among Pashtuns as a way to get around the structural problems inherent in getting rival tribes to cooperate. There were two patterns. In the first rival tribes would agree to cooperate in the name of Islam to expel non-Islamic invaders. Resistance fighters became known generically as *mujahidin,* or holy warriors, a title that obscured tribal differences. Though their rhetoric was Islamic, the key leaders were not themselves clerics. However, there was a second religious model of warfare practiced by Pashtuns in which clerics, usually Sufi saints (*pirs*), took command and organized armies in which they were the leaders. They could work around the tribal system because they owed their power to religious charisma, and could claim their authority was through God and not any tribal affiliation. These groups arose primarily to lead rural revolts against the Kabul government's attempts to centralize power and in frontier areas before 1947 against the British (who labeled them "mad mullahs"). The first type of war was approved by the state because it served to keep the country free of foreign occupiers. The second was treated much more unfavorably because these revolts were directed against its own authority. Such revolts rarely proved successful when the central government was strong and could suppress uprisings with a regular army. But when governments were weak (such as during the civil war against King Amanullah in the late 1920s) they had better success. It was the first tradition that underlay the Afghan resistance against the Soviet Union's occupation and it was the second that created the climate for the emergence of the Taliban.

MODERNISTS VERSUS ISLAMISTS

For the past one hundred years Afghan politics has been split between those who wished to see Afghanistan transformed and those who opposed the process. While this has often been portrayed as a battle between modernists and Islamists, the division was more complex. It has had as much to do with conflict over the limits of power of the central government, the cultural gap between elites in Kabul and the inhabitants of the countryside, and questions of taxation and conscription. It is this very crosscutting set of issues that prevented Islam from becoming a distinct ideology. Factions that would raise the Islamic banner in one context would ignore it in another. For example, rural revolts against changes in the legal status of women imposed by urban-based Kabul governments would be decried as un-Islamic. But the same people studiously ignored complaints by orthodox clergy that many their own tribal customs concerning women's inheritance rights and marriage procedures violated *shari'ah* law.

Neither the status of Islamic tradition nor social change was a pressing issue when Abdur Rahman created the Afghan state in the late-nineteenth century by building a strong national army equipped with modern weapons: he was interested in building state power, not transforming the Afghan people. He centralized Afghanistan to an extent never seen before, and over the twenty years of his reign he crushed all opposition to his government. While reining in the autonomy of the *'ulama*, he carefully portrayed himself as a defender of Islam because he had kept Russia and Britain out of Afghanistan. He was also careful to have the *'ulama* issue *fatwa*s giving justification for all of his acts, including wars of conquest against the Shi'i Hazara in central Afghanistan. In contrast to his active state building (Kakar 1971), Abdur Rahman was keen to see that his modernizations have as little impact on the population as possible. He imported foreign experts into Afghanistan to provide technical aid but did not introduce Western styles of education into Afghanistan itself. The economy actually declined as a consequence of the Amir's policies of taxing and controlling international transit trade and banking himself. He had a deliberate policy of keeping the country's natural resources undeveloped and refused to allow railroads in order to keep Afghanistan isolated (Hanifi 2001). By the end of his reign the former crossroads of Central Asia had developed the reputation of a hermit kingdom.

Although isolated, Afghanistan was caught up in the ferment of the Islamic world after the First World War and the dissolution of the Ottoman Empire. Under King Amanullah (1919–28) Afghanistan saw itself in two different ways. As the only Muslim state not under colonial domination (the country had gained complete independence from the British Raj in 1919), the religiously minded pushed Amanullah to proclaim himself successor to the Ottoman sultan as leader of world's Sunni Muslims. On the other hand, the world around Afghanistan was presenting new models. A revolution had destroyed the czars and created a new Soviet Union to the north. Turkey and Iran in the west had new leaders who declared that Islam was not the solution but the problem that had led to the region's loss of power. It was these latter movements that soon fascinated Amanullah. Following the lead of Ataturk and Reza Shah, Amanullah decided that Afghanistan needed to be modernized. By contrast with Ataturk's radical secularism that attempted to expel Islam from the public sphere in the Turkish Republic or Reza Shah's use of the military and economic projects to transform Iran, changes in Afghanistan were minimal but significant. Amanullah declared that state law would supersede religious law in his new law code, he sent Afghan students abroad for Western education, and he began some economic development programs. Religious opponents argued that his changes to family law were unIslamic and he was abandoning his role as defender of the religion. Such social issues figured prominently in a revolt by the eastern Pashtuns in 1924 that forced Amanullah to pull his reforms when the army proved too weak to put down the revolt without mobilizing the tribes for help (Nawid 1999). It should be noted, however, that these reforms were never implemented in the rural areas and that new taxes, as opposed to social issues, were more likely the spark of the revolt. While issues of taxation may also have sparked the American revolution, in Afghanistan the religious justification for revolts always took precedence even when the fundamental issue was in fact economic or political.

Amanullah was inspired to make another attempt at reforms immediately after he took a world tour in 1928 that included stops in India, Egypt, Britain, Italy, Germany, Turkey, the Soviet Union, and Iran. Upon his return he declared a whole host of reforms but was immediately faced with revolts by the eastern Pashtuns. This time he was unable to put down the rebels, and as other ethnic groups rose up to oppose his government, he abdicated the throne (Poullada 1973). A bandit Tajik rebel from north of Kabul, Habibullah, took the throne for nine months and rescinded the former king's attempts at modernization. This was seen as a victory for conservative elements in the country, but the old elite reasserted itself when Nadir Khan deposed Habibullah in 1929 and restored the royal dynasty to power with himself as king. During his short reign (he was assassinated in 1933) he took a more conservative approach, putting contentious reforms aside and rebuilding the state's armed forces. Only when the state power was more secure in the 1950s did reforms begin again.

During the long reign of Zahir Shah (1933–73) government power was largely in the hands of his father's brothers and his cousin Daud Khan, who was prime minister from 1963 to 1973. It was during this period that Afghanistan underwent a major transition. The Cold War conflict provided the Afghan government with aid from both the Soviet Union and the United States. The army was modernized by the Soviets and the West provided aid in the fields of education. Both helped build the first paved roads in Afghanistan and created its first system of communications. Daud's policy was to make changes quietly, beginning in Kabul, and then see them spread to the provincial cities and rural areas over time. For example, policies that encouraged the end of veiling in the 1960s protected women who dropped them and jailed clerics that openly opposed the policy, but did not make veiling a political issue as had been done in Iran and Turkey. Similarly, Western-style education was expanded and included women, but this was voluntary. In dealing with the clerics, the state began to demand certification through training at the state-run Kabul University if they wished to be employed by the government. The 1964 constitution also exemplified the gradual policy of modernization by declaring that all state laws must be compatible with Islam, but that in the event of a disagreement, the state laws would take precedence. But no court had the power to nullify state laws on the grounds that they violated Islamic principles (Dupree 1978, 559–69).

It was at Kabul University where these policies were most hotly debated. Afghanistan has always had a very small elite, and while the expansion of education brought many new people into politics, the numbers involved were only in the thousands and almost all of them resided in the capital. At the university politically active students divided into two opposing factions. The leftist faction favored faster reform and a greater break with Afghanistan's past. They formed two parties, Khalq (Masses) and Parcham (Banner), which became the core of the future People's Democratic Party of Afghanistan (PDPA). Islamist students who wanted to move the government in a more religious direction opposed them. Given Afghanistan's history Daud's government was more concerned about opposition from the religious right than the secular left. In 1973 when Daud overthrew Zahir Shah in a coup and declared himself president of a new Republic of Afghanistan, the leftists initially supported him. The Islamists attempted to move against him in 1975 by mounting some small revolts against the government in the rural areas. Because they had no local support these quickly failed and the most prominent Islamists fled to Pakistan while others were jailed. However, the leftist parties were soon disappointed in Daud and his failure to take more radical steps to change Afghanistan. In 1978 they mounted their own coup, murdered Daud, and declared their intention to create a new socialist Afghanistan (Dupree 1978, 761–68).

THE SOVIET INVASION, DEFEAT, AND ITS AFTERMATH

The radical Khalq party was the dominant faction in new PDPA government, and they were not just interested in ruling Afghanistan but in transforming the country through revolutionary policies of land reform, education, and changes in family law. They moved to destroy all who opposed them, including many of their leftist Parcham rivals, the traditional rural landowners, the old military establishment, and the Islamic clergy. They abandoned Afghanistan's historic policy of neutrality for a direct alliance with the Soviet Union. The regime also rejected the country's traditional Islamic symbols of legitimacy by striking religious salutations from their speeches and decrees and changing the color of the flag to red. As revolutionaries they justified themselves and the legitimacy of their government in Marxist terms. This rhetoric was alien to most of the rural population, except in the north, where it was all too familiar to the descendants of refugees who had originally fled from Soviet Central Asia in Stalin's time. The Khalq regime was the first (and only) Afghan government to explicitly reject Islam within its governing framework. This proved an unwise move since the PDPA membership numbered fewer than ten thousand countrywide and made it an easy target to attack not just by Islamist parties but by ordinary Afghans for whom no government was legitimate if it was not run by believing Muslims (Arnold 1983).

When the PDPA went beyond policy pronouncements and attempted to implement its policies in the countryside, it met with resistance. The government responded with military force and the country's provinces erupted in rebellion. These uprisings were uncoordinated and tended to focus on local rather than national issues, but they soon became widespread (Shahrani and Canfield 1984). The Soviet Union, which distrusted the Khalq leadership and had attempted to remove it, became concerned that the situation was getting so out of control that the regime itself was in danger of collapse. In an attempt to restore stability the Soviet Union invaded at the end of 1979, deposed the ruling Khalq faction after murdering its leader, Hafizullah Amin, and installing a Parchami, Babrak Karmal, as his replacement. The Soviets then engaged in a wholesale war against the Afghan population in an attempt to force it into submission or to run the resistance out of the country. Eventually 3 million Afghans fled to Pakistan and Iran, over 1 million were killed, and millions of others were displaced internally. In spite of having no centralized command, being divided by ethnic and sectarian differences, and being hopelessly outmatched in equipment by Soviet and Afghan government forces, a war of resistance—financed with billions of dollars in aid and training obtained from the United States and Saudi Arabia and administered by Pakistan—wore down the Soviets, and in 1989 they withdrew. Their regime in Kabul collapsed three years later.

The Soviet invasion created a national opposition unlike any seen before. The collapse of central authority and the rise of locally based resistance groups transferred real power into the hands of local communities previously ruled by distant officials assigned by the central government. By framing the conflict as a *jihad,* a holy war, it was possible to unite a very large number of people and to deprive the Kabul government of legitimacy. While the Afghan resistance was unable to win set-piece battles against its Soviet enemy because of its better organization, firepower, and air superiority, the Russians found it impossible to permanently suppress the opposition in spite of inflicting heavy casualties. Since the Afghan definition of victory consisted of a Soviet withdrawal, all the resistance needed to do was to make the country ungovernable and a drain on Soviet resources. With the acquisition of American-supplied Stinger antiaircraft missiles in 1986, the rebels were able to reduce a key Soviet advantage and drive the price for staying even higher. By the late 1980s losses in men and material were enough to make the war profoundly unpopular in Moscow. The Soviets under Gorbachev concluded that the best policy was just to let the Afghans keep their country and bring the troops home (Hyman 1992).

The Soviet occupation lasted a decade and did immense damage to the country and its people (Kakar 1995). More significantly, both sides in the anti-Soviet war were to a large extent creations of their funders rather than mass indigenous political movements. The PDPA received its support from the Soviet Union, a cost estimated at about $5 billion a year during its occupation period. The *mujahidin* would not have been competitive without access to similarly large sums of money and arms, which were supplied by the United States and Saudi Arabia. This meant that the Afghan resistance was as dependent on international aid as its Soviet supported rival was. As a result the Afghan *mujahidin* found themselves sucked into two larger conflicts: the ongoing Cold War struggle between the United States and the Soviet Union, and a new struggle by Saudi Wahhabis to make the war in Afghanistan the vanguard of a transnational *jihad* that they hoped would bring about Islamic revolutions in the Sunni Arab world and beyond. Unfortunately for their patrons, the Afghans had little interest in either struggle. In particular the only *jihad* the Afghans were willing to fight was in Afghanistan itself, and that would end when the Soviets withdrew.

The interference of outsiders was clear in the organization of the resistance. While there was a broad coalition of Afghan parties opposed to the Soviet invasion that included royalists, nationalists, and regional groups and even non-PDPA leftists, only the Islamist parties had access to money and arms. This was because foreign aid to the resistance was distributed through the Pakistan government, and only the seven Sunni Islamist parties it formally recognized were eligible for support. (The Shi'i parties received aid from Iran's Islamic government.) These parties had not been particularly influential inside Afghanistan before the Soviet invasion. Indeed, many of their leaders had been living in exile in Pakistan because of their participation in a series of failed Islamic uprisings against the Daud government in the mid-1970s that had received little or no popular support. By making them conduits of aid, Pakistan raised their profile and power. Local resistance groups within Afghanistan had to affiliate with one of these Islamist parties in order to get weapons. Because the groups fighting in Afghanistan had little or no interest in the political ideologies of these parties or their leaders, party affiliation was most often based on personal relationships or regional and ethnic ties. Thus in choosing between the two most powerful parties, the Tajiks and northerners in general tended to align them themselves with Rabbani's Jamiat-i-Islami while Pashtuns and others in the south and east joined more often with Hekmatyar's Hizb-i-Islami. But given the complex nature of Afghan politics, locally rival groups would often join different *mujahidin* parties regardless of ethnic ties or would defect from one party to another if they could get a better deal (Roy 1990).

Because outsiders financed the war, they naturally interpreted the struggle in Afghanistan as a Manichaean conflict of competing ideologies (e.g., Islam vs. atheism, socialism vs. capitalism, freedom vs. oppression, feudal reactionaries vs. progressive patriots, modernists vs. traditionalists).

The lack of ideology that underlay traditional Afghan politics was thereby hidden. The *mujahidin* parties, for example, had good connections with Kabul government bureaucrats throughout the war and could generally get any information they needed from them. PDPA troops struck deals with local resistance groups to avoid fighting. Even at the national level the philosophical differences between the resistance and the Kabul regime that had originally sparked the war were soon blurred. The PDPA government itself denounced its earlier radical policies as mistakes after the Soviet invasion. They rid themselves of the Soviet style red flag, pointedly reintroduced Islamic phrases into their decrees and speeches, and made sure their leaders were seen at prayer with supportive clergy. But the continuing opposition to the legitimacy of the PDPA government was not based on its policies but because it allowed the occupation of the country by Soviet troops who remained actively at war with the population.

When the Soviet Union withdrew in 1989 this bedrock objection to the PDPA's legitimacy was removed but so also was the protection of their troops. At the time it was assumed (even by the Russians themselves) that the Kabul regime would fall within weeks or months. However, its leader, Najibullah (who had replaced Karmal in 1986), proved surprisingly successful at keeping his troops intact and holding the regime together. This support was based not on ideology but on Najibullah's continuing access to Soviet money, weapons, and food that he could distribute to his followers. This included a large growth in the regime's rural militias that numbered over 100,000 people. Many former *mujahidin* groups defected in return for arms and money. They saw little reason to fight against his regime if their own needs were met and the Soviets were gone. Najibullah even reorganized his administration by opening it up to noncommunists and proposed reserving positions for *mujahidin* leaders in a future coalition government (Giustozzi 2000).

Pakistan and the United States, both of which wanted to see an outright *mujahidin* military victory, rejected Najibullah's overture. But although they had expected to topple the PDPA government easily when the Russians withdrew, the *mujahidin* proved unable to take fixed military positions and that failure produced a stalemate. With the Soviets gone, far fewer Afghans were willing to take up arms against the government as long it did not trouble them. It was only when the Soviet Union disintegrated and Russia refused to continue large-scale aid that Najibullah's government collapsed in April 1992. Although it was still well armed, had its forces intact, and had enough stored supplies to survive in the short term, factions within the PDPA decided that their long-term prospects were bad. Now was the opportune moment to negotiate their futures from a position of strength, and they all cut deals and switched sides largely on the basis of ethnic ties. Thus the PDPA regime was less defeated militarily than reorganized as its components defected to various *mujahidin* factions.

With the fall of the Kabul regime the last remaining thread that had bound the *mujahidin* into a marriage of convenience snapped. Their leaders had no clear goals because their unity had been based on resistance against the Soviet Union and its client Afghan government, not on any common political platform (Roy 1995). Perhaps more important, none of the seven recognized faction party leaders who were supposed to form a new government had done any significant fighting inside Afghanistan themselves or created a national political base. They were naturally opposed to any open system of government that might expose their unpopularity or narrow base of support. They were particularly vehement in their insistence that the former king, Zahir Shah, should play no role in government, not even a symbolic one. Royal legitimacy through recognized tribal lineage still held enough sway among ordinary Afghans so that it threatened to undermine the Pakistani backed *mujahidin* party leaders because the most powerful of them (Rabbani, Hekmatyar, and Sayyaf) lacked prestigious social origins.

A *mujahidin* power struggle was therefore inevitable once the PDPA dissolved. Each faction leader realized that if he did not obtain power now, he never would. And since the parties were based more on personality than ideology, there was very little basis for compromise, particularly since the rise of a predominate leader would mean an end to all the smaller factions. Thus the agreed-upon distribution of power failed almost immediately. The "prime minister," Hekmatyar, refused to enter the capital and remained encamped on the hills south of Kabul from where he shelled the city, and the troops of his "president," Rabbani. Kabul, which had been spared any fighting during the war because of its many lines of defenses, was devastated over the next three years and large parts of the city were reduced to rubble. As a result many of its residents fled the city seeking safety elsewhere and twenty-five thousand people were believed to have died as a result of the fighting. A stalemate ensued in which neither side was able to dislodge the other. In an attempt to break the deadlock Hekmatyar cut a deal in January 1994 with the Uzbek leader Dostam, who once again betrayed former allies to join what he hoped would be the winning side. This was an odd couple: the most fundamentalist *mujahidin* commander embracing the former communist general. The venture failed to bring down Rabbani's government, and the fighting in and around Kabul intensified as the Tajiks led by Masud in one part of the city continued to fight bitter battles with the Hazaras led by Ali Mazari in the other (Barfield 1996).

The inability of the factions to find any common agreement about what a future government should look like, let alone who should run it, made it impossible to unify the country politically. And because each of the factions was strong only in its home region and could not displace its rivals elsewhere, there was no real prospect of unifying the country militarily. Nor did the any of the factions have the same access to resources as they did during the anti-Soviet war for coalition building. The swift end of Najibullah's regime after the Soviet Union collapsed demonstrated dramatically how dependent he was on outside funding to stay in power. Less well noticed was that the victorious *mujahidin* parties soon faced the same problem. The United States, which had been matching Soviet aid to Kabul with its own support to the *mujahidin* (negative symmetry), was only interested in funding a Cold War struggle that had suddenly been rendered moot. Saudi Arabia was generous in funding a *jihad* against unbelieving invaders, but showed little interest in the civil war that was now raging among fellow Muslims. The international community that might have stepped in to help with rebuilding the country instead focused on the more the immediate problem of relieving the suffering caused by faction fighting in the country (Rubin 1995, 2002).

THE RISE AND DEMISE OF THE TALIBAN

In previous periods of turmoil Afghan leaders had arisen to reestablish political order in the country by combining some recognized claim of political legitimacy with substantial aid from the outside world. Because Afghanistan had been a rentier state whose successive central governments (regardless of ideology) had all been dependent on extracting outside resources to maintain their stability for close to two centuries, attempting to create a new central government without substantial outside aid would have been a daunting task under the best of circumstances. In their absence it proved impossible.

The Taliban leader, Mullah (later Amir) Omar, was a local cleric in Kandahar with an honorable war record in the anti-Soviet *jihad*, but he was neither an important figure in that war nor a player in any of the postwar factions. In 1994 a group of Pashtun Islamic students, trained in Pakistan but having moved to Kandahar, complained to Mullah Omar about the local warlords who had abused the population by committing crimes that included robbery, rape, and extortion. Omar instructed his student followers (or *taliban,* hence the name) to confront these bands and disarm them. After capturing and executing some of the most notorious of these groups they then unblocked the roads around Kandahar, seized power from other local warlords, and brought a high degree of order to the territories they took under their control. The movement was widely popular locally because it promised security of life and property to a region that lacked both. Its ideology was of secondary importance. Upon seeing the Taliban's strength among the Pashtuns, Pakistan switched its backing to the new movement with the hope that it would have more success than its previous clients. After helping them take control of Kandahar, the Taliban expanded quickly with additional Pakistani aid and destroyed Hekmatyar's Hizb-i-Islami to become the dominant Pashtun faction in 1995. A year later they seized Kabul, and by 1998 all but northeastern Afghanistan was under their control. While the Taliban were initially lauded for bringing peace and security to the regions they captured, their social and religious policies were widely unpopular. In some ways they were a mirror image of the PDPA, intent on imposing radical doctrines of foreign origin (this time religious) on a population that was strongly opposed to them (Rashid 2001).

Although the Taliban was a religious movement, its attraction to the Pashtuns as opposed to other ethnic groups was not surprising. While their emergence was sudden, their movement's dynamic followed a well-worn path: scholars have long noted that religious leaders could transcend tribal boundaries and unite people in the name of religion who would not otherwise cooperate. Commenting on the structurally similar Bedouin tribes (in the thirteenth century!), Ibn Khaldun argued that religion was uniquely suited to bringing tribes together:

> The Bedouins are the least willing of nations to subordinate themselves to each other, as they are rude, proud, ambitious, and eager to be leaders. Their individual aspirations rarely coincide. But when there is religion [among them] through prophethood or sainthood, then they have some restraining influence on themselves. The qualities of haughtiness and jealousy leave them. It is, then, easy for them to subordinate themselves and unite (as a social organization). (Ibn Khaldun 1967, 120)

The Taliban had used the failures of the *mujahidin* warlords to attract a wide following among the Pashtuns. An advantage of a religious movement for rival Pashtun leaders was that there was no honor or prestige lost in subordinating oneself to the will of God or God's agents. The movement also served to give the Pashtuns the dominant role they expected to play in Afghan politics without having to cede any ground to rival tribes. The Taliban expansion into Pashtun areas was largely peaceful, with tribal leaders and local *mujahidin* commanders defecting to their cause in return for maintaining their local power under a Taliban administration. When they moved out of Pashtun regions they relied more on force. But, after losing a series of battles in 1995 that forced them to retreat back almost to the gates of Kandahar, they reverted to a policy of co-optation and bribery that resulted in the rapid fall of such major centers as Herat, Kabul, and then Mazar-i-sharif without major fighting. Their attempts to implement policies based on genuine military coercion generally failed, as when their heavy-handed occupation of Mazar in 1997 led to a disastrous defeat in which they were driven out of the region with the loss of an estimated three thousand troops. Their second occupation in 1998 was much more cautious and successful. However, even with outside support they were unable to completely displace Ahmad Shah Masud's Northern Alliance in northeastern Afghanistan in the years that followed (Goodson 2001).

The Taliban in Historical Perspective

The Taliban brought something new to the Afghan scene. Although they proclaimed themselves to be the defenders of traditional Islamic values, their movement marked a clear break with the past in that it was the first successful political movement in the country led by clerics. All previous Afghan regimes of whatever orientation had secular leaders.

Two types of charismatic leaders had led previous Afghan religious movements. The first were long established holy figures, sometimes representing a long lineage, who could draw on a network of disciples and relationships with particular tribes or ethnic groups to become the focus for organizing opposition to a central government. Visionaries who claimed to be acting on God's command to bring about some radical and divinely inspired change led the second type of more ephemeral movement. The leaders of the first type of movements held recognized positions of influence that persisted regardless of whether their opposition was successful. The leaders of the second had no such recognized positions (indeed, their socially marginal origins often were taken as a sign that they must be inspired by God). Failure of their movements ended their careers and often their lives. The Taliban was a larger and unusual variety of the second category. They began not in opposition to a central government or an invader but rather in response to the anarchy that enveloped Afghanistan with the fall of the PDPA regime.

Breaks with the Afghan Past

The Taliban broke with Afghan tradition not only in the clerical origin of its leaders, but perhaps most importantly in its refugee origins. The Soviet war lasted for so long and the refugee flow into neighboring countries was so great that over time it created a new class of people: refugee Afghans born in Pakistan or Iran who had never seen the country or experienced life there. Refugee camps are notorious hotbeds for radical movements of all types because they are generally poor, they provide few opportunities for young people, and the political factions that control them can manipulate their populations. The hope of recovering a lost homeland is a particularly powerful ideal, but as time passes the view of this homeland becomes more and more mythic because refugee children know of it only by hearsay. The past is idealized because the present is so miserable and the future is so uncertain. Groups with extreme messages, whether their ideologies are political, ethnic, or religious, galvanize their followers not only with the visions of reclaiming a lost homeland but of then transforming those followers. Examples of such movements are numerous and include the radical political movements of the PLO among the Palestinians, exile-based movements of both the Tutsi and Hutu in Central Africa, or sectarian movements such as the Taliban. In all of these cases, the groups involved focused on what they had lost because they were not incorporated into the areas to which they had fled. They sustained a separate and distinct identity in part because the world community isolated them and fixed them in space and time with permanent refugee or alien labels that may have been appropriate initially but that became more problematic as the decades wore on.

Refugees in Afghanistan did better than most: they experienced a tactical victory when the Soviets withdrew and, in theory, they could return to their homeland. But the fighting among the *mujahidin* meant that for most the option of returning home was difficult. Even when they did arrive, the homeland was not what they had known when they left it. Although poor before the war, the Afghan economy at least functioned and there was general security for life and property. Now there was none. The *mujahidin,* who had been heroes in the anti-Soviet *jihad,* lost respect when they became faction leaders engaged in self-interested and violent struggles for power with other similar groups. The Taliban drew on this discontent in two ways. First, they recruited young men who had been too young to participate in the anti-Soviet war and gave them an opportunity to participate in a new *jihad,* one that would bring a "truer version" of Islam to Afghanistan. *Jihad* had been the focal experience for young men throughout the Soviet war, and those too young to participate were looking for a goal that was equally as idealistic. That the Taliban's view of Islam was far more radical and conservative than any existing in Afghanistan previously meant little to people who had nothing to compare it with. For them it was far easier to imagine an ideal Afghan way of life, and to enforce it on others, because they drew their lessons from religious schools and not the give and take of everyday life. Second, the Taliban drew on the discontent of the population at large with the continuing anarchy in the country. Any ideology and regime that promised stability would be given the benefit of the doubt if it could bring about that stability. For most Afghans, it was the success of the Taliban in bringing about order that mitigated the fact that it was both a clerical movement and one whose vision of Islam (particularly its puritanical banning of practically all forms of entertainment) was not widely shared or appreciated.

The Soviet war and the *mujahidin* civil war that followed left Afghanistan devastated, not only physically but also in its social and political structure. Before the war it would have been very difficult for any movement of the Taliban type to cover so much territory so easily. The power of local landed elites, rival tribes, and the power of a functioning central government prevented the easy spread of any national movements. The war and the massive outflow of refugees disrupted traditional Afghan society to such an extent that it was now vulnerable to rapid changes because the local power structures now lacked cohesion. To use an ecological analogy, the old Afghan system was a climax state: a self-perpetuating stable set of political relationships in which rival forces in the country remained in equilibrium until they were disrupted by an outside force. Such climax states, once destroyed, take a long time to rebuild or reach a new climax state. The Taliban represented a political movement characteristic of such a transitory phases where anarchy is the greatest problem and political power is weak. Although in power for more than five years they did little to transform themselves into a government. The only new institution they introduced was a religious police force that took charge of enforcing the regime's draconian policies.

CONTINUITIES WITH THE AFGHAN PAST

If the Taliban did represent one great continuity, it was in continuing the long-standing struggle for power between Afghan modernists and the Afghan traditionalists. The modernists were primarily urban based and sought a more secular and socially liberal environment that would integrate Afghanistan into the larger world community. The traditionalists had a more conservative vision based on a combination of deeply rooted rural values and traditional religious beliefs. The twentieth century was a continuing struggle between them in which neither was able to eradicate the other, and over time each got more extreme. The communist parties that overthrew Daud in 1978 argued that he had not been radical enough in pursuing a modernist vision. When their own attempts at a radical transformation of society failed and the Soviet Union invaded to keep Afghanistan socialist, the modernists were discredited in the eyes of most Afghans. Islamist parties that had failed to arouse much sympathy when they were persecuted by Daud's government rode high in opposition to the Soviets and reinvigorated Islam as a political force in Afghan national politics. But both sides had in common a mission to transform a population that had no desire to be transformed. The opposition between the Taliban and the local populations was therefore most intense in cities such as Kabul and Mazar that were the strongholds of the modernists, in part because Taliban policies drew as much inspiration from rural Pashtun Afghan values as they did from Islam.

THE TALIBAN AND *JIHAD*

The Taliban made *jihad* one of the strongest elements of their struggle. It provided a religious justification for warfare against their enemies. But the Taliban were quite careful to restrict their *jihad* to one country: Afghanistan. They attempted to reassure the secular post-Soviet Central Asian states that they had no intention of spreading their struggle northward. While such a promise might seem simple good politics (the Taliban were isolated enough without making new enemies), it also reflected an Afghan ethnocentrism. They had contempt for most of their neighbors and did not really care what they did. It was certainly not their responsibility to change them. And far from identifying with the many Muslim foreigners who fought in Afghanistan, the Taliban appeared to take the view that if they wanted to conduct a *jihad* against their own governments that was their own affair, but it had nothing to do with the Afghans. Indeed the only place that a Taliban style *jihad* was likely to spread outside of Afghanistan with Taliban support was Pakistan because that was where it had originated. Because Pakistan had its own large population of co-ethnic Pashtuns, there was a close connection with Islamist parties there who were part of an existing debate within Pakistan itself on how much more Islamic the country needed to become. Successive Pakistani governments played with fire by so closely identifying themselves with such a radical Islamist movement in order to influence Afghanistan's politics when its own society was more vulnerable to its spread than any of the other neighboring states.

ISLAM AS THE ONLY WAY

The Taliban saw Islam and its *shari'ah* law as the fundamental basis for proper social life. They also believed that since God's law was superior to state law, the state itself was not ultimately sovereign. Thus to their way of thinking, only Islamic principles could be used to judge rights. If these came into conflict with internationally recognized norms, such as the treatment of women, the Taliban argued that Islam must be followed. The difficulty was that Islamic scholars in other countries did not accord their interpretation of Islam much validity. Their interpretations were often idiosyncratic and tended to dress local custom in the guise of religion. On the other hand, many aspects of Taliban policy were not local custom at all. The puritanical strain of Wahhabism that induced them to ban all forms of entertainment, seclude women, enforce beard codes, and demand the harshest forms of Islamic punishments were all alien to Afghanistan. It was here that the influence of foreign Muslims, conservative Pakistani madrasas where the Taliban had been trained, and the financial support of the movement by the Gulf Arabs introduced an ideological edge to the movement that ultimately undermined its legitimacy.

This could be seen when the Taliban ordered the destruction of the standing Buddhas in central Afghanistan in March 2001 (Barfield 2001). The decree was issued by an assembly of clerics and confirmed by Mullah Omar as a religious issue and did not appear to have been run past any Taliban government officials before it was announced. The logic behind the decision was explained in a Taliban newspaper editorial in *Shari'at* (February 28, 2001) published just after the edict was issued. It stated that "the objects of worship, which had been considered as sacred and worshipped in their time in the past, are filthier than everything else and thus it is necessary that our beloved country should be cleansed of the existence of such false objects." That other Islamic scholars rejected this line of interpretation had no impact on Mullah Omar. When informed that of their objections he boasted that "Muslims should be proud of smashing idols. It has given praise to God that we have destroyed them" (*Times,* March 6, 2001). But the Taliban regime's inability to justify their action in strict Islamic legal terms undermined their claim. A set of Egyptian clerics who went to visit Mullah Omar in Kandahar were later scathing in their opinion of Taliban legal reasoning and condemned the decree as fundamentally flawed:

> because of [the Taliban's] circumstances and their incomplete knowledge of jurisprudence they were not able to formulate rulings backed by theological evidence. The issue is a cultural issue. We detected that their knowledge of religion and jurisprudence is lacking because they have no knowledge of the Arabic language, linguistics, and literature and hence they did not learn the true Islam. (*Al-Sharq al-Awsat,* March 23, 2001)

But who were they to tell Mullah Omar, the man who named himself Amir-ul Momineen, or Commander of the Faithful, that he did not know his business? Omar's only overt response to all the criticism was to order the sacrifice of one hundred cattle and to give the meat to the poor to express his regret for taking too long to get the job done and not having done it earlier.

The Taliban were also hostile to other religions. Earlier, in December 2000, they had issued a decree declaring that that "any Afghan who converts to the rescinded religion of Christianity will be sentenced to death." The Afghan newspaper *Hewad* (January 13, 2001) had gone on to warn, "Anyone caught selling literature promoting Christianity or Judaism or degrading Islam, its personalities would be subjected to five years' imprisonment." After they had destroyed the Buddhist monuments, the Taliban turned their attention to the small Kabul Hindu community in May 2001 and demanded that they wear a badge to distinguish themselves as non-Muslims. In June the Taliban announced that at all non-Muslim international aid workers and journalists must agree to abide by their version of Islamic law (including punishments such as stoning for adultery) and accept the authority of the Taliban religious police. In August they arrested a group of foreign aid workers and charged them with being Christian missionaries. But in September 2001 the Taliban found themselves confronted by an enraged United States when its Arab Afghan allies launched attacks on Washington and New York and they were driven from power before the year ended.

THE END OF THE TALIBAN

Over the course of their rule in Afghanistan the Taliban had become more and more dependent on al-Qaeda and the Pakistani government for financial and military support. Unlike other Afghan factions, the Taliban was willing to lose large numbers of men in battle. This created a manpower shortage as losses mounted and they found it harder to recruit Afghans into their ranks. Instead they depended more and more on the so-called Arab Afghans (foreign Muslims mostly from the Arab Gulf states and Central Asia) and Pakistanis. The use of these troops in an Afghan civil war alienated the local population. They saw these troops as foreigners who had no business in Afghanistan. Because they were engaged in a war of Muslims against other Muslims, the Taliban portrayal of their struggle as a type of *jihad* was seen as illegitimate. Pakistan's role was particularly distrusted because they were seen as invaders keen to incorporate Afghanistan into Pakistan.

On a cultural level the Taliban's increasing adoption of Wahhabi interpretations of Islam also alienated the population. Afghan Islam had never been dogmatic. Strong Sufi influences, the veneration of saints and their tombs, and poor religious education gave Islam in Afghanistan an eclectic flavor. Even the Taliban had difficulties in sorting out what was religiously based and what came from Pashtun custom because they rarely bothered to learn Arabic. The success of the Wahhabist movements in

other countries had played on people's insecurity and the role that religion should play in society. In Afghanistan, where religion was still seen
as a natural way of life and not a political ideology, attempts by visiting
Arabs to tell the Afghans how to be better Muslims fell on deaf ears.
Afghans were so secure in their faith that they could not be bullied into
believing that they needed to be better Muslims. And their contempt for
foreigners meant that they were least likely to take advice from Arabs or
Pakistanis on what they saw as their own religion.

The roots of this cultural certainty, that they knew Islam better than
anyone else, went deep, and I had often observed it during my own anthropological fieldwork in Afghanistan during the 1970s. One small example I remembered vividly occurred when I was living in a summer
nomad camp and discussing religion with a young shepherd because
there was nothing else to do and this was always considered a good subject for conversation. We were debating the comparative advantages of
Islam over other religions when he moved into a favorite topic of plural
marriage. "Yes," he declared, "one of the advantages of Islam is that a
man can have seven wives." And I replied, "No you can't; the *shari'ah*
limits a man to only four wives." "No, you're wrong," he objected. We
continued to argue back and forth with no resolution when who should
happen along the trail but a mullah whom we immediately invited to
drink tea with us. The shepherd then said, "Mullah, sir, this foreigner
says that a Muslim can't have seven wives! Go on. Tell him he is wrong."
But the mullah replied, "Well he can't. The foreigner is right. You can
only have four." Now, you might have thought that an answer by an authoritative religious figure would have ended the argument, but it did
not. The shepherd paused only to sip some more tea and then countered
by declaring that Haji so-and-so had seven wives. The mullah said he
must be mistaken, "Perhaps some died or he divorced some, but I am
sure he has no more than four wives." The shepherd was not deterred.
"No, no, I know it to be true. Besides, it is well known that those Muslims who may have to fight *jihad* are allowed three extra wives." Now,
the mullah practically choked on his tea and said, "No, there is no *jihad*
exception in *shari'ah*!" But the shepherd simply declared, "Oh yes there
is," and that ended the discussion. The shepherd was illiterate and had no
formal religious education, but he was quite sure of what he knew about
his own religion, and having a mullah contradict him was merely an an-
noyance that had no effect on his belief.

Thus although the Taliban were known to the outside world for their
imposition of a puritanical Islam, the assertion that only their interpretation of Islam had validity did not take root in Afghanistan. Instead
people looked upon these new rules as a form of oppression. This was

reinforced by the traditional Afghan prejudice against village mullahs, who generally lacked social prestige, and the ruling Taliban councils consisted almost entirely of ill-educated mullahs whose knowledge of Islamic theology and the wider world was very limited. Had they had better information, they would likely have been more aware of the risks they took in allowing Osama bin Laden to use Afghanistan as a base for his international *jihad* against the United States and the West in general. However, the Taliban had shown little interest in the affairs of al-Qaeda. Although it was the training base for that movement, few Afghans were involved. Afghans were willing to die in a *jihad* to free their own country, but they were unwilling to die in other people's *jihads*. Also, because they saw martyrdom as a consolation prize and not a goal to be sought, they had no use for plots that were suicidal.

Even before the 9-11 attacks on the United States, the Taliban were isolated by the world community for harboring terrorists and their dependence on revenue from the international drug trade. As a result they became even more dependent on financial and political support from Pakistan and Osama bin Laden. This was to prove their undoing following the September 11 attacks on the United States. Pakistan immediately deserted them, and their alliance with al-Qaeda made them a direct target of the United States. At the beginning of the war Mullah Omar threatened the United States with the same fate as the Russians and British if they dared to enter Afghanistan and called on the Afghan people to rise up against an American attack. The Western press ran many stories of "unconquerable Afghanistan" and the invincibility of Afghan guerillas. However, within weeks of war's beginning, Taliban positions unraveled completely. They first collapsed in the north and west, where Pashtun control had always been most resented. Kabul fell immediately after the Taliban abandoned the city, hoping to regroup in the Pashtun heartland. But this proved no sanctuary when the traditional Pashtun tribal leaders used the opportunity to regain power and expel the Taliban from Kandahar. While Mullah Omar has attempted to rally Taliban remnants who fled to Pakistan, their major tactic has been one of terror: to disrupt attempts to reconstruct Afghanistan and prevent the return of civil order. Far from heeding the Taliban call to rise up en masse against the infidels and demanding the foreign troops leave, the Afghan population appeared more inclined to ask for a larger international force to ensure stability and prevent the country's return to anarchy and civil war.

One reason that United States forces failed to draw the same level of resentment that Soviet troops had received was that the Taliban had already introduced foreign forces into the county: those of the so-called Afghan Arabs and Pakistanis. These groups were widely resented in

Afghanistan, so it was not hard for the United States to build a coalition against them. The American invasion also exposed the weakness of the Taliban even in the Pashtun region. At the time the Taliban collapsed there were probably fewer than a thousand American troops actually inside Afghanistan. In a very real sense this was merely a continuation of an Afghan fight where the winning side now had access to enough American cash to buy out most of its opponents and enough American air power to decimate the Arab Afghans and Pakistanis who chose to fight. Using one foreign invader to rid the country of another fell well within the Afghan political tradition. And the Americans could be counted upon to leave the country at some point, while it was widely feared that Pakistanis and Arabs would not, so in this case using a non-Muslim power to rid the country of unwelcome foreign Muslims was deemed acceptable. In the short run at least the pragmatism of the Afghans proved more significant than any religious ideology.

Rebuilding Afghanistan

In spite of its many problems, the current political leadership of the Afghanistan has proved remarkably pragmatic. The Bonn Accord meetings and the subsequent Loya Jirga in 2002 laid the foundation for a government that incorporated all major ethnic and regional groups. In this process, choosing cooperation rather than conflict was not a vote for idealism.

Rather, the decision was forged by necessity: in nearly a quarter century no faction ever proved capable of dominating the whole country on its own militarily, even with outside help. This experienced reality means that the chances of actually creating a broad-based government are much better than they were in 1992 when the Soviet-backed Najibullah regime collapsed and each faction struggled for supremacy. What will be the role of Islam or Islamists in this process?

Although the number of clerics was far fewer than in previous national Loya Jirgas, conservative Islamists still demanded explicit recognition of *shari'ah* law and the creation of Afghanistan as an Islamic state. Their demands were not rejected outright but instead were finessed. Of course the government could be called an Islamic state; was it not a nation of Muslims? As to *shari'ah* law, the new government pointed to the 1964 constitution, which had been reinstated and had already declared that all national laws would be in accord with Islam, so that issue was moot as well. Both in the 1964 constitution and in the new draft constitution, this assertion that a government run by Muslims is an Islamic government remains a typically Afghan way of avoiding conflict on this issue. The reason that it serves as an acceptable compromise is rooted in Afghanistan's maintenance of an older form of Islamic society in which it is not easy to tease out separate strands of religious belief from other aspects of life. The very importance of Islam as parts of people's everyday identity paradoxically reduces the power of the *'ulama* because most Afghans reject their claim of having a monopoly on defining religious orthodoxy to the rest of society. This allows political leaders, as long as they stay within the broad outlines of the faith, considerable flexibility in the policies they pursue. For example, for the first time in Afghan history, Shia legal schools are recognized in the draft Afghan constitution for disputes among Shias where no national law applies, although the Hanafi legal interpretation retains its dominance elsewhere. This increased recognition of minority rights, however, has less to do with a newfound tolerance than a recognition of the de facto autonomy of the country's regions and religious minorities.

There are great difficulties, however, in looking at the prospects for democratic pluralism because the one set of key players in civil society, political parties, are still lacking. Political factions of course exist, but these are based primarily on personal, regional, or ethnic interests. There is a striking absence of the intellectuals who formerly played a strong role in laying out their visions for an Afghan future, and the former political elite in Kabul that used the ideological party model is all but defunct. While parties will emerge in time, they are not players now. And with all current factions claiming some Islamic justification for their actions, Islam itself becomes a locus of contest and not the basis of a distinct political ideology. As a result, civil society in Afghanistan is still very much a work in progress. The idea of popular sovereignty and individual civil rights are far from being accepted as a given, let alone firmly established. In this regard most Afghans are more in sympathy with the traditional *'ulama* view that no democratic majority, however large, can change laws established by God (Zaman, this volume). But precisely because of the wide variety of crosscutting ties that make politics in the country so complex, this respect for God's authority does not immediately transfer itself to the Islamic parties or leaders as God's agents. As long as Islam is seen as bound into Afghan life at every level, it will be difficult to tell any individual Muslim how to live his life. While respect for individual autonomy is far from the extensive sets of individual rights embodied in various international human rights conventions, the Afghan view of the individual's role in society does provide a space for debate and contest that is very real.

However the country develops, Afghanistan is likely to march to its own drummer to a tune of its own making.

References Cited

Arnold, Anthony. 1983. *Afghanistan's Two-Party communism: Parcham and Khalq*. Stanford, Calif.: Hoover Institution Press, Stanford University.

Barfield, Thomas. 1996. "The Afghan Morass." *Current History 95*, no. 597: 38–43.

———. 2001. "Idol Threats." *Religion in the News* 4, no. 2: 4–7.

Dupree, Louis. 1978. *Afghanistan*. Princeton, N.J.: Princeton University Press.

Economist, The (London). 2001. "The Monster." May 26, p. 12 (U.S. edition).

Giustozzi, Antonio. 2000. *War, Politics and Society in Afghanistan, 1978–1992*. London: Hurst.

Goodson, Larry. 2001. *Afghanistan's Endless War: State Failure, Regional Politics, and the Rise of the Taliban*. Seattle: University of Washington Press.

Hanifi, Shah Mahmoud. 2001. *Inter-regional Trade and Colonial State Formation in Nineteenth-century Afghanistan*. Ph.D. dissertation, University of Michigan.

Hewad (Kabul). 2001. "Afghan Taleban: Conversion to Christianity in Muslim society against UN charter." Translated by BBC Worldwide Monitoring. January 13, pp. 1–2.

Hyman, Anthony. 1992. *Afghanistan under Soviet domination, 1964–1991*, 3rd ed. Hampshire, U.K.: Macmillan Academic and Professional.

Ibn Khaldun, 'Abd al-Rahman b. Muhammad. 1967. *The Muqaddimah: An Introduction to History*. Translated by Franz Rosenthal. Abridged ed. Princeton, N.J.: Princeton University Press.

Kakar, M. Hasan. 1971. *Afghanistan: A Study in International Political Developments, 1880–1896*. Kabul: Government Printing House.

———. 1979. *Government and Society in Afghanistan: The Reign of Amir 'Abd al-Rahman Khan*. Austin: University of Texas Press.

———. 1995. *Afghanistan: The Soviet Invasion and the Afghan Response, 1979–1982*. Berkeley and Los Angeles: University of California Press.

Kamali, Mohammad Hashim. 1985. *Law in Afghanistan*. Leiden: Brill.

Nawid, Senzil K. 1999. *Religious Response to Social Change in Afghanistan, 1919–1929: King Aman-Allah and the Afghan Ulema*. Costa Mesa, Calif.: Mazda Publishers.

Olesen, Asta. 1995. *Islam and Politics in Afghanistan*. Richmond, U.K.: Curzon.

Poullada, Leon. 1973. *Reform and Rebellion in Afghanistan, 1919–1929; King Amanullah's Failure to Modernize a Tribal Society*. Ithaca, N.Y.: Cornell University Press.

Rashid, Ahmed. 2000. *Taliban: Militant Islam, Oil, and Fundamentalism in Central Asia*. New Haven, Conn.: Yale University Press.

Roy, Olivier. 1990. *Afghanistan: Islam and Resistance in Afghanistan*. 2nd ed. Cambridge: Cambridge University Press.

———. 1995. *Afghanistan: From Holy War to Civil War*. Cambridge: Cambridge University Press.

Rubin, Barnett R. 1995. *The Search for Peace in Afghanistan: From Buffer State to Failed State*. New Haven, Conn.: Yale University Press.

————. 2002. *The Fragmentation of Afghanistan: State Formation and Collapse in the International System*. 2nd ed. New Haven, Conn.: Yale University Press.

Shahrani, M. Nazif, and Robert L. Canfield, eds. 1984. *Revolutions and Rebellions in Afghanistan: Anthropological Perspectives*. Berkeley: Institute of International Studies, University of California Press.

Shari'at (Kabul). 2001. Editorial. Translated by BBC Worldwide Monitoring. February 28, pp. 1–2.

Al-Sharq al-Awsat (London). 2001. "Egypt's Mufti Wasil Interviewed on Recent Visit to Afghanistan." Translated by BBC Summary of World Broadcasts. March 20.

Times (London). 2001. "Taleban Boasts of Smashing 'Idols.'" March 6.

Chapter 10

ISLAM AND THE CULTURAL POLITICS

OF LEGITIMACY: MALAYSIA IN THE

AFTERMATH OF SEPTEMBER 11

Michael G. Peletz

Four weeks after the attacks on the World Trade Center and the Pentagon that occurred on September 11, 2001, the American government began a massive bombing campaign in Afghanistan to dislodge the Taliban and root out and destroy the al-Qaeda network that was believed to be responsible for the September 11 carnage. As was widely expected, the days immediately following the beginning of the U.S. bombing saw major protests throughout the Muslim world. October 12, for example, witnessed a demonstration involving over three thousand people in front of the heavily fortified U.S. Embassy in Kuala Lumpur, the federal capital of the Muslim-majority nation of Malaysia. By the time the demonstrators attained a critical mass, they were dispersed with water cannons and the threat of rubber bullets and other forms of retaliation by security forces under the direction of Prime Minister Mahathir Mohamad, a (relatively) secular nationalist who is well known throughout the world for his liberal economic reasoning and authoritarian governance. Also by this time, leaders of the major Islamist opposition party (the pan-Malaysian Islamic party, or PAS), whose supporters include over a million registered voters, had called for a *jihad* or "holy war" against the United States. Not surprisingly, sidewalk vendors in certain parts of the country boasted brisk sales of T-shirts bearing Osama bin Laden's face and the phrase "Man of the World."

Many Americans who followed these stories on CNN or through sensationalistic reports in the *New York Times* and other media outlets experienced an unsettling sense of déjà vu. To them—and of course to many others—it seemed that with regard to attitudes toward the West and America specifically, Muslims in Malaysia partake of the same sensibilities as "fundamentalist" or "extremist" Muslims associated with al-Qaeda, the Taliban, Hamas, Hezbollah, and the like.

These impressions were reinforced in the months that followed when intelligence experts and media specialists repeatedly referred to Malaysia in the Western press as a "staging area" or "launching pad" for terrorist attacks against the United States. To bolster this claim, Western intelligence officials invariably point to the existence of (classified) photographic evidence of a January 2000 meeting in Kuala Lumpur at the condominium owned by a Malay Muslim (Yazid Sufaat) and his wife (Sejahratul Dursina). The thirty-eight-year-old Yazid, a biochemist turned businessman trained at California State University–Sacramento as well as a former captain in the Malaysian army, is believed to be a local supporter of al-Qaeda and to have hosted a meeting in his condominium with at least three al-Qaeda operatives. Two of these latter men (Nawak Alhazmi and Khalid al-Midhar) were among the hijackers of American Airlines Flight 66, which crashed into the Pentagon. The third, Zacarias Moussaoui, is the Moroccan-born French citizen who is assumed to have been "the twentieth hijacker" and is currently on trial in the United States on charges of conspiring in the September 11 attacks.

Yazid, who was arrested in Malaysia in December 2001 and has been in detention ever since, is often referred to as the "money man," since he is believed to have supplied Moussaoui with the funds and official papers that enabled him to travel to the United States and collaborate with the other hijackers. Yazid's wife was arrested along with thirteen others in April 2002, in a series of raids by Malaysian authorities that are said to have turned up military training notes, computers, and a map of Malaysia's largest port (Port Klang). These arrests were widely reported in the Western media. So, too, were the arrests of alleged Islamic militants in neighboring Singapore in December 2001 and August 2002, which yielded information suggesting they intended to bomb U.S. interests and a variety of "soft targets" in Singapore, Malaysia, and beyond.

The sense one might get from afar that Malaysia is a hotbed of terrorist activity and that large numbers of Malaysia's Muslims are violent militants is bolstered by government accounts of the organization known as Jemaah Islamiyah, roughly, "the Islamic group" (see Hefner, this volume). The sixty-five-year-old Indonesian-born cleric who is the spiritual leader of this group, Abu Bakar Bashir, is an unabashed admirer of Osama bin Laden. Perhaps more germane is that he seeks the creation, by whatever means necessary, of a territorially expansive Islamic state in Southeast Asia that includes southern Thailand, Malaysia, Singapore, Brunei, Indonesia, and the southern Philippines. Abu Bakar Bashir fled his Indonesian homeland during the early 1980s, at which point he settled in Malaysia, where he is believed to have begun recruiting local Malays, Indonesians, and others—some of whom fought alongside Mujahidin forces against the Soviets in Afghanistan—and training them in the basics of guerrilla warfare and terrorism. The fact that Abu Bakar Bashir lived in Malaysia for some fourteen years has taken on new meaning

following the deadly blasts in Bali on October 12, 2002, which many authorities in Southeast Asia and the West attribute to his organization (Jemaah Islamiyah). Indeed, it is widely assumed, at least in government
circles, that Jemaah Islamiyah has numerous cells in Malaysia, and that
the months and years ahead could see bombings in Malaysia on a scale as
devastating as those in Bali.

The accounts of government officials and journalists are by no means
the only phenomena that might give the outside observer cause for alarm.
Even the casual traveler to Kuala Lumpur will come across bookshops
and sidewalk vendors selling pamphlets, books, audiocassettes, and CDs
depicting Osama bin Laden in heroic terms. Similarly, anyone wandering
around the Masjid India area of Kuala Lumpur is likely to encounter
sidewalk merchants selling Osama bin Laden T-shirts emblazed with images of the fiery explosion and collapse of the World Trade Center. Amid
the endless variety of cell-phone holders and other cheap plastic goods
hawked on sidewalks throughout the city, one can also find toy tanks
marketed as replicas of the tanks used by the Taliban. Impressions along
these lines are likely to be reinforced if one journeys to the east coast state
of Terengganu, which, like the neighboring state of Kelantan, is under the
control of PAS. In Terengganu one cannot miss the billboards along the
roadside that endorse the local government's efforts to implement laws
known as *hudud*. These laws entail the harsh punishments specified in
the Qur'an for certain criminal offenses, such as amputation of limbs for
theft, flogging and imprisonment for fornication, stoning to death for
adultery, and so on.

Appearances, though, are not always what they seem. One of the main
points I emphasize in this chapter is that despite the embassy demonstration and other external signs that might suggest a radicalization of Islamic sensibilities in Malaysia in the wake of September 11, most Muslims
in Malaysia continue to be quite moderate and democratically oriented.
A second point is that global dynamics set in motion by the events of September 11 have altered the political playing fields in Malaysia in a variety
of deeply significant ways, some rather predictable, others definitely not.
On the one hand, they greatly strengthened Prime Minister Mahathir's
hand vis-à-vis his political opponents, including PAS supporters and others committed to the creation of an Islamic state as well as those of a
more liberal and cosmopolitan bent who have focused their reformist energy on restoring the integrity of the secular judiciary and expanding
the space of civil society. In the process these dynamics have undercut
opportunities for the expansion of civil society and the pluralistic sensibilities underlying them. On the other hand, dynamics associated with
September 11 and its aftermath have enhanced the legitimacy of increasingly high-profile Muslim feminist organizations, such as Sisters in Islam,

who have worked to bring about reforms in the Islamic courts and other Islamic institutions so as to improve the legal options and overall living standards of Muslim women. This is an exceedingly important development, but it has come at considerable cost to the most visible spokespersons of such groups and others who have questioned one or another official version of Islam.

A third point I underscore is that analysis of the larger context in which the embassy demonstrations occurred indicates that Muslims in Malaysia are not all that concerned with positioning themselves against the West. More pressing than any such "inter-civilizational" clashes, to invoke Samuel Huntington's (1996) highly problematic terminology and prophecy, are the struggles over which contested visions of Islam should prevail in Malaysia in the present and the future. The key debates—and certainly the ones that are most intensely felt—in other words, bear on *intra*-civilizational clashes, not those of an inter-civilizational variety. The same is true of neighboring Indonesia and many other parts of the Islamic world (Hefner 2000; Eickelman and Piscatori 1996; Lawrence 1998; Kepel 2002).

To put some of this in slightly different terms, the politics of legitimacy has reached unprecedented levels of intensity in Malaysia. One result has been the intensification of discursive wars of position built around Manichaean contrasts between "good Muslims" on the one side and "bad Muslims" on the other. Partly because certain categories of "bad Muslims" are defined as apostates, infidels, or both, these wars of position have heightened the salience of divides between Muslims and non-Muslims. More generally, all such dynamics make clear that the main challenges to the state come not from territorial or other claims made by ethnic or religious minorities, but from competing claims within the demographically and politically dominant Malay Muslim community.

BACKGROUND AND CONTEXT

Malaysia is frequently described in travel brochures and academic treatises as "the crossroads of Asia," owing to the country's rich cultural and ethnic diversity. The ethnic mosaic is usually discussed in terms of four major categories.[1] "Malays," all of whom are Muslims, make up about 51 percent of the total population. "Chinese," who are usually described as practicing a syncretistic blend of Buddhism, Confucianism, and Taoism, compose about 26 percent. "Indians," most of whom are Hindus, though some are Sikh, Christian, or Muslim, account for about 7 percent. And "Others," including hill-dwelling aborigines, Eurasians, and the like, make up the remaining 16 percent (Government of Malaysia 2000).

The legal system is frequently glossed as pluralistic to highlight the diversity and variegated provenance of its three major traditions of law: Malay customary law (*adat*), which pertains only to Malays; Islamic law (Malay, *syariah,* Arabic, *shari'a*), which is relevant to Malays and all other Muslims, albeit to a limited range of their affairs; and national (statutory) law introduced by British colonists in the nineteenth century, which bears on all citizens and others in Malaysia. Malaysia's political institutions include a system of parliamentary democracy and a constitutional monarchy, much like the British system upon which it is modeled. They also include an indigenous (Malay) polity of precolonial origin, which has been stripped of most of its power but is formally intact.

Malaysia has a population of some 24 million people. I would argue, though, that the Malaysian case is of much greater significance than the country's demographic girth might suggest at first glance. One set of reasons for this is that Malaysia is among the most successful of the "non-Confucian" Asian tigers and has also sustained a pace of rapid development that is probably second to none in the Muslim world. Another is that Malaysian Prime Minister Mahathir (r. 1981–2003), far more than any of his predecessors, successfully projected both the Malaysian case and his particular ideas on political-economic modernization as an emulable model for other regions of the world. The seventy-eight-year-old Mahathir has frequently claimed, for example, that the Malaysian model of growth-led development that is simultaneously informed by transcendent Islamic values and "smart partnerships" linking the civil service, the private sector, and political leaders is a preferred alternative to Western-style development in other Muslim-majority nations and in much of the southern hemisphere as a whole. In his "role as 'emissary' for the South," Mahathir has also offered "a post-Bandung discourse of Malaysian-style 'economic nationalism' for peripheral states to follow [that is] fashioned around themes of political solidarity with poor and developing countries" (Hilley 2001, 99). Mahathir's messages have been well received in many quarters, both at home and abroad. This is partly because in the course of a mere generation or so Malaysia has catapulted itself into the slender ranks of Muslim countries with appreciable middle classes and burgeoning if still precarious civil societies (Abdul Rahman Embong 2002). Circumstances such as these help explain why Malaysia has become a locus of nationalist, transnational, and academic discourses concerning "Muslim modernities," "Asian modernities," and "alternative modernities" generally (Ong 1999; Peletz 2002; see also Appadurai 1996; Eickelman and Piscatori 1996; Rofel 1999; Hefner 2000).

It remains to emphasize that ethnic distinctions and antagonisms in Malaysia are infused with far-reaching religious, political, and economic significance and have been exacerbated by development strategies of the postcolonial government. This is most evident with the New Economic Policy (NEP, 1971–90), which sought to eradicate poverty among all Malaysians and to "restructure society" by undermining the material and symbolic connections between ethnic categories on the one hand and economic standing and function on the other. By pursuing policies to help the predominantly rural and agricultural Malays "catch up" economically with Chinese and Indians, the government has placed tremendous emphasis on "race" (on being a Malay or a non-Malay) as a criterion in allocating government loans and subsidies and other scarce resources (university scholarships, contractors' licenses, start-up funds for businesses, etc.). These policies have heightened the awareness of distinctions between Malays and non-Malays and made them all the more politically and economically salient.

The NEP also exacerbated class antagonisms within the Malay community. Although its programs helped create a Malay middle class and enriched some Malays quite substantially, they left other Malays no better (and, in some cases, relatively worse) off than before in terms of material standing and access to social justice. Reactions to the NEP have taken many forms, including active and passive resistance to the Green Revolution implemented as a key feature of the NEP in many areas, and disaffection from the central clique of the ruling political party and from the party in its entirety.

Dissatisfaction with the government's commitment to modernity and the NEP in particular has fueled Malaysia's Islamic resurgence. The resurgence is known as the *dakwah* (Arabic *da'wa*) movement. The term *dakwah* means to invite or call one to the Islamic cause, or to respond to the invitation or call, hence missionary work, including making Muslims better Muslims. The resurgence is usually said to date from the early 1970s, even though it is most appropriately viewed as an outgrowth of earlier developments in Islamic nationalism and reform, such as those associated with the Kaum Muda (Young Group) movement of the 1920s and 1930s (Roff 1967). The *dakwah* movement is thoroughly homegrown but has also been inspired by Islamist groups and Islamic revivalism in Indonesia, Pakistan, Egypt, Libya, and other parts of the Muslim world.

Most scholars approach the resurgence as response, indeed a form of resistance, to one or more of the following analytically related and culturally interlocked sets of developments. The first development concerns the postcolonial state's Western-oriented modernization policies (noted above), which entail a heavily interventionist role for the state with respect to economic planning, distribution, and capitalist processes as a whole. These policies are widely seen as contributing to Malaysia's overdependence on Western capital; to the economic success of Chinese and Indians relative to Malays; and to upper-class corruption as well as deracination and moral and spiritual bankruptcy throughout the Malay community. The second development involves the simultaneous shifting and hardening of class interests and animosities, especially between the newly emerged middle class and an entrenched (aristocratic) ruling class. The third development is the tightening of ethnic boundaries, particularly those separating Malays and Chinese. These boundaries have become increasingly pronounced and freighted in recent decades, owing largely to NEP-era practices highlighting race in the allocation of scarce government resources. The NEP is commonly regarded as having encouraged cultural assertiveness—some would say chauvinism—among Malays (Chandra Muzaffar 1987; Zainah Anwar 1987). This cultural assertiveness is especially evident as regards Islam, the practice of which, along with speaking the Malay language and observing Malay "custom" (*adat*), is a defining feature, and increasingly *the* key symbol, of Malayness. More broadly, scholars generally view the *dakwah* movement as a powerful vehicle for the articulation of moral opposition to government development policies, traditional as well as emergent class structures, other ethnic groups, or some combination of these or related phenomena (Shamsul A.B. 1983; Nagata 1984; Chandra Muzaffar 1987; Zainah Anwar 1987; Muhammad Abu Bakar 1987; Husin Mutalib 1993; Peletz 1997, 2002).

Dakwah organizations are highly diverse and their objectives are in certain respects mutually incompatible. However, they all share an overriding concern to revitalize or reactualize (local) Islam and the (local) Muslim community by encouraging stronger commitment to the teachings of the Qur'an and the *hadith,* in order to effect a more Islamic way of life (*din*). The main groups have included the following: (1) Darul Arqam, a communal, land-based organization that enjoined its members to emulate the life of the Prophet and that strove for economic self-sufficiency by establishing its own schools, clinics, mosques, business enterprises, and shopping centers; it was banned by the government in 1994; (2) Jamaat Tabligh, a loosely structured Delhi-based missionary organization seeking to revitalize the spirit of Islam by means of one-on-one contacts, informal discussion groups, and the personal examples set by its itinerant missionaries; and (3) ABIM (Angkatan Belia Islam Malaysia; the Muslim Youth Movement of Malaysia), which emphasizes formal education and is extremely popular among university students, former student leaders, and youth generally, and encourages lobbying efforts, active participation in party politics, and otherwise "working within the system."

Also worthy of mention here is the major opposition party, PAS (Parti Islam Se-Malaysia; the Pan-Malaysian Islamic Party), the successor to the

Hizbul Muslimin (Islamic Party) formally inaugurated in 1948, which has a decidedly populist orientation and has been a key player in Malaysian politics since shortly after its formation in 1951 (Kessler 1978; Safie bin Ibrahim 1981; Firdaus Haji Abdullah 1985). Strictly speaking, PAS is not part of the *dakwah* movement, though many of its objectives are espoused by some segments of the movement. The most basic of these objectives is the creation of an Islamic state with the Qur'an and the Sunnah as its constitution.

The relationships between the various segments of the movement and the state merit careful consideration, for they have fueled many political and religious dynamics in contemporary Malaysia. As far as most scholars are concerned, Darul Arqam has never posed an appreciable threat to the state (its banning by the government in 1994 notwithstanding). But ABIM and PAS clearly have, particularly since their leaders have frequently charged the ruling party (UMNO, the United Malays National Organization) with failing to safeguard the interests and well-being of the Malay community, especially with regard to Islam. PAS in particular has also claimed that the ruling party has sold out to local Chinese and Indians as well as foreign capitalists, all of whom are seen as having contributed both to Malaysia's underdevelopment and dependence on foreign markets and to its moral decadence and spiritual bankruptcy.

In such a religious and political climate the ruling party has to work overtime to validate its Islamic credentials—relegitimize the party and the state—and thus co-opt, or at least undercut, both the Islamic resurgents and the opposition party. This means going forward with its own far-reaching but ultimately rather moderate Islamization program, which is simultaneously a consequence of the *dakwah* phenomenon and a key factor in its promotion along state- and regime-friendly lines. This program to "out-Islamicize" the opposition, which does at times have those qualities of an arms race that Gregory Bateson (1936), in a very different context, referred to as "schismogenesis," has included: the creation of an international Islamic university, an Islamic stock market, and a nationwide system of Islamic banking and insurance (all geared ultimately toward meeting the material and other needs of the urban middle classes and assuring them that one can be both authentic Muslims and members of a modern middle class); the building and refurbishing of prayer houses and mosques; and the passage of myriad legislative measures bearing on Islam and Islamic law specifically. The government's Islamization program has also entailed the co-optation of charismatic Muslim intellectuals, partly by offering them influential posts in the administration. The most stunning success in this regard occurred in 1982 when Mahathir succeeded in converting then ABIM President Anwar Ibrahim to the cause of UMNO, thus fracturing the Islamist opposition. (In subsequent years Anwar rose through the ranks to become deputy prime minister, a position he held until he was ousted and jailed in 1998). Broadly speaking, state strategies overseen by Mahathir have succeeded in undercutting PAS and ABIM, and in retaining the support of urban middle-class Malays who are most responsive to *dakwah* appeals. But they have also seriously alienated non-Malays, who make up nearly half of Malaysia's multiethnic population, just as they have intensified ethnic antagonism. Indeed, Chinese and Indians see the Islamic resurgence as an overtly political movement with strong xenophobic overtones bent on eroding the rights of non-Muslims and subjecting them to the dictates of Islam.

As should be clear, many of the organizations associated with Malaysia's Islamic resurgence are embroiled in struggles with different groups of national elites concerning the role, scope, and force of Islam in Malaysia's modernity project, as is the main Islamic opposition party (PAS). Also centrally involved or directly implicated in such struggles are activist-oriented Muslim feminists who reject PAS-style Islamization as misguided and misogynist; and "ordinary Muslims" (or "ordinary Malays"; the two terms are used here interchangeably), who are not in the forefront of contemporary religious or political developments but are among the more enduring targets of resurgents' efforts at cultural cleansing. Ordinary Muslims compose the majority of the Muslim population and are most directly affected by the changes sought in Islamic law, though the themes of broader significance are the pluralistic nature of Malaysian Islam and the highly contested nature of Islamic legal institutions and their role in modernity in contemporary Malaysia.

THE AFTERMATH OF SEPTEMBER 11

I noted earlier that the events of September 11 greatly strengthened Mahathir's hand vis-à-vis his political opponents, especially the Malay Muslims among them. This is largely because in the weeks and months following September 11, Mahathir and his ruling party deftly painted their PAS adversaries as "extremists" with Taliban, if not al-Qaeda-style, sensibilities and aspirations. In addition, Mahathir and other UMNO elites engineered the high-profile arrests of dozens of political opponents—nearly all of them Malay Muslims—who were detained under the dreaded Internal Security Act (ISA), on the grounds of "national security." Some of those arrested may have been passive supporters or active members of Jemaah Islamiyah or a shadowy organization known as the Malaysian Militant/Mujahidin Group (Kumpulan Militan/Mujahidin Malaysia, KMM), whose professed goals resonate in important ways with those of al-Qaeda (Abuza 2003). But many of the arrests seemed to have had little if anything to do with real or imagined threats to national security and everything to do with Mahathir's obsessive concerns to undercut his political rivals and silence the rest of the population via self-censorship.

Overall, Mahathir's actions helped convince the electorate that PAS supporters are dangerous, violent extremists capable of harboring if not working directly with groups such as al-Qaeda. But UMNO still has to work very hard to win elections. Indeed, some knowledgeable observers contend that they must work ever more strenuously—by hook or by crook—in each election in order to emerge victorious. So the point here is not that because of September 11 and its aftermath the ruling party has been in a position to sit back and coast. It is, rather, that the dynamics of September 11 enabled UMNO to stem the electoral shift toward PAS that occurred as a result of the enduring crises that Mahathir created in the latter part of 1998 by his sacking, jailing, and pillorying of his former heir apparent, Anwar Ibrahim, on largely trumped-up charges of sodomy, corruption, and bribery. As many readers may recall, Anwar was convicted in the secular courts and sentenced to fifteen years in prison after a mockery of a trial characterized by gross irregularities on the part of government prosecutors and judges. The Anwar trial and the ensuing crises it created dealt a serious blow to the independence and integrity of the judiciary, and were partly responsible for the electoral shift toward PAS—and the growth of a multiparty opposition coalition consisting of PAS, the National Justice Party (Parti Keadilan Nasional, headed by Anwar's wife, Wan Azizah Wan Ismail), the (predominantly Chinese) Democratic Action Party, and the socialist-oriented People's Party of Malaysia (Parti Rakyat Malaysia, or PRM)—that was evident in the national elections of November 1999. But the more relevant point, to repeat, is that September 11 halted the electoral shift toward PAS just as it undercut the opposition alliance and the *reformasi* (reform) movement associated with it. The paramount dilemma for PAS, as one of the party's intellectuals expressed it to me in an interview in August 2002, is that "people are afraid of us now." The understandably triumphant UMNO perspective is succinctly conveyed in the words of the press secretary of an UMNO politician from Kelantan whom I interviewed (in August 2002 as well); "September 11 was a godsend for us."

UMNO's ascendancy since September 11 has contributed to heightened political stability, at least in the short run. It also signals the willingness of Malaysians to work with the United States in pursuing policies of mutual interest, some of which reflects the more pervasive sense that UMNO and its national leaders speak for the majority of Malays and the majority of Malaysians; and that the fortunes of Malays and Malaysians as a whole are very much intertwined with those of the United States. The

United States is Malaysia's largest trading partner and largest foreign investor, and many people in Malaysia are well aware that they benefit directly from the stability and strength of America's economy and other institutions.

There is, however, a major downside to the closer relationship that has developed between U.S. leaders and Mahathir since September 11. The unprecedented coziness that now characterizes relations between Washington and Kuala Lumpur has dealt a terrible blow to local and international campaigns geared toward pressuring Malaysian authorities to reduce corruption, restore the integrity of the judiciary, and clean up their record on human rights. One of the consistent themes that emerged from my (August 2002) interviews with lawyers, judges, and other professionals is that when it comes to Malaysia, U.S. policy makers are single-mindedly preoccupied with insuring that its leaders join the U.S. "war against terror." Consequently, the United States stopped exerting pressure on Mahathir to reestablish the autonomy and integrity of the judiciary and to expand human rights and civil society. Haji Suleiman Abdullah, who is one of the most prominent legal experts in the country as well as the head of the Syariah Bar Council and former head of the Malaysian Bar Association, told me quite emphatically that with little or no U.S. pressure on the prime minister to "clean up his act," the judiciary will be further eroded and human rights will continue to suffer. He added that in the aftermath of the Anwar affair, reformers had attained a critical momentum, which had dissipated in the wake of September 11. Worse, though, is what Suleiman and some of his colleagues ruefully refer to as the "ASEANization" of basic Malaysian institutions. What is meant by this turn of phrase is that once reputable Malaysian institutions like the judiciary and the civil service have deteriorated to the levels characteristic of their counterparts in neighboring ASEAN countries such as Indonesia and the Philippines.

Suleiman and many others see the U.S. Patriot Act as a complete vindication of Mahathir's heavy-handed use of the dreaded ISA to deal with his critics. One pro-Mahathir line of reasoning I encountered runs as follows: "The United States has been a democracy for over two hundred years and you still need these kinds of laws. Malaysia has only been independent and democratic for about fifty years, so of course we still need them." Mahathir was in fact emboldened by U.S. policy to the point of claiming that the Patriot Act is modeled on Malaysia's ISA! Many Malaysians, moreover, see the Patriot Act and related measures as profoundly hypocritical, and as one more example of U.S. hostility toward Muslims. Perhaps more important, they emphasize that the prolonged detentions of Muslim minorities, without trial or specific charges, sets an abysmal example and sends a terribly disheartening message to those throughout the world who are engaged in struggles to enhance pluralistic sensibilities and democratic institutions. With regard to these issues, then, and perhaps more obviously U.S. cocreation and support of Israeli policies toward Palestinians, the U.S. bombing of Afghanistan, and the U.S.-led war against Iraq, Muslim professionals and others in Malaysia evince significant hostility toward the United States that could easily grow and solidify in the months and years ahead. This is all the more likely if the United States proceeds with the establishment of a regional counterterrorism center on Malaysian soil and the promotion throughout the Muslim world and beyond of Mahathir as an exemplary Muslim leader who represents the best of Islam and modernity if not *"the* shining light of moderate Islam"* (Shamsul A.B. 2001, 4709, emphasis added).

Muslim Feminists and the PUM Controversy

I mentioned earlier that events since September 11 have augmented the legitimacy of high-profile Muslim feminist organizations like Sisters in Islam. In the process these events have drawn positive attention to the activities and agendas of such groups, which are geared toward improving the legal options and living standards of Muslim women in accordance with contemporary reinterpretations of sacred religious texts. The enhanced legitimacy has come about partly because organizations like Sisters in Islam have long been highly critical of PAS and other Islamist groups on the grounds that they are backward-looking, intolerant, misogynist, extremist, and otherwise dangerous. As a result of post-September 11 developments, Muslims and non-Muslims alike are listening more carefully to what the Sisters in Islam have to say about the Qur'an, Islam, and policies toward women, as well as issues of equality, justice, and democracy generally. Dynamics such as these bode well for Muslim and other women in Malaysia, particularly since they are drawing women into public and specifically political arenas in new and productive ways.

Like university-educated Muslim feminists in many other parts of the world (Ahmed 1992; Afkhami 1995), the women involved in Sisters in Islam have endeavored to promote alternative readings of foundational Islamic texts such as the Qur'an and the *hadith.* These scholarly efforts are aimed at recuperating the egalitarian ethical and legal sensibilities of early Islam that were stifled by more hierarchical readings of classic texts, the latter of which gained ascendancy in the course of the formal codification and official elaboration of Islamic law and "custom" that occurred in the centuries after the deaths of the Prophet and his companions. Drawing also on the liberal sensibilities of global feminism and transnational NGOs concerned with women's issues and human rights, Sisters in Islam have campaigned vigorously to insure greater legal and basic

human rights for Muslim women. They have done so mostly by organizing high-profile workshops and conferences, by writing letters to the editors of major dailies, by publishing pamphlets and books (with titles such
as *Are Muslim Men Allowed to Beat Their Wives?*), and by formal and
informal lobbying efforts of various kinds. Much of their energy has been
devoted to ameliorating problems associated with polygyny, abandon-
ment, and the mistreatment of women in the context of marriage and
divorce. They have also forced the government to respond with various
legislative and policy measures, including the passage in 1994 of a national law against domestic violence that has informed judicial process in
the Islamic courts and has also had salutary effects in Malaysian society
as a whole.

Sisters in Islam is a very small organization with perhaps only a dozen
or so formal members (part of a deal struck with the government that
they would not attempt to create a mass movement). Despite their small
numbers, the Sisters in Islam have extensive networks with other progressive NGOs, both local and transnational, and are frequently featured
in the local media. The bottom line is that because of their adept engagement in coalitional politics, their influence is enormous (see also Singerman, this volume). They work closely with officials in various ministries,
including but not limited to the Ministry of Women and Family Development, and they are in direct communication with the prime minister himself on legislative and policy matters concerning women and religion. The
Sisters in Islam are also taken quite seriously by high-ranking officials in
the indigenous polity, like the Sultan of Selangor, though some ordinary
Muslims regard them as too radical, too feminist, and/or too Western in
their approaches to textual interpretation, advocacy, and reform. More
generally, the Sisters in Islam promote a vision of Islam that is highly
principled, inclusive, and pluralistic. In these and other ways they have
contributed a great deal to the cultivation and "scaling up" of sentiments
and dispositions that are conducive to the expansion of civil society. In all
likelihood, they will continue to do so in the months and years ahead.

To better appreciate where the Sisters in Islam are situated in the playing fields of contemporary Malaysian Islam, we might consider some of
the points that emerged in interviews I conducted with members of the
organization in August 2002. One of the program directors, Ruzana
Udin, underscored that the Sisters in Islam is the only group in Malaysia
that is fighting within an Islamic framework for women's rights; that they
are caught in the middle of the struggle between UMNO and PAS; and
that Mahathir and UMNO are not really "pro-women" but are quite liberal compared to PAS. Mahathir "gave space" to Sisters in Islam partly
because the government needs moderate voices like theirs to help them
undercut PAS. This relationship leads moderate Muslims to support Sis-

ters in Islam, but it also contributes to the view that Sisters in Islam is "linked to" (managed by) the government.

My conversation with Zainah Anwar, the extremely articulate and highly personable executive director of the organization, focused largely on PAS. This is not surprising since like many others involved with Muslim feminist groups and progressive NGOs, she sees PAS as the chief impediment to the realization of her objectives to win the hearts and minds of the new Muslim middle classes. "We were against the World Trade Center bombings, but we are also against the U.S. bombing in Afghanistan. [That said,] most moderate Muslims do not support PAS's call to *jihad* against the U.S." By way of contextualizing PAS's foreign policy views in more expansive terms, she mentioned that "*Harakah* [the PAS newspaper] is very anti-American," to which she added, "PAS felt that the Taliban were a good Islamic government, partly because they 'protected' women":

> Since September 11, many human rights NGOs that had been allied with PAS have abandoned them [because] much that PAS has done has backfired: the declaration of *jihad* against the U.S.; the PUM controversy [about which more below]; and the *hudud* law issue . . . Their positions on music, women, culture, dance, *hudud*—all of this puts them on the intolerant, extremist side of Islam. They have unleashed and helped legitimize a [Malay] mindset of 'everyone has to defend Islam,' that 'Islam is under siege.' They don't believe in *ijtihad* [independent reasoning], . . . have medieval, ahistorical minds . . . [and] no ability to deal with differences of opinion within Islam.

Turning to some of the broader issues, Zainah observed that "there is a huge middle class here. With so much at stake, they don't want to take to the streets [like Indonesia]; they're committed to the democratic process . . . [even though] both PAS and UMNO have in different ways tried to break the social contract. . . . The Sisters in Islam want a consistent, principled, liberal, progressive Islam," a goal shared by some in the government. The problem, though, is that due to "police abuse, corruption, the ISA," and the like, "the government lacks the moral authority to bring about change." So "we are building a broad base through public education, working with single mothers, Puteri UMNO [the wing of UMNO devoted to young women], young lawyers, religious people, and others, and targeting future leaders."

Despite their enhanced legitimacy in many circles, the leaders of groups like Sisters in Islam have paid a heavy price for their high-profile critiques of the Islamic courts and various other contemporary Islamic institutions that they see as having developed in ways that are out of keeping with the egalitarian sensibilities of the Prophet's original message. Zainah Anwar in particular has come under repeated fire from PAS leadership as well as the Persatuan Ulama Malaysia (Association of Malaysian Ulama; PUM), which claims to be a national organization of *'ulama,* or religious scholars. In the early part of 2002, leaders of the PUM—the majority of whom appear to be PAS stalwarts—accused her and five other public intellectuals of insulting the Prophet and disgracing Islam, both of which are grave offenses according to Islamic doctrine and Malaysian state law alike and could result in lengthy prison sentences.[2] In addition, the PUM petitioned the sultans, who are the official heads of Islamic affairs in their respective states, to have religious experts issue an authoritative legal opinion, or *fatwa,* that would condemn all six of the individuals involved and declare that the five of them who are Muslims are guilty of apostasy, an offense that many Muslims in Malaysia and elsewhere feel should result in the death penalty. The individuals thus targeted include (in addition to Zainah Anwar): Patricia Martinez, a well regarded scholar of Islam; Kassim Ahmad and Akbar Ali, both of whom are respected journalists; Malik Imtiaz Sarwar, an accomplished lawyer specializing in human rights; as well as Farish Noor, an incisive and outspoken political scientist, human rights activist, and journalist who perhaps more than any of the others has been vilified for his controversial remarks about the need for an Islamic reformation in Malaysia and elsewhere in the Muslim world. Some of these individuals have had their cars vandalized and have received anonymous threats that they will be raped or killed or both if they persist in their criticisms of official views of Islam. Needless to say, this kind of retaliation has taken a tremendous toll. Certain of the individuals thus targeted are understandably loath to remain in Malaysia, and at least one of them has become despondent to the point of contemplating suicide.

Hudud *Law and Moral Reasoning*

A related but analytically distinct dynamic has to do with the previously noted fact that in the aftermath of September 11, Mahathir along with other UMNO leaders and the heads of various NGOs including but not limited to Sisters in Islam have successfully painted PAS and other Islamists into a corner. One consequence has been a hardening of PAS's positions on many fronts, including the necessity of creating a state apparatus of Islamic design (an "Islamic state"). As a step in the direction of establishing a system of Islamic government and spirituality in Malaysia, the PAS-controlled state government of Terengganu passed legislation in July 2002 to implement *hudud* law, much as the PAS-controlled state government of Kelantan did in 1993. *Hudud* law deals with crimes and punishments that Muslim jurists have conventionally viewed as derived from foundational Islamic texts such as the Qur'an and the *hadith.* In

Malaysia, the main crimes include theft, highway robbery, fornication, adultery, and apostasy. The key punishments are corporal: amputation of limbs for theft, whipping and imprisonment for fornication that does not involve adultery, stoning to death for adultery, and so forth.

The current *hudud* controversy is exceedingly complex, partly because many textual, interpretive, procedural, evidentiary, and jurisdictional issues are both unsettled and very much contested (An-Na'im 1990; Rose Ismail 1995; Mohammad Hashim Kamali 1995, 2000). Most important to bear in mind here is that the Terengganu legislation to introduce *hudud* law is *state*-level legislation; in order for it to become effective law, it must be approved by the *federal* government. The federal government vehemently opposes PAS's version of *hudud* for all sorts of reasons; hence the situation is stalemated, with a showdown likely to develop between the state and federal governments that could well trigger a constitutional crisis.

The *hudud* controversy is also contributing to a politicization of the otherwise generally nonpoliticized police forces. This is because PAS officials in Terengganu have made clear to local police that they must enforce all religious and other laws passed by the state. Federal officials, for their part, have reminded the police in no uncertain terms that they are federal employees and thus beholden to the federal government's laws and directives, which forbid them enforcing *hudud* laws. PAS leaders have declared amid much fanfare that they expect the cooperation of local-level police and prison officials, and that if such cooperation is not forthcoming, they will train and deputize volunteer forces both to enforce the law and to build the jails necessary to hold suspects and convicted criminals.

The building of such new penal facilities seems unlikely; but not surprisingly, proclamations pro and con *hudud* laws are in the papers daily and very much on people's minds. The more general point is that the largely politically driven circulation of impassioned and dichotomous discourses on *hudud* is contributing to further polarization within the Muslim community. The cultural political situation that has developed in this community is such that one's stance on *hudud* law has become *the* litmus test of whether or not an individual is, depending on one's perspective, either an authentic or legitimate Muslim or a backward-looking, dogmatic, and bigoted one.

To refer as I have to the largely politically driven circulation of impassioned discourses on *hudud* is not to reduce one's position on *hudud* to a narrow political calculus. Powerful moral sensibilities animate many of the debates at issue. Both for this reason and because there is a significant and perhaps growing minority of Muslims—both among PAS supporters and among Malays who do not necessarily line up behind PAS platforms—who endorse the implementation of *hudud* law, it is important to understand *hudud*'s moral appeal, especially the symbols and idioms in which it is cast and interpreted.

Consider, for example, the views of a middle-aged Malay taxi driver, whom I shall refer to as Ahmad. Concerning Ahmad's background and social location, I know only a few of the basics: that he served for many years in and is now retired from the armed forces, that he earns a living driving a taxi in and around Kota Baru (Kelantan's capital), that he has two wives and ten children, and that he solemnized his second marriage across the border in Thailand so as to circumvent state laws requiring that he obtain the permission of the local Islamic court to take a second wife. He was later fined M $300 (U.S. $79) for this breach of state law, but in recounting the circumstances of this marriage to me, he shrugged off the fine as a token fee. More relevant in the broader scheme of things is that his violation of the law did not invalidate the second marriage—a situation that is particularly distressing to Muslim feminists and others who have sought, with mixed success, to reform laws bearing on polygyny (Peletz 2002).

Ahmad, who identifies with and votes for PAS, welcomes the implementation of *hudud* law primarily because "these are God's laws, not human laws; they are written in the Qur'an and people cannot tinker with them." More generally, according to Ahmad, he and others support the laws for two reasons. The first is that "this is what God wants; hence the laws must be followed." The second is that introduction of the laws will help eliminate corruption and vice. He added that women are safer under *hudud*, presumably because of the deterrent effect of harsh penalties for rape, but we did not pursue this matter. When I asked about UMNO's stance against *hudud*, Ahmad replied that many "ministers, rich guys, and big shots," including Prime Minister Mahathir, do not back the introduction of *hudud* laws because the enforcement of such laws would result in their being arrested and punished for the crimes they habitually commit, like adultery (*zina*) and drinking alcohol.

One of the basic topoi that emerged from our conversation is that UMNO is an organization of "ministers, big guys, big shots," corruption, and vice, and that PAS takes a principled stand against corruption, vice, and abuse of privilege. The populist critique that runs throughout these comments merits note (Kessler 1978, 1980), as does the fact that such critiques have broad resonance in areas like Kelantan and Terengganu that have been marginalized or largely bypassed by state-sponsored modernity. "Per capita income in Kelantan [is] only a quarter that of the national average, and foreign investment one-tenth the size of adjoining Perlis" (Hilley 2001, 190); things are not much better in Terengganu. The broader theme is that the climate of corruption, vice, and abuse of privilege created by UMNO politicians and their policies goes a long way toward helping to explain why so many Malays support PAS candidates and/or the Islamic resurgence, and the implementation of *hudud* laws in particular.

Let us proceed to a consideration of the perspectives of an extremely urbane up-and-coming PAS politician, Haji Husam Musa. The forty-four-year-old Husam graduated from the University of Malaya (with a degree in economics), is a member of parliament from a rural district of Kelantan as well as political secretary to Haji Nik Aziz bin Haji Nik Mat (chief minister of Kelantan) and chief of PAS Youth in Kelantan, who occasionally writes for *Harakah,* PAS's bimonthly newspaper. When I asked Husam to describe PAS's major objectives, his short answer was "justice and brotherhood [*keadilan* and *persaudaraan*] throughout society." He went on to explain that "justice must be based on divine instruction, and that the Almighty is the most just in the universe." People "must base their struggle on the Holy Books . . . be they the Qur'an, the Bible, or the Old Testament; . . . for Muslims [it must be] the Qur'an." Husam added that in contemporary Malaysia, corruption and other crime are endemic; hence there can be no justice. "Look at all the rapes and murder reported in the newspapers. The existing laws do nothing; they are rubbish. . . . There is no justice without *hudud.* . . . The idea of deterrence is very important here; [*hudud* laws] put fear in the hearts of criminals." Husam also spoke of protection, of the protection that Islam affords to non-Muslims: "liberty, freedom of belief, the right to speak, the right to lead social lives [to socialize and fraternize] as they wish. Mutual respect. We want to establish that again. Brotherhood and justice have been destroyed by UMNO . . . because of its emphasis on pragmatism, nationalism, racial sensibilities, and discriminatory affirmative-action policies. The Chinese, for example, have suffered greatly. . . . But we all come from Adam."

Husam's belief that the existing laws "do nothing" and "are rubbish," coupled with his view that corruption and crime are endemic in Malaysia partly because extant laws have no bite, is obviously key to his support of *hudud,* which he sees as a gift from God that can serve as a powerful deterrent to corruption and criminality of other kinds. Support for *hudud* is all the more critical since criminality precludes the development of the peace, justice, ("pan-racial") brotherhood, and universalistic mutual respect that God offers not just to those who have submitted to Islam but to the human community in its entirety.

A broadly congruent set of rationales for the support of *hudud* is espoused by Haji Suleiman Abdullah who is in his early sixties and, as mentioned earlier, is the former head of the Malaysian Bar Council and one of Malaysia's most respected lawyers. Our conversation turned to *hudud* law after a discussion of what Suleiman sees as overwhelmingly negative developments in the secular judiciary since the Anwar crisis and September 11 in particular. This context must be borne in mind, for as Husam Musa's previously noted comments make clear, one's position on *hudud* needs to be examined in the light of one's perspectives concerning the relative integrity of the secular judiciary and the state apparatus in its entirety, including its capacity to create a social and spiritual climate conducive to a moral reign of "law and order."

Hudud "is a covenant with God; if you question it, you're an apostate. . . . The adultery and theft provisions of *hudud* address the sanctity of the family and property, the security of an individual in society, which are core values in most if not all societies. The penalties are not all that severe if they are viewed in light of the damages to society that would occur if the crimes [they are meant to deter] were committed." The crimes are "a major outrage to society, hence you must have a punishment that is comparable. . . . Drug use, incest—in Malaysia, these are highest among Muslims. . . . [They are an] index of 'progress.' . . . Our leaders see privatization and economic development . . . [but] I worry about the future of society, the drift, and deculturalization, . . . [the consequences of] policies of unmitigated economic development." To understand support for *hudud* we need to bear in mind that "most [people] prefer the framework and certainties of religion; it provides answers and enables people to be part of a community of believers. . . . [In Malaysia] most people are basically good, but [we] must strengthen [that]; society needs reminders."

At this juncture I would like to step back from the specifics of the three sets of comments discussed here and draw attention to the strong emphases (however variably inflected) on restorative—as opposed to retributive—justice. I underscore this theme for three (related) reasons. First, it is of central importance both in Islamic doctrine bearing on jurisprudence and in the actual workings of Islamic law "on the ground," in Islamic courts (Rosen 1989; Hirsch 1998; Sachedina 2001; Peletz 2002). Second, it is usually overlooked in Western discussions of Islamic law, which typically focus on vengeful, maiming retribution. And third, if we fail to appreciate the moral appeal of restorative justice, we will also fail to grasp why Muslims in Malaysia and elsewhere are increasingly supportive of local and transnational programs aimed at introducing Islamic laws and Islamic states apparatuses in their entirety.

Some of the more general dynamics at issue here have been well described in a recent article on Islam and globalization by Farish Noor (who, as we have seen, has been targeted by the PUM and others owing to his outspoken views on the need for Islamic reformation). Since Farish's commentary is relevant both to Malaysia and far beyond, I quote at length:

Sharia laws and *hudud* criminal punishments [are] finding increasing appeal in the Islamic world . . . [due to] the collapse of the secular development paradigm in so many post-colonial Muslim states. Despite the economic gains from globalization in many countries, in some post-colonial states globalization has taken a toll on the state's capacity to govern and manage society. . . . Externally imposed structural-adjustment policies, a growing dependence on foreign capital and relentless pressure on local governments by global agents have all helped to discredit many Muslim governments— because they failed to reform domestic arrangements adequately to address the . . . issues that globalization demands. The net result is they are no longer able to cater to the interests and welfare of their respective con-stituencies. . . . The encroachment of market forces and neoliberalism turns the secular legal system into a market for goods and services. . . . Moreover, corruption endemic in poorer countries takes a large bite out of justice.

By contrast, traditional religious courts appear accessible, cheap, reli-able, and consistent. The beauty of sharia law—as seen by many ordinary Muslims—is that it at least offers some legal protection with clear verdicts. While many ordinary Muslims will not agree with the actual punishments, and few would relish the thought of . . . watch[ing] convicted criminals whipped, stoned, or mutilated, the fact remains that sharia is seen as a cred-ible alternative to a civil/secular legal system alienated from the masses.

This, then, is the predicament faced by many Muslim governments and activists who want to hold back the calls for strict sharia laws and hudud punishments. By failing to improve on the secular legal system . . . , they find themselves bereft of an alternative when confronted by . . . hardline Is-lamists who call for religious law. . . . The way out of this impasse is obvi-ous: reform the civil-law apparatus and make courts open, transparent, just and accessible. . . . This in turn should be linked to the wider project of re-forming the structures of the post-colonial state itself, so that the other in-stitutions of government—the police, legislature and executive—all perform their respective duties as well. . . . Failure to reform would mean opening the way for more demands for an alternative paradigm. The rise of political Islam, which was an urban, global, and modern phenomenon from the be-ginning, reads as an index to the failure of many modern post-colonial Mus-lim states. Rather than demonizing hudud, the political elites of much of the Muslim world would do well to take care of the mess in their own back-yards. Only then will faith in the civil legal system be restored. (Farish Noor 2002, 23)

The essay by Farish quoted here makes no specific reference to Malaysia, even though the Malaysian-born Farish has written much about cultural politics and religion in his homeland. The essay is framed instead in relation to Pakistan, Iran, Sudan, Nigeria, and the Muslim world as a whole. That said, there is much in Farish's social scientific framing of the globalizing dynamics at issue that resonates with the remarks of the three Malaysian Muslims cited earlier (Ahmad, Husam Musa, Suleiman Abdullah)—though the latter individuals also invoke issues of sanctity, divine will, God's covenant, and so forth whereas the more secular Farish does not.

Hudud, *Apostasy, and the Cultural Politics of Legitimacy and Enforced Quietism*

As should be clear, there is much heartfelt and powerful debate in Malaysia on the subject of *hudud*. Somewhat less obvious but no less crucial to appreciate is that most of the public debates concern certain issues and dynamics but not others. The focus is typically on one or more of the following themes: whether the laws should be introduced; why they should or should not be introduced; how and when they might be effectively implemented; what the implications of the laws will be for Muslim women; whether non-Muslims should or will come under their jurisdiction; and why certain groups and broad sectors of society support or oppose the laws. Conspicuously absent from (or at least rather far down toward the bottom of) this list are debates on the ontological status of the laws in quintessentially foundational Islamic texts such as the Qur'an.[3]

There are many reasons for this absence. One has to do with the fact that the Qur'an tends to be available in Malaysia only in Arabic, which the vast majority of Malays cannot actually read (as opposed to recite). Another exceedingly important one in terms of its cultural salience is suggested by Suleiman's remark that to question God's covenant in the form of *hudud* is to be guilty of apostasy (*keridahan, kemurtadan*), a crime of such gravity that (as noted earlier) it merits the death penalty as far as many Muslims in Malaysia and beyond are concerned. The irony here, though, is that while apostasy is invariably subsumed under the rubric of *hudud,* scholars of Islam do not universally agree on the precise entailments of apostasy or whether the Qur'an specifies in unqualified terms that apostasy is (or should be) a capital offense. Some learned scholars of Islam in Malaysia and elsewhere, for instance, contend that the Prophet's message on the latter issue has been distorted by centuries of conservative juristic interpretation and political expediency, and that the Prophet intended the death penalty for apostasy *only* when it *also* involved "blasphemy and rebellion against the [Islamic] community and its legitimate leadership" (Mohammad Hashim Kamali 2000, 29, passim). According to this view, the death penalty is not mandated by the Qur'an or any other Islamic source if apostasy does not entail such blasphemy and rebellion, especially if the only transgression at issue involves philosophical or other questioning of one or another conventional or official interpretation of Islam. That said, there is a strong current throughout the entire Muslim community in Malaysia that questioning any aspect of Islam could well lead to divisions within the *ummah,* and that exposing or widening divisions of the latter sort amounts to "letting down the side" and thus an erosion of Muslim (hence Malay) sovereignty, which is necessarily tantamount to treason. The scope and force of this constrictive current are amplified by the secular policies and strategies of UMNO, including not only Mahathir's use of the ISA to quell real or imagined dissent cast in religious or other terms, but also the government's well-honed strategy of convincing the Muslim electorate that Malaysian Islam is always under siege and that extraordinary policing measures are perforce always justified. This is to say that there is an overdetermined reluctance to debate the ontological status of apostasy and many other issues linked to religion.

Another reason for the general absence of debate in Malaysia about the ontological status of *hudud* in sources such as the Qur'an has to do with matters of intellectual and moral authority and legitimacy. These themes suffused an interview that I conducted in August 2002 with Syed Muhammad Naquib Al-Attas, one of the leading intellectuals in Southeast Asia and one of the world's most accomplished and respected scholars specializing in Islamic philosophy and metaphysics, Islamic education, and "the Islamization of knowledge."

Al-Attas is the founder and director of the Kuala Lumpur–based International Institute for Islamic Thought and Understanding (ISTAC), a highly influential (and architecturally stunning) degree-granting institution whose daily classes, weekly seminars, and other activities are devoted to "analysing, clarifying, [and] elaborating ... the key terms 'relevant to the cultural, educational, scientific, and espistemological problems encountered by Muslims in the present age' " (Wan Mohd. Nor Wan Daud 1998, 99–100). He is also the main spiritual and intellectual inspiration for the Islamic Youth Movement of Malaysia (ABIM), which has been one of the most powerful and high-profile of the organizations promoting Islamic resurgence in Malaysia since its founding in the early 1970s. In this connection it warrants emphasis that ABIM provided the institutional context in which a steady stream of charismatic Muslim intellectuals who went on to make their mark in national political arenas honed their organizational and other skills and otherwise "cut their teeth." Such intellectuals include: Anwar Ibrahim, who (as mentioned earlier) was head of ABIM before Mahathir recruited him to UMNO and rewarded him with a succession of prestigious political posts; Fadzil Mohamed Noor, the longtime leader of PAS and the head of the opposition alliance in its entirety at the time of his death in June 2002; Haji Abdul

Hadi Awang, the chief minister of Terengganu who assumed the mantle of PAS leadership on the death of Fadzil Mohamed Noor; and scores of other nationally prominent Muslim intellectuals who command important positions both within and outside state-run (or state-friendly) Islamic institutions. In sum, Al-Attas's ideas and sensibilities have played a dominant role in shaping the intellectual and political contours of contemporary Malaysian Islam.

The author of more than two dozen books and monographs and scores of articles (many translated into Arabic, Persian, Turkish, Urdu, French, German, Russian, etc.), the seventy-two-year old Al-Attas has a commanding presence but is also both charming and avuncular. Among the first questions he put to me after confirming that I had written scholarly works about Islam in Malaysia were, "Who are your authorities? Which authorities have you been speaking to? And why have you never come to see me until now?"

While Al-Attas was extremely cordial and generous with his time, he spent most of the interview railing against the West, specifically "the Orientalists, positivists, relativists, secularists, post-modernists, and social scientists, all of whom distort and diminish Islam" and presumably religion, spirituality, and ethics in general. His main objection to positivism has to do with "its insistence that God can only be known or proven to exist through the senses," though he added that "we oppose positivistic, post-modern, and secular perspectives that view religion as nothing more than culture. It is not modernity per se [that we oppose]."

One of his initial remarks had to do with Westerners trying to understand why "we [Muslims] behave the way we do; it's not because we are 'fundamentalists' or 'hate the West.'" He went on to say, "It's not our problem, it's your problem, a Christian problem," the "it" here referring to Westerners' difficulties understanding "the lack of separation between church and state in Islam," which from Al-Attas's perspective means primarily that "there can be no separation of the ethical and the political."

The conversation turned to September 11. "The moment it happened your president started talking about [the need for] a crusade; he's an idiot, and so is Margaret Thatcher. . . . [And then there is] the Italian Prime Minister who said we've produced no Cellinis, no Michelangelos, no Mozarts." Mentioning that he had heard something about Michelangelo being homosexual, Al-Attas remarked, "Your church . . . , the robes, the music; so much paganism, isn't it?" adding "[Western] scholars are spreading much of the havoc. . . . You need to ask the *right* authorities. Otherwise, you confuse and destroy and set up false authorities among Muslims. . . . The scholars one should study and respect are the al-Ghazalis, the Sufis—the higher ones—[and] Ibn Khaldun, the father of modern sociology," though he was quick to underscore that "too many books can also confuse."

"There are [in any case] different kinds of knowledge: true knowledge, useful knowledge, and dangerous knowledge. We want to concentrate on useful knowledge. We [humans] are only here for a few years. Some knowledge is for one's own salvation; some is for development in subsequent generations. Muslims must know about their history [and] civilization, and culture, [about] what happened to them. It's all been confused by the colonialists. [But] we oppose extremism."

Al-Attas brought up the idea of "Islams" (in the plural), rejecting outright that any such phenomena exist. By way of illustration he insisted "there is no such thing as a Malaysian Islam that is distinct from other kinds of Islam. There are only different levels of intelligence." In an effort to more thoroughly address the relationships that exist in different societal contexts between local culture on the one hand and Islam on the other, I cited an aphorism I heard many times in the course of fieldwork in the state of Negeri Sembilan during the late 1970s and 1980s: *adat bersendi hukum, hukum bersendi kitabullah,* which means (roughly) "custom/tradition" hinges or depends on [God's] law, just as [God's] law hinges or depends on the book or word of God. This aphorism was often cited by villagers as a way of asserting what they took to be the broad compatibility between their matrilineally inflected kinship institutions and the basic values (if not specific legal injunctions) of a patricentric Islam. While much ink has been spilled on such matters (see Peletz 1988), the most germane issue here is that the vast majority if not all of the villagers I encountered in over two years of fieldwork consider themselves to be "good Muslims," despite what their detractors may say. Yet Al-Attas's reactions to my invocation of this expression was unequivocal and altogether dismissive: "These people don't understand." He proceeded with a critique of British and Dutch colonial scholars, and of Orientalism generally, intimating that any local variation in the practice, experience, or understanding of Islam was due to Orientalist distortion. Implicitly acknowledging that not all such distortion need be intentional, he delineated some of the challenges of translation in the study of religion, adding that "academics, journalists, and politicians" are also part of the problem, as are "lax Muslims." Al-Attas went on to register an exceedingly important point, which he effectively retracted a few moments later (as we shall see): "But as long as they don't actually deny they're Muslims, then they're still Muslims," to which he added, it's "not like . . . [your] Inquisition."

Al-Attas's solution to these problems and to the dilemmas of marginalization and injustice encountered by Muslims the world over is to promote the development of sound pedagogy and scholarship: to provide the Muslim community, especially at the university level, with "an education that is religiously self-conscious and conservative, yet prescriptive, practical and futuristic" (Wan Mohd. Nor Wan Daud 1998, 169); to decolonize knowledge and create truly Islamic understandings of metaphysics, ontology, and epistemology; and thus to restore *adab,* which he defines as recognition "that knowledge and being are ordered hierarchically according to their various grades and degrees of rank, and . . . [that one has a] proper place in relation to that reality and to one's physical, intellectual and spiritual capacities and potentials" (137). These goals are not surprising, given Al-Attas's life's work and the nature of the teaching and research institutes into which he has poured so much of himself. Education clearly has the potential to liberate Muslims in Malaysia and elsewhere from the circumstances in which they find themselves, but the relationship between education and liberation or freedom is complicated, partly because, in Al-Attas's opinion, those who lack education should not be accorded the same basic freedoms as those who are educated. Justice, not equality, is his overriding concern, and a reign of justice defined in terms of *adab* and things being in their "right and proper place" need not entail equality as understood in the West. He elaborated briefly on whether "an ignorant person" had a right to speak and whether a journalist would have enough sense to recognize that such an individual did not deserve a forum. Though he did not state explicitly that those without religious knowledge of the sort he deemed legitimate should be prevented or discouraged from expressing their views in public, his position on such matters was obvious: "Yes, there should be freedom of expression, but not on certain matters," the bottom line being, "and if you're in doubt, you're not a Muslim."

What is especially revealing about this latter statement is not that it contradicts Al-Attas's earlier contention that "as long as Muslims don't deny they're Muslims, they're still Muslims." It is, rather, its illustration of the tension and exceedingly thin line between religiously or existentially inflected doubt on the one hand and denial and renunciation of one's faith, loyalty, identity and membership in a moral community (defined both locally and transnationally) on the other. Of particular interest here are the remarks Al-Attas offered to help convey his position: even "to pose the question, 'How do I know that God exists?' requires proper understanding—a proper understanding of who God is, of what knowing is, and of what existence means." These remarks were followed by, "If people are honest and sincere, they will stop asking such questions."

To summarize these perspectives: anyone who asks questions of the latter ("doubting") sort risks being considered an apostate (*murtad*) and a dishonest and insincere one at that. Dynamics such as these help explain why many members of the Muslim community in Malaysia display a marked reluctance to engage in debate concerning the ontological status of *hudud* laws in the Qur'an or to question other aspects of conventional

or official interpretations of Islam. So too of course do mutually reinforcing dynamics of govermentality emanating from the upper echelons
of the executive branch, such as the well-documented willingness of Mahathir and his supporters to define "unorthodox" religious beliefs and
practices as treasonous, seditious, or simply "deviationist" and thus best
dealt with through the use of the ISA, which can result in indefinite detention without specific charges or even the pretense of a trial.

It remains to underscore that the themes to which Al-Attas returned
again and again were those bearing on knowledge and power; more precisely, the key theme that Al-Attas emphasized in our conversation was
that textually based knowledge of Islam is a prerequisite for the authority to speak. To this I would add two points. First, that Al-Attas's scholarship and teachings have played an extremely influential role in the
development of the variably inflected organizations and movements whose
institutional structures and ideologies help define the contours of contemporary Malaysian Islam—the Islamic Youth Movement of Malaysia,
the Pan-Malaysian Islamic Party, the Association of Malaysian Ulama,
and the International Institute for Islamic Thought and Civilization,
among others. The second point is more general and more directly relevant to the central thesis of this chapter: most of the struggles over
Malaysian Islam that we see at present are being waged via pen, discourse, and debate, not through physical coercion or violence. This has
always been true of Malaysia and has not changed since September 11,
notwithstanding recent media and intelligence reports depicting angry
demonstrators at the U.S. embassy in Kuala Lumpur and suggesting that
Malaysia is a "staging ground" or "launching pad" for terrorist actions
against the US.

Mahathir's Islamic State

No account of changes in the fields of Malaysian cultural politics since
September 11 would be complete without brief mention of the now famous comments about Malaysia being an Islamic state that were made
by Prime Minister Mahathir on September 29, 2001, just a few weeks
after the attacks of September 11. Mahathir's pronouncements were intended partly as a response to President Bush's derogatory and inflam-
matory generalizations concerning the extremism and other dangers of
Muslim regimes, rogue states, and the like. The gist of Mahathir's remarks was that Malaysia is a predominantly Muslim nation that em-
braces a moderate, forward-looking, and inclusive Islam, and that Bush's
generalizations were thus both empirically problematic and deeply offen-
sive to Malaysian Muslims and moderate Muslims the world over. The
problem, though, is that Mahathir's comments included the arguably

ambiguous assertion that "Malaysia is an Islamic state." The latter assertion was immediately reported by local and international media and quickly became the focus of intense, overdetermined debates among Malaysia's public intellectuals, as well as political and religious elites, and ordinary Muslims and non-Muslims from all walks of life. Many of the Muslims who participated in the debates at issue are not recognized as traditional *'ulama* and do not have extensive scholarly familiarity with Islamic religious texts or the Arabic language, which religious experts and scholars of Islam (like Al-Attas) generally regard as an absolute necessity if one is going to offer legitimate perspectives on Islam. The views of all such individuals are thus deeply suspect as far as *'ulama* and other religious scholars are concerned—as of course are the commentaries and analyses of all non-Muslims (such as Patricia Martinez) who have weighed in on the issues. Worse, since all such views have the potential to create divisions within the *ummah* or Muslim community, they raise the twin specters of sedition and treason. The more encompassing dynamic here is what Eickelman and Piscatori (1996) refer to as the "fragmentation of authority," which, as they make clear, has occurred throughout the Muslim world during the twentieth century. In the Malaysian case, as elsewhere, this fragmentation of authority is a consequence of the erosion of traditional class and religious hierarchies coupled with the spread of mass education and modern media and technology that have gone hand in hand with the ascendance of new, predominantly urban middle classes and the attendant emergence of new loci of power, prestige, and moral anchorage.

Mahathir's pronouncements about Malaysia being an Islamic state signaled a major watershed in Malaysian politics. The comments themselves, along with the discourses they spawned, exacerbated fears and anxieties among non-Muslims in particular that the ruling party is willing to abandon its support of long-established multicultural and multireligious practices in its efforts to fend off Western rhetoric and outmaneuver PAS. In some ways far more distressing to non-Muslims is their feeling that the social contract among the major ethnic groups that was engineered with the help of the British as they relinquished their colony in 1957 might be tossed to the wind for the sake of political expediency.

To convey a sense of non-Muslims' feelings of distress concerning their secondary status vis-à-vis Muslims I might mention the thoughts expressed to me in the course of a two-day conference by a distinguished Sikh gentleman whose extensive engagement in civic affairs includes high-level involvement in the Malaysian Consultative Council of Buddhism, Christianity, Hinduism, and Sikhism, as well as leadership roles in various NGOs concerned with the educational well-being of the Sikh community. A highly respected religious official who is thoroughly conversant in Malay, English, Punjabi, Hindi, and Urdu, Mr. Singh (as I shall call him) spoke to me in whispers, all the while looking over his shoulder to make sure that no one else could hear what he was saying. "I'm a taxpayer and citizen too. But we [Sikhs and non-Muslims generally] get no airtime. . . . In America, Muslims [religious minorities] have outlets, the government supports them. In Malaysia there is nothing like that. Once a year we can have cultural events, but we can't talk about religion. . . . And the government has admitted that most of the tax revenue comes from non-Muslims. . . . [Do they give us] land and money for temples? No. But the government will contribute how many hundreds of thousands [of ringgit] for mosques in places like New Zealand? The Muslims want equality and justice, but where is the justice?"

Singh's heavily freighted misgivings are all the more instructive when we bear in mind that he is decrying a state of affairs under a relatively *secular* (but nonetheless strongly pro-Malay Muslim) regime. Given the justifiable concern on the part of non-Muslims that the imposition of *hudud* law and the creation of an Islamic state will exacerbate NEP-type policies that discriminate against all non-Muslims, it stands to reason that there is virtually no support among non-Muslims for *hudud* law or the creation of an Islamic state. Sensibilities expressed along the following lines are typical: the "DAP [the predominantly Chinese Democratic Action Party] fervently opposes the setting up of an Islamic state. We will never assist PAS in the setting up of an Islamic state"; and "If we allow these Islamic fanatics to rule the country, the peaceful and harmonious country . . . built by our predecessors will be destroyed."[4]

One could easily provide numerous other examples of non-Muslims' views in the same vein, but this seems unnecessary. Suffice it to say that the fallout from Mahathir's remarks about Malaysia being an Islamic state (along with other dynamics described here) have sharpened the lines and antagonisms between Muslims and non-Muslims. They have also helped bring about a situation in which distinctions between Muslims and non-Muslims have come to override all other axes of difference and inequality, including those cast in ethnic, racial, and class terms. This is all the more significant since by most accounts the last few decades, and the last few years in particular, have seen an increased segregation and polarization of Malays, Chinese, and Indians. Owing to September 11 and its aftermath, the pronounced racialist discourses that long framed all such dynamics have given way to deeply divisive discourses of Muslim versus non-Muslim, many of which are animated by contestations among different groups of Malays over which deeply contested version of Islam should be accorded legitimacy.

Conclusion

On October 31, 2003, as this essay was moving toward publication, Mahathir made good on his pledge (variably articulated since mid-2002) that before the general elections scheduled for 2004 he would step down as Malaysia's head of state and hand the reins of governance to Deputy Prime Minister Abdullah Ahmad Badawi, the soft-spoken, nationally prominent career civil servant (and former head of the ministries of defense and foreign affairs, among others) whom Mahathir had carefully groomed as his successor since the sacking of Anwar in September 1998. In some ways the formal retirement from public life of one of the longest serving elected leaders that the world has ever seen marks the end of a truly remarkable era in the history of Malaysia and the broader region. It is obviously too soon to tell, though, if the ritualized transfer of authority signals a real passing of the baton let alone a true changing of the guard. For Mahathir may well remain on (or behind) the scene as an extremely influential player, assuming a role analogous perhaps to that played by Singapore's Lee Kuan Yew, who after relinquishing the post of prime minister, which he held for over three decades, became "senior minister" in the famed city-state.

It is clear, however, that the direction of future political and religious developments in Malaysia will depend a good deal on how sixty-four-year-old Prime Minister Abdullah and his entourage and successors handle the challenges to their authority that arise in the months and years ahead. This in turn will depend in no small measure on U.S. policies in the region, including those associated with our current administration's "war on terror." These latter policies could well prompt ruling elites in Indonesia, the Philippines, and elsewhere to introduce sweeping versions of Malaysia's ISA, thus further emboldening both their Malaysian counterparts and their supporters and successors.

Another set of variables figuring into the future in rather unpredictable ways has to do with the existence of an estimated 2.1 million Malaysian youth who are eligible to vote but are currently unregistered (*New Sunday Times*, August 11, 2002). Large numbers of these youth live in the multiethnic and heavily urban Klang Valley region, which includes Kuala Lumpur, and which tends to benefit more from state-driven development than PAS-controlled areas of the Malay heartlands, such as Kelantan and Terengganu. All things being equal, one might therefore expect this critically important group of young Malaysians to lean toward UMNO rather than an opposition party like PAS, which has long derived much of its support from predominantly Malay rural areas (such as Kelantan and Terengganu) that are marginalized or largely bypassed by state-sponsored modernity. On the other hand, the massive increase since September 11 of Muslim tourists visiting Malaysia from Middle Eastern countries like Saudi Arabia, Lebanon, Syria, the United Arab Emirates, Kuwait, Oman, and the like (Prystay 2002), could result in a partial "radicalization" of youthful sensibilities, especially if, as has occurred in neighboring Indonesia since the fall of Suharto in 1998, well-connected proponents of one or another variant of Salafi-Wahhabism are able to make common cause with groups of disaffected youth.

As for the recent past and the present, it is worth stepping back from all the discursive and other divisiveness that I have outlined here in order to appreciate an exceedingly important generalization bearing on the major carriers of Malaysian Islam (UMNO, PAS, ABIM, Sisters in Islam, Al-Attas/ISTAC, etc.). The majority (though clearly not all) of the contests over Islam and other key symbols and institutional resources that we see in Malaysia are occurring in relatively democratic ways: through elections, court battles, weekly seminars and educational outreach, legitimate lobbying efforts, PR blitzes, letters to the editors of local newspapers, and so on, not through disappearances, torture, assassinations, suicide or other bombings, coup d'etat, and the like. PAS, for example, which promotes and seeks to instantiate a very conservative "*syariah*-oriented" vision of Muslim society and politics and has enjoyed successes at the polls partly because of a reputation for clean government, fair play, and relative transparency, tends rather consistently to play by the rules of the electoral game, though this is not to suggest that party leadership has embraced—or in the future would seek to nourish—a culture of democratic pluralism. Some of these generalizations also apply to Al-Attas/ISTAC and ABIM, who are strongly committed to education and justice, though not necessarily to equality as commonly understood in the West. The Sisters in Islam, for their part, as well as many of the other NGOs and political parties that I have glossed over here, have established viable working relationships with the ruling party and have capitalized on the administration's efforts to portray itself as the carrier of a progressive Islam. The more salient point, though, is that these organizations have pledged themselves both to electoral politics and to the "scaling up" of values and sensibilities conducive to democratic pluralism. The same cannot always be said of UMNO, or at least of Mahathir and his inner circle, which in recent years has certainly included Abdullah, who now stands at the helm of the ship of state. While Mahathir deserves much credit for Malaysia's stunning economic transformation and merits inclusion among the burgeoning ranks of the Muslim world's relatively progressive prodevelopment modernist leaders, he and his inner circle have a well-deserved reputation for ruthlessness both in their dealings with rivals and detractors and in their willingness to subvert democratic systems of checks and balances when they feel the need to do so. One can hope that newly anointed Prime Minister Abdullah will build on Mahathir's reputation as the proponent of a relatively progressive Islam and simultaneously distance himself from the antidemocratic practices for which Mahathir has also long been well known.

There is no simple black and white here, and as in many other parts of the Muslim world (Indonesia, Pakistan, Saudi Arabia, Jordan, Kuwait, Egypt, and Turkey come quickly to mind), the main obstacles to the expansion and strengthening of pluralist sensibilities and democratic institutions have little if anything to do with Islam per se. Scholars and others concerned with identifying impediments to reform-oriented policies might thus focus their attention elsewhere. It might be most productive to begin with questions about the institutionalized arrangements that enable political elites in control of top-heavy executive branches to manipulate overwhelmingly secular organs of governance and all varieties of cultural phenomena. One part of the puzzle is the critically important symbolic capital and institutional support provided to such elites by American and other Western allies. Without such capital and support, things would look very different. But that is another essay.

NOTES

This essay draws on extensive fieldwork (1978–80, 1987–88) and subsequent research in Malaysia (1993, 1998, 2001, and 2002). Robert Hefner and Shamsul A.B. provided helpful comments on an earlier draft of this essay, for which I am most grateful. I spell Malay terms in accordance with the conventions of standard Malay, but alternative spellings are still found in the literature and in contemporary Malaysia. Thus *syariah* (Islamic law) is sometimes rendered as *shari'a, syari'ah,* or *shari'at.* When quoting published material, I retain the author's original spelling.

1. Some of the material in this section is adapted from Peletz 2002.
2. Many of the charges are outlined in PUM/PUK 2002.
3. See An-Na'im 1990, chap. 5; cf. Rose Ismail 1995 and Mohammad Hashim Kamali 2000.
4. The first quote is from Chen Man Hin, DAP Chairman (1991); the second is from Chan Kong Choy, MCA [Malaysian Chinese Association] Youth President (1992); they appear, along with mostly similar views, in an anonymous (1999) pamphlet, *"Islamic State": What Are We Afraid Of?*

REFERENCES CITED

Abdul Rahman Embong, ed. 2002. *State-Led Modernization and the New Middle Class in Malaysia.* London: Palgrave Macmillan.

Abuza, Zachary. 2003. *Militant Islam in Southeast Asia: Crucible of Terror.* Boulder, Colo.: Lynn Rienner.

Afkhami, Mahnaz, ed. 1995. *Faith and Freedom: Women's Human Rights in the Muslim World.* Syracuse, N.Y.: Syracuse University Press.

Ahmed, Leila. 1992. *Women and Gender in Islam: Historical Roots of a Modern Debate.* New Haven, Conn.: Yale University Press.

An-Na'im, Abdullahi Ahmed. 1990. *Toward an Islamic Reformation: Civil Liberties, Human Rights, and International Law.* Syracuse, N.Y.: Syracuse University Press.

Appadurai, Arjun. 1996. *Modernity at Large: Cultural Dimensions of Globalization.* Minneapolis: University of Minnesota Press.

Bateson, Gregory. 1936. *Naven: A Survey of the Problems Suggested by a Composite Picture of a New Guinea Tribe Drawn from Three Points of View.* Stanford, Calif.: Stanford University Press.

Chandra Muzaffar. 1987. *Islamic Resurgence in Malaysia.* Kuala Lumpur: Fajar Bakti.

Eickelman, Dale, and James Piscatori. 1996. *Muslim Politics.* Princeton, N.J.: Princeton University Press.

Farish Noor. 2002. "Negotiating Islamic Law." *Far Eastern Economic Review,* September 19, p. 23.

Firdaus Haji Abdullah. 1985. *Radical Malay Politics: Its Origins and Early Development.* Petaling Jaya: Pelanduk Publications.

Government of Malaysia. 2000. *Buku Tahunan Perangkaan Malaysia* (Yearbook of statistics, Malaysia). *2000.* Kuala Lumpur: Jabatan Perangkaan Malaysia/ Government of Malaysia.

Hefner, Robert W. 2000. *Civil Islam: Muslims and Democratization in Indonesia.* Princeton, N.J.: Princeton University Press.

Hilley, John. 2001. *Malaysia: Mahathirism, Hegemony, and the New Opposition.* London: Zed.

Hirsch, Susan. 1998. *Pronouncing and Persevering: Gender and the Discourses of Disputing in an African Islamic Court.* Chicago, Ill.: University of Chicago Press.

Huntington, Samuel. 1996. *The Clash of Civilizations and the Remaking of World Order.* New York: Simon and Schuster.

Husin Mutalib. 1993. *Islam in Malaysia: From Revivalism to Islamic State?* Singapore: Singapore University Press.

"Islamic State": What Are We Afraid Of? 1999. Kuala Lumpur: Vinlin Press.

Kepel, Gilles. 2002. *Jihad: The Trail of Political Islam.* Cambridge, Mass.: Harvard University Press.

Kessler, Clive. 1978. *Islam and Politics in a Malay State: Kelantan, 1839–1969.* Ithaca, N.Y.: Cornell University Press.

———. 1980. "Malaysia: Islamic Revivalism and Political Disaffection in a Divided Society." *Southeast Asia Chronicle* 75:3–11.

Lawrence, Bruce B. 1998. *Shattering the Myth: Islam beyond Violence.* Princeton, N.J.: Princeton University Press.

Mohammad Hashim Kamali. 1995. *Punishment in Islamic Law: An Enquiry into the Hudud Bill of Kelantan.* Kuala Lumpur: Ilmiah Publishers.

———. 2000. *Islamic Law in Malaysia: Issues and Developments.* Kuala Lumpur: Ilmiah Publishers.

Muhammad Abu Bakar. 1987. *Penghayatan Sebuah Ideal: Suatu Tafsiran Tentang Islam Semasa* (Appreciation of an ideal: An interpretation of contemporary Islam). Kuala Lumpur: Dewan Bahasa dan Pustaka.

Nagata, Judith. 1984. *The Reflowering of Malaysian Islam: Modern Religious Radicals and Their Roots.* Vancouver: University of British Columbia Press.

New Sunday Times. 2002. "Only 10,000 of 2.1 Million Youths Registered as Voters." August 11.

Ong, Aihwa. 1999. *Flexible Citizenship: The Cultural Logics of Transnationality.* Durham, N.C.: Duke University Press.

Peletz, Michael G. 1988. *A Share of the Harvest: Kinship, Property, and Social History among the Malays of Rembau.* Berkeley and Los Angeles: University of California Press.

———. 1997. "'Ordinary Muslims' and Muslim Resurgents in Contemporary Malaysia: Notes on an Ambivalent Relationship." In *Islam in an Era of Nation-States: Politics and Religious Renewal in Muslim Southeast Asia,* edited by Robert W. Hefner and Patricia Horvatich, pp. 231–73. Honolulu: University of Hawaii Press.

———. 2002. *Islamic Modern: Religious Courts and Cultural Politics in Malaysia.* Princeton, N.J.: Princeton University Press.

PUM/PUK (Persatuan Ulama Malaysia and Persatuan Ulama Kedah/Malaysian; Ulama Association and Kedah Ulama Association). 2002. *Kontroversi Mengenai Memo Kepada Majlis Raja-Raja Melayu–Islam Dicabar, Rasulullah s.a.w. dan Ulama Dihina* (Controversy concerning the memo to the Malay rulers—Islam challenged and the Prophet and ulama insulted/degraded). Pinang: Jutaprint.

Prystay, Chris. 2002. "Malaysia Pitches Itself as a Safe Place for Mideast Tourists." *Asian Wall Street Journal,* August 28.

Rofel, Lisa. 1999. *Other Modernities: Gendered Yearnings in China after Socialism.* Berkeley and Los Angeles: University of California Press.

Roff, William. 1967. *The Origins of Malay Nationalism.* Kuala Lumpur: University of Malaya Press.

Rose Ismail, ed. 1995. *Hudud in Malaysia: The Issues at Stake.* Kuala Lumpur: SIS Forum.

Rosen, Lawrence. 1989. *The Anthropology of Justice: Law as Culture in Islamic Society.* Cambridge: Cambridge University Press.

Sachedina, Abdulaziz. 2001. *The Islamic Roots of Democratic Pluralism.* Oxford: Oxford University Press.

Safie bin Ibrahim. 1981. *The Islamic Party of Malaysia: Its Formative Stages and Ideology.* Kuala Lumpur: Nuawi bin Ismail/University of Malaya Press.

Shamsul A.B. 1983. "A Revival in the Study of Islam in Malaysia". *Man,* n.s., 18, no. 2:399–404.

———. 2001. "Shadow of Afghan War." *Economic and Political Weekly,* December 22, pp. 4708–9.

Wan Mohd. Nor Wan Daud. 1998. *The Educational Philosophy and Practice of Syed Muhammad Naquib Al-Attas: An Exposition of the Original Concept of Islamization.* Kuala Lumpur: ISTAC.

Zainah Anwar. 1987. *Islamic Revivalism in Malaysia: Dakwah among the Students.* Kuala Lumpur: Pelanduk Publications.

Chapter 11

MUSLIM DEMOCRATS AND ISLAMIST
VIOLENCE IN POST-SOEHARTO INDONESIA

Robert W. Hefner

When, in another generation, historians look back at the end of the twentieth century in search of historical antecedents to Muslim democratization, Indonesia probably deserves to be given a pride of place on par with countries like post-Khomeini Iran and contemporary Turkey. Although often overlooked in surveys of the Muslim world, the Southeast Asian country of Indonesia is the largest Muslim-majority country in the world, with some 88.7 percent of its 215 million people professing Islam. Equally important, in the final years of the authoritarian Soeharto regime (1966–98; see Elson 2001), Indonesia witnessed the creation of a movement for a democratic Muslim politics that was second only to post-Khomeini Iran in scale and intellectual vigor. The coalition that united to topple President Soeharto in May 1998 included Indonesians from varied religious backgrounds (Forrester and May 1999; Hefner 2000). Among its Muslim proponents, however, a key role was played by a new class of intellectuals intent on devising solid Islamic grounds for democracy and civil society (see Abdillah 1997; Barton 2002; Effendy 1994). Although philosophical materialists may dismiss such things, a key feature of Muslim politics everywhere is that, at some point, political initiatives must be justified in relation to religious discourses that comprise the "underlying framework that, while subject to contextualized nuances, is common to Muslims throughout the world" (Eickelman and Piscatori 1996, 5).

Indonesia in the 1990s had a wealth of activists and intellectuals involved in this effort to effect a foundational reorientation of Muslim politics. Moreover, the initiative showed one of the main features political theorists like Guillermo O'Donnell and Philippe Schmitter identify as most important for a successful transition to democracy: a coalitional structure linking "exemplary individuals" and intellectuals to mass-based organizations in society (O'Donnnell and Schmitter 1986, 48–56). By these measures, Indonesia in the late 1990s was one of the most important centers of Muslim reformation in the world.

Sadly, Indonesia's achievement may never be widely recognized because the movement for a democratic Muslim politics was soon overshadowed by a rash of sectarian violence. From 1999 to 2002, battles between Christians and Muslims in the eastern province of Maluku took some eight thousand lives (Klinken 2001). During roughly the same period, the central highlands on the nearby island of Sulawesi saw bloody skirmishes between Muslim and Christian gangs, causing a thousand deaths (Aragon 2001; Human Rights Watch 2002). Equally alarming, in the months following Soeharto's resignation in May 1998, radical Islamist paramilitaries sprang up in cities and towns across Indonesia. Although democratic Muslims and progressive nationalists had hoped to press for deeper reforms after Soeharto's resignation, by late 1998 they found themselves outflanked and outgunned by the radicals. Many of the latter made no secret of their ties to powerful patrons from the ancien regime.

Although the Islamist paramilitaries were best known in the international press for vandalizing bars, discothèques, and other alleged centers of vice, their more decisive political effect was to take back the streets from democratic Muslims and blunt the drive for political reform. In November 1998, the armed forces commander, General Wiranto (a Soeharto ally), worked with radical *ulama* to mobilize 100,000 Islamist militiamen, in an effort to prevent prodemocracy students from disrupting the special session of the People's Consultative Assembly, which had convened to set the ground rules for special parliamentary elections to be held the following year (Dijk 2001, 340–50). On June 23, 2000, hundreds of activists from one of the largest paramilitaries, the Islamic Defenders Front (FPI), ransacked the headquarters of the National Commission on Human Rights. Their action just happened to coincide with the commission's opening of investigations into the involvement of the Indonesian military in the 1999 violence in East Timor. On other occasions, the paramilitaries raided bookstores for left-wing literature, intimidated unveiled women, and used machetes to break up prodemocracy meetings. Although the sectarian violence in eastern Indonesia showed that non-Muslims too played a major part in post-Soeharto violence, the ascendance of the Islamist paramilitaries, and the seeming inability of the country's large moderate groupings to contain them, greatly tarnished Indonesia's reputation as a center of civic-pluralist Islam. The Bali bombings in October, 2002, in which two hundred people died, and the bombing of the Marriott Hotel in Jakarta in August 2003, in which thirteen more were killed, seemed only to confirm the impression that Indonesia was no center for progressive Islam, but was on the verge of becoming a second front for Osama bin Laden's al-Qa'ida (Abuza 2002, 2003).

In this chapter, I will suggest that things were not quite so grim as the second-front thesis implies. However, although relatively small compared to their mainstream rivals, parmilitarized Islamists did seize the initiative from moderate and prodemocracy Muslims in the months following Soeharto's overthrow. This chapter aims to examine just why this occurred, and why a country with such a promising legacy of democratic Muslim politics has had such difficulty in its post-Soeharto transition. The example of armed Islamists outflanking a moderate majority has relevance for the study of Muslim politics in other parts of the world as well.

The evidence I present here suggests that the most critical obstacle to the democratic transition has had as much to do with the legacies of Indonesian state and society as it has any specific quality of Muslim politics. Certainly, some features of contemporary Indonesian politics, such as the ideals of the *jihadi* movement, can only be fully explained with reference to the pluralism and contests of Muslim politics. But the *specific* effect of these variables was determined by two more general features of state-society relations: the relative weakness and segmentary divisions of civil society, and the habit of some in the political elite (both at the national and provincial level) of neutralizing their opposition by inflaming sectarian passions and mobilizing supporters along ethnoreligious lines. During the post-Soeharto period, this sectarian trawling across the state-society divide, as I shall call it, allowed otherwise small groups of armed militants to exercise a political influence disproportionate to their numbers in society.

Since the late 1990s the struggle for the hearts and minds of Indonesian Muslims has been complicated by a third development: the expansion of armed Islamist groupings with ties to the al-Qaʻida into the country. Reports in the Western media have made much of al-Qaʻida's infiltration into the Southeast Asia region. There is such a presence, and, as was amply demonstrated by the Bali and Jakarta bombings, some of its promoters have the desire and capacity to make bloody mischief indeed. Nonetheless, in Indonesia if not the southern Philippines (cf. Chalk 2002), al-Qaʻida has until recently been a secondary influence on Islamist paramilitarism by comparison with the paramilitarists' domestic sponsors. The rapid spread of religious violence and the state's inability to contain it caught the mainstream Muslim leadership off guard and momentarily allowed the radicals to scale up their influence in society. But this contest is far from over.

Ironically, the Bali and Jakarta bombings may prove to have been a blunder as far as the radicals are concerned. The attacks were linked to one of the smaller paramilitaries, the Jemaʻah Islamiyah, an organization that, as my own interviews in Central Java have indicated, has indeed had contacts with al-Qaʻida. By unleashing a bombing campaign, however, the Jemaʻah Islamiyah galvanized the moderate Muslim leadership into action and dispelled moderates' reluctance to accept U.S. claims that terrorist networks were operating in Southeast Asia. Whether this shift proves to be enduring and allows a sustained scaling up of Muslim resources for civil peace and pluralism, however, will depend on domestic political developments, as well as the outcome of ongoing international conflicts.

Sectarian Trawling, Unsolidary Surges

In their *Transitions from Authoritarian Rule*, Guillermo O'Donnell and Philippe Schmitter (1986, 54) have noted that some transitions from authoritarianism are eased by a "popular upsurge" in which interest groups in society put aside their differences and rally to the idea that they are a people united by a common commitment to democratic reform. In Indonesia after the fall of President Soeharto, observers had hoped for just such a solidary surge. However, the hope was dashed with the outbreak of bitter factional squabbles among members of the political elite and, shortly thereafter, of communal violence between Christians and Muslims in several parts of the country.

The elite factionalism and communal tensions had complex genealogies, elements of which date back to the colonial period and imbalances between Muslims and non-Muslims, as well as Javanese (Indonesia's largest and most politically influential ethnic group) and non-Javanese. However, the more immediate influence on these tensions was the fact that rather than building a consensus on the terms of citizenship or the procedures of public politics, Soeharto's "New Order" regime (1966–98) kept contenders for power off balance by playing rival ethnic, religious, and ideological groups against each other. From this perspective, there was a vast difference between the inclusively pluralist spirit of the country's official doctrine, the Pancasila (Five Principles), of which Soeharto was an avid promoter, and the blatantly sectarian practice of state politics (see Aragon 2000, 309–13; Bowen 1993, 125; Kipp 1990). The Soeharto regime played ethnoreligious groups against each other, moreover, at a time when migration, population growth, and economic development were straining ethnic relations in several provinces. In Maluku, Central Kalimantan, Central Sulawesi, and Papua, in particular, hardworking Muslim migrants from Java and Sulawesi displaced indigenous people, many of whom were non-Muslim, from their once-dominant position in the marketplace and society. This displacement caused great resentment among indigenous peoples, Christian as well as Muslim, and in some provinces fueled tensions that were to figure in the post-Soeharto violence.

Another influence on this volatile mix of elite factionalism and communal tension was that the New Order government also conducted much of its political business offstage and extralegally rather than through official channels, relying on an odd assortment of gangsters, local toughs, and paramilitaries (see, e.g., Cribb 2000; Ryter 1998). Soeharto and his allies had first honed this tactic during their rise to power in 1965–66, in the aftermath of a failed left-wing junior officers' coup against the country's senior military leadership. The Soeharto group portrayed the coup as an irreligious communist plot against the nation, and mobilized the country's Muslim organizations, as well as smaller groupings of Christians and Hindus, into an efficient campaign of mass killing (Cribb 1990; Hefner 1990, 193–227; Robinson 1995). No sooner had Soeharto come to power, however, than he marginalized the Muslim parties on whom he had earlier relied, surrounding himself with advisers drawn from the secular Muslim, Christian, Chinese, and Javanese mystical communities. Western analysts were so struck by this preference that they concluded Soeharto was a nominal Muslim or "Hindu-Buddhist," more interested in a conservative variant of Javanese tradition than in Islam (see Emmerson 1978; Pemberton 1994).

Although he dabbled in Javanese mystical arts, however, Soeharto's primary concern was never Javanese tradition as such, even in its conservative forms. His passion was power, and he showed considerable ideological flexibility in pursuit of that end. When political circumstances demanded he change his public religious garb, he did so unhesitatingly. In the late 1980s, the Roman Catholic commander of the armed forces, Benny Moerdani, expressed reservations about the scale of first-family corruption. The challenge infuriated Soeharto, and, true to his divide-and-conquer manner, he responded by ousting the Catholic general and promoting conservative Islamic officers in place of Moerdani's secular Muslim and Christian allies (Schwarz 2000, 146, 175). During these same years, an Islamic resurgence gathered momentum across Indonesia. My interviews with Soeharto advisers during these years showed that the president was keenly aware of the change, as well as the news of radical Islamist challenges in Iran, Algeria, and Egypt. The president responded by throwing himself into Qur'anic study, deserting his Javanese-mystical friends, and launching a series of cooptative ventures in the Muslim community (Hefner 2000, 19, 71).

When, in the course of the president's outreach to the Muslim community, some in the moderate Muslim leadership indicated they were as interested in democratic reforms as they were in Soeharto patronage, the president again changed tack. Rather than wooing moderate Muslims, he reached out to hardline Islamist groups, including some that had been previously among Soeharto's most virulent Muslim opponents (Bruinessen 2002; Hefner 2000, 59–93, 167–207). In addition to keeping his opponents in the armed forces and moderate Muslim elite off guard, the president's turn to conservative Islam had the additional benefit of throwing an obstacle in the path of the country's fledgling democracy movement. In the 1990s, that movement was gaining momentum, buoyed by the end of the Cold War and transitions under way in East

Asia and Eastern Europe. Although its leading lights were Muslim, the Indonesian movement was exuberantly pluralist in spirit. The president and his allies responded by portraying the democracy movement as the creation of an international cabal of Jews and Christians. The sectarian trawling for an uncivil Islam had taken a new and darker turn.

The president's new alliance with conservative Islamists caused great unease in elite political circles, including the ruling party, Golkar. Although for most of its history Golkar had been a broad alliance that included Christians and secular nationalists as well as pious Muslims, in 1994 President Soeharto awarded control of the party's powerful "strategy bureau" (Litbang Golkar) to conservative hardliners who, not coincidentally, had close ties to the small Islamist faction in the armed forces. In collaboration with these commanders, the strategy bureau helped craft the most spectacularly sectarian propaganda tracts ever deployed by the Soeharto regime. Several widely circulated documents accused the United States, the Vatican, Israel's Mossad, nominal Muslims, and Chinese Indonesians of engineering the 1997–98 financial crisis so as to ruin the economy and drive Soeharto from power. In the final months of the Soeharto era, Chinese Indonesians were the target of fierce attacks, with several Soeharto aides describing Chinese Indonesians as "disloyal rats"; one regime document called for the Chinese to be driven from Indonesia once and for all. During the riots of May 13–14, 1998, Chinese Indonesians were the victims of awful social violence, including mass rapes and killing (Hefner 2000, 201–7). An independent commission established in the aftermath of the violence accused a cabal in the armed forces of having played a role in the organization of the violence (TGPF 1998).

If indeed it was organized by Soeharto supporters, the May violence proved to be a serious strategic blunder. The riots provoked mass resignations by unhappy members of the Soeharto cabinet, and eventually led to the president's resignation on May 21, 1998. But the president's ouster did not put an end to elite factionalism or sectarian trawling. No sooner had the president stepped down than street battles broke out between prodemocracy students and ultraconservative Islamists; some of the latter had direct ties to military hardliners. Moderate Muslims and the democracy students soon discovered that, however broad their support in the Indonesian public, they were no match for the urban toughs mobilized by conservative Islamists.

The Great Hope

In June 1999, Indonesia held its first parliamentary elections since Soeharto's fall. The results of the elections showed that there was still little public support for conservative Islamism. Only about 16 percent of the national vote went to parties advocating the establishment of an Islamic state. By comparison, during the country's last free and fair elections in 1955, 44 percent of the electorate cast their vote for parties advocating some form of Islamic state (Feith 1957).

The contrast in the outcome of the two elections is all the more interesting when one recalls that the Muslim public in contemporary Indonesia is, by most measures, considerably more pious than in the 1950s, when Clifford Geertz and Robert Jay carried out their pioneering research on Islam and politics (Geertz 1960; Jay 1963). In an important unpublished survey of several thousand voters taken just after the 1999 elections, the political scientists William Liddle and Saiful Mujani (2000) found that only 3.6 percent of those surveyed self-identified as syncretic or nominal Muslims (known as *abangan* in Javanese). In the 1950s about half of the country, and a full two-thirds of all Javanese, were thought to be nominal or syncretic Muslims. An additional 17.3 percent of the Muslims in the 1999 survey identify themselves as secularists who never or rarely perform Islamic devotions. Conversely, a full 81 percent of respondents claimed to be faithful in the performance of religious obligations. These data resonate with ethnographic studies that confirm that there has been a resurgence in public piety since the late 1970s (see Bowen 1993; Bruinessen 2002; Hefner 1987, 2000; Woodward 1989).

Notwithstanding this great change in religious attitudes, Liddle and Mujani (2000, 17) found that some 60 percent of pious Muslims cast their vote for non-Islamic or secular parties. Indeed, a full two-thirds of the voters who chose the biggest vote getter in the 1999 elections, Megawati Sukarnoputri's secular nationalist Democratic Party-Struggle, identified themselves as pious Muslims (Liddle and Mujani 2000, 37). This information suggests that the elite squabbling and street fighting taking place in late 1998 and early 1999, pitting conservative Islamists against Muslim democrats and progressive nationalists, did not reflect an equally pervasive sectarianism in the public as a whole.

The People's Consultative Assembly's election of Abdurrahman Wahid to the presidency in October 1999 raised hopes that this factional divide might yet be bridged and the moderation reflected in the elections could be channeled into a revived program of political reform. Leader of the prodemocracy Democracy Forum during the 1990s, Wahid had long been regarded as a democratic nationalist and Soeharto opponent. Eccentric in manner and independent in spirit, the near-blind leader was also popular among Chinese, Christians, and Hindus as a result of his statements on ethnoreligious tolerance (Barton 2002). What made Wahid an especially attractive choice for the presidency, however, was that he was also the chief executive of the country's largest Muslim organization, the 35 million strong Nahdlatul Ulama, a traditionalist organization with roots in the country's great network of Qur'anic schools (*pesantren;* see

Feillard 1995). In the MPR elections of October 1999, then, Wahid edged out Megawati Sukarnoputri, the leader of the secular-nationalist Indonesian Democracy Party-Struggle. He did so in part because, after the defeat of Soeharto's hand-picked successor (B. J. Habibie), conservative Muslims opted to cast their votes for Wahid rather than Megawati, a secular-nationalist and a woman (Barton 2002, 264–84; Doorn-Harder 2002).

Rather than abating, however, infighting among the political elite only increased after Wahid's election, as Muslim conservatives joined forces with remnants of the ancien regime to scuttle Wahid's efforts at political reform. Tactical blunders by the new president helped to solidify the anti-Wahid alliance. Three measures had a particularly deleterious impact. First, the president's plan to establish limited commercial relations with Israel infuriated even moderate Muslims. Second, his effort to lift the ban on the Indonesian Communist Party mobilized old regime conservatives and even many moderate Muslims, for whom fierce anticommunism had long been a guiding principle. And third, his unsuccessful effort to reform the armed forces, beginning with the removal of the powerful armed forces commander (and Soeharto ally), General Wiranto, stiffened antireform resistance in the military. Combined with the president's intemperate habit of taking swipes at even his own allies, these measures cemented the anti-Wahid alliance of Islamists, old-regime anticommunists, and antireform military commanders. Well before the People's Consultative Assembly formally ousted him in July 2001, Wahid's coalition had disintegrated, and he had effectively ceased to govern.

With the democracy movement stalled, efforts to reform the political establishment weakened, and most of the old regime remained securely in place. This was especially true in the provinces, most of which had experienced less reformist tumult than Jakarta. Despite the continuity in the state apparatus, however, the impact of Soeharto's departure and continuing discord in the armed forces heightened tensions among rival provincial elites. Rather than strengthening "civil" society, local bosses took to squabbling among themselves for the spoils of state and market. More alarming yet, in regions divided along ethnoreligious lines, some leaders exploited sectarian tensions to mobilize their base. In this way, the sectarian trawling already practiced in the New Order came to be deployed in an even more pervasive and destabilizing form—not just by Jakarta actors and "the state," but by provincial elites and nonstate actors.

This, then, was the background to the ethnic and religious violence that broke out in parts of Indonesia in the early post-Soeharto period. In a few provinces, like Yogyakarta and East Kalimantan, local administrators worked hard to keep the populist rivalry within bounds, and incidents of violence were few. However, in regions that had experienced widespread immigration and demographic change, like Maluku, Central

Kalimantan, and Central Sulawesi, many contenders for power showed no such hesitation, exploiting ethnic and religious tensions with a verve that made Soeharto look like a moderate.

The populist sectarianism was exacerbated by local bosses' reliance on another category of actor to have come of age during the Soeharto era: the organized gangsters known as *preman*. Soeharto and his allies had made regular use of *preman* throughout the New Order period. Most groupings were given an ideological makeover so as to look like ardent regime supporters, but their underworld ties remained operative just the same. It is notable that whereas the dominant gangs in the early New Order were nationalist (Ryter 1998), by the end of the region the largest groups were radical Islamist (Yunanto 2003). Where, as in Maluku or Central Sulawesi, post-Soeharto contention involved this flammable mixture of elite factionalism, gangsterism, and ethnoreligious tensions, the result could be deadly indeed.

UNCIVIL SOCIETY

One reason it is important to understand this background to the recent spate of violence in Indonesia is that, in the aftermath of the September 11, 2001, attacks in the United States, some foreign analysts have assumed that Indonesia's main problem is radical Islam, and that the most important influence on radical Islam was al-Qa'ida. Armed Islamist radicals have indeed been part of post-Soeharto Indonesia's problem. As the above discussion indicates, however, many (though not all; see below) of the radicals had initially benefited from the support of regional bosses and remnants of the Soeharto regime more than they had any international Islamist network.

Equally important, the politics of divide and conquer (known in Indonesian as *politik pecah-belah,* lit., "slice and separate" politics) did not just have a baleful effect on political Islam. This uncivil legacy also reinforced paramilitarist tendencies among Christians and other minorities in provinces like Maluku, Central Kalimantan, Central Sulawesi, and Irian (Papua). Indeed, in the first three of these provinces, non-Muslim paramilitaries sprang into action shortly after Soeharto's departure. One of the worst initial outbreaks of violence took place in the province of Central Kalimantan on the island of Borneo, where hundreds of hapless Madurese immigrants, who happened to be Muslim, were massacred by gangs of indigenous Dayaks, who happen to be nominal Christians or animists (ICG 2001; see Schiller 1997 for background). The fact that Dayaks involved in the campaign did not drive Muslim Malays from these same territories shows that the violence was not primarily a

Christian-Muslim conflict. In fact, in some instances Malays joined
Dayaks in attacking Madurese villages.

The worst violence pitting Muslims against Christians occurred in the
eastern Indonesian province of Maluku. In the beginning, this conflict
looked as if it might avoid the abyss of Christian-Muslim communalism,
and unfold according to a more complex ethnic logic, similar to that seen
in Central Kalimantan. During the first phase of the Maluku violence, for
example, Catholics were able to hold themselves apart from the conflict,
which pitted local Protestants against Muslim immigrants. In the northern portion of the old province, local Protestants had become involved in
conflicts over land with Muslim refugees from Makian Island, recently
relocated to the region. However, illustrating the crosscutting nature of
local alliances, the Protestants were themselves longtime supporters of
the Muslim Sultan of Ternate (see Klinken 2001, 6).

Sadly, however, as the Maluku conflict escalated, local bosses discovered that it was easier to mobilize large followings by portraying the conflict in religious terms, rather than political-economic. The resulting
communalization of the violence was, of course, not an entirely empty in-
vention. Tensions between Christians and Muslims had long been growing in the province, especially around the capital city of Ambon. As Gerry
van Klinken (2001) has shown, these tensions had risen steadily in the
1980s and 1990s with the migration of Muslim Buginese, Butonese, and
Makassarese to the once-Christian territory. In the late-nineteenth century the province was almost exclusively Christian; it was still majority
Christian as late as 1971. By the early 1990s, however, the influx of migrants had created a Muslim majority. Worse yet in the eyes of indigenous Christians, the hardworking immigrants had the networks and
commercial acumen to displace locals in the marketplace. By 1990, it was
only in government and the police that local Christians still enjoyed an
edge over Muslims. With the Soeharto regime's shift toward a more pro-
Islamic policy during the 1990s, however, even this changed. The appointment of the first Muslim Ambonese to the governorship of Maluku
in 1992 "coincided with a new readiness on the Part of President Soeharto, who felt under pressure from the armed forces, to play the religious card" (Klinken 2001, 18).

In his study of ethnonationalist conflicts and collective violence in
South Asia, the Harvard anthropologist Stanley J. Tambiah has observed
that if scattered incidents of local violence are to become full-blown communal wars, the tensions and resentments of everyday life must be removed from their place of origin and generalized into encompassing
narratives of ethnic victimization and enmity. Tambiah refers to this
process as "focalization" and "transvaluation." "Focalization progres-

sively denudes local incidents and disputes of their contextual particulars, and transvaluations distorts, abstracts, and aggregates those incidents into larger collective issues of national or ethnic interest" (Tambiah 1996, 81). It is precisely this process that gave the conflict in Maluku such an incendiary quality after 1999. What had begun as local grievances and a patchwork of alliances was gradually abstracted and focalized into a narrative of a clash of religious civilizations.

In Maluku as in South Asia, state officials played a central role in some of the violence, but it would be a gross oversimplification to ascribe the conflict to an all-powerful state. Such blame-the-state generalizations are especially unhelpful here in Indonesia, because a key symptom of the post-Soeharto crisis was that the state itself had lost its cohesiveness, as opposed factional elites struck coalitional bargains with rival entities in society. A similar segmentary fissioning of state and society, known in Indonesian as *aliranisasi* (lit., "streaming"), had taken place earlier in the country's history, in the period leading up to the mass killings of 1965–66 (see Hefner 2000; Schrauwers 2000).

Equally important, and contrary to a certain romanticism widespread in the 1990s (see chap. 1), it is clear that actors in "civil" society were also complicit in the violence. Whether in Indonesia, India, Rwanda, or the United States, real-and-existing civil societies—the realm of voluntary associations between the household and the state (Hall 1995; Hefner 1998)—are *always,* not merely occasionally, crosscut by ethnic, religious, class, and gender tensions (see Hansen 1999; Hefner 2001; Keane 1996, 10). Although in the 1980s democratic activists had hoped that civil society might provide a kinder and gentler road to democratization, civil society is no more capable of fulfilling the democratic dream on its own than the communities earlier assigned that same mythically heroic role: the community of believers, the proletariat, the middle class, the nation.

If elements of both state and society were complicit in the Indonesian violence, the role of the Islamist paramilitaries nonetheless merits special mention. This is so not because the Islamist paramilitaries played a larger role in the violence than non-Muslim bosses, but because the former dealt such a severe blow to the hopes of democratic Muslims. Tambiah's remarks on focalization and transvaluation are again helpful in this regard (see also Hansen 1999). Focalization and transvaluation require the active presence of agents who have the discursive resources and social authority to disseminate a metanarrative of communal peril and riposte. This discursive legerdemain also requires that voices of moderation within the target community be silenced. What made the Islamist paramilitaries such a potent force in post-Soeharto Indonesia is that, for a while, they seemed close to meeting both of these conditions.

THE *JIHADI* ADVANCE

In the months following Soeharto's fall, hundreds of Islamist paramilitaries sprang up in cities and towns across Indonesia. In the city of Solo alone (a hotbed of political activity in Central Java), there were more than seventy militias operating by late 1999. Most of these paramilitaries had no more than a few dozen members recruited from among neighborhood youth. The largest, however, mobilized tens of thousands of followers in cities and towns across the country. Armed Muslim activism on this scale had not been seen since the anticommunist killings of 1965–66. Unlike the mobilization during that period, however, state patrons had direct influence over only the largest paramilitaries. Many smaller paramilitaries rejected the post-Soeharto state outright, demanding it be replaced with an Islamic state.

The three largest paramilitaries of the post-Soeharto period provide a clear illustration of the varied ideologies and alliances that underlay Islamist paramilitarism. The three are the Islamic Defenders Front (FPI, Front Pembela Islam), the Jihad Paramilitary, or Laskar Jihad, and the Laskar Mujahidin, the paramilitary wing of the Council of Indonesian Mujahidin (MMI, Majelis Mujahidin Indonesia).[1] In early 2003, the leader (*emir*) of the last group, Abu Bakar Ba'asyir, was accused by Indonesian authorities of complicity in the Bali bombings, as well as earlier attacks on dozens of Christian churches on Christmas eve 2000. Although he was eventually cleared of these charges (though convicted for a lesser infraction), activists linked to his organization were found guilty of the Bali bombings. The bombings and subsequent trials were eventually to bring about a tectonic shift in the paramilitarists' public fortunes.

The Islamic Defenders Front

Until its suspension in October 2002, the Islamic Defenders Front, or FPI, was the largest of Indonesia's Islamist paramilitaries. On several occasions the FPI leadership boasted that they had a half million fighters, but my own observations suggest the active membership was actually closer to forty thousand to fifty thousand, most of it concentrated in a handful of large cities. Five thousand of the best-coordinated and aggressive FPI units, however, operated in and around the capital city of Jakarta. From its founding on August 17, 1998, to its "suspension" in October 2002 (see below), the Jakarta FPI was the most potent paramilitary force in the capital, striking fear even among the local police.

Unlike their Jakarta counterparts, FPI units outside the capital had a reputation for militancy combined with poor coordination and indiscipline. The provincial units' recklessness reflected the fact that the national organization was stitched together in the months following Soeharto's downfall through alliances between bosses from already-existing paramilitaries, many of which had only nominal ties to the FPI's Jakarta leadership. Another complicating influence on the FPI was that, unlike the Laskar Mujahidin and the Laskar Jihad, the FPI recruited much of its membership from poor urban neighborhoods and, in particular, from the ranks of petty gangsters and ready-for-hire political hooligans. The FPI leadership made no secret of its rank and file's populist background, since this only enhanced the militia's image as a formidable street force. But the gangland reputation also fueled allegations that some of the organization's celebrated attacks on bars, discothèques, and brothels were as much concerned with securing protection money as they were controlling vice.

Although the rank and file come from lumpenproletariat backgrounds, the FPI's national leadership consists of middle-age religious scholars of Hadrami-Arab background. The FPI's founder, Al-Habib Muhammad Rizieq bin Hussein Syihab, is a Hadrami Arab, as are his lieutenants. The supreme commanders of the other two large paramilitaries, the Laskar Jihad and the Laskar Mujahidin, also happen to be Hadrami Indonesians. However, unlike the FPI, these organizations recruit most of their officers from among people of non-Arab background.

Of all Indonesia's large paramilitaries, the FPI has also been the least reluctant to advertise its ties to high-ranking security officials, including the commander of the post-Soeharto armed forces, General Wiranto, and the police chief for the capital district, Nugroho Jayussman. Jakarta journalists whom I interviewed in 1999 and 2000 stated flatly that Wiranto and Jayussman were responsible for creating the FPI. Wiranto and Jayussman themselves, however, have repeatedly denied having any more than a friendly relationship with Rizieq.

Despite the denials, there is ample evidence of elite backing for at least some of the FPI's actions. It was at the invitation of General Wiranto, for example, that the FPI in November 1998 helped to mobilize a 100,000-strong "voluntary security force" (pam swakarsa) to protect the Consultative Assembly and the Habibie government from prodemocracy demonstrators (Dijk 2001, 341). In June 2000, the FPI ransacked the headquarters of the National Commission on Human Rights when the latter body issued statements implicating members of the armed forces command in the 1999 violence in East Timor. Police stood by during the attack, and later made no attempt to arrest the action's organizers, although their identity was widely known. In March and April 2001, finally, the FPI joined with conservative members of the military and former ruling party, Golkar, in a campaign of "anticommunist" actions that attacked leftist students and ransacked bookstores selling socialist literature, accusing President Wahid of sanctioning both.

However extensive the FPI's ties to military and civilian elites, it is nonetheless clear that the FPI leadership always had its own interests and ambitions. On November 2, 1999, several hundred FPI activists burned a Protestant church south of the capital. On December 13, 1999, four thousand FPI militants broke into and occupied Jakarta City Hall, demanding that the city government close discos, cinemas, restaurants, and massage parlors during the Muslim fasting month. On October 10, 2000, hundreds of FPI militants announced their intention to kill a delegation of Israelis scheduled to visit Indonesia for the 104th Inter-Parliamentary Union conference. (The Israelis withdrew from the conference.) The FPI also spearheaded fierce demonstrations against the United States after the attacks of September 11, 2001. In October 2001, the FPI chief even threatened to shut down the American embassy and conduct sweepings of hotels to flush out Americans and British "spies."

These latter actions led to several violent confrontations with the police. In December 2000, the police command in Jakarta announced that it would no longer tolerate FPI's unilateral actions against cafés, restaurants, and bars. A day later, machete-wielding FPI members invaded a government housing complex in North Jakarta, only to be repelled by its residents. On December 11, 2000, the police took firmer measures, firing bullets into the tires of a van carrying attackers who had just ransacked four entertainment centers in West Jakarta and were hauling away booty (five air conditioners). Angered by the police action, on December 13 hundreds of FPI militants attacked a police station east of the capital, seriously injuring three officers. The next day FPI members attacked a prostitution complex in Subang, West Java, killing a guard. Angry locals reacted by burning down the house of the district FPI leader.

As police pressure increased in early 2001, the FPI scaled back its attacks on alleged centers of vice, concentrating its energies on the campaign against President Wahid. Once Wahid was forced from power in July 2001, however, the FPI ratcheted up its public actions again, sponsoring demonstrations in support of the implementation of Islamic law. In the weeks following September 11, 2001, the FPI also led the fiercest demonstrations against U.S. actions in Afghanistan, and publicly declared its willingness to attack Americans. By this time, however, it was becoming clear that many government officials were growing tired of FPI recklessness. When, in early 2002, American officials raised the issue of renewing limited collaboration with the Indonesian armed forces (contacts that had been frozen for several years), many Jakartan observers predicted—rightly, as it would turn out—that the FPI's days were numbered.

The Laskar Jihad

The Yogyakarta-based Laskar Jihad (*jihad* militia) has had a similar history of on-again-off-again cooperation with establishment figures. Until its sudden dissolution three days after the Bali bombings in October 2002, the Laskar Jihad (LJ) was the second largest of Indonesia's paramilitaries. It was also the best funded and best coordinated, and it was well armed. Although the LJ cooperated with other paramilitaries in attacking alleged centers of vice, its primary concern was always to respond to what were described as Christian acts of aggression against Muslims in Maluku and Central Sulawesi. When I interviewed the Laskar Jihad leader, Jafar Umar Thalib, at the end of July 2001, he said quite bluntly that he intended to extend this armed *jihad* to other areas of the archipelago, including Central Kalimantan, Aceh, Papua, and "anywhere else the enemies of Islam have not learned they must relent." At its peak in September 2001, the organization had two thousand fighters in Maluku, eight hundred to one thousand in Central Sulawesi, and several hundred operating under a different Islamist uniform in Papua.[2]

The Laskar Jihad grew out of an earlier conservative religious movement known as the Sunna Communication Forum (FKAWJ, Forum Komunikasi Ahlus Sunnah wal Jamaah), founded in Yogyakarta in 1994. The founder and spiritual leader of the FKAWJ was a young (b. December 1961) Arab Indonesian by the name of Jafar Umar Thalib. Thalib's career began in Saudi-backed Salafiyah organizations, including the Institute for Islamic and Arabic Studies (LIPIA) in Jakarta, where Thalib studied in the early 1980s, and the Indonesian Council for Islamic Predication (DDII), where he worked in 1983–84.[3]

Awarded a scholarship by the DDII, Thalib traveled in 1986 to Saudi Arabia. From there, under the sponsorship of the Saudi-based Muslim World League, he traveled to Afghanistan, where he met briefly with Osama bin Laden. In his interview with me, Thalib insisted he never directly collaborated with bin Laden, choosing instead to join a faction of the Afghan *mujahidin* with ties to the Saudi government. After the events of September 11, 2001, Thalib publicly distanced himself from bin Laden. He did so, however, not because of the attacks on the United States, but because of bin Laden's opposition to the Saudi government.

Between 1989 and 1993, Thalib made several trips back to Yemen to continue his *salafiyah* studies. Upon returning to Indonesia in 1993, he founded a religious boarding school (*pesantren*) north of the city of Yogyakarta. Unlike most *pesantren*, Thalib's school catered not to adolescent youth, but to the middle-class university students active in the Islamic study circles (*halaqah*) for which Yogyakarta was famous. The more radical among these students were organized into not only religious study groups, but secretive political cells known as *usrah* (lit., "family"). Modeled on the radical wing of the Egyptian Muslim Brotherhood (Mitchell 1969; Wickham 2002), the *usrah* were small operational cells consisting of five to fifteen people linked to a vertical command structure. The senior command coordinated the *usrah* that made up any single organization; they also directed the membership's weekly religious and political lessons. Some groups also engaged in paramilitary training. The *usrah* movement as a whole instilled a spirit of militancy and exclusivity, emphasizing that Islam is a total way of life. Members dressed in a distinctive South Asian *salafiyah* style, and shunned contact with "nonbelievers," an expansive category that included ordinary Muslims regarded as insufficiently pious. Although their memberships were distinct, both the Laskar Jihad and the Laskar Mujahidin (below) mobilized their membership using this pattern of secretive *usrah* cells.

Although some writers have insisted that Thalib was "nonpolitical" until he founded the Laskar Jihad in February 2000, in separate interviews with me, he and one of his chief lieutenants, Ustadh Umar Budihargo, acknowledged their ambitions were political as well as religious from the start. Their purpose, both said, was to counteract the stream of "deviationist" thinking being propagated by Muslim democrats in the university town. Yogyakarta in these years was second only to Jakarta as a center of prodemocracy Muslim activism. During 1999, when I lived in the city, no Muslim activists with whom I spoke had any illusions about Thalib being apolitical. Thalib was known not only for his opposition to democratic Muslims, but for his cordial ties to hardline patrons in Jakarta. The more specific charge leveled at Thalib was that a member of the Soeharto family, who also happens to own a home near Yogyakarta's sultan's palace, had provided the financing for Thalib's *pesantren* in 1994. In his interview with me, Thalib flatly denied this charge.

Whatever the truth of this accusation, what is clear is that from late 1999 on there were regular and high-level meetings between Thalib and representatives of a faction of the armed forces. A former midlevel field commander of the Laskar Jihad, whom I interviewed on August 3, 2001, just after he had left the organization, explained that discussions had increased in January 2000, when retired members of the armed forces, with ties to a still-active commander, approached Thalib indicating they were prepared to support his efforts to mobilize Muslims to respond to Christian attacks in Maluku. Like Thalib, these agents blamed President Wahid for the Maluku conflict and accused the embattled president of being a communist sympathizer. The terms of cooperation were agreed on in February 2000. Soon thereafter a campaign was launched among leading Muslim families in Jakarta, directed by two former Soeharto ministers, to raise money for arms and medical supplies.

The International Crisis Group's report on the violence in Maluku, "Indonesia: The Search for Peace in Maluku" (issued on February 8, 2002), notes that after the founding of the Laskar Jihad in February 2000, out-of-uniform members of the Indonesian National Military (TNI) helped to train its fighters at a camp outside of Bogor, West Java. Tactical support of this sort was also apparent in the Laskar Jihad's startling display of weapons in front of the presidential palace on April 7, 2000, as well as the militants' unimpeded travel across Java to the port of Surabaya several weeks later. Although the president, minister of defense, and governor of Maluku province all appealed to security officials to stop the militia from traveling to Maluku, the militants not only moved freely but were given security escorts along much of the route. In Surabaya they boarded state-owned ferries for Maluku. A Muhammadiyah activist who was in the province at the time told me in July 2000 that upon their arrival in Maluku, the fighters were escorted into the port city of Ambon and provided with weapons shipped in separate containers from Surabaya. Showing once again that there was no consensus among security officials on policy toward the Laskar Jihad, however, provincial police seized one of the weapons containers upon its arrival in the port.

Tactical collaboration between factions of the elite and the Laskar Jihad was also apparent in the "antivice" campaigns in which the organization participated in Yogyakarta during early 2001. As with the FPI's attacks in Jakarta, the Yogyakarta campaign targeted discothèques, bars, brothels—as well as meetings of prodemocracy activists. By July 2001, attacks by machete-wielding militants had paralyzed the local democracy movement. In their antivice actions, Laskar Jihad militants were joined by militants from the Movement of Ka'abah Youth (GPK), an affiliate of one of the country's largest Muslim parties, the United Development Party, or PPP. In Yogyakarta in August 2001, a former officer of the GPK who disagreed with the campaign's targeting of democracy activists described its origins:

> The whole strategy to use the GPK to attack places of immorality and the democracy movement wasn't something simply *tolerated* by security officials. It was *designed* by district officials in a series of meetings I attended during early 2001. The meetings involved officials from Golkar, military officials, Laskar Jihad, and the PPP [the Islamic party]. The campaign's purpose wasn't just to combat vice. It was also intended to mobilize conservative Islamists and undermine support for Abdurrahman Wahid and the democracy movement.

If there is evidence of a coordinate relationship between the Laskar Jihad and at least some members of the security elite, the organization's three-year history also offered numerous examples of conflict with security officials. In June 2000, responding to what it claimed was police bias, the Laskar Jihad mounted an armed assault on a mobile police armory in the Tantui region of Ambon, Maluku, seizing ammunition and seven hundred automatic weapons. In August 2000, a special "Joint Battalion" made up of soldiers drawn from the army, marines, and the air force exchanged gunfire with Laskar Jihad fighters. Other clashes took place in January 2001 and, most seriously, June 14, 2001, when Joint Battalion soldiers attacked a Jihad polyclinic, killing twenty-three militants. Thalib responded to this incident by posting a *fatwa* on the Laskar Jihad Web site calling for the Maluku military commander to be killed. Shortly thereafter, the commander was transferred and the Joint Battalion was replaced by army special forces (KOPASSUS) regarded as more sympathetic to the Laskar Jihad.

Despite these last actions, official opposition to the Laskar Jihad continued to grow. On May 4, 2001, Thalib was arrested after returning from Maluku, on grounds of inciting religious hatred (a prosecutable offense in Indonesia) and condoning the execution by stoning of a Laskar Jihad fighter accused of adultery (the militant had conceded the accusation and agreed to the punishment). In the face of protests from Muslim conservatives, Thalib was quickly released. A year later, however, he was arrested again. This time Thalib was charged with defaming the president and fomenting hatred, in relation to remarks that he had made opposing a recently negotiated peace settlement for Maluku.

Thalib's arrest sparked bitter accusations in the Muslim community that Indonesian authorities were caving in to U.S. pressures. But the incident also revealed growing divisions in the Laskar Jihad leadership itself. These pitted a hard core determined to press forward with the *jihad* campaign against accommodationists, including Thalib, who insisted that there was no point to armed struggle if the group no longer enjoyed the backing of politicians and military officials. In the aftermath of the Bali bombings in October 2002, this split grew, with hardliners deserting Thalib's organization to form militias dedicated to continuing *jihad*. By July 2003, Thalib was speaking openly of his disenchantment with politics and his determination to dedicate himself to religious education. My interviews with former Laskar Jihad militants in that month indicated that militant defectors from Thalib's organization had regrouped into separate *usrah* cells. They made no secret of their determination to renew armed *jihad* when circumstances allowed, with or without Jafar Umar Thalib.

The Laskar Mujahidin

Unlike the Laskar Jihad and the Islamic Defenders front, the leadership of the third and smallest of the Islamist paramilitaries to be discussed here, the Laskar Mujahidin, has long had an antagonistic relationship with Indonesia's armed forces and political establishment. The Laskar Mujahidin is the armed wing of the Indonesian Mujahidin Council (Majelis Mujahidin Indonesia, MMI). The MMI was founded in Yogyakarta in August 2000, and is dedicated to the implementation of Islamic law and the establishment of an Islamic state. The council includes among its leadership a heterogeneous assortment of intellectuals and politicians from mainstream pro-*shari'a* groupings as well as armed militants. However, some officials in the organization are regarded as having sympathies for the Jema'ah Islamiyah, a group with ties to al-Qa'ida and blamed for the Bali and Marriott bombings.

In their earlier years, the men who were to become the leaders of the MMI were associated with the Darul Islam (DI, "abode of Islam") movement. The DI is an old armed Islamist movement that declared an Islamic state in 1948, and then did battle with government forces until 1962 (Dijk 1981). In military circles, even pro-Islamic ones, the Darul Islam has long been regarded as a traitor to the national cause because it turned against the Republican government when the latter was struggling against the Dutch. This legacy did not prevent the military from making occasional use of DI activists. In the anticommunist campaign of 1965–66, DI veterans were recruited to assist in the roundup and killing of communists in West Java. As anticommunist forces in Vietnam teetered toward collapse in the early 1970s, Soeharto's intelligence chief, Ali Moertopo, sponsored the revival of clandestine DI networks, with an eye toward mobilizing them should there be a renewed communist threat (Feillard 1995, 119; ICG 2002, 5). During the 1970s and early 1980s, there were allegations that several bombings blamed by the government on a shadowy Islamist group, the Komando Jihad, may really have been the work of Ali Moertopo double agents working with the DI.

During the 1970s and 1980s, a new network of DI activists gradually came into existence, organized around the activities of an influential Qur'anic boarding school, the Pesantren al-Mu'im, in the village of Ngruki outside of Solo, Central Java. The school was founded in 1973 by two *ulama* of Hadrami-Arab descent, Abdullah Sungkar and Abu Bakar Ba'asyir. Neither man had been directly involved in the Darul Islam rebellions, but both shared that movement's ambition of replacing Indonesia's existing government with an Islamic state. In the 1970s, both men threw themselves into the task of creating communities of believers, or *jema'ah,* dedicated to the implementation of Islamic law. Much like the founders of the Laskar Jihad, the two men relied on an underground network of training cells (*usrah*) to achieve this aim. As the Soeharto regime ratcheted up its pressure on Islamic groupings in late 1978, both men were arrested and accused of involvement in Komando Jihad violence. Held in prison for four years, they were tried and eventually released on time already served. Three years later, when they got wind of government prosecutors' plans to rearrest them, the pair fled to Malaysia. There they continued to raise funds and recruit members to their network, focusing much of their effort on Malaysia's large expatriate Indonesian community (ICG 2002, 12). In the 1980s, some activists in the Jakartan wing of the movement were linked to acts of criminal violence, including bank robberies and murder, but these actions were condemned by Sungkar and Ba'asyir.

In the final years of the Soeharto regime, Sungkar and Ba'asyir are said to have come under the influence of the Egyptian al-Jama'a al-Islamiyya, a breakaway faction of the Egyptian Islamic Brotherhood committed to armed struggle (Sullivan and Abed-Kotob 1999, 82–86). Not everyone in the Indonesian JI network agreed with the leadership's more militant tack. However, in the mid-1990s, as hardline groupings like KISDI and the DDII, to which Sungkar and Ba'asyir had once been close, reconciled with President Soeharto, the two men remained unreconstructed critics of the president. Together with the prominence of veterans of the Darul Islam rebellion in the organization's leadership, this legacy explains why Ba'asyir and the MMI have always been regarded with suspicion in military and old regime circles.

Another consequence of the hardening of Sungkar and Ba'asyir's position, however, was that during the late 1990s, several hundred Jema'ah Islamiyah militants traveled to camps in Afghanistan and Pakistan to receive guerrilla training with internationalist *jihadis* supporting the Afghan *mujahidin*. In his study of al-Qa'ida networks in Southeast Asia, Zachary Abuza makes the prescient observation that these years happened to coincide with the expansion of the al-Qa'ida into Southeast Asia. Al-Qa'ida agents had first appeared in the region in the early 1990s. By 1995, they were participating in secret preparations to bomb U.S. airliners over the Pacific (the attack was thwarted). Al-Qa'ida operatives also traveled to and fought in Maluku and the southern Philippines in the late 1990s and 2000s (Abuza 2003; ICG 2002, 12).

One issue that came to divide JI activists centered on whether the state to which the movement aspires is to coincide with Indonesia's present territorial boundaries, or will include Malaysia, the southern Philippines, and southern Thailand as well. The dispute split the organization in two, but the factions are said to have reconciled shortly after Ba'asyir and Sungkar returned to Indonesia in 1999. Both groups participated in the Mujahidin Congress in Yogyakarta on August 5–7, 2000, at which the Indonesian Mujahidin Council was formed (see Awwas 2001). Both also endorsed the formation of a Laskar Mujahidin to fight Christians in Maluku and Central Sulawesi.

Although their electronic media facilities are not as sophisticated as those of the Laskar Jihad, the MMI and Laskar Mujahidin have nonetheless demonstrated an aptitude for print and electronic media. Most of their media activities have been concentrated in Yogyakarta, at the Wihdah Press. The Wihdah Press was founded and is today still directed by Irfan S. Awwas (born Irfan Suryahardi in 1960), whose brother has been identified as a major JI operative. An intelligent and fiercely independent militant who served nine years in prison for opposing Soeharto policies, Awwas was the prime force behind the convening of the August 2000 congress that led to the establishment of the Majelis Mujahidin Indonesia. During the first three years of the post Soeharto period, Awwas's press published some of Indonesia's most influential radical tracts. Wihdah Press was the publisher, for example, of one of the most influential hardline accounts of the Maluku violence, Rustam Kastor's *The Political Conspiracy of the South Maluku Republic and Christians to Destroy the Muslim Community in Ambon Maluku* (Kastor 2000). This work and two sequels make the case that the violence in Maluku was instigated not just by Maluku Christians, but by Israel and the United States. This, of course, was an Indonesian variant of the conspiracy theories common in *jihadi* circles around the Muslim world since the 1980s. Equally telling, while laying blame for the Maluku violence on Christians, Kastor—himself a former army officer—also accuses the democracy movement of having prepared the ground for the conflict by weakening the army.

Although after its founding in August 2000 the MMI established branches across Indonesia, Jema'ah Islamiyah cadre tied to the organization fell into factional infighting shortly thereafter. A faction led by Riduan Isamuddin, alias Hambali, pressed for armed struggle against the United States in the aftermath of the September 11, 2001, bombings. In February 2002, Hambali was identified by Singapore authorities as one of the masterminds of a plot to attack Western embassies and U.S. naval ships in the Singapore region. Malaysian authorities have also identified Hambali as the person who, in January 2000, arranged accommodations in Malaysia for two of the hijackers of the American Airlines Flight 77 that crashed into the Pentagon on September 11. Philippine authorities have also alleged that Hambali was involved in the 1995 plot to bomb U.S. passenger jets. Finally, the International Crisis Group also implicated the Hambali wing of the Jamaah Islamiyah in a series of bombings of Christian churches across Indonesia on Christmas eve 2000, in which some nineteen people died (ICG 2002, 12). In February of 2003, Indonesian authorities brought formal charges against Ba'asyir and his colleagues for these actions (Ba'asyir was eventually cleared of the charges).

It was the bombings in Kuta, Bali, on October 12, 2002, however, that finally brought the JI into glaring public scrutiny. Individuals linked to the JI confessed to the attacks, explaining the action was designed to kill Americans and American allies. Police interrogations confirmed that after Abdullah Sungkar passed away in November 1999, many of the organization's younger militants were unhappy with the selection of Abu Bakar Ba'asyir as the JI leader. Although Ba'asyir agrees with the long-term necessity of armed struggle and was alleged to have approved the Christmas 2000 church bombings, he is said to have disagreed with the plan for escalated violence after September 11, 2001. The disagreement was one of tactics, not principle. Ba'asyir worried that an escalation of the violence would only invite a government crackdown and push the Megawati government toward closer cooperation with the United States.

In retrospect, if these were Ba'asyir's fears, they appear well founded. Three days after the Bali bombings, the Laskar Jihad announced its dissolution. Although several Western analysts claimed the organization's dissolution was caused by financial problems, sources close to the organization told me in October 2002 that the organization had come under "intensive pressure" from former supporters in the armed forces. Two weeks later, the Islamic Defenders' Front suspended its activities as well.

Abu Bakar Ba'asyir's Laskar Mujahidin, however, remained defiant, rejecting government demands that it dissolve. Press coverage of JI involvement in the Bali violence, however, shocked and angered the mainstream Muslim public. Until the Bali bombings, the Indonesian public had been skeptical of Western, Malaysian, Singaporean, and Philippine claims of the Jema'ah Islamiyah's existence and its alleged campaign of violence. The Bali bombing dispelled some of that skepticism and galvanized Indonesia's two large mainstream organizations, the Nahdlatul Ulama and the Muhammadiyah, into a concerted campaign against extremist violence. The violence also shifted the balance of opinion among political leaders in Jakarta. Prior to Bali, they too had been skeptical of charges that the Jema'ah Islamiyah was planning acts of violence.

By early 2003, then, the Islamist paramilitaries' fortunes had declined drastically, and Muslim moderates were reasserting themselves with a new vigor, hopeful that the paramilitaries' backers had deserted the organizations once and for all. Nonetheless, militants in the national Islamic leadership, including a few well-placed figures with ties to Golkar, continued to speak of an international conspiracy of Jews and Christians against Islam and against Muslim Indonesia. The U.S.-led invasion of Iraq in March 2003 was universally condemned by Muslim moderates, not least of all because they feared the American campaign would put new wind in extremist sails. Moderates in the NU and Muhammadiyah moved quickly to take control of the antiwar movement, however, and the success of their efforts insured that the impact of the war proved less destabilizing than many had feared.

Conclusion

The Indonesian example reminds us that for a transition from authoritarianism to take hold, it is not enough that there be a tolerant and participatory civil society. For the transition to succeed, democratic actors in society need partners in the state to work with rather than against society's civil currents. It is this positive synergy across the state-society divide that has proved so elusive in post-Soeharto Indonesia. Rather than building on resources in the Muslim community for moderation and participation, political bosses in the state *and* local society engaged in sectarian trawling that provided Islamist paramilitaries with an influence greatly out of proportion with their numbers in society.

In light of the top-heavy and state-centric analyses long popular in Indonesian studies, it is important to emphasize that this failure was not just a matter of an all-controlling and ne'er-do-well state. State-based actors may have played a central role in some of the worst trawling, such as that which fueled the street battles in the capital in the months just after Soeharto's resignation. But these elite-sponsored intrigues were soon followed by equally bitter trawling expeditions by "civil-societal" actors in the provinces.

There is a larger political lesson here. Contrary to the romanticized characterizations commonplace in the 1990s, civil society in Indonesia and elsewhere has long been crosscut by ethnoreligious divides. In Indonesia during the 1980s and 1990s, economic growth and migration reshaped the social landscape, and pushed ethnoreligious tensions in some provinces to heights that would have strained the capacities of even the most democratic state. The Soeharto regime's habit of playing ethnoreligious groupings against each other compounded these social tensions considerably. However, the regime did not invent societal tensions where otherwise there would have been none. On the contrary, "civil" society itself was torn by sectarian resentments and divisions. Even worse, in the aftermath of Soeharto's resignation, aspiring bosses in state *and* society did not hesitate to exploit these uncivil divides for their own ends.

There were, however, other vulnerabilities in Indonesian society more specifically related to features of Muslim politics. One was that, during the 1980s and 1990s, the Muslim community's great mass organizations, the Nahdlatul Ulama and the Muhammadiyah, had protected themselves from Soeharto manipulation by distancing themselves from formal politics and deepening their commitment to civic and educational tasks. When, a few month's after Soeharto's fall, radical paramilitaries arose on the fringes of the Muslim community, the NU and the Muhammadiyah moved quickly to call for peace, the rule of law, and civic moderation. However, neither of these organizations was organized in such a way as to allow it to act as a centrally coordinated political machine. Neither, then, was able to fill the vacuum created by, so to speak, the regime's desertion of its civil functions.

There was another aspect of the Indonesian crisis also related to the peculiarities of Muslim politics. Like most of the Muslim world, Indonesia had been swept by an Islamic resurgence in the 1970s and 1980s. The resurgence took place in the aftermath of growing popular disillusionment with a long-dominant secular nationalism. It also occurred, however, after programs of mass education made ordinary Muslims eager to assume responsibility for their religion (Eickelman 1992). As discussed in the introduction and several other essays in this book, one consequence of the resurgence was a great pluralization in popular understandings and social professions of Islam. In most countries, the majority of resurgent Muslims were moderate or apolitical in their views. However, often there was also an ultraconservative minority eager to respond to the competitive pluralism of public life by playing up divisions between Muslims and non-Muslims, as well as Muslims regarded as less than pious in their profession of the faith. Among other things, the conservatives demanded that Muslims turn their back on citizenship ideals and avoid all contact with "infidels." Fueled in part by publications and predication programs sponsored by Salafiyah organizations in Saudi Arabia (see Abuza 2003), this conservative stream also insisted that Islam is a total and "complete" system, alone capable of resolving the modern world's problems. This claim effectively denies the relevance of other forms of knowledge for dealing with social problems. Not coincidentally, the claim also legitimates patriarchal and authoritarian arrangements antithetical to democratic citizenship.

During the early years of the Soeharto regime, the Indonesian Council for Islamic Predication (DDII, Dewan Dakwah Islamiyah Indonesia) was the main conduit for Saudi-Salafiyah ideas. Soon after its establishment in 1967, the DDII forged close ties with the Saudi-sponsored Islamic World League (Rabitat al-'Alam al-Islami). Already in the 1970s, the DDII had begun to translate and publish Saudi-Salafiyah tracts, some of which were notable for their anti-Christian and anti-Jewish diatribes (Bruinessen 2002; Hefner 2000). With the *jihadi* mobilization against the Soviets in Afghanistan, and with the growing irritation in many Arab capitals with U.S. policies in the Middle East, this propaganda took on an even more militantly *jihadist* tone. With the end of the Afghanistan campaign and the outbreak of violence in Bosnia, Kashmir, Chechnya, and other Muslim lands, the literature escalated its critique into a full-blown attack on alleged "Jewish and Christian" conspiracies against Islam. Although for most of the Soeharto era proponents of these theories remained marginal to the mainstream Muslim community, they nonetheless survived. More serious, their theories came to play a central role in the ideological training of the secretive *usrah* cells that sprang up in cities and on campuses across Indonesia in the 1990s.

For Indonesia's moderate and democratic Muslims, then, a central challenge of postresurgence politics was the effort to pacify the sectarian and authoritarian fervors of the *jihadi* fringe so as to channel the energies of the resurgence in a pluralist and democratic direction. Whether in contemporary Turkey, post-Khomeini Iran, or elsewhere, one of the most common instruments for resolving this problem involves efforts by members of the educated new Muslim middle class to demonstrate the compatibility of Islam with modern democracy and pluralism. In other words, a key feature of modern Muslim politics involves moderates' efforts to constrain and "civil-ize" the patriarchal and authoritarian tendencies of conservatives unconvinced of the benefits of modern pluralism.

Unfortunately, in the case of Indonesia, the economic crisis of 1997–98 converged with the collapse of state authority and the outbreak of ethnoreligious violence to make this civic-pluralist project deeply problematic. With the country facing a dual political and economic crisis, the *jihadis'* claim that the country's plight was the result of an international Jewish and Christian conspiracy began to resonate with some angry urban youth. In a nation of almost 200 million Muslims, the total number of *jihadis* remained minuscule. But antidemocratic violence is not a matter of majority rule. The *jihadis'* militancy and secretive *usrah* organization gave them an enormous advantage over their civic pluralist rivals. Worse yet, the *jihadis'* willingness to collaborate with provincial bosses and old regime conservatives provided them with access to a social and political capital with which they could scale up their influence and strike at their moderate rivals.

What went wrong in post-Soeharto Indonesia had some Islamist colors, then, but its driving force also showed something all too familiar from other troubled settings: a transition from authoritarian rule staggering under the weight of economic crisis, a corrupted political culture, and, finally, rampant violence stoked by unscrupulous political bosses. There was indeed a measure of international terrorism laced into this potent brew, and it helped to provoke some of the most awful acts of recent terrorist violence. It may yet again. But any analysis that sees Indonesia's crisis as primarily the result of al-Qa'ida or other internationalist machinations will have missed the more serious lesson to be learned from the Indonesian example. It is that the seeds for Indonesia's difficulties, and, in particular, the seeds for the *jihadis'* post-Soeharto ascent, were sown by thirty-two years of divide-and-conquer authoritarianism. This politics wreaked havoc with Indonesia's tradition of moderate Islam, and destroyed public trust and pluralist collaborations at a time when, as a result of the changes sweeping Indonesia, the country needed new avenues of participation and citizenship more than ever.

Despite the violence of the past few years, the social resources for a culture and practice of citizenship have not been exhausted. Although each faces opposition from a hardline minority within, the Muhammadiyah and Nahdlatul Ulama remain pillars of Islamic moderation and civic-pluralism. In parliamentary debates that raged in the National Assembly in 2001 and 2002, both of these organizations took principled and courageous stands against proposals that would have obliged the state to implement Islamic law. The two organizations did so on the ground that such a measure would damage the country's pluralist heritage.

As this example shows, Indonesia still commands significant resources for democratic citizenship and pluralist participation. The main challenge in the years to come—and it is a serious one—will be whether actors in civil society can at last find democratic partners in the state and among the country's fractious political parties. If such a coalition across the state-society divide can be devised, then this troubled nation may yet make good on its civil-Islamic promise.

NOTES

1. I carried out interviews on and with the membership of the Laskar Jihad and Majelis Mujahidin Indonesia in Yogyakarta Indonesia during July–August 2000 and 2001, and again during June–July 2003. My Indonesian research assistant conducted an additional forty interviews from October 2001 to June 2003. The information I present here on the Islamic Defenders Front is based on press reports, interviews with Muslim activists (none of whom were members of the FPI), and an important report by the Research Bureau of the Center for Language and Culture at the National Islamic University in Jakarta (Tim Peneliti 2000).

2. The Laskar Jihad had also planned to send troops to the province of Aceh, where separatists were gaining ground against the government. With the clear backing of elements in the armed forces command, in January 2002 Jafar Umar Thalib traveled to the troubled province to establish his forces. His presence was denounced by the Acehnese fighters, who accused him of being a stooge of the armed forces command.

3. Although its meanings have changed over time, "salafiyah" in the Indonesian context refers to a variant of puritanical Islamic reform ostensibly modeled on the first generations of Muslims. On the term's varied meanings see Shahin 1995.

REFERENCES CITED

Abdillah, Masykuri. 1997. *Responses of Indonesian Muslim Intellectuals to the Concept of Democracy (1966–1993)*. Hamburg: Abera Verlag Meyer and Co.

Abuza, Zachary. 2002. "Al-Qaeda's Asian Web of Terror." *Time (Asia)* 160, no. 22 38–40.

———. 2003. *Militant Islam in Southeast Asia: Crucible of Terror.* Boulder, Colo.: Lynne Rienner.

Aragon, Lorraine V. 2000. *Fields of the Lord: Animism, Christian Minorities, and State Development in Indonesia.* Honolulu: University of Hawaii Press.

———. 2001. "Communal Violence in Poso, Central Sulawesi: Where People Eat Fish and Fish Eat People." *Indonesia* 72 (October): 44–79.

Awwas, Irfan S. 2001. *Risalah Kongres Mujahidin I dan Penegakan Syari'ah Islam* (Proceedings of the First Congress of Mujahidin and for the implementation of Islamic law). Yogyakarta, Indonesia: Wihdah Press.

Barton, Greg. 2002. *Gus Dur: The Authorized Biography of Abdurrahman Wahid.* Singapore: Equinox Publishing.

Bowen, John R. 1993. *Muslims through Discourse: Religion and Ritual in Gayo Society.* Princeton, N.J.: Princeton University Press.

Bruinessen, Martin van. 2002. "Genealogies of Islamic Radicalism in post-Suharto Indonesia." *South East Asia Research* 10, no. 2:117–54.

Chalk, Peter. 2002. "Militant Islamic Extremism in the Southern Philippines." In *Islam in Asia: Changing Political Realities,* edited by Jason F. Isaacson and Colin Rubenstein, pp. 187–222. New Brunswick, N.J.: Transactions Publishers.

Cribb, Robert, ed. 1990. *The Indonesia Killings, 1965–1966: Studies from Java and Bali.* Clayton, Australia: Monash Papers on Southeast Asia no. 21, Centre of Southeast Asian Studies, Monash University.

———. 2000. "From *Petrus* to Ninja: Death Squads in Indonesia." In *Death Squads in Global Perspective: Murder with Deniability,* edited by Bruce B. Campbell and Arthur D. Brenner, pp. 181–202. New York: St. Martin's Press.

Dijk, C. van. 1981. *Rebellion under the Banner of Islam: The Darul Islam in Indonesia.* The Hague: Martinus Nijhoff.

———. 2001. *A Country in Despair: Indonesia between 1997 and 2000.* Leiden: KITLV Press.

Doorn-Harder, Nelly Van. 2002. "The Indonesian Islamic Debate on a Woman President." *Sojourn* 17, no. 2 (October): 164–90.

Effendy, Bahtiar. 1994. "Islam and the State: The Transformation of Islamic Political Ideas and Practices in Indonesia." Ph.D. dissertation, Department of Political Science, Ohio State University.

Eickelman, Dale F. 1992. "Mass Higher Education and the Religious Imagination in Contemporary Arab Societies." *American Ethnologist* 19, no. 4 (November): 643–55.

Eickelman, Dale F., and James Piscatori. 1996. *Muslim Politics.* Princeton, N.J.: Princeton University Press.

Eickelman, Dale F., and Jon W. Anderson. 1999. *New Media in the Muslim World: The Emerging Public Sphere.* Bloomington: Indiana University Press.

Elson, R. E. 2001. *Suharto: A Political Biography*. Cambridge: Cambridge University Press.

Emmerson, Donald K. 1978. "The Bureaucracy in Political Context: Weakness in Strength." In *Political Power and Communications in Indonesia*, edited by Karl D. Jackson and Lucian W. Pye, pp. 82–136. Berkeley and Los Angeles: University of California Press.

Feillard, Andrée. 1995. *L'Islam et armée dans l'indonésie contemporaine*. Paris: Cahier d'Archipel 28, Éditions L'Harmattan.

Feith, Herbert. 1957. *The Indonesian Elections of 1955*. Interim Report Series, Modern Indonesia Project. Ithaca, N.Y.: Southeast Asia Program, Cornell University.

Forrester, Geoff, and R. J. May, eds. 1999. *The Fall of Soeharto*. Singapore: Select Books.

Geertz, Clifford. 1960. *The Religion of Java*. Glencoe, Ill.: Free Press.

Hall, John A. 1995. "In Search of Civil Society." In *Civil Society: Theory, History, Comparison*, edited by John A. Hall, pp. 1–31. Cambridge: Polity Press.

Hansen, Thomas Blom. 1999. *The Saffron Wave: Democracy and Hindu Nationalism in Modern India*. Princeton, N.J.: Princeton University Press.

Hefner, Robert W. 1987. "Islamizing Java? Religion and Politics in Rural East Java." *Journal of Asian Studies* 46, no. 3: 533–54.

———. 1990. *Political Economy of Mountain Java: An Interpretive History*. Berkeley and Los Angeles: University of California Press.

———. 1998. "On the History and Cross-Cultural Possibility of a Democratic Ideal." In *Democratic Civility: The History and Cross-Cultural Possibility of a Modern Political Ideal*, edited by Robert W. Hefner, pp. 3–49. New Brunswick, N.J.: Transaction Publishers.

———. 2000. *Civil Islam: Muslims and Democratization in Indonesia*. Princeton, N.J.: Princeton University Press.

———. 2001. "Introduction: Multiculturalism and Citizenship in Malaysia, Singapore, and Indonesia." In *The Politics of Multiculturalism: Pluralism and Citizenship in Malaysia, Singapore, and Indonesia*, edited by Robert W. Hefner, pp. 3–58. Honolulu: University of Hawaii Press.

Human Rights Watch. 2002. "Breakdown: Four Years of Communal Violence in Central Sulawesi." New York: Human Rights Watch Papers, vol. 14, no. 9C.

ICG. 2001. "Communal Violence in Indonesia: Lessons from Kalimantan." Brussels: ICG Asia Report no. 19.

———. 2002. "Al-Qaeda in Southeast Asia: The Case of the 'Ngruki Network' in Indonesia." Brussels: ICG Asia Briefing, August 8.

Jay, Robert T. 1963. *Religion and Politics in Rural Central Java*. New Haven, Conn.: Cultural Report Series no. 12, Program in Southeast Asian Studies, Yale University.

Kastor, Rustam. 2000. *Konspirasi politik RMS dan Kristen menghancurkan ummat Islam di Ambon-Maluku* (The political conspiracy of the RMS and Christians to destroy the Muslim community in Ambon-Maluku). Yogyakarta: Wihdah Press.

Keane, John. 1996. *Reflections on Violence*. London: Verso.

Kipp, Rita Smith. 1990. *Dissociated Identities: Ethnicity, Religion, and Class in an Indonesian Society.* Ann Arbor: University of Michigan Press.

Klinken, Gerry van. 2001. "The Maluku Wars: Bringing Society Back In." *Indonesia* 71 (April): 1–26.

Liddle, R. William, and Saiful Mujani. 2000. "The Triumph of Leadership: Explaining the 1999 Indonesian Vote." Department of Political Science, Ohio State University, manuscript.

Mitchell, Richard P. 1969. *The Society of the Muslim Brothers.* New York: Oxford University Press.

O'Donnell, Guillermo, and Philippe C. Schmitter. 1986. *Transitions from Authoritarian Rule: Tentative Conclusions about Uncertain Democracies.* Baltimore, Md.: Johns Hopkins University Press.

Pemberton, John. 1994. *On the Subject of "Java."* Ithaca, N.Y.: Cornell University Press.

Robinson, Geoffrey. 1995. *The Dark Side of Paradise: Political Violence in Bali.* Ithaca, N.Y.: Cornell University Press.

Ryter, Loren. 1998. "Pemuda Pancasila: The Last Loyalist Free Men of Suharto's Order." *Indonesia* 66 (October): 45–73

Schiller, Anne. 1997. *Small Sacrifices: Religious Change and Cultural Identity among the Ngaju of Indonesia.* New York: Oxford University Press.

Schrauwers, Albert. 2000. *Colonial "Reformation" in the Highlands of Central Sulawesi, Indonesia, 1892–1995.* Toronto: University of Toronto Press.

Schwarz, Adam. 2000. *A Nation in Waiting: Indonesia's Search for Stability.* 2nd edition. Boulder, Colo.: Westview.

Shahin, Emad Eldin. 1995. "Salafiyah." In *The Oxford Encyclopedia of the Modern Islamic World,* edited by John L. Esposito, 3: 463–69. New York: Oxford University Press.

Sullivan, Denis J., and Sana Abed-Kotob. 1999. *Islam In Contemporary Egypt: Civil Society versus the State.* Boulder, Colo.: Lynne Rienner.

Tambiah, Stanley J. 1996. *Leveling Crowds: Ethnonationalist Conflicts and Collective Violence in South Asia.* Berkeley and Los Angeles: University of California Press.

TGPF. 1998. "The Final Report of the Joint Fact Finding Team (TGPF) on the May 13–15, 1998, Riot." Jakarta: TGPF.

Tim Peneliti. 2000. *Radikalisme Agama dan Perubahan Sosial di DKI Jakarta* (Religious radicalism and social change in Jakarta). Jakarta: Pusat Bahasa dan Budaya, IAIN Syarif Hidayatullah.

Wickham, Carrie Rosefsky. 2002. *Mobilizing Islam: Religion, Activism, and Political Change in Egypt.* New York: Columbia University Press.

Woodward, Mark R. 1989. *Islam in Java: Normative Piety and Mysticism in the Sultanate of Yogyakarta.* Tucson: University of Arizona Press.

Yunanto, S. 2003. *Gerakan Militan Islam di Indonesia dan di Asia Tenggara* (Militant Islamic movements in Indonesia and Southeast Asia). Jakarta: Ridep Institute.

Chapter 12

SUFIS AND SALAFIS: THE POLITICAL

DISCOURSE OF TRANSNATIONAL ISLAM

Peter Mandaville

THE NATURE AND CHARACTER OF CONTEMPORARY TRANSNATIONAL ISLAM defy easy description. Recent coverage of this topic in both the popular media and in academic discourse has tended to emphasize the prevalence of highly radical and militant tendencies at the core of those Islamic movements whose activities cross national borders. Some of the more alarmist voices today go so far as to claim the existence of something like an "Islamic Comintern" set on the destruction of Western society and its allies in the Muslim world. In the wake of September 11, the rush to identify enemies and targets—particularly among policy makers and media pundits in the United States—has produced an image of transnational Islam as inherently malignant. Occasionally accurate in their analyses, such depictions of transnational Islam are, however, highly partial and often presented outside of context and in a worryingly dehistoricized manner. We are sometimes given to believe, it seems, that a highly coordinated global network of militant fanatics sprang up fully formed in diverse locales across the Muslim world on September 10, 2001.

Such accounts do much to obscure the complex realities of Muslim transnationalism. It is certainly fact that there exist today Islamic movements—and, moreover, lines of communication and coordination between them—with the willingness and capacity to use violence in the name of religion. It is also the case, however, that the vast majority of transnational connections between individuals and groups in the Muslim world have nothing whatsoever to do with militancy and revolution. Indeed, in global communications forums on the Internet, and in the activities of a growing number of Muslim NGOs, we find evidence of a transnational Islam whose agenda is organized instead around themes such as education, human rights, and gender equality. Even more perplexing it would seem is the fact that the boundaries between these two categories of Muslim transnationalism are not always clearly delineated. Funds from otherwise legitimate charities, for example, can through the exigencies of global exchange find their way into nefarious hands. In short, to understand transnational Islam is, by necessity, also to be comfortable with manifold shades of gray.

This chapter will provide a comparative overview of several manifestations of contemporary transnational Islam. By examining the history, ideology, and practices of several movements—including both "radicals" and "moderates"—I will engage the widely held assumption that transnational Islam is not conducive to discourses of political civility, pluralism, and democracy. In contrast to many of the other contributions in this volume, I will be covering groups who reject religious and political pluralism as it has been defined for the purposes of this project. My aim in doing so stems from the assumption that calculating the most effective way to "scale up" moderate discourses in the absence of an understanding of why more radical tendencies find significant transnational appeal will never produce a comprehensive analysis. Indeed, the ability of radical groups to articulate themes that resonate at times with large portions of worldwide Muslim audiences needs to be regarded as one of the chief obstacles to the wider dissemination of civil, pluralist Islam. In this regard it becomes vital to understand the complex interplay between various groups and movements of sometimes quite different dispositions—or, more properly, to understand that these dispositions, always contingent and subject to rapidly changing and fluid circumstances, often escape easy characterization. The approach I adopt must also therefore reject easy categorizations of "good" and "bad" variants of Islam and, moving away from an exclusively geopolitical orientation, it will seek instead to provide something closer to a discursive analysis of the intellectual and social dimensions of Muslim transnationalism in a globalizing world.

The general plan and structure of the chapter is as follows. I begin by identifying some of the major trends in transnational Islam today. Developing a specific focus on European-based sociopolitical movements, I offer a description and analysis of three of the more radical groups— Hizb ut-Tahrir, al-Muhajiroun, and the Supporters of Shari'ah—who claim significant transnational support for their political agendas, all of which are organized around the principle of reestablishing a global Islamic polity. While these groups are only tangentially linked to networks such as al-Qaeda, there is a large degree of intellectual and ideological overlap between the former and latter. They are hence worth studying in order to better understand the "precursor" social sources of support for transnational militant Islam.

The chapter next moves on to an examination of social movements that represent trends in transnational Islam far more compatible with civil, pluralist norms—and, as I will argue, better socially positioned to scale up their influence over the next generation. This section describes and analyzes social and educational movements, such as the Gülen and

Nur groups organized out of Turkey, whose religious orientation draws heavily on modernist neo-Sufi (mystical) sources. I also examine Tariq Ramadan's discourse on European Islam and the jurisprudential bases for communal pluralism and coexistence with non-Muslim others.

I conclude by, to some extent, deliberately disrupting the ideal type categories of "radical" and "moderate" Islam developed in preceding sections in order to make the point that the reality of contemporary transnational Islam is such that it resists the analyst's and policy maker's desire for straightforward typologies. The program of scaling up transnational civil Islam, I argue in the end, is one that cannot be definitively located. It is a quite literally movable feast, and one that requires a sensitivity to rapidly changing contingencies within and across numerous layers of Muslim society. In this regard, also, we are required to rethink the conventional notions and boundaries of what constitutes democratic politics.

CONTEMPORARY MUSLIM TRANSNATIONALISM

The scope and diversity of the Muslim world, combined with technologies of communication and travel, produce enormous variety in transnational Islam today. This runs the gamut from highly personalized intellectual linkages between individuals to the high diplomacy of Islamic intergovernmentalism in the OIC and state-sponsored *da'wa* (Arab, "call," religious propagation) work via organs such as the Muslim World League (Schulze 1990, 213–65). When it comes to the question of transnational social movements, there is not only a wide range to contend with, but considerable variation in scale, style, and activities. We can think, for example, of the enormous Tablighi Jama'at, a largely apolitical faith movement whose annual conferences in India represent the second largest world gathering of Muslims after the *hajj*. Transnational *da'wa* work is one of the group's main pursuits, and to this end it maintains coordination centers in South Asia, the Middle East, Europe and North America (Masud 2000). Other groups are oriented toward social and economic development issues. Women Living under Muslim Law and Sisters in Islam (see Peletz, this volume), for example, style themselves as international solidarity networks. MuslimAid is a leading global charity. Far-flung diasporas, such as the Chinese Uygar community in Turkey, organize on behalf of Muslim kin and brethren back home (Shichor 2003), while new media spaces provide opportunities for discussion and debate among Muslim youth groups in the European Union and the United States (Mandaville 2001; Allievi 2003).

The political forms of contemporary Muslim transnationalism—that is, those groups whose explicit aim is the establishment of Islamic polities—are somewhat less diverse. Olivier Roy identifies two major networks that encompass many of the nationally oriented Islamist movements: one affiliated with the Muslim Brotherhood and covering mainly the Arab Middle East (e.g., HAMAS in Palestine, al-Nahda in Tunisia) and the other organized around Pakistan's Jama'at-i Islami (Roy 1994). It is more accurate, however, to say that these connections, for the most part, are ones of general ideological orientation and intellectual lineage rather than active, coordinated sponsorship and coordination. It should be emphasized again that these groups are, in the main, working locally to establish Islamic states in particular countries. Their political aspirations do not extend beyond national borders, and in this sense I do not regard them as transnational movements per se. However, this does not mean that certain of these groups—particularly the more radical among them—are not at times implicated in the agendas and activities of actors whose political aspirations extend beyond the state. Ayman al-Zuwaihari, for example, former leader of Egypt's Islamic Jihad, effectively folded his group into Usama bin Laden's al-Qaeda in the mid-1990s. The Brotherhood and Jama'at both also have a history of ties to and sponsorship of groups abroad.

When we move on to deal with transnational political movements whose goals are more global in scope, things become murkier still. Linkages and relationships can be highly informal, nebulous, and rather ad hoc, contributing to an aura of uncertainty in terms of scale and breadth of geographic coverage. That groups such as al-Qaeda appear to be constituted by cells on virtually every continent, cropping up in such seemingly unlikely locales as South America (Whitbeck and Arneson 2001), lends their activities an aura of omnipresence. By cultivating this image of ubiquity, and through a careful public relations strategy involving media sound bites that seemingly appear out of the ether, a relatively small number of such groups have managed to catapult themselves to the forefront of transnational Islam in the eyes of the public. The spectacle of September 11 and a series of smaller-scale attacks in multiple countries have all served to reinforce this image in recent months. Since these events, the public discourse on transnational Islam has focused almost exclusively on shadowy militant networks, many of which are described as inspired by Wahhabism, a hardline variant of Islam usually seen to emanate from Saudi Arabia. In the wake of the October 2002 bombing in Bali, Indonesia, for example, significant attention focused on Jemaah Islamiah, described as an al-Qaeda "franchise" seeking to establish a Pan-Islamic state encompassing Muslims in Indonesia, Malaysia, the Philippines, Singapore and Brunei (Abuza 2003; Wain and McBeth 2002; see also Hefner and

Peletz in this volume). Much is made of the fact that ideologues associated with the group had studied Islam in Saudi Arabia or other parts of the Middle East, supposedly confirming the transnational Wahhabi agenda.

While speculation about transnational Islamic militancy has reached a fevered pitch, our understanding of these groups and the individuals (often only tangentially) affiliated with them has progressed very little. While it should be clear by now that radical groups with violent agendas constitute the marginal fringes of transnational Islam, this does not mean that they should be dismissed as insignificant. It is in part their willingness to adopt extreme methods that compensates for their relatively small numbers. Likewise, skillful use of rhetoric and symbols that resonate with Muslims worldwide affords them a constituency that, while not always supportive of their militant tactics, identifies with many of the issues that constitute their discourse of resistance. While groups such as al-Qaeda have been analyzed extensively from strategic, security, and geopolitical perspectives (Alexander and Swetman 2001; Gunaratna 2002; Paz 2003), relatively little attention has been paid to them or their affiliates as *social phenomenan* (cf. Bruinessen 2002). At the outset of this chapter I sought to argue that before moving to an analysis of how civil, pluralist Islam might be more effectively scaled up, we need first to understand how the discursive landscape of political Islam—particularly in its transnational aspect—has seemingly come to be so dominated by radical tendencies. In the next section of this chapter, therefore, I will undertake to describe and analyze a complex of sociopolitical movements based largely in the United Kingdom whose goals for the establishment of Islamic polity are more global in scope, and which represent a hardline, conservative approach to religion. Because these groups are peripheral to the activities of an organization such as al-Qaeda—while still sharing many of the same general ideological orientations—they represent interesting examples of the "intermediate milieu" of radical Islam. Their activities constitute a space in which antipluralist agendas can be organized and propagated, while stopping short (for the most part) of adopting coercive methods. These groups vary greatly in terms of the support they command (rarely, it would seem, nearly as much as they claim) and the extent to which they are able to coordinate transnational activities, yet they are certainly qualitatively, in terms of their ideological appeal, if not necessarily always quantitatively, significant.

Diasporas of Radical Islam

Over the last decade several social movements espousing radical political agendas have emerged as a small but vocal camp within the British Muslim community. These groups are similar enough in their general aims and in the tenor of their discourse to be commonly lumped together as a single tendency. While elements of a shared agenda can indeed be identified, a closer examination soon reveals considerable differences in emphasis and method. Furthermore, some among their leaderships go to considerable lengths to differentiate themselves from each other—particularly insofar as in one case at least, a group was founded as an offshoot of one of the others following a significant disagreement over matters of theology. Shared between them in terms of political vision, however, is an emphasis on the need to eventually reestablish the Islamic caliphate (*khilafah*), the original Muslim polity that existed in one form or another until its abolition at the hands of Mustapha Kemal Ataturk in 1924. In other words—and this is in part why I treat them as transnationally oriented groups—these groups seek to achieve not isolated Islamic states, but rather a global Muslim polity under a single caliph (*khalifah*) charged with the duty of ensuring the practice and enforcement of *shari'ah* (religious law). All three have, or claim to have, branches and followers in multiple countries and their U.K.-based leaderships have all been involved in political activism in the Middle East, South Asia, and elsewhere. Because their programs depart from a different *aqeedah* (tenets of belief or "creed"), the location and importance of the caliphate varies between their respective discourses. In seeking to identify an emphasis on the caliphate as the distinguishing aspect of their political agendas, however, I use the generic label *khilafist* to set these groups apart from those Islamists, such as the Muslim Brotherhood or Jama'at-i Islami, seeking to establish individual Islamic states. In what follows I shall provide a description account of the background, intellectual orientation, political program, and transnational reach of each group, followed by an analysis of why and how their political discourses have selective appeal today.

Hizb ut-Tahrir

Hizb ut-Tahrir (Party of Liberation—hereafter HT) is the oldest and probably the most widespread in its transnational activities of the three groups under examination in this section. Founded in Jerusalem in 1952 by Taqi ud-Din al-Nabhani, HT emphasized from the beginning the importance of establishing a single party (*hizb*) through which Muslims could work for the reestablishment of *khilafah*. In the eyes of Nabhani and his followers, it was only through revolutionary action in concert that the world's Muslims could restore themselves to a position of global power. In this sense, the founding of Nabhani's movement marks a reincarnation of certain elements found in earlier discourses on Pan-Islam, yet with a stronger emphasis on the importance of a single Muslim polity. Nabhani faced considerable opposition from the Jordanian state (which

still controlled Jerusalem at that time), and also found it difficult to develop a mass following for his party. With Arab nationalism gathering
strength as the dominant political ideology of the day, appeals for a new
caliphate fell largely on deaf ears. HT found itself moving underground
at the same time as it began to establish small footholds in other Arab
countries. Noted to be particularly strong in Turkey, where memory of
the Ottoman caliphate still endures to some extent, the group's activities
in the Middle East and Asia (outside the reach of anti-HT propaganda in
the Arab world) have been well documented during the first decades of its
existence (Taji-Farouki 1996).

The structure of HT, while highly fluid in practice, is organized around
a series of hierarchical committees. The party maintains a worldwide
central leadership committee headed by an *amir* (leader), currently Abdul
Qadeem Zalloon. The group does not disclose the location of the central
committee, but it is widely believed to reside in Lebanon. Each nation
(or "province" since the party does not recognize the validity of the
nation-state model) in which HT operates possesses a five-to-ten-member
committee headed by a *mu'tamad*. These national leadership councils
subspeciate into smaller local (usually urban) committees under a *naqib*
and neighborhood study circles guided by a *mushrif*. In countries where
it has been subject to persecution by authorities, HT has been known to
adopt a rigorously enforced cell structure.

Sporadic references to crackdowns on HT branches in North Africa
and Turkey can be found throughout the 1970s and 1980s, and the group
resurfaced to a torrent of negative publicity in Britain in the early- to
mid-1990s. Having engaged in a heavy recruiting drive at U.K. universities, HT found itself banned from British higher education campuses by
the National Union of Students following accusations of anti-Semitic activities. The group's *mu'tamad* in the United Kingdom, Shaykh Omar
Bakri Muhammad, emerged during this time as a controversial public figure, challenging all Muslims in the United Kingdom to adopt the pursuit
of *khilafah* as the only possible authentic course of political action available to Muslims. Although its beliefs and program remained a minority
tendency, the radical political position adopted by the group managed to
effectively polarize the British Muslim community for a short period
(Mandaville 2001). Seeking to label all who rejected the caliphate as
Western collaborators—or in Bakri's terms, "chocolate Muslims"—HT
prompted a vigorous debate about the political imperatives of Islam as a
minority community. In 1996, after significant disagreements arose within
the U.K. leadership of HT as to the theological basis for the group's political activities and the scope of its work, Bakri left the group to found
al-Muhajiroun (see below). Severely discredited in the eyes of Muslims
and non-Muslims alike, HT retreated from the public eye for several

years, leaving the limelight in the United Kingdom to groups such as al-Muhajiroun. Attention to HT's activities increased again in the summer of 2001, but this time centered on Central Asia, where reports had emerged of active cells organized out of Uzbekistan that authorities were trying to link with al-Qaeda (Rashid 2002: 135). Although London remains an important site of fund-raising, recruitment, and coordination for the group, HT's political activism seems increasingly to be focused elsewhere, with Pakistan, Jordan, and Palestine claimed as major areas of focus at the present time.

Sources of support for HT vary considerably from context to context, and in this sense it is difficult to produce something like a profile of a "typical" party member. It has proven itself skillful in adapting its discourse to local conditions and at appealing to particular grievances. In the early 1990s, for example, it was particularly successful in recruiting among second- and third-generation South Asian immigrants in the United Kingdom, many of whom had been raised with a form of Islam they regarded as disengaged from worldly issues and political imperatives. Alienated by their parents' "village Islam" (i.e., oriented toward the sectarian idiosyncrasies of the villages in Pakistan and Bangladesh from which they had migrated) and socially adrift in a society into which mainstream integration proved difficult, the discourse of radical resistance offered by HT appeared highly attractive. By placing *khilafah*—a marginal ideal at best in mainstream Muslim political thought—firmly at the center of its religious discourse, HT was able to take advantage of a relative lack of religious knowledge on the part of its young recruits. When asked about the extent of desire in the *ummah* for a new caliphate, group members often give a general answer about Muslims desiring greater unity. When it is put to them that such a desire does not necessarily translate into support for *khilafah,* and that those seeking a political order based on Islam might prefer groups such as the Muslim Brotherhood (the most popular Islamist tendency in the Arab world), HT supporters tend to explain that Muslims will eventually realize that the correct political implementation of Islam must necessarily lead to *khilafah.*

So how, in HT's view, will this new caliphate come about? The party's political discourse begins by recognizing the lack of any "executive structure" in the Muslim world as a major problem and one that must, according to a *shari'ah* obligation impingent upon all Muslims, be rectified. In terms of its methods, it seeks to style itself as nonderivative in the sense that it does not study and emulate the approaches taken by previous Islamist movements. Instead, it seeks to go back to the basic legislative sources of the religion—the Qur'an, *hadith,* and *usul al-fiqh.* The correct method for establishing *khilafah* is fixed and can, it claims, be found in the *shari'ah,* but this should be distinguished from "means and style," which are necessarily specific to place and time. HT, at least in the United Kingdom, explains that its work is intellectual and political, and in this regard they reject militant methods. Realizing the close relationship between force and power, however, HT does speak of actively seeking *nussrah*—support from the armed forces or those responsible for the security of citizens—in countries where it operates, but claims that this is a form of activity controlled exclusively by the party's central leadership. While appealing to a young and generally well educated audience, the group finds support for its program by simultaneously adopting a populist rhetoric designed to link socioeconomic disenfranchisement to religiosity. For example, HT's publicity literature in the United Kingdom defines capitalism as "the detachment of religion from life." Regarding the geographic scope of its activities, the group expresses a willingness to work anywhere and everywhere, but suggests that the caliphate has the best chance of being reestablished in those lands where a precedent already exists (i.e., the Middle East and former Ottoman territories). While global *khilafah* remains the party's ultimate goal, it espouses a gradualist approach.

Al-Muhajiroun

Al-Muhajiroun emerged publicly in Britain 1996 after its founder, Omar Bakri Muhammad, split with HT. A Syrian by birth, Bakri gained his qualifications as an *'alim* in Damascus and Beirut, where he was affiliated with the Muslim Brotherhood and several other Islamist tendencies before joining HT. Bakri spent several years in Saudi Arabia in the 1980s, until his ties with HT landed him in trouble with the kingdom's authorities.

Many broad aspects of HT's program are duplicated in al-Muhajiroun's political discourse, including the emphasis on *khilafah* and the movement's general organizational structure (not to mention several key HT texts, which Bakri presumably authored during his time with the party). There are, however, also several significant points of divergence. First, Bakri cites HT as following a fundamentally different *aqeedah*—in other words, of subscribing to separate tenets of religious belief. Al-Muhajiroun, he claims, is a *salafi* group, meaning that it orients itself with the traditional teachings associated with the first few generations of Muslims after Muhammad. Developments in theology and jurisprudence that came later are regarded by this school of thought as dangerous innovation (*bid'a*). Bakri's teaching identifies *salafiyya* as a methodology or way of thought rather than a tendency associated with any particular group or movement. Central to salafi thought is an emphasis on *tawhid*, the unity of God, a trait shared by the revivalist project of Muhammad Ibn Abdul Wahhab in eighteenth century—hence the tendency for many contemporary salafi groups, particularly those advocating the strict application of *shari'ah,* to be labeled Wahhabi. Bakri accuses HT, by contrast, of following an "Asha'ri" creed, meaning that they subscribe to latter theological innovations that allow for a modicum of human reason to enter into matters of religion. In Bakri's view, what passes for reason is usually nothing more than selfish desire, and hence inherently dangerous. A literal application of jurisprudential knowledge produced by the earliest generations of Muslims is therefore the only safe method by which to conduct human affairs. For the *salafiyyun,* in Bakri's view, Islam was not a text or culture that can be objectified (as Muslims try to do today); rather, theirs was a living, active knowledge. The doctrinal orientation of HT, according to Bakri, means that they have developed an incorrect obsession with *khilafah* and have lost sight of *tawhid* as the central duty of all Muslims.

The second major difference between HT and al-Muhajiroun concerns the geographic scope of their activities. Bakri criticizes the gradualist tendencies of HT that permit it to focus on one particular country or *mijaal* ("area of work") at a time. By contrast, al-Muhajiroun, he claims, works throughout the *ummah,* seeking *nussrah* at all times. Bakri's group, he claims, does not actively pursue *jihad* (religious struggle—which for Bakri carries a militant connotation in this context), although he believes—unlike HT—that Muslims have a duty to support *jihadi* groups wherever they may be fighting. He criticizes HT's claim that *jihad* is an activity that can only be legitimately promulgated by a caliph and hence cannot be supported until such time as *khilafah* is reestablished. That said, Bakri is careful to distance himself from some of the contemporary *jihadi-salafi* groups. He argues that some among them do not have sufficient regard for the sanctity of all human life and are wrong to regard the entire world, including non-*salafi* Muslim regimes, as *dar al-harb* (i.e., the abode of war—lands in which Muslims are engaged in violent struggle with unbelievers). Regarding its global support, al-Muhajiroun claims to have members and affiliated groups in Saudi Arabia, the United Arab Emirates, Kuwait, Yemen, Lebanon, Sudan, Pakistan, South Africa, Mauritius, Central Asia, and the United States. *Da'wa* links to Southeast Asia are also cited. The group declines to put any numerical figure on the level of its support, claiming only that it is "growing significantly." Bakri has actively sought to forge alliances with other movements in the United Kingdom and abroad, another point of disagreement between him and the leadership of HT at the time of their separation. On its publicity literature, for example, the group lists twenty-seven "organs" of al-Muhajiroun. It actively seizes opportunities to appear with other Islamist groups, even those that do not share a strictly *salafi* orientation. In this regard there is a sense in which al-Muhajiroun can also be thought of as an umbrella group.

The political discourse of al-Muhajiroun shares much with HT, although Bakri goes to considerable lengths to articulate a *salafi* basis for the *khilafah*. Invoking the notion of *tawhid al-hakimiyyah* (oneness of the law) as the link between the unity of God and governance on earth, he outlines various forms of authority (*sultah*) which translate, according to his interpretations, into legislative, executive, and judicial functions. Democracy, however, is identified as the opposite of that for which al-Muhajiroun (and, incidentally, HT) strives. Asserting that the notion of rule by the people contradicts the Islamic dictum that sovereignty is reserved for God alone (Qur'an 6:57, 12:40), Bakri emphasizes that ultimate authority must always lie within the divine alone—or, on this earth, within the *shari'ah* that represents divine will. Al-Muhajiroun, like many contemporary Islamist—and particularly *khilafist*—movements, is subject to considerable criticism that suggests their program consists of nothing beyond vague appeals to a rather utopian vision of the caliphate. What would this look like in institutional form? How would it be structured? How would issues of economic regulation, taxation, and international relations be dealt with? Realizing that a lack of specifics has been a shortcoming of Islamist groups in the eyes of many, Bakri has sought to answer some of these questions in a recent pamphlet that tries to outline in greater detail the structure of a *khilafah*-style government (Bakri Muhammad 2002).

As with many *salafi* scholars, Bakri is exhaustive in terms of laying out the concepts, categories of analysis, and textual evidence in which he finds support for the positions he advocates. Indeed, this sort of rigorous taxonomy is a hallmark characteristic of *salafi* discourse, and one of the many points of criticism leveled at it by opponents. *Salafis,* in the eyes of many, are obsessed with establishing hard-and-fast categories and labels that differentiate in stark terms between "good" and "bad" beliefs and practices. There seems to be little gray area, in Bakri's discourse, for example, between heaven's eternal reward and the damnation of hellfire. While this rigidity—and, at times, obscurantism—is alienating to most Muslims, leaving as it does little room for ambiguity, reflection, or creative interpretation, its moral clarity nevertheless proves appealing to others.

The Jihadis: Abu Hamza al-Masri and the Supporters of Shari'ah

The third and final group to be examined, the Supporters of Shari'ah (SOS) is also the most highly personalized of the movements. It centers almost exclusively around Shaykh Abu Hamza al-Masri, imam, until recently, of the North London Central Mosque in Finsbury Park—widely held to be the leading center of radical Islam in Britain. A group de-

scribed by its leader as "deliberately diffuse and loosely organized," SOS
is the U.K.-based public relations face for a wider transnational network
with connections to Algeria's Groupe Islamique Armé (GIA) and other *jihadi* movements. Abu Hamza, born in Alexandria, Egypt, fought alongside the Afghan *mujahideen* against the Soviet occupation. He came to
the United Kingdom in 1979 and took British citizenship. Along with
Abu Qatada, another *jihadi* shaykh recently arrested by the U.K. authorities, Abu Hamza is generally regarded as the figure most likely to be involved in active recruitment for militant groups abroad. September 11
suspects Zacharias Moussaoui and James Ujaama as well as attempted
shoe-bomber Richard Reid are all said to have been under his tutelage at
some point in recent years.

Insofar as the move from Hizb ut-Tahrir to al-Muhajiroun contained
elements of both continuity and rupture, we find the same dynamic at
work in the shift from Bakri's group to Abu Hamza's SOS. Where HT
emphasizes a gradualist approach to establishing *khilafah* via persuasion
before *jihad* can be legitimately enjoined, Abu Hamza represents the opposite end of the spectrum. *Khilafah* per se is not so much his concern;
rather, the active propagation of *shari'ah*—by *jihad* if necessary—is the
political imperative. The caliphate, in Abu Hamza's view, will flow naturally from correct implementation of the *shari'ah*. In this regard he is
more concerned with general religious orientation than any one specific
institution, bringing his approach closer to that of al-Muhajiroun. The
triumph of righteous Muslims, in other words, will naturally bring about
righteous governance.

That is not to say, however, that Abu Hamza and Omar Bakri Muhammad see entirely eye to eye. Although the two appear together frequently
at rallies and press conferences, one also gets the sense that they position
themselves with respect to each other somewhat tactically. An association
with SOS allows Bakri to emphasize his transnational activist credentials,
while al-Muhajiroun provides Abu Hamza the opportunity to articulate
his agenda alongside an umbrella of social movements with a predominantly intellectual orientation. Bakri has at times criticized aspects of the
jihadi agenda, while Abu Hamza has let it be known that he has not always been satisfied with the *aqeeda* of al-Muhajiroun's leader. That said,
cooperation between the two groups and joint public appearances have
increased significantly of late, and they are increasingly identified as advocating the same general political program.

It is difficult to make any definite determination as to the extent of any
linkages between these movements and the more actively militant networks such as al-Qaeda. Accusations of recruiting for terrorist training
camps in Afghanistan have been leveled at both groups at various times,
and some reports have their leaderships boasting of sending thousands of

eager volunteers to *jihad* in Chechnya, the Philippines, and elsewhere (see also Robert Hefner's discussion of *jihadi* groups in Indonesia in this volume). Omar Bakri and Abu Hamza, for their part, deny being involved in any such activities. When asked about this topic, they emphasize their role as religious scholars, saying that they offer nothing more than opinions as to whether *jihad* in a particular country or situation is justified. The choice to enjoin *jihad* is, in their claims, left entirely up to the individual in question. Regardless of whether or not SOS and al-Muhajiroun function as active recruiters, it is undoubtedly the case that the forums and spaces they occupy are known as places people can go to find like-minded individuals and to become affiliated with figures whose public persona is not so prominent as Bakri's or Abu Hamza's. It is in the sense of a legitimizing intellectual discourse, then, that the activities of the more active *khilafist* groups become most interesting. They provide ideologues and an intermediate social milieu—an interstitial space of sorts—that seeks to organize Muslim consciousness toward, in their view, "higher" (and often transnational) purposes.

Several points emerge out of this overview of the main tendencies within the U.K.-based radical movements. While all three share a broadly *khilafist* orientation, and have at various times been described as "Wahhabi," there exist significant differences between them in terms of the relative importance of the caliphate in their discourses and the correct means of achieving it. Hizb ut-Tahrir might be seen as the advocates of *"khilafah* in one country" in contrast to the Trotskyite al-Muhajiroun and SOS, who favor something closer to a permanent worldwide revolution. Some among the leadership of these movements have also traveled ideologically over the course of their careers. Omar Bakri Muhammad, for example, has been fairly comfortably associated—it would seem—with a diverse range of political movements and doctrinal orientations. Looking at their overall political goals, however, certain common themes certainly arise. It can be said that all three groups seek to render the worldviews of local Muslims more global, but not in a cosmopolitan, tolerant sense. Promulgating Islam as a higher order identity, would-be supporters are asked to deemphasize national affiliations in the name of the *ummah* and to understand the suffering of Muslims in other lands as their own—and as circumstances into which they are obliged by their religion to intervene. In this sense, the *khilafist-jihadi* agenda might be said to hold the greatest appeal for those whose sense of belonging is already in flux—those disjunct from mainstream society and somehow adrift. Radical Islamist discourses structured around a strong antagonism to prevailing social orders hence serve to crystallize political identities and affiliations. The clarity of vision and moral certainty of *salafi* Islam becomes more attractive to some than the indeterminacy and relativism of more moderate, pluralist approaches.

The political discourse of all three groups also makes frequent use of the notion of *kuffar* (unbelievers, infidels) as a technique of moral othering. This is where the obsession with normative categories begins to take on a social reality. Non-Muslim others are figured as those beyond the pale of social responsibility. Although, contrary to popular belief, *salafi* discourse does not require Muslims to engage in armed conflict with *kuffar* wherever they may be found (unless they are themselves laying siege to Muslims—which, today, in the view of many *salafi* groups they are), unbelievers are understood to be located outside the normative remit of social relations. By placing the unbeliever in a category of radical difference, the possibility of coexistence premised on cultural pluralism and political civility is precluded.

Toward Islamic Cosmopolitanism

When we move on to deal with the moderate discourses of Muslim transnationalism, our task becomes considerably more difficult due to the sheer volume of linkages that exist. It is not at all difficult today to identify an enormous number of Muslim intellectuals engaged in an assertion of pluralism and sensitivity to the other as the bases of an Islamic social ethics. From the hermeneutics of tolerance and gender characterizing the work of Khaled Abou El Fadl (2002) and Amina Wadud (1999) to the democratic pluralism of Abdolkarim Soroush (2002) and the Islamic liberation theology of Farid Esack (1997) to the cosmopolitan human rights of Chandra Muzaffar (2002), Islam is rife with discourses that seek to protect spaces of alterity. It also gives renewed credence to the notion of the *ummah* that a mapping of the names just mentioned would trace a line from Los Angeles to Virginia in the United States across to Iran down to South Africa and over to Malaysia. It is also interesting to note that the bulk of these intellectuals are operating in environments that are highly multicultural and transnational in nature—the problem of difference is hence necessarily one of their primary concerns.

In order to limit my discussion for purposes of a meaningful comparison, I will focus in this section on several social and intellectual networks that might be understood to represent the contours of an Islamic cosmopolitanism. These groups can be differentiated from the *salafis* in three important respects. First, their discourse is characterized by an inherently pluralist orientation to religious sources and their interpretation. In contrast to the *salafi* emphasis on hard-and-fast categories, these moderate tendencies are much more eclectic in their reading and understanding

of textual sources—a fact that also permits enormous latitude in the social
dimensions of their work. Second, the discourse of the pluralist groups is
characterized by a rather different conception of "politics." Rather than
locating the correct and necessary practice of the political within a Muslim state of universal jurisdiction (*khilafah*), these moderate groups seek
to foreground Islam's emphasis on individual morality and responsibility
toward others—the idea being that good governance, regardless of what
institutional form it takes, will naturally emerge from such an orientation.
Finally, and in another direct contrast to the salafi groups, the non-Muslim
other occupies a fundamentally different place in pluralist discourse. Rather
than serving to disrupt the moral order, the non-Muslim in pluralist Islam
figures as an invitation to responsible social (and political) engagement.
Coexistence within a civil society premised upon notions of tolerance
becomes the sociopolitical imperative.

Fethullah Gülen's Transnational Education Network

The best example today of a successful transnational effort to "scale up"
moderate Islam is probably to be found in the network of educational institutions associated with Fethullah Gülen's movement in Turkey. Gülen's
work, in the eyes of one observer, is tantamount to a replacement of political Islamism with an "educational Islamism" (Agai 2002, 29). The
overall orientation of Gülen and his groups draws heavily on the thought
and teachings of Said Nursi (1876–1960), a reformer and pan-Islamist
who stressed the compatibility of modernity and religion. Contrary to
many of his contemporary Islamists who sought to reject the West, Nursi
taught that there was much of value to be learned from Europe. Stressing
individual piety in the context of reaching toward others, pluralist interpretations of the Qur'an, religious knowledge as "light," and an understanding of nature and materiality as evidence of the presence of God,
Nursi can be seen to draw strongly on the mystical tradition within
Islam. According to Hakan Yavuz (2000a, 7), "Nursi's teachings have
helped to create a neo-Sufism in Turkey. His books have freed Islamic
knowledge from the hegemony of the ulema and have thus democratized
this knowledge."

Gülen's movement has placed Nursi's emphasis on education and
knowledge firmly at the center of its discourse on Islam. Having established a series of private schools and colleges throughout Turkey starting
in the 1970s, Gülen began reaching overseas during the last decade.
There are now close to three hundred educational institutions affiliated
with the movement operating across the world, with particular strength
in the Middle East, Central Asia, the Caucuses, and many areas of Central and Eastern Europe. Particularly notable about these schools is the

fact that they are not primarily—and some not even at all—in the business of religious education. Rather, they stress a modern curriculum and the notion that all knowledge, whether religious or otherwise, brings one closer to God. The teachers in these schools are normally pious followers of Gülen, seeking to set an example through their relatively socially conservative lifestyles. The model that Gülen adopted for these schools in the 1970s was deliberately designed to carve out a new space for religion in Turkish society. By adopting the official state curriculum, Gülen's movement managed to avoid invoking the wrath of the heavily secular state. His goal was to produce a generation of highly educated (according to modern norms) young Turks who were also religiously oriented and who would be able to go on and constitute a new professional class. In this sense, Gülen is commonly seen to have succeeded in creating a middle path between the more overt political Islamism of the Refah party (and its successors) and the official secular orientation of the Turkish state. Gülen's sights seemed more set on gaining influence among the "businessmen, teachers, students and journalists" (Yavuz 2000b) of Turkish society rather than on occupying the organs of state power.

Indeed, it was an emphasis on transnational philanthropy that first allowed him to expand operations beyond the confines of Anatolia. By deemphasizing the nationalist dimensions of his early discourse, Gülen has become an effective global operator over the past decade. He has always stressed the importance of reaching out toward and exchanging ideas with other faith systems and non-Muslim peoples. For him knowledge serves as an intermediary space in which disparate communities are able to coexist—even if one is simultaneously grounded as a Turk and a Muslim. "The movement argued," according to Bekim Agai, "that one who has a firm sense of identity based on knowledge does not fear contact with others. Thus, a solid national and religious identity was not seen as being in contradiction to participation in the process of globalization" (Agai 2002, 34).

In recent years, Gülen has sought to duplicate his Turkish successes elsewhere. These efforts, combined with a significantly higher profile in Turkey itself, have made him a rather controversial and polarizing figure. Not only the Turkish authorities, but a number of other governments have investigated his network, looking mainly for evidence of attempts by Gülen to "infiltrate" the state (Semyonov 2002). Yet there is also a sense in which his movement has been embraced both at home and abroad as a positive force working for Turkish Islam. Former Prime Minister Bulent Ecevit has praised Gülen for his efforts in raising the profile of Turkish Islam as tolerant and moderate, and the governments in a number of countries in which his schools operate have, after an initial period of suspicion, realized that his schools provide a high quality education and important social services. In Central Asia, for example, the schools enjoy widespread support among parents due to their success rates in preparing students for the entrance exams required to gain entrance to prestigious universities (Balci 2002, 21).

One of the most successful aspects of Gülen's approach in terms of scaling up the propagation and influence of his movement has been the extent to which sharp divisions between Muslims and non-Muslims are absent from his discourse (cf. the *salafi* approach, discussed above). While firmly grounded in Islam and with religiosity as a major animating impulse, the Gülen movement's emphasis on education as a global space of interfaith ecumenicism has allowed its appeal to extend not only to Muslims outside of Turkey, but even to non-Muslims, many of whom are enrolled in its schools. The group's immediate prospects in Turkey seem promising given the recent success of religiously oriented (but, again, not necessarily politically Islamist) parties in recent elections. There have been a few observers, including some whose voices figure in policy-making circles in Washington D.C., claiming that Gülen and the Nurcu movement (i.e., those based on the teachings of Said Nursi) more generally represent the future of a moderate social Islam (Fuller 2002). If able to allay the fears it sometimes prompts abroad as insidious "Turkish religious radicals," the Gülen movement also has good transnational prospects—particularly in postsocialist countries seeking to complete the transition to fully functioning civil societies.

Tariq Ramadan's Europe as Dar ash-Shahadah

A somewhat different trend, yet with a similar emphasis on the need for coexistence and social integration alongside non-Muslims, is to be found in the work of the Swiss-based philosopher Tariq Ramadan (see Bowen, this volume). Called at times a "Muslim Martin Luther" (Donnelly 2002), he has been at the forefront in recent years of an emerging, deeply hybridized idiom of European Islam. Ramadan's work, best typified by his *To Be a European Muslim* (Ramadan 1999) calls for a new pragmatism in Muslim thought and jurisprudence, particularly among Muslims living as minorities in the West. He encourages young Muslims, in particular, to regard their position in non-Muslim homelands not as one of weakness, but rather as a source of strength. He observes that in many Muslim majority countries (e.g., Turkey and Iraq), the state is actually more militantly secular than in the West—hence the position of diaspora becomes one that allows for greater freedom in the practice of religion. This point of view is certainly to some extent a product of Ramadan's own background and upbringing. He is the grandson of Hassan al-Banna, founder in 1928 of the Muslim Brotherhood—one of the Islamic world's largest and most influential sociopolitical movements. Ramadan's parents had to leave Egypt precisely because of the idea, so dominant in Nasser's Egypt of the late 1950s, that religion should have no place in public discourse.

Yet Ramadan's emphasis on the European Muslim is not an invocation to insularity and "ghettoization." Rather he suggests that as a minority community, Muslims possess a set of responsibilities and duties as regards their relations with non-Muslim others. Through what amounts to a radical reinterpretation of the traditional Islamic dichotomous cosmology that divides the world into *dar al-Islam* (lands where Muslim rulers and *shari'ah* law are in place) and *dar al-harb* (those lands in which Muslims struggle to achieve the former), Ramadan refigures the political and ethical geography of minority Islam. If Islam in Europe is seen instead, he would argue, as an example of *dar ad-da'wa* (the abode of call)—or, better yet, as *dar ash-shahada* (the space of testimony)—then we have a situation in which Muslims are required to interact responsibly and equitably with non-Muslims (cf. Bowen's discussion of Ramadan elsewhere in this volume). Withdrawal and introspection are not options; rather, civic participation, coexistence, and outreach all become imperative. As Ramadan puts it:

> [This] approach ... therefore enables us to define the European environment as a *space of responsibility* for Muslims. . . . Muslims now attain, in the *space of testimony*, the meaning of an essential duty and of an exacting responsibility: to contribute, wherever they are, to promoting good and equity within and through *human brotherhood*. (Ramadan, 1999, 150, emphasis added)

Accompanying this call for political engagement is an emphasis in Ramadan's work on the need to reinvigorate and reinterpret the classical sources of Islamic jurisprudence such that the emphasis is not on blind adherence to dogmatic tradition, but rather on a pragmatic search, above all, for the achievement of *maslaha*—"public good." In this scheme, one or another interpretation of Islamic textual sources is not correct simply because it accords with the classical tradition, but rather is *only* correct if it speaks to the issues and problems of the present time (cf. the *salafi* emphasis on jurisprudential immutability). The good of the community—and this community must be understood to encompass not only Muslims, but also non-Muslims—is, in the end, of paramount importance. As Ramadan writes:

> Muslims will henceforth have to ask questions, not alone, not *against* the whole society, but now *with* their fellow citizens through a sincere and genuine shared preoccupation. . . . The Muslims' religion commands them to strive for more justice, but this certainly does not mean that they should be concerned only with themselves and not collaborate with all those who try

to reform society for the better, in the name of human dignity and respect. (Ramadan 1999, 230–32)

This trend in Ramadan's work represents what I have elsewhere termed "critical Islam" (Mandaville 2003), a dual connotation that suggests a need for historicism with regard to Islamic tradition but which also presents the possibility of regarding Islam as a form of critique (vis-à-vis, for example, Western neoliberalism). Ramadan's idiom of Islam, I think, helps us to transcend the impasse between critique and solidarity, where the former is figured as a threat to the latter. Rather, he demonstrates that a new hermeneutics of the other in Islam—necessarily, at times, entailing critique—can actually produce a variant of solidarity premised upon coexistence and testimony to core ethical values: the actuality of *dar ash-shahada*.

It is important to note, then, that Ramadan's is not an ethics based on sameness. It is quite insistent on the fact that Islam is different, and in some cases, critical of the norms of mainstream Western society. Although cognizant of the fact that proximity breeds responsibility, it nevertheless seeks to pose Islam as an alternative vision. This ability to engage in a spirit of civility while maintaining a critical distance from certain Western norms is perhaps the greatest strength of Ramadan's approach. Where Gülen is perceived by some to be insufficiently critical of the West and too strongly influenced by the relative heterodoxy (by traditional Sunni standards) of Nurcu thought, Ramadan's work—solidly based in mainstream sources of jurisprudence (and hence more difficult for traditionalists to dismiss outright)—represents the possibility of recovering from the *usul al-fiqh* the contours of a pluralist, democratic Islam.

Taken together, Gülen and Ramadan offer us the intellectual and social foundations for a new form of Islamic cosmopolitanism—and, moreover, one that has the potential to be attractive to a wide range of religiopolitical orientations in the Muslim world. Pluralism and social civility figure prominently in the religious discourses they embrace, and both have found a growing audience in recent years. The approach they represent, however, takes root and blossoms most effectively in those contexts where the religious landscape is less developed or already significantly pluralized. The greatest challenge these discourses face is to supplant ingrained orthodoxies and the vested interests of the religious establishment in those Muslim majority countries dominated by other varieties of Islamism.

CONCLUSION: NEITHER *SALAFI* NOR SUFI

What I have really done in this chapter is to describe something closer to two *ideal types* of transnational Islam: one seeking the establishment of a global Muslim polity through a strict interpretation and implementation of jurisprudential sources, the other promulgating a pluralist discourse that emphasizes dialogue and coexistence with the non-Muslim other through a tradition of intellectual reformism. While each of these two poles certainly has its adherents within the *ummah* today, the future of transnational Islam actually lies in the far more ambiguous religiopolitical landscape occupied by the Muslim masses. In this regard our attention returns very quickly to the question not only of what kind of Islam "travels" best, but the need to (re)contextualize even the more cosmopolitan orientations as we see they take hold within specific societies. Teachers in conservative Deobandi madrasas in Pakistan, while they may share certain of his views, do not disseminate the *fatwas* of Omar Bakri Muhammad from London. Student reading groups at universities in Indonesia, while they may share Tariq Ramadan's emphasis on the democratic, multicultural possibilities of Islam, have never read his books. We are, in other words, reminded that it is important not to overstate the case when it comes to transnational Islam. While we can identify tendencies and general varieties of discourse, it becomes much more difficult to establish direct causal linkages.

When we want to understand, for example, why the *salafi* project that commonly goes by the name of "Wahhabism" seems so successful in reproducing itself internationally, I would argue that it is much more important to concentrate on the conditions of its reception in a particular setting rather than on the supposedly intrinsic qualities of its discourse. This means that we need to spend as much time studying the local circumstances that allow violent discourses of antihegemonic resistance to gain a foothold in distance climes. While Wahhabism can certainly be seen to contain the intellectual resources, we need to ask how it is—by particular actors in particular social locations—that this orientation becomes articulated to specific political projects. What I am arguing for, then, is an approach to transnational Islam that is highly sensitive to the interplay of global and local: one that understands the mechanisms through which universal normative discourses are rendered meaningful to the predicaments of a particular social milieu.

The temptation to comprehend the transnational Muslim world according to sharply delineated notions of "good Islam" and "bad Islam" must also be resisted. In so politically charged a climate, such strict divisions can produce dangerous polarizations and create an environment in which it becomes even more difficult for moderate, pluralist discourses to find a voice. Even the seemingly quite specific themes of transnational *salafism* and sufism that structure this chapter are, in reality, far messier than my easy categories would suggest. Sufi movements have certainly figured historically in violent political struggles (Kemper 2002), while in some cases social movements of a generally *salafi* orientation represent the only available form of democratic resistance to highly authoritarian governments in the Middle East (as is the case in Saudi Arabia; see Okruhlik, this volume) and elsewhere. Muslims themselves tend not to define each other in such stark terms, and in this sense the ethos of the *ummah* can be said to have some meaning today. The crosscurrents of transnational Islam mean that these various tendencies sometimes flow through each other, with radical agendas transmitted via moderate circuits. Islam teaches one to aid and assist a fellow Muslim rather than to evaluate and categorize—particularly among the more moderate tendencies, and hence the ease with which they can be exploited by those with more sinister agendas.

This intermingling or hybridity even finds an intellectual expression in particular religious figures today. Indeed, there is a sense in which the most successful contemporary transnational Islamic discourse might be identified with Shaykh Yusuf al-Qaradawi, an Egyptian religious scholar based in Qatar. His work is to be found, literally, everywhere in the Muslim world. Through popular religious programs on al-Jazeera and via the translation of his books into languages such as Bahasa Indonesia and Urdu, Qaradawi has found a truly global audience. What appeals, it would seem, is the way he brings traditional methods of Islamic scholarship to bear on the complex issues of global life (e.g., multicultural marriages, medical ethics, the Internet). Qaradawi produces a discourse that seems modern and moderate at the same time as its formal dimensions (utilizing traditional *fatwa* methodology) retain the authenticity of Islamic traditionalism, winning him admirers from the *banlieus* of Paris to the *pesantren* of Southeast Asia (see John Bowen on Qaradawi elsewhere in this volume).

What emerges from this chapter, then, is the importance of a sense of caution when dealing with transnational Islam. By placing radical and moderate discourses side by side, I have sought to make the point that it is not and will never be possible to identify a single form of civil, pluralist Islam that can be promoted globally. While there do exist important moderate discourses that produce the kind of social capital that Putnam and others have identified as a cornerstone of civil societies (Putnam 1993), other individuals have found it equally expedient to invest themselves in groups for whom democratic pluralism represents the greatest of dangers. In short, even as we discuss the grander contexts of transnational networking and global communications, attendance to local circumstances becomes all the more important. This is why it becomes important to understand how it is that the more radical Islamist groups manage to exploit some Muslims' desire for resistance against corrupt governments, foreign hegemony, and socioeconomic deprivation. The transnational propagation of a civil democratic Islam will hence depend upon having spaces into which it can flow. This means understanding and extinguishing the conditions that feed support for radical militancy while simultaneously encouraging the spread of a religious pluralism and a "civil Islam" (Hefner 2000) that speaks directly to the pragmatic concerns of daily life in the increasingly global *ummah*.

As regards the future of radical and moderate tendencies, particularly among Muslims in the West, much will depend on the changing circumstances of both local and global contexts. The comments and pronouncements of public officials and other opinion makers are carefully monitored by Muslims in the West, and these contribute significantly to the discursive environments in which social movements and political groups of all persuasions operate. September 11 polarized Muslim communities in the United States and Europe—an effect rendered even more extreme, perhaps unconsciously, by the official rhetoric emanating from policy makers in Washington, D.C. While the Bush administration went to considerable lengths to emphasize that a "War on Terrorism" should not be understood as a war on Islam, it simultaneously recast the world in Manichaean terms, seeking unequivocal statements of support for the United States ("with us or against us"). Such worldviews leave no room for the shades of gray that characterize Muslim transnationalism. It becomes difficult for Muslims—or anyone, for that matter—to criticize aspects of U.S. foreign policy without appearing suspicious to newly hyperactive security regimes in Washington. In short, if one does not leave space for Muslim opponents of Usama bin Laden to voice complaint (and to be heard rather than dismissed as "unpatriotic") about other aspects of American conduct abroad, one creates an environment that favors recruitment by the radicals. Likewise, short-sighted and ignorant comments by American right-wing religious leaders, such as Pat Robertson, Franklin Graham, and Jerry Falwell (Barisic 2002), about the violent nature of Islam serve only to confirm the suspicions of Muslims in the West that they are a misunderstood and alienated segment of society.

As had been made clear in the latter half of this chapter and by other contributors to this volume, there exists significant scope for the scaling up and propagation of civil pluralist variants of Islam in the West and in the wider Muslim world. There is also good reason to argue that the moderate orientation represents Islam's "natural" course. Yet this process proceeds *relationally* within wider global contexts. In this sense, then, we are not charged only with seeking to shift Islam toward a more progressive orientation, but rather—and perhaps more importantly—we are also seeking to create the conditions that allow Islam's rich history of pluralist tolerance to flood into the present. This task requires us to be attentive to the paths that enable the spread of civil Islam, but also to recognize that public and policy discourses can simultaneously serve to hinder pluralism.

Notes

The author would like to thank Fatima Ayub and Allen McDuffee for their invaluable research assistance during the preparation of this chapter.

References Cited

Abou El Fadl, Khaled. 2002. *The Place of Tolerance in Islam*. Boston: Beacon Press.

Abuza, Zachary. 2003. *Radical Islam and Terrorism in Southeast Asia*. Boulder, Colo.: Lynne Rienner.

Agai, Bekim. 2002. "Fethullah Gülen and His Movement's Islamic Ethic of Education." *Critique: Critical Middle Eastern Studies* 11, no. 1 (Spring): 27–47.

Alexander, Yonah, and Michael S. Swetnam. 2001. *Usama bin Laden's al-Qaida: Profile of a Terrorist Network*. Ardsley, N.Y.: Transnational Publishers.

Allievi, Stefano. 2003. "Islam in the Public Space: Social Networks, Media and Neo-communities." In *Muslim Networks and Transnational Communities in and across Europe,* edited by Stefano Allievi and Jørgen Nielsen, pp. 1–27. Leiden: Brill.

Bakri Muhammad, Omar. 2002. "24 Hours after the Khilafah." London: al-Muhajiroun Publications.

———. N.d. *Jihad and the Method to Establish the Khilafah.* London: al-Muhajiroun Publications.

———. N.d. "Sharing Power with Kufr Regimes or Voting for Man-Made Law Is Prohibited *Haram.*" London: al-Muhajiroun Publications.

Balci, Bayram. 2002. "Fethullah Gülen's Missionary Schools in Central Asia and Their Role in the Spreading of Turkism and Islam." Manuscript.

Barisic, Sonja. 2002. "Pat Robertson Describes Islam as Violent Religion That Wants to Dominate," *Associated Press,* February 22, 2002.

Bruinessen, Martin van. 2002. "Genealogies of Islamic Radicalism in Post-Suharto Indonesia." *South East Asia Research* 10, no. 2: 117–54.

Donnelly, Paul. 2002. "Tariq Ramadan: The Muslim Martin Luther?" *Salon.com,* February 15.

Esack, Farid. 1997. *Qur'an, Liberation, and Pluralism*. Oxford: Oneworld.

Fuller, Graham. 2002. "The Future of Political Islam." *Foreign Affairs* 81, no. 2 (March/April): 48–60.

Gibb, H.A.R., and J. H. Kramers eds. 1991. *Shorter Encyclopaedia of Islam*. Leiden: Brill.

Gunaratna, Rohan. 2002. *Inside al-Qaeda*. New York: Columbia University Press.

Hefner, Robert. 2000. *Civil Islam: Muslims and Democratization in Indonesia*. Princeton, N.J.: Princeton University Press.

Husain, Mir Zohair. 2002. *Global Islamic Politics*. 2nd ed. New York: Longman.

Kemper, Michael. 2002. "Khalidiyya Networks in Daghestan and the Question of Jihad." *Die Welt des Islams* 42, no. 1: 41–71.

Mandaville, Peter. 2001. *Transnational Muslim Politics: Reimagining the Umma*. London: Routledge.

———. 2003. "Towards a Critical Islam: European Muslims and the Changing Boundaries of Transnational Religious Discourse." In *Muslim Networks and Transnational Communities in and across Europe*, edited by Stefano Allievi and Jørgen Nielsen, pp. 127–45. Leiden: Brill.

Masud, Muhammad Khalid, ed. 2000. *Travellers in Faith: Studies of the Tablighi Jama'at as a Transnational Islamic Movement for Faith Renewal*. Leiden: Brill.

Muzaffar, Chandra. 2002. *Rights, Religion, and Reform: Enhancing Human Dignity through Spiritual and Moral Transformation*. London: Curzon Press.

Paz, Reuven. 2003. *Tangled Web: International Networking of the Islamist Struggle*. Washington, D.C.: Washington Institute for Near East Policy.

Putnam, Robert. 1993. "The Prosperous Community: Social Capital and Public Life." *American Prospect* 4, no. 13 (Spring): 35–42.

The Holy Qu'ran. Translated by A. Yusuf Ali. Leicester: Islamic Foundation.

Ramadan, Tariq. 1999. *To Be a European Muslim*. Leicester: Islamic Foundation.

Rashid, Ahmed. 2002. *Jihad: The Rise of Militant Islam in Central Asia*. New Haven, Conn.: Yale University Press.

Roy, Olivier. 1994. *The Failure of Political Islam*. Cambridge, Mass.: Harvard University Press.

Schulze, Reinhard. 1990. *Islamischer Internationalismus im 20. Jahrhundert: Untersuchungen zur Geschichte der Islamischen Weltliga (Rabitat al-'Alam al-Islami) Mekka*. Leiden: Brill.

Semyonov, Vladimir. 2002. "Islamic Extremist Lyceum Closed in Karachai-Cherkessia." *ITAR-TASS Newswire*, May 28.

Shichor, Yitzhak. 2003. "Virtual Transnationalism: Uygur Communities in Europe and the Quest for Eastern Turkestan independence." In *Muslim Networks and Transnational Communities in and across Europe*, edited by Stefano Allievi and Jørgen Nielsen, pp. 281–311. Leiden: Brill.

Soroush, Abdolkarim. 2002. *Reason, Freedom, and Democracy in Islam*. Oxford: Oxford University Press.

Taji-Farouki, Suha. 1996. *A Fundamental Quest: Hizb al-Tahrir and the Search for the Islamic Caliphate*. London: Grey Seal.

Wadud, Amina. 1999. *Qur'an and Woman: Rereading the Sacred Text from a Woman's Perspective*. New York: Oxford University Press.

Wain, Barry, and John McBeth. 2002. "A Perilous Choice for the Presidents." *Far Eastern Economic Review*, October 3, 17–19.

Whitbeck, Harris, and Ingrid Arneson. 2001. "Terrorists Find Haven in South America." *CNN International*, November 7.

Yavuz, Hakan. 2000a. "Being Modern in the Nurçu Way." *ISIM Newsletter* 6 (October): 7, 14.

———. 2000b. "Cleansing Islam from the Public Sphere." *Journal of International Affairs* 54, no. 1 (Fall): 21–42.

Chapter 13

PLURALISM AND NORMATIVITY
IN FRENCH ISLAMIC REASONING

JOHN R. BOWEN

As MUSLIMS CREATE NEW, STABLE COMMUNITIES in Europe and North America, they have asked how best to adapt their normative and legal traditions to their new settings. These traditions are central to Islam. The root meaning of *islâm* is "submission" to the will of God, and scriptures communicate to humans the norms and forms for that submission. These norms have multiple sources, from the Qur'ân (the revealed word of God), to the collections of *hadîth* (the reports of statements and actions of the Prophet), to the decisions of qualified jurists and judges. In Muslim-majority countries they have been the basis for creating political, legal, and social institutions: councils of jurists, courts of law, mosques for worship, places for ritual sacrifice. Muslims living in countries without such institutions have begun to reconsider these norms. Should there be new sets of norms for Muslims living as minorities? Is Islam a matter of general principles that one might find to be common across Muslim and non-Muslim societies? Or is Islam perhaps best understood as a matter of individual, ethical behavior rather than compliance with legal traditions?

I consider a range of Muslim responses to these questions in France, a country of relatively new Muslim immigration. I focus on the ways in which the social and political structures of that country have shaped the direction of Islamic reasoning, and to underscore this shaping effect I consider the contrast between British and French experiences. In each country certain directions of reasoning are, I argue, more likely to be adopted and accepted by Muslims. I also emphasize that Islam has faced issues of pluralism from its beginning. Early Muslim authorities acknowledged the legitimacy of multiple traditions or schools of normative reasoning (*madhhab*)—before Christian jurists did so, one might well add. Muslim jurists see normative or legal reasoning, *fiqh,* as a human, fallible practice, an inevitably partial effort to comprehend God's plan for humans, the *sharî'a.* Judges took into account local values and practices to the extent that these did not violate God's commands. It is thus perfectly within the historical legacy of Islamic reasoning to develop norms that would accord with life in new social situations.[1]

CONTRASTING CONDITIONS FOR MUSLIMS IN EUROPE

That said, the sudden growth of resident populations of Muslims in Europe has presented new challenges for Muslim scholars. Since the 1960s, considerable numbers of Muslims have immigrated to countries in Western Europe.[2] Most of these Muslims have come from the countries of northern and western Africa, Turkey, and southern Asia. During the 1950s and 1960s, European governments encouraged the immigration of workers to serve the expanding industrial sector as inexpensive laborers. Many of these early immigrants were single men or married men whose families remained behind. Both the immigrants and the host countries thought that the stay was temporary. Some governments built large housing projects, both in city suburbs and in relatively isolated areas, to encourage the eventual repatriation of the immigrant workers and, indeed, to encourage their isolation from the cultural mainstream. France, for example, offered instruction in languages of origin for immigrant children in order to facilitate their expected "return" to their countries of origin.

Two things went wrong with this policy. First, the host economies suffered recession in the 1970s, and the immigrants quickly went from being useful instruments in national growth to hostile competitors for low-paying jobs. Political parties of the far right played on these sentiments. Secondly, and notwithstanding the economic reversals, many immigrants stayed on in their new countries and either brought their families to Europe or created new families in Europe. The children were Europeans in culture and language, whether or not they were granted citizenship. They began to demand rights of citizenship, including their right to practice their religion unimpeded: to build mosques, to carry out public rituals, and to dress in an Islamic way. These demands were not always welcomed by other residents, and the resentment over economic competition that fueled the far right in the 1970s and early 1980s had become, by the late 1980s and 1990s, resentment over cultural difference, an unalterable newness on the part of the Muslim families.

This economic, cultural, and political conflict was increasing in intensity at the moment when "political Islam" took world center stage. The Islamic Revolution in Iran and the rise and repression of Islamic parties in North Africa and Turkey led to a worldwide excitement among younger Muslims about the possibilities for constructing new kinds of nations, ones in which Islam would play an important public role. These same possibilities frightened ruling parties in these same countries, and they found sympathetic listeners among political leaders in Europe and the United States. Violence increased in the 1990s, carried out by Muslims and non-Muslims. In France, the military wing of the Algerian Islamist movement planted bombs in public places; in Germany, neo-Nazi groups attacked Turks. After the attacks of September 11, 2001, popular fears of Islam focused on the network of al-Qaeda supporters that extended through Asia, North America, and Europe, and on the growing problems of violence in poor areas of the larger cities.

Less noticed during this period have been the creative efforts by European Muslims to adapt religious practices to their new social conditions. These conditions include distinct political cultures: laws regarding who may form what sort of association, policies about state recognition of and aid to religious groups, and norms about where and when one may publicly express religious beliefs (Rath et al. 1999).

The contrast of France and Britain serves to illustrate the relevant differences. In France, a long struggle between the Catholic Church and partisans of a secularist and revolutionary heritage eventuated, early in the twentieth century, in the regime of *laïcité*. The political culture of laïcité requires the elimination of religion from public forums: from schools, state enterprises, and government. This culture also suffuses teacher education, creating not only a heritage of militant anticlericism, but also a militant antireligious stance that often goes well beyond the strict requirement of French law. Parallel to the history of laïcité is that of *francité*, "Frenchness," the idea that full citizenship requires cultural assimilation to a French model of comportment: European dress, good command of French, and socialization with French people (Bowen 2003a). The close association of laïcité and Frenchness helps explain the strong support in France for laws banning girls from wearing head scarves in public schools, despite the equally strong French political support for freedom of religious expressions (Bowen 2004).

Laïcité and francité in turn shape French ideas of citizenship. Despite the fact that commentators often emphasize the distinction of legal nationality (*nationalité*) and citizenship (*citoyenneté*)—the former merely indicating the government to which one owes obedience, the latter indicating a willingness and capacity to participate in civic life—throughout French history the two have been intertwined. As a general rule, to be given nationality one has had to demonstrate citizenship, and, conversely, full rights of civic participation have been limited to French nationals.[3] Prior to 1981 and the ascension of François Mitterrand to power, it was relatively difficult for noncitizens to form legally recognized associations and thus to gain legitimacy in the eyes of the state. Moreover, until 2003 no national Islamic body existed that could take part in the national-level decision making so critical to French affairs.[4]

On the dimensions signaled in France by laïcité and francité, Britain offers a marked distinction. Religion is present in public life; indeed, Tariq Modood (1993) has argued that maintaining the established Church of England keeps secularism from controlling public space (he might have had the negative example of France in mind). The demands made on residents or subjects are minimal, consistent with Hobbes's ideas about the proper role of the state in guaranteeing order (Favell 2001). Indeed, to speak of "the state" makes much less sense in Britain than France; residents encounter myriad local agencies and boards. Immigrants from South Asia to Britain began forming diverse associations soon after their arrival, and some of these associations have worked with local school boards to press for changes in diet, religious education, and so forth, with little direct appeal to officials in London (Lewis 1993; Vertovec 2002; Werbner 2002).

In these and other countries, Muslims have correctly seen that they must forge collaborations with non-Muslim political leaders if they are to develop workable Islamic social and religious institutions: schools that need recognition and financial aid; Islamic chaplains to prisoners and soldiers who require state certification; the simultaneous sacrifice of thousands of animals on the Feast of Sacrifice that requires state health board approval. The relationships between Muslim public intellectuals and political leaders may be uneasy and unstable, but they shape the direction of Muslim social, political, religious, and intellectual life in each country. Muslims in France have become used to looking for a single, national resolution to a problem; Muslims in Britain value allowing local accommodations to resolve disputes. As Muslims develop more effective Europewide institutions, they probably will realize that they have become less "European" than they have become French, British, Danish, and so forth, and that they have adapted their religious and cultural institutions to these respective political cultures.[5]

THE SOCIOLOGY OF ISLAM IN FRANCE

Although France keeps no statistics on the religious beliefs or practices of its inhabitants, estimates of the number of Muslims resident in France range from 4 to 5 million people, nearly all of them immigrants and their children.[6] About 60–70 percent of Muslim immigrants to France have come from three countries of North Africa, the Maghreb: Algerians and Moroccans have contributed the largest numbers, followed by Tunisians. Turks and West Africans form the next largest groups.[7] The dominance of North African Muslims in the public sphere is even greater than these numbers might suggest, for a number of reasons. The North African countries had historically close colonial ties to France, and Algeria was part of France until 1962. North African immigration in the 1960s and 1970s was massive and concentrated in industrial cities.[8]

Muslim men who came to France in the 1960s and 1970s found themselves living with Muslims from a variety of countries, often in large public housing units. In urban neighborhoods as well, or in the poorer suburbs of Paris or Lyon, one finds Moroccans, Malians, and poorer French families living together. Certain ties can reinforce country allegiances, as when an association or a mosque is predominantly associated with one country, or a Sufi order preserves ties to a particular saint. Algerians may vie with Moroccans for control of a mosque, or each, along with Comorians and others, may have their own mosque and associations. Foreign countries (in particular Morocco, Algeria, and Saudi Arabia) have financed mosques, reinforcing country-based rivalries. But even those mosques, religious schools, or associations sponsored by Muslims from a particular country rarely are exclusivist, because they usually do not seek to reproduce a particular theological or ritual tendency. Moreover, for many in the generation of Muslims born in France (the *beurs*), it is the experience of being discriminated against as "Maghrebin" or "Arab" that creates their sense of "ethnicity" (Cesari 1998, 56–57).

The common Arabic language has facilitated some degree of cooperation across the three North African communities, as has a relatively shared degree of religious jurisprudential reasoning (following the Mâliki *madhhab*) and religious practices. This cooperation exists both at the national level—for example, in the activities of the largest national organization, the Union des Organisations Islamiques de France (UOIF)—and in some cases at the local level in the forms of shared worship in mosques. In cities or neighborhoods where cross-ethnic cooperation is high, the shared Arabic language facilitates common participation by North Africans (but not others) in congregational prayers. Indeed, the growing distinction, and sometimes tension, is between the Arabic of the older generation and the French of the younger Muslims as the language of the sermon.

By contrast, Turks have not had the same historical ties to France, and the centers of Turkish diasporic activities are in Germany. Many of the Senegalese and Mali immigrants have distinct forms of religious practice and social organization, in particular the Sufi orders focused on specific teachers in West Africa. Other Muslims, from the West Indies or the Indian Ocean islands, for example, have organized into ethnically specific associations and formed a grab-bag national organization to represent their interests as "non-Maghrebis."

Within the North African category, although Algerians are numerically dominant (one-half of North Africans, one-third of all Muslim immigrants), and they control the important Paris mosque, Tunisians and Moroccans play important leadership roles in a number of national organizations. Tunisians have taken on major roles as leaders of religious schools, particularly around Paris. Moroccans make up 40 percent of all *imams* (sermon givers at Friday prayers) in France.[9] Thus in France no one country group is predominant across categories, the way that Pakistanis dominate Muslim affairs in Britain and Turks play the predominant role in Germany.

Who are the authorities among these Muslims? Because the traditional Islamic institutions that defined the roles of specific authorities are virtually absent from Europe, it is difficult to use the Islamic vocabulary of *muftis, ulamâ,* or *faqîhs.* I prefer to speak of Muslim public intellectuals, each with specific claims to legitimacy and specific bases in social institutions. Teachers at religious schools, mosque officials, and leaders of Islamic associations all can claim some degree of legitimacy as Muslim public intellectuals because of their institutional roles—but ratification of those claims by ordinary Muslims depends on the religious knowledge these intellectuals can demonstrate. The public realm of Islamic knowledge in France is characterized both by the importance of these religious institutions and by the refusal of ordinary Muslims to assume that someone has Islamic credibility just because he (or she) occupies a leadership position in a religious institution.

Private Islamic schools or institutes offer classes on weekends and evenings for Muslims who wish to learn more about their heritage. Those who occupy the principal positions at these schools usually also contribute to public discussions about Islam, for example, by writing in magazines or speaking at gatherings. They may have training in Islamic jurisprudence, but they are evaluated by other Muslims more in terms of their abilities to plausibly represent themselves as learned in Islam matters than in terms of their formal training. In any case, none have the level of formal Islamic education that would earn them a position as a jurist or expert in a Muslim-majority country.[10] Some of these teachers also developed a second, advanced track within their schools that is intended to train future scholars, teachers, and religious officiants for mosques. [11]

Mosques may be directed by persons with or without a high degree of religious training. Some mosque officials occupy entirely administrative roles; such is the case with the heads (*recteurs*) of the Paris "great mosque" and the largest mosque in Lyon, both of whom have the ear of the state and the French media. Other mosque officials also act as imams, as ritual leaders for prayer and other ritual events, as in the case of the large mosque in Paris's Nineteenth *arrondisement,* the Mosquée Ad-Dawa, and for major mosques in Marseille and Toulouse. These imam-officials often develop large and stable followings, and sponsor an array of associated activities, including religious courses, neighborhood associations, and women's groups. In a third category are the vast majority of mosques, including the many small ones housed in nondescript settings, where imams come and go, subject to the support of a mosque committee and the will of the regular worshipers. In the smaller mosques something like a free market in imams prevails: someone may appear and give Friday sermons for several weeks or months, until he loses local support. It is the coming and going of these imams, particularly those who have received training in Saudi Arabia and have brought "radical" *salafiste* ideas to France that most concerns both the French state and the more established mosque leaders. Because mosques now have become the basic electoral unit for the national Islamic representative body, the control of mosques has taken on great political importance.

Finally, there are leaders of the many local and national organizations and federations claiming to represent the interests of Muslims. Their legitimacy in the eyes of the state rests on the numbers of followers or affiliated mosques they can claim; their legitimacy in the eyes of those followers has to do with their ability to show themselves as having a political voice in France and to present an attractive version of Islam. A few can claim nationwide standing; most important are the Union des Organisations Islamiques de France (UOIF), and the "great mosque" of Paris, which functions as an umbrella organization as well as a mosque. The Paris mosque is controlled by Algeria, although it also receives Saudi funds. The UOIF leadership comes from Morocco and to a lesser extent Tunisia and Algeria. The popular legitimacy of the UOIF lies less in its political role than in its success in sponsoring the annual "Islamic fair" north of Paris at which are displayed books, videos, and clothing, and at which speak religious authorities from throughout the world (Bowen 2004).

A very few Muslim public intellectuals operate in a free-floating way, seeking financial support where they can find it. The best known speaker on Islam in Europe, Tariq Ramadan, derives his authority from his personal gifts at speaking to the social concerns of everyday Muslims, while drawing on the intellectual and to some extent political legacy of his grandfather, Hassan al-Banna, a founder of the Muslim Brotherhood. Ramadan delights audiences by cutting to the chase: urging Muslims to get involved in schools, neighborhoods, and elections. In 2003, his argument that one can be completely Muslim and European also has earned him the suspicion of an increasingly secularist and unified French media. And yet even Ramadan's success proves the rule concerning the importance of religious and social institutions to the new Muslim public intellectuals, in that he has benefited from the wide promulgation of his audio- and videocassettes through the Tawhid publishing network and the local organizing activities of his several support groups, especially Présence Musulmane in the Paris region.

The ordinary Muslims who attend lectures, listen to cassettes, or ask advice of these public intellectuals are preoccupied by the question with which I began this chapter, reformulated for the individual Muslim: How should I live my life in France so as to not violate Islamic norms? Must I wear a head scarf in school? How should I find a spouse? Is it accepted to work at a bank, to eat in a non-Muslim home, to perform the sacrifice by sending money to Algeria? Precisely because the norms of Islam can no longer be taken for granted, because each individual both can and must make choices, ordinary Muslims are demanding that public intellectuals give them guidance. In order to offer that individual guidance, however, Muslim intellectuals in France are themselves searching, and debating, about the directions and limits of Islamic normativity in a secular, plural- ist society.

Reworking Fiqh to Fit France

In their writings and public discussions on normative questions, Muslim intellectuals in France have followed one of two broad two types of rea- soning: one that starts from the traditions of practical jurisprudence (fiqh), and another that seeks to ground Islam on general principles. As I will discuss below, this division is not specific to France or to Europe; in- deed, parallel discussions are to be found throughout the Islamic world. However, these lines of reasoning take on socially specific values in the French context, as the example below illustrates.

One of the more pressing questions for Muslims who are planning to reside permanently in Europe is whether they may take out loans at in- terest to purchase homes. The Islamic prohibition against lending or bor- rowing at interest would seem to prevent them from so doing, but in the late 1990s some Muslims living in Europe put the question to the Euro- pean Council for Fatwa and Research, a collection of jurists of various nationalities who now reside in Europe.[12] The council is led by the highly influential Egyptian jurist Sheikh Yûsuf al-Qardâwî, who lives in Qatar. In 1999, the council responded to the question in the form of a fatwâ, a nonbinding legal opinion issued by a qualified person or group. The ju- rists stressed that the prohibition on usury does mean that Muslims everywhere should take steps to avoid borrowing from banks that charge interest, and should devise alternative ways of financing homes, such as paying more than the stated price but in installments. However, if

Muslims in Europe could not practice such alternatives, then they could take out a mortgage for a first house.

In their argument the jurists cited two considerations. First, the doctrine of extreme necessity (*darurat*) allows Muslims to do what otherwise is forbidden under compulsion or necessity. Why is it a necessity to own a house? Renting keeps the Muslim in a state of uncertainty and financial insecurity, stated the council. Owning a house allows Muslims to settle in close proximity to a mosque, and to modify their house to accommodate religious needs. Moreover, Muslims living in Europe had reported to the council that mortgage payments were equal to or lower than rents. The jurists also referred to the idea that while in non-Muslim countries, Muslims may make contracts that violate Islamic law. In support of this argument they cited the opinions of past jurists who belonged to two of the traditional schools of Sunni legal interpretation, the Hanafī and the Hanbalī.[13] Muslims cannot change the institutions that dominate life in their host countries, stated the council members, and thus Muslims are not responsible for the existence of an interest-based financial system. If they were forbidden to benefit from banking institutions, then Islam would have weakened them, a result that would contradict the principle that Islam should benefit Muslims.

The ruling did not change the traditional prohibition of lending at interest, but exempted Muslims living in Europe from the prohibition because of a combination of empirical circumstances: the importance of owning a house, the high level of rents, and the absence of viable alternatives. These circumstances allow the jurists to apply the principles that necessity allows for exemption, and that Muslims may use otherwise invalid financial instruments when they live in "non-Islamic countries." The ruling generated considerable interest among Muslims living in Paris, even though many of them either were not in a financial position to apply for a bank loan or, because they were in Europe only for a brief period of study, would probably return to their home country to seek work and raise a family. Muslims found the ruling important because it implied that Muslims in Europe could legitimately create a new set of Islamic rules, valid only in Europe. This heady possibility excited some and disconcerted others.

In 2001 and 2002 I sought the opinions of Islamic scholars in France on the ruling. I began with one of the jurists making up the European Council, Dr. Ahmed Jaballah, who now is recognized as the chief jurist for the UOIF. Jaballah explained that the council decided that Muslims could best provide for their children by moving out of poor neighborhoods and buying houses. "The only way to improve family life is to move out, and the loan helps them do that. But many in the Muslim world objected to the fatwa because it approved interest. They do not understand what social life is like here." Later the same day, I attended Jaballah's evening class on *fiqh*. He directs and teaches at the Paris branch of the Institut Européen des Sciences Humaines, an evening school for Muslim men and women sponsored by the UOIF. The school is located in Saint Denis, an easy train ride from Paris. That evening, Jaballah emphasized the flexibility of the sharî'a. Islam is "valid for all places and times," he explained (writing out the phrase in Arabic), but it is also adaptable to all contexts. There are universal elements and those which we change. Most things are neither prescribed nor proscribed, thus they are in the large domain of *le licite*, the permitted, which in his model constituted a legal vacuum. He drew a circle, with a shaded portion being those acts for which there are texts, and the much larger remainder being that vast area of "le licite."

This general approach to understanding Islamic norms emphasizes the place within Islam for creativity. However, other Muslim scholars were opposed to the ruling precisely because it stifled creativity among Muslims. Hichem El Arafa is the director of another school in the Paris region, CERI, the Centre d'Études et de Recherches sur l'Islam (formerly the Institut des Études Islamique de Paris), also located in Saint Denis. He was asked frequently to speak about the council's ruling. "Everyone had heard about it; if you played 'micro on the sidewalk' and asked people coming out of a mosque if they had heard of it [the fatwa] they would have. So they asked me about it." [JB: And were you opposed?] "I am not entirely against it, but I wanted to consider other arguments. I think that it does not lead to creativity in thinking about these issues. For example, the few experiments we do have in Islamic banking, we would not have had them if Muhammad 'Abduh [the important late-nineteenth-century reformer] had said that you did not need to come up with something new. And the experimentation is good, many fail and some succeed and we have new institutions" (interview 2001). In his classes on *fiqh* (which I have attended beginning in 2001), El Arafa stresses the importance of looking for the consensus of Islamic scholars, *ulamâ*, in deciding on a difficult question, an approach that in this case leads him to remain on the side of the majority of Muslim scholars in the world who oppose these concessions to banks and mortgages.

Echoing El Arafa's pragmatic arguments were those proposed by Dhaou Meskine, a scholar who also runs an evening and weekend school, "La Réussite," in Aubervilliers, north of Paris and east of Saint Denis. "There are too many families in France who live in debt," he said, "and four million who have been unable to repay their debts." He went on to explain that there are other, creative ways of obtaining money, such as repaying the seller of the house gradually, perhaps at a higher price, and that he had successfully experimented with such arrangements. Meskine also objected to the very idea of different laws for different places: "Syeikh Qardâwî says that interest in Europe is acceptable because Europe is not a Muslim land. But laws must be universal: if it is forbidden to steal, or lie, or falsify papers, or to make illegal marriages in Muslim lands, then it is also the case for Muslims living in Europe, in the *"dâr al-'ahd,"* land of treaty. That is the nature of religion; it is intended to apply everywhere" (interview 2001).

Although they all agreed that statements about Islamic norms should be based on jurisprudential reasoning, these scholars emphasized not the legal arguments but the socially pragmatic ones. What would be the social consequences of permitting mortgages or forbidding them? Some hold that bank mortgage gives Muslims the ability to realize their duties to their families, a positive value in Islam. Others counter that retaining the prohibition leads to fruitful experimentation and maintains the moral power of the law. For someone such as Dhaou Meskine, who has lived through years of difficult negotiations with a left-wing local government, many of the problems faced by Muslims come from their not following the rules that are common to Islamic law and French state law.

The claim that there could be distinct Islamic norms for Europeans draws on an old debate in Islamic jurisprudence as to whether differing social conditions justify creating new or different Islamic rules. In the early centuries of Islam scholars developed a distinction between two realms, the *dâr al-islâm,* or abode of Islam, versus the *dâr al-harb,* or abode of war. The former included the countries ruled under Islamic principles; the latter referred to all other places, where, presumably, Muslims would not be free to worship. Today, many Muslims find discomfort in this way of viewing the world. How is one to define "Muslim societies," the *dâr al-islam?* Does one look to the correctness of the government, the piety of the people, or simply the fact that most people living in the country profess Islam as their religion? Is a majority-Muslim country whose government represses its people and prevents the free expression of religious ideas to be considered part of *dâr al-islâm?* Conversely, why should countries not governed by Islamic laws but where Muslims are free to worship be considered as belonging to an "abode of war?"

Some Muslims have proposed alternatives. Referring to the protection given to religious minorities by international law, some scholars have proposed *dâr al-'ahd,* "abode of treaty," as a better way of designating non-Islamic states that offer religious freedom. Others have proposed *dâr al-da'wa,* "abode of predication," or *dâr ash-shahâda,* "abode of witness," emphasizing the possibilities open to Muslims in these lands (Ramadan 2002).

Reasoning from Islamic Principles

The range of alternative interpretations discussed above remains quite narrow, and the accommodations made to European social conditions remain negative ones, under which one does (or does not) allow an exemption to an otherwise universally valid rule. A second, quite different way of adapting Islamic norms to European social life is to shift focus from rules to principles or general ethical values. This shift leads some Muslim scholars to ask whether a positive Islamic value can be accorded features of French, and more broadly European, social life. Should Muslims consider certain French institutions to be valuable in Islamic terms, to provide legitimate answers to problems of social life? Perhaps these institutions provide moral and legal equivalents of Islamic institutions. So arguing would require emphasizing the general meaning or intent of an Islamic rule rather than the social form that a rule has taken in what are considered as "Muslim countries."

Approaching Islamic norms in this way is hardly unique to Europe; throughout the Muslim world, scholars interested in reforming Islamic law often have based their arguments on claims about the principles or general intentions behind Islamic rules. Of continuing importance to modern debates is the work of the fourteenth-century scholar al-Shatibi, who distinguished between the timeless principles, *maqâsid,* found in the Qur'ân, and the historically changing products of jurisprudence (Masud 1977).[14] In Indonesia, generations of legal scholars and historians have argued that one must separate the Arab cultural content of Islamic law from the universal principles contained in the Qur'ân and *hadîth* (Bowen 2003b).

In Europe, scholars who take this approach often criticize the approach taken by the Council of Qardâwî as too unimaginative, overly trapped in an old style of fiqh. Tariq Ramadan, for example, considers the council as engaging in a juristic *bricolage,* an effort to lighten *fiqh* without rethinking it in European terms. Ramadan agrees with Meskine that *fiqh* should be universal, but he would locate the universal dimension at the level of general principles.[15] Consider, for example, Ramadan's approach to the question of marriages performed according to European law. Many Muslims in Europe consider marriages to be religiously valid only if performed in a private, "Muslim" context, after the legal marriage has been performed at city hall. For Ramadan, thinking in this way is to preserve the traditional forms of marriage without examining the nature of marriage itself, which is a contract. "A civil marriage already is a Muslim marriage, I think, because it is a contract, and that is what a Muslim marriage is." More generally, the European law of contracts corresponds to the Islamic law of contracts, and Muslims are just as obliged to respect contracts with non-Muslims as with Muslims; "that is a universal element of *fiqh,* valid anywhere. If we take this step then we can accept much of European law" (interview, 2001).

A similar approach, but with a slightly different conceptual base, is taken by the director of the Bordeaux mosque, Tareq Oubrou. In an innovative interpretation of the basic structure of Islamic normativity, Oubrou distinguishes between obligatory ritual (*ibâdât*) on the one hand, and social norms (*mu'âmalât*) on the other. The former does not change, but the latter may be realized either as law (*droit*) or as ethics, depending on the political context within which one lives. In a country with Islamic law and social institutions, social norms are realized as law. In countries such as France, where such realization is impossible, Muslims must "ethicize" these norms. He offered an example: "If a woman comes to me and says, 'My husband beats me; do I have the right to ask for a divorce,' I say yes, divorce; and when the judge pronounces the divorce they are divorced, ethically speaking, religiously speaking. So we 'ethicize' the Islamic law on divorce, same values, but we choose the idea from one or another of the legal schools that is more subtle, for example from the Mâliki, or another, which ever can best respond to the spirit of the *sharî'a* and also to the society into which Muslims integrate sociologically and anthropologically in French citizenship" (interview, 2002).

This search for general principles as a bridge across cultural and legal divides sometimes is developed as the study of the "reasons, objectives, goals" of the sacred texts, the *maqâsid* of the Qur'ân. Scholars such as Oubrou suggest the idea of a hierarchy or priority of obligations and norms, and ask whether we may discard certain lower-order obligations in order to better accomplish higher-order ones. Oubrou has applied this approach to a range of questions. For example, he (2000) has argued that a Muslim may eat meat whether or not he or she knows that it was killed according to Islamic procedures, because the purpose of the dietary rules were those of health and hygiene. "Why does Islam refuse to eat meat that has not been cleansed of its blood? Precisely because the blood contains unhealthy germs" (2000, 43). If one is assured that a butcher is an honest person and follows health rules, then the meat is acceptable.

This second approach to norms is hotly contested by those urging continued reliance on the traditions of fiqh. For example, from their positions at the University of Damascus, Sheikh Ramadân al-Boutî and his son, Tawfik al-Boutî, condemn roundly the idea of an Islamic law based either on the special conditions confronting Muslim minorities in Europe or on the principles of the Qur'ân, which they call "this new Islamic 'jurisprudence' that has never been a part of Islamic law."[16]

The Future of Islamic Normative Reasoning in France

The development of one or more distinctive French, or European, approaches to normativity is at its beginning. I believe that the particular form of political culture in each country will continue to shape Muslims' responses to specific social problems. For example, in France the taken-for-granted importance of the central state in regulating social life has led Muslims to automatically turn to Paris to demand assistance in obtaining *halâl* food, ensuring safe travel to Mecca, creating religious schools, and so forth.

Despite the strong mutual suspicions professed by the many associations and public figures in France, most have supported, in principle, the efforts to create a national Islamic body. That the state would have the right and the obligation to "organize Muslims" is accepted by most Muslim public intellectuals. This acceptance will continue to shape the way scholars carry out normative innovation, by exerting pressure for nationwide, uniform decisions to be taken about issues affecting Muslims, and pressure for these decisions to conform to French social norms. Such pressures are less felt in, say, Britain, and a greater range of normative positions are publicly promoted. (One cannot imagine a French Hizb ut-Tahrîr publicly urging all Muslims in France to refuse all participation in politics, as their British counterpart did at the 2002 assembly I attended.) Put another way, Muslims living in France experience more political and social pressure to "scale up" their institutions to a national level than do Muslims living in Britain (or, probably, Muslims living in any other European country).

The pressure for national uniformity makes it quite difficult to propose that Muslims in France should follow a particular Islamic legal school, or even that a subgroup should do so. It also lends support to those scholars who urge Muslims to draw on several legal schools or to employ an approach to normativity that is not confined to the traditional methods of jurisprudence. If there is a consensus among the new generation of teachers, it is on this point. Dhaou Meskine, who was trained in Tunisia where the Mâliki legal school is followed, described the situation: "In *fiqh* there are legal schools, and in the Muslim world each country follows one, but there is none for France, so you have to teach all of them, even though that is not a very good solution. You cannot just choose one. So, we leave it up to the teacher. He can either choose one school and then also teach some of the comparisons, or teach *fiqh* based on the *hadith*. Last year we had a Hanbalî teacher, this year we had a Mâliki one" (interview, 2002).

In his plans to create a new institute to train religious scholars, Tareq Oubrou proposes a similar approach: "We will teach them law as well as the other topics; law will include French law. It is eclectic, with sociology, theology, law, with the hope that the imam will have some classical knowledge, but that he will have a very specific orientation. We have no specific books or references; we work on the texts, practical work, looking at all the possible sources, Hanafî, Hanbalî, etc., and also knowing French law."

But how does a jurist or other scholar then choose among the several legal schools? Oubrou's answer to this question reveals the particular effects of the pluralism in social institutions on normative reasoning. This pluralism introduces new constraints, in this case those of French social norms and law, and possibilities, into jurisprudence. Oubrou reasons by beginning with the norms of French culture and requirements of French law, and then looks for the Islamic legal alternative that offers the best fit with these parameters. In many cases it is the Hanafî or Mâliki school that meets this conditions, and the Hanbalî legal school that is the strictest (the Saudi Arabian jurists follow that school), but Oubrou pointed out that sometimes this is not the case: "Sometimes there are zones in Hanbalî law that are more supple than in Hanafî or Mâliki law, for example on polygamy. Mâliki law says the husband has to receive the permission of the first wife [to take a second], but the Hanbalî position is by way of the needs of society (*maslahat*), that if the culture is monogamous, then so is the sharî'a on this point. I always say, if the first wife accepts the second, then why should I interfere? We accept homosexuality, polyandry, why not a man and a woman? It is scandalous."

Oubrou's argument on this point exemplifies what we might call the bidirectional reasoning pursued by many of these scholars. He and others seek to develop an Islamic normative base for a way of life that would be in accord with French social norms and French law. Thus, if the broad society is monogamous, then Islamic norms also point toward monogamy as the appropriate marital form. But he also insists that Islamic norms might on some counts improve on French ones. If French men can have mistresses as well as wives, as do many prominent public figures, then would it not be better to legalize these relationships by permitting polygamy?

Within what might become a consensus there are, however, some important tensions. One lies between those scholars who identify with North African legal traditions and those who advocate looking directly at the Qur'ân and *hadîth*. This tension is not as sharp as that which, in some majority Muslim countries, has opposed advocates of *taqlîd*, following a specific madhhab, to advocates of a direct reinterpretation, an *ijtihâd*, based on Qur'ân and hadîth. In contemporary France, none of the public scholars and teachers can advocate taqlîd, for the reasons pointed out by Meskine. Nor is it possible to reject legal schools per se, because those schools have become part of the background heritage of many immigrants, because the foreign states that provide financial assistance would not look kindly upon such rejection, and because those French scholars who did have training in jurisprudence generally were trained within a *madhhab*.[17] The difference among scholars is more one of relative emphasis, as I will try to convey with some excerpts from interviews.

Dhaou Meskine, for example, prefers to remain within a *madhhab*, and complains that those teachers who teach only from Qur'ân and *hadîth*, and those who teach the stricter Hanbalî *madhhab*, are less likely to be criticized by younger Muslims than are those who teach from within the more "flexible" Hanafî or Mâliki schools (the fourth, the Shâfi'î, is not taught by North African Muslims): "The problem is that if you teach Hanbalî or salafite [meaning strict, approximately Hanbalî] approaches to *fiqh*, it is all right, but if you teach Mâliki or Hanafî, people object. There is a wind from the Orient bringing texts and television programs from Saudi Arabia, all of which promote Hanbalî or worse, all of which is quite different from Maghrébin *fiqh*. The Medina and Meccan scholars are dominant, even in the style of reading the Qur'ân. The worst approach is in the book of *fiqh* by al-Jazaïri, who was born in Algeria but then moved to Saudi Arabia. [JB: Is he a Hanbalî?] He is worse than Hanbalî, because he has to show that he is even more strict than the Arabian scholars, as he is from elsewhere."

His former co-teacher of *fiqh* classes (until the early 1990s) and fellow Tunisian, Hichem El Arafa, criticized Meskine's preference for Mâliki texts, and preferred the *fiqh* book by al-Jazaïri, as "not good but better than Meskine's preferred text." El Arafa's method of teaching *fiqh* (as I have followed it in his courses in Saint Denis) is to base instruction directly on Qur'ân and *hadîth*, as do al-Qardâwî and al-Jazaïri. He studied in Saudi Arabia, and although he describes ways of thought there as very rigid, this experience may have made teachings "from the Orient" more palatable to him than to Meskine.

And yet others find that these disagreements ignore the larger context of Islamic thought. "We cannot just work with *fatwâ*," argues Tareq Oubrou, "because we have to think not just normatively but in terms of theology, tolerance, the person, the society, liberty and determinism, and ethics. We are required in emergencies to respond to questions about what is harâm and halâl, but we have to carry out a long term effort to rethink what Islam should be in a very secularized society, as France, which is not like in the US. The normative has to respond to what I call the *maqâsid*, the broad vision of Islam, design, objectives; this goes beyond the normative. Ethics are central to Islam. We did not have to undergo what Christianity did to overthrow the power of the Church; it was already people who developed Islam; it is Protestant" (interview 2002). Although in print (Babès and Oubrou 2002) he has been more cautious, insisting on the continued importance of Islamic norms for all

Muslims against a more secularized, one could say Kantian, view, Oubrou's position could lead to a more rationalized and internalized version of Islam than most European Muslim scholars would publicly favor.

In this review of some of the more prominent scholars and teachers active in France today, I have emphasized the positions taken with respect to two distinct, but related, questions. The first question concerns whether different norms should apply either ethically or in some sense legally in different countries. This question is an old one, but it has renewed immediacy as Muslims set out to rethink the proper form of social life in countries of new immigration. It admits of a wide array of responses. Some of these responses, such as those given by Dhaou Meskine, Hichem El-Arafa, and Yûsuf al-Qardâwî on the issue of mortgages, fit into long-standing ways of thinking about Islamic normativity in terms of jurisprudence. One may argue that norms ought to differ in Europe, or that they ought to be the same as in, say, Qatar, but in either case the argument is based on principles of jurisprudential reasoning.

And it is here that the second question arises: Should normative reasoning be carried out in that manner or should it be based entirely on the general values or objectives of the Qur'ân? Tariq Ramadan argues that general principles contained in scripture or in the traditions of fiqh often find their equivalents in European social norms or law, and that this equivalence should be the starting point for rethinking normativity. Tareq Oubrou emphasizes the ethical dimension of norms, but his conclusions resemble Ramadan's. Other scholars, especially those based outside Europe, find this way of thinking to be too radical a departure from the traditions of Islamic jurisprudence; the Syrian scholars Ramadan and Tawfik al-Boutî, for example, explicitly take the emphasis on "objectives" to task.

I find that it is the answers to this second question that most fundamentally divide Muslim scholars in Europe—and not only in Europe. Those scholars who emphasize their roots in the traditions of jurisprudential reasoning argue that Muslims, and not only Muslims, have a lot to learn from the traditions of Islamic normative thought. Those scholars who emphasize the points of convergence between European and Islamic traditions argue that Muslims need to creatively and continually adapt their religion to their conditions of social life. These positions inevitably orient their advocates differently: in the first case, toward the classical sources of authoritative Islamic jurisprudence; in the second case, toward other public intellectuals, Muslim and non-Muslim, in Europe and North America. In France, at least, it is this choice of starting point—fiqh or France—that provokes the loudest cries of approval or suspicion from Muslims and non-Muslims. For some Muslims, at least, the greatest challenge is to find a way of doing both at the same time, to rhetorically as well as substantively root reasoning in both the traditions of fiqh and those of Europe.

NOTES

1. On the development of the theory of jurisprudence in Islam, see Hallaq 1997, 2001; on the practice of rendering judgments in early modern Muslim societies, see Johansen 1999 and Powers 2002.
2. Many recent works provide overviews of Muslims in Europe. Among the most interesting in English, see the following: Vertovec and Peach 1997, for a collection of studies on processes of adaptation; Nielsen 1999, for an analysis of issues facing Muslims in Europe, with a focus on Britain; Kastoryano 2002, for a comparative study of immigration to France and Germany; and (in French) Roy 1999, for a French view on what Muslims ought to do to become European.
3. See Brubaker 1992 and Kastoryano 2002; this close association has impeded efforts to give nonnational residents the right to vote in local elections.
4. In April 2003, a new body, the Conseil Français du Culte Musulman (CFCM), was organized and charged with coordinating policy regarding the training of imams, the certification of *halal* food, the provisions for Muslims in cemeteries, and other matters.
5. For an extended contrast of Britain and France see Bowen 2003c.
6. On Islam in France see Cesari 1998; Souilamas 2001; and Venel 1999 for interviews with younger Muslims, and Cesari 2002 for a brief English-language article. The somewhat older work by Kepel (1991) retains a great deal of interest for its fine attention to sociological detail.
7. Haut Conseil 2001, 36–39 follows earlier scholars in estimating the number of Muslims at slightly over 4 million but insists that the number of people "of Muslim religion" would be closer to 1 million the rest being "of Muslim culture." They base their estimate of religious Muslims on surveys concerning how often Muslims pray in mosques. Because the census is not allowed to gather data on "faith," figures in France always have to do with immigration history and various religious practices as determined by surveys.
8. Contrast the pioneering and thus socially salient role played by "black" West Indian immigrants to Britain (Modood et al. 1997).
9. It is very difficult to generalize about these three populations, since in fact there have been distinct migrations, each involving different socioeconomic segments, from these countries. A group at INED (Institut National des Études Demographiques) is currently developing the relevant analyses. Also shaping these histories are the very different orientations of the three governments. Both Algeria and Morocco have strong, direct presences in France, through local "amicales," through funding of mosque projects, and through direct negotiations with the French government. Algeria's relationship is particularly direct because of its role in directing the Paris mosque.
10. Tunisians play a preponderant role as teachers for reasons not yet well analyzed, but which probably have to do with the suppression by the Tunisian government of Islamic education, and the fact that far more Moroccans and Algerians came as unskilled workers to France.
11. Examples of teachers developing this dual track are Tareq Oubrou in Bordeaux,

Ahmed Jaballah and Hichem El Arafa in Saint Denis, and Dhaou Meskine in Aubervilliers, all mentioned below.

12. A French-language collection of the council's *fatwâs* recently was published (Conseil 2002); the *fatwa* discussed here appears on the council's Web site in the list of resolutions taken at the 1999 session: *http://www.fioe.org/ask_the_scholar/fourth%20statement.htm.*

13. On the early modern Hanafî position, see Abou El Fadl 1994, 173–74.

14. As a rough and ready indication of continued importance, the Web site islamonline.net has nine *fatwas* in its current *fatwa* bank that refer to al-Shatibi as an authority.

15. See Ramadan 1998 for his most extensive analysis of the heritage of Islam.

16. Al-Bouti 2001; I have seen the two al-Boutîs, at different times, make this argument in conferences at a major Paris mosque; see Bowen 2004.

17. It is thus not accidental that the teachers in France who place more emphasis on questioning the assumptions behind jurisprudence, such as Tareq Oubrou and Tariq Ramadan, were not themselves trained as jurists, whereas teachers who emphasize working within legal schools to the extent possible, such as Dhaou Meskine and Ahmad Jaballah, did have such training.

References Cited

Abou El Fadl, Khaled. 1994. "Islamic law and Muslim minorities: The Juristic Discourse on Muslim Minorities from the Second/Eighth to the Eleventh/Seventeenth Centuries." *Islamic Law and Society* 1, no. 2: 143–87.

Babès, Leïla, and Tareq Oubrou. 2002. *Loi d'Allah, loi des hommes: Liberté, égalité et femmes en islam.* Paris: Albin Michel.

Al-Bouti, Sheikh Mohammad Sa'îd Ramadân Al-Boutî. 2001. "La confluence de la 'jurisprudence des minorités' et le fractionnnement de l'islam n'est nullement une coïncidence," at *http://www.islamophile.org/spip/article.php3?id_article=107*

Bowen, John R. 2001. "Shari'a, State, and Social Norms in France and Indonesia". ISIM Papers no. 3. Leiden: Institute for the Study of Islam in the Modern World.

———. 2003a. "Two Approaches to Rights and Religion in Contemporary France," in *Rights in Global Perspective,* edited by Jon Mitchell and Richard Wilson, pp. 33–53. London: Routledge.

———. 2003b. *Islam, Law, and Equality in Indonesia: An Anthropology of Public Reasoning.* Cambridge: Cambridge University Press.

———. 2003c. "The Articulation of Religion, Culture, and Ethnicity for Muslims in Europe" Social Science Research Council Working Paper.

———, 2004. "Does French Islam Have Borders? Dilemmas of Domestication in a Global Religious Field." *American Anthropologist* 106, no. 1. (March 2004): pp. 44–55.

Brubaker, Rogers. 1992. *Citizenship and Nationhood in France and Germany.* Cambridge, Mass.: Harvard University Press.

Cesari, Jocelyne. 1998. *Musulmans et républicains: Les jeunes, l'islam et la France*. Brussels: Éditions Complexe.

———. 2002. "Islam in France: The Shaping of a Religious Minority." In *Muslims in the West: From Sojourners to Citizens*, edited by Yvonne Yazbeck Haddad, pp. 36–51. Oxford: Oxford University Press.

Conseil européen des fatwâs et de la recherché. 2002. *Receuil de fatwas*. Lyon: Tawhid.

Favell, Adrian. 2001. *Philosophies of Integration: Immigration and the Idea of Citizenship in France and Britain*. 2nd edition. Houndmills, U.K.: Palgrave.

Hallaq, Wael B. 1997. *A History of Islamic Legal Theories: An Introduction to Sunnî usûl al-fiqh*. Cambridge: Cambridge University Press.

———. 2001. *Authority, continuity, and change in Islamic law*. Cambridge: Cambridge University Press.

Haut Conseil à l'Intégration. 2001. *l'Islam dans la République*. Paris: Documentation Française.

Al-Jazaïri, Abubaker Jaber. 2001. *La Voie du Musulman* (trans. of *Minhaj al-Muslîm*). Paris: Maison d'Ennour.

Johansen, Baber. 1999. *Contingency in a Sacred Law: Legal and Ethical Norms in the Muslim fiqh*. Leiden: Brill.

Kastoryano, Riva. 2002. *Negotiating Identities: States and Immigrants in France and Germany*. Princeton, N.J.: Princeton University Press.

Kepel, Gilles. 1991. *Les banlieues de l'Islam: Naissance d'une religion en France*. Paris: Seuil.

Lewis, Philip. 1993. *Islamic Britain: Religion, Politics and Identity among British Muslims*. London: I. B. Tauris.

Masud, Muhammad Khalid. 1977. *Islamic Legal Philosophy: A Study of Abu Ishaq al-Shatibi's Life and Thought*. Islamabad: Islamic Research Institute.

Masud, Muhammad Khalid, Brinkley Messick, and David S. Powers. 1996. "Muftis, Fatwas, and Islamic Legal Interpretation." In *Islamic Legal Interpretation: Muftis and their Fatwas*, edited by Muhammad Khalid Masud, Brinkley Messick, and David S. Powers, pp. 3–32. Cambridge, Mass.: Harvard University Press.

Modood, Tariq. 1993. "Establishment, Multiculturalism, and British Citizenship." *Political Quarterly*.

Modood, Tariq, et al. 1997. *Ethnic Minorities in Britain: Diversity and Disadvantage*. London: Policy Studies Institute.

Nielsen, Jorgen S. 1999. *Towards a European Islam*. London: Macmillan.

Oubrou, Tareq. 2000 "Le 'minimum islamique' pour l'abbatage ritual en France." *La Médina* 5:42–43.

Powers, David S. 2001. *Law, Society, and Culture in the Maghrib, 1300–1500*. Cambridge: Cambridge University Press.

Qardâwî, Yûsuf. 1997. *Le Licite et l'Illicite en Islam* (trans. of *Al-halâl wa al-harâm fi Islam*). Paris: Al-Qalam.

Ramadan, Tariq. 1998 *Aux Sources du Renouveau Musulman*. Paris: Bayard Editions.

———. 2002. *Dâr ash-shahâda: L'Occident, espace du témoignage*. Lyon: Tawhid.

Rath, Jan, Rinus Penninx, Kees Groenendijk, and Astrid Meyer. 1999. "The Politics of Recognizing Religious Diversity in Europe: Social Reactions to the Institutionalization of Islam in the Netherlands, Belgium and Great Britain." *Netherlands Journal of Social Sciences* 35, no. 1: 53–68.

Roy, Olivier. 1999. *Vers un Islam Européen*. Paris: Editions Esprit.

Souilamas, Nacira Guénif. 2001. *Des "beurettes" aux descendantes d'immigrants nord-africains*. Paris: Grasset.

Ternisien, Xavier. 2001. *La France des Mosquées*. Paris: Albin Michel.

Venel, Nancy. 1999. *Musulmanes françaises: Des pratiquantes voiles à l'université*. Paris:L'Harmattan.

Vertovec, Steven. 2002. "Islamophobia and Muslim Recognition in Britain." In *Muslims in the West: From Sojourners to Citizens,* edited by Yvonne Yazbeck Haddad, pp. 19–35. Oxford: Oxford University Press.

Vertovec, Steven, and Ceri Peach, eds. 1997. *Islam in Europe: The Politics of Religion and Community*. Houndmills, U.K.: Macmillan.

Werbner, Pnina. 2001. *Imagined Diasporas among Manchester Muslims*. Oxford: James Currey.

INDEX